The Puncher & Wattmann
Anthology of Australian Poetry

The Puncher & Wattmann
Anthology of Australian Poetry

Edited by John Leonard

PUNCHER & WATTMANN

First published in 2009 by Puncher and Wattmann
PO Box 441
Glebe NSW 2037

http://www.puncherandwattmann.com
puncherandwattmann@bigpond.com

National Library of Australia
Cataloguing-in-Publication entry:

Leonard, John
The Puncher & Wattmann Anthology of Australian Poetry
ISBN   9781921450297

I. Title.
A821.3

Cover design by Matthew Holt
Page design by Sophie Gaur

Printed in China by Everbest Printing Company

Set in Adobe Jenson 11 pt

The publisher and editor are grateful to Allan and Maria Myers, and to Newman College, for financial assistance which made this book possible.

Contents

vii

viii

≈

The ordering of poets by year of birth has been varied for Giles, Neilson, 'E', Gilmore and Lang in order to place their poems near to other poems that are contemporaneous.

The year of first publication in a book by the author is given at the foot of most of the poems. Where the year is bracketed, the reference is to other publication, such as a newspaper or a journal. Usually this is because a book has not been published. For interest's sake, a year for both is sometimes given. Some very new poems near the beginning of the anthology, which are as yet not in a book, are without a year.

≈

INTRODUCTION

This book has grown out of my 1998 *Australian Verse: An Oxford Anthology* and makes, in important respects, a new selection. It catches up with an unusually rich period: more than a hundred poems are added from 1999-2009, forming a sizeable survey of the contemporary art. And this process inevitably has altered the vision further back: in all, about seventy percent of the poems by living poets — both fresh and familiar names — are new. The choices from earlier twentieth-century and colonial generations have been adjusted on a lesser scale to absorb a number of second thoughts.

I include some contemporary performance poems and the words of old convict songs and bush ballads along with the 'literary' — by which I mean poems that are just as ready for utterance (even if it be silent), but are aimed for the slow savour that printed publication invites. Of course 'performance' works in some instances have just that effect if printed. The literary is in any case most of the field here, in a gamut of styles running from surreal prose poems to early topical newspaper verse. I will refrain from giving a version of the usual story of the evolution of Australian poetry in terms of influences, movements in poetics, and sheer personal alliances. A reader can easily search for this elsewhere. The ghost of its scaffolding is discernible in the selection here, but my instinct is not to trammel the poems. Poems can interestingly outgrow their first labels.

Any such story is itself in evolution. In recent decades, for instance, its look has been altered by fuller recognition of poetry by women. We have also become accustomed to the fact that Australians write in many languages. This anthology, however, stays almost entirely with work created in English.

The book begins with the newest poets and traces back to the earliest. It travels, that is, from where we stand. Of course we stand in history, and for the reader who travels along (or skips back and forth) vistas of history are opened. Just to consider Australia: a little over two centuries hold a very busy social history which often plays into these poems directly or at a tangent — to do with invasion, settlement, Federation, enfranchisements and rights, and the twentieth-century-long project of a marginal country's affiliation with the globe. Poetry, indeed, may be a long-standing example of such affiliation — not necessarily in the sense of world recognition, but in its being. One thing that strikes me about Australian poetry, as with other arts in this country, is how confidently, since about the middle of the nineteenth century, it has taken on the modern Western assumption that art is both local and international in its entanglements.

Our artistic traditions, including poetry, tend to accommodate a physical setting in the pre-history of land, and also to mark inheritances, whether of dreamtime or of imported cultures. The latter – including many besides the English and Celtic with which immigration started – all carry cargoes of archaic complication. The connection made may be personal or it may be a generalised awareness: transactions with ancientness of one sort or another are palpable in much Australian poetry from early on until now. In a sense this is a suggestion about poetry itself, which often carries a pungent awareness that language is an inheritance we accept for alteration and renewal. In any case, the poems here generally have a confident reach that doesn't countenance either the anxious or the blasé note with which Australian society at times has encountered the ambivalences arising from colonisation and geographical position.

An interesting twist on this is that, characteristically, an Australian poem may present itself implicitly as an utterly fresh thought or impulse. The choice of traditional or free forms seems to make no difference to this. A certain brazenness and venture is probably traceable not just to Pound's famous injunction (of 1934) to 'Make it new', but to colonial beginnings and the freedom of distance. There is, moreover, a fair amount of Romanticism in Australian poetry, even up to present times, but it is generally cut with that sharpness of intelligence which goes under the heading of wit. And of course the skilful comic poem is a treasured genre for its verbal and social send-up.

It needs to be said too that an interest in inheritance has been downplayed in Australian poetry at least twice: in the themes of nation-making that occupied the years around Federation in 1901, and again in the poetics of poets who were influenced by the international ferment of youth in the 1960s.

The question of the nature of Australian perspectives is rarely far from the surface in much of the poetry of the nineteenth century. In the twentieth, and since, poets have by and large been happy to write democratically about almost anything, among which the local naturally has a part. Harris, Walwicz, Wright, David Campbell and Hope have poems here with 'Australia' in the title, each very different. But amid the currents and turmoils in Australian and world experience that signify the twentieth century, one demarcation in Australian poetry stands out. It is a formal one. Starting with a generation born around (or shortly before) the 1930s, most poets of recent and present times adopt free verse; earlier generations used traditional forms in similar proportion. Exceptions can be found of course on either side of the divide, and a number of poets have been ambidextrous, such as Wright. Harwood and Buckley, among others, shifted to free verse in mid-career. The change was effectively in place by the early 1970s, about a decade after free verse gained dominance in the USA: but in that country formal and free verse had by then been running side by side for a long time – and this had been the case also in the UK.

The slowness to change can be fairly described as conservative, but this needs to be nuanced. Many of those writing in metre were not socially or politically conservative in their time. It seems to me that the issue was mainly one of craft, which Australian poets have generally tended to be fierce about. It was plain (and still is) that the mantle of free verse tempts some poets to indulgence: mere cuteness becomes easy, as does a rushed prosiness that flicks the reader's eye down a page without the grip on syllables that makes for an involving rhythm. Poets committed to metre, and able at handling its own temptations to stiffness or triteness, were suspicious of the loose aura of free verse – probably for longer than they needed to be – until its capabilities of complexity were undeniable.

The joy of this for present readers is a concentrated field of lucid, formal complexity stretching from Neilson and Slessor on through the 1960s (and still, for some poets, continuing). Then, arising around the poetry of the young Dawe and Peter Porter (who doubles as a noted formalist), and of Murray and others soon after, for four decades the subtle rhythms of good free verse have proved just as wonderful.

With one exception, I follow my previous volume in regretfully omitting translations of indigenous poetry. By every account, this is a rich domain: a diverse heritage in at least 250 distinct languages. It is an oral tradition involving ceremonial narrative and song in which every region of the land was culturally and spiritually named, along with the day-to-day, long before the first colonists arrived in 1788. As with oral traditions elsewhere, poems have been able to last with little change over many generations while new ones have been added.

Although much has been lost, a living tradition remains in some places. The attractive translations of relatively recent examples from several regions in *The honey-ant man's love song* and *Little Eva at Moonlight Creek*, both edited by Martin Duwell and R.M.W. Dixon, are recommended. These two books and others like them can instil confidence by including illuminating commentary – which would be cumbersome if it were tried in the present anthology. The mythology, symbols and cultural assumptions are complex, and meaning can depend partly on aspects of delivery and music, and sometimes dance. Moreover, regional and formal variations are extensive. Any large or small representation here (from the small fraction that has actually been translated) must inherently signal its inadequacy.

'Song Cycle of the Moon-Bone' is nevertheless included. Although it first emerged into print in Ronald M. Berndt's translation in 1948, this powerful poem is placed at the book's end where its evocation of belonging – a cyclic gathering of thought and connection – shows in telling contrast to much of the nineteenth-century poetry of immigrants in the pages that precede it. I will simply add that authoritative opinion rests with readers who know the work in its original language. I would personally like to see such poetry in an anthology of its own, companion in size to this one, taken from the best annotated translations existing and to come, and drawing of course on an understanding of custodianship and of the elements of necessary secrecy.

I take it that an anthologist reads very widely, and particularly knows the full oeuvre of each poet whose work is selected. That's a fair pact with the reader. Regarding contemporary poets, it means considering earlier and recent work with equal care – selection might span across both if space allows. Yet the one or more poems that seem best to open a window onto the peculiar freshness of a writer's work can leap up from any period in it. My priority has been to watch for such, anticipating that some readers will be intrigued into googling or browsing in a library or shop to discover more. This is one of the prospective pleasures of a survey anthology: a stirring of readerly interest in poets who may go on to become personal favourites. It goes with experiencing an individual's overview of the most interesting directions and byways that the art has taken over a period. I am hoping that, to both those ends, this is a bookful of poems to delight in.

That said, although this editor likes every poem here chosen (none from mere duty of representation), it is rare for an individual's selection to feel entirely right to someone else. An anthology, therefore, like any other poetry book, is testing ground. We come to poetry knowing what kind of poem we most respond to, with a hope of finding our expectations not only met but expanded.

Some inclusions and absences may surprise, of names both past and present: the point is worth making that, usually, omission is neither more, nor less than, a judgement of preferences given a limited space. This applies especially in the crowded contemporary scene. For me, the number of current poets whose work makes them certainties for selection might be somewhat above a dozen (the thought is necessarily fluid); beyond that, I think the number of poets writing original and high-quality work is larger than at any time in this country's history.

To an observer, the present community of Australian poets comes across as a mutually encouraging and inclusive one. No special group forms a recognisable 'establishment'. Rather, new names keep attaining an accepted niche as 'significant' among peers, to be joined at a fair rate by other names, forming a kind of quasi-establishment of many. And plenty of poetry is published. The downside has been an almost total collapse of critical debate, as the reflexes of PR become prevalent. Whether or not the quotient of inflated reputations is higher under this inclusive regime than it has been in more critically oriented times is a moot point, probably not worth dwelling upon. A real problem, though, is the outright distancing of a potential core readership: that is, the many lovers of books and of a range of arts for whom engagement is inseparable from hearing and reading spirited discussion. Our best current poetry is ripe for that.

It is good fortune that several survey anthologies of Australian poetry are appearing almost simultaneously a decade into the new century, each shaping preferences from a different vantage point. There is a tacit invitation for critically minded readers to renew the idea of debate and assessment, of comparing excitements and otherwise. A renaissance in reading, I believe, could follow.

Waking: for Kafka

It is a mandible language, ours; one of release
or grasp; a byzantine binary of yes, no (yes);
the shellac click of stag beetles all het up.
Dear Franz you should love whom you want to
and hard – forget about the world's wanton
fathering and mothering . . . both will bear on
past your little momentous death.
Our parents always outlive us in a sense;
at our end we call for them from the darkest night
of our first own bedroom –
even if they do not come
there will be Breakfast. Waking is the bare minimum
or miracle. There's no telling what you'll be,
or how you'll be loved. Release, now grasp.

Man is Wolf to Man

Until the consummation of things:
man, wolf, man. A man hangs
like an amulet. His death to counter-
weight the deaths by his hand,
assuming God has a sense of balance.
The skeleton in the sand of Ash Sham
wears its clothes. Shirt unbuttoned
to show a cage of sand, the blindfold
blown off his three eyeholes.
Men's muscles did minutely grow

as they dug their holes to waste in.
Napoleon loves his soldiers, as do
the ravens, the first *guerrilla* said
with his purse of French ringed fingers.
From that time we knew little-wars
will be stockpiled as one great cause.
Dusk, once aimless little peace:
now all is animal, aimed in sights.
Sometimes the enemy knocks before
entering. A baby is hidden in the drawer.

2007

Mythos

We had read the books. We wanted to believe
it could happen in rooms like ours: white walls;
novels beside the bed.
Outside: the snowdrift, wind raking the black birch.

Solace of the real, of the body.
Instead, immense silence, then that hingeless cry
breaking the animal darkness like a spike.   *2008*

Winter Harmonica

In blackberry, in lightwood, a bird
needlepoints itself into the idea of a field: I am here.
Combs of blue-tipped speargrass brush
the back of my hand like a gray foal
shaking and shaking its mane.
The bird and I watch each other calmly.
The bird is composed and still
as a pheasant on a Chinese silkscreen.
Its eyes are soft and dark as caviar,
its body rivered with lemon brushstrokes.
I want to say the triplets in its throat
are smooth as creekstones, marbles,
some image of scribbled black water –

Inferno

You couldn't get much further from
the physical, the earth,
than Dante's selva oscura:

a forest dark with another language.
Than his garden of Limbo,
his burning sands, disembodied caves.

The suicide gets closer: incarnated
in her tree, her carcass
hung on it at judgment day – she got nearer

to the earth by truly hating it. Let's believe
her victory – that she knew
by dying, she would die.

But Dante turns away, from death
in the body to death in the mind:
eternal outside time. Can't change – you

are written.
He seems distracted, but really he accepts it,
for that is art, and that is hell.

Proverb

'In the room
where onions are frying
even the cat weeps.'

No more allegories – let's agree
proverbs help nobody.
No parables, I beg of you.

But then, who could love detail for its own sake?
Surely a gentle mind turns straight
away to symbol?

'Fact is the Kingdom of God.
Precision polishes the narrow heart.
Stories set us free.'

The enemies of complexity prefer such
companionable summaries.
But, Mother Doubt, you early laid on me

your threefold cradle-gifts:
sadness, restlessness,
and foremost of these, a hopeless

passion of reality. And so
my beloved cat, weep.
No more parables – let's just disagree.

2007

Winnowing

It was a definite change, a migration.
It was a paring down to something lone and lashless –
autumn, a lunar season.
It moved through the traffic,
and ate early dinners in the restaurants,
and got shorter in the afternoons.
It was like someone who saw themselves
in the mirror and got sad;
who grew their hair long, then cut it off.

The trees were blatant, letting themselves go,
leaving dull eyes spread in the gutters.
And a builder had left a radio in the rubble,
and the music moved, and the wind got a song in its head
and couldn't forget it, till the wind *was* the song,
and the wind was just something the song   .
had known once, and the song was worried by the gust
it felt, sometimes, inside, moving it along,
a white wave, a moving thing.

It was part of a philosophy:
things on top of other things
the city with its greenery
and the offices built of paper
and the harbour that holds its own shelved city
with the living
drowned in the boats of their collarbones.

Walk out a little and on the edge of the city
there are green half-fields, and buildings
in a shuttered sleep, and gathering animals.
Where one thing, there, becomes another –

(Or, just give in to it, the problem –
the coloured, colouring thing –
Newspaper report: different country, country scene.
Twenty years on, windy field, exhuming the bodies,
mass grave, trench number three: the bones
of a foetus in the bones of a woman:

'tiny bones, femurs, thighbones the size
of a matchstick.'
Spread babushka –
rainy season, 'the time for winnowing'.
Drowsy season. The bombs grow like blue flowers.)

2009

GRAEME MILES (b 1976)

Two Guesses at Immortality

The match has always just been lit,
smell of phosphorus is heavy with old birthdays
which are all today.
Everything is here and everyone.
You're home once and for all
at the moment when it's all new again.
And it's absolutely still.
There's nowhere else to go,
everything is sated and even the moan
of the frogs doesn't sound needy.
The room sits in the music, the music
in the room. Whatever fine hairs
your inner ear has shed
have been returned to you
and there's no forever
for this to last through.

Or the one day repeats itself
with its long night to be slept through
while the world returns to how it was.
A loop long enough to hold
all the old lusts and violence
while the island is washed clean
by a flood each night.
It all returns like a song to the chorus
like a waltz to the heavy beat
at the start of the bar.

Trampolining

The fattest eternity is childhood,
minutes stuffed with waiting
and the just-there world
deferred to an afterlife of joy
where magically we outgrow
what could tell us what to do:

we sat cross-legged on the floor, quiet
as the glad-wrapped biscuits on the supper-table,
a summer school-night boiling over
with nightmare prayers
in somebody's Adelaide living-room,
fed air by a cooler on rollers,

our pastor bellowing at the helm,
hell's ore in his flame-cheeks.
Gorby, Reagan and Thatcher went
chasing round his head with bombs:
explode the world and bring
the roaring-back of God-the-parent!

The grown-ups stamped their thonged
and sandalled feet on the carpet:
the mortgages and what they worked for,
the chip pan bubbling every night at six,
the hand-me-downs all forced to fit:
oh take it Satan, it's all yours . . .

Any day we'd be whooshed up to heaven;
and the kids at school, their parents,
cousins, dogs,
sucked up and funnelled
into hell's gated suburb, far out
where no public transport would travel.

But my brother and I were saving up
for a trampoline: its coming required
every cent of our faith
that we might be allowed to remain
in the human world a bit longer,
to have it and jump on it: to believe

in the leaden feet sunk in the cool summer grass,
the springy canopy shooting us up
above the apple trees, all day and well into dusk,
touching heaven with our hair,
our tongues, our fingertips, then somersaulting,
shrieking and tumbling

back down into the miracle, or whatever
it was: the thing not yet taken, the present-tense,
cast off by the adults for the kids to play with.

Kangaroos

The idea of a desert is somewhere beyond our little camps.
Some kangaroos watch until I get very close, their nucleic eyes
slipping down the other side of the incline,
their slow heavy silent mechanical
hindquarters clenching, unclenching them away.

All along the roadside their bodies lie open like fruit,
stiff legs in the air, the puddling fur going khaki in lifeless grass,
a long fence of skulls saying *do not enter this desert . . .*

But each death looks momentary, one wrong leap against
thousands of right ones; thousands of hours
lived hurtling through space with no notion of obstacle.

Quick-jumps, paws dipped, their tail-sailing
walloping gait a conqueror's dream, their gestures
so almost-human, almost-comical, we might think
they saw themselves in us, answered us with *like, like.*

Always turning to leave, wider to go –
they emerge in dissolving light as if they carry
the Earth in their skins, as if they are the land they inhabit . . .
it stares at you through them, looks through you
in the shared-breath stillness, their telepathic here now
group hesitation. As if something's deciding
whether to let you in, or through. As if there was an opening,
a closing. Then turning away again, loping off
into that open where death stands to one side (you imagine)
and each leap is a leap into deeper life, deeper possession.

2007

Flight

After a flight and a bus ride,
a change both of money and language,
here you were standing with me at dusk.
We stepped straight out to see the place –
all narrow stairs, and doors of different sizes,
and then the garden held back
by lawns about the house –
when with a cry of joy you jumped
forward and ran a few paces ahead,
down the pathway canopied with yews,
and into the evening. Elated
at last it seemed so easy to break
from that poise which had
borne the weight of times past.
And my heart jumped behind you, startled
at having to catch up, busy collecting
the slipstream of new intent.

2007

The Translation

We woke with the crook of our arms empty.
Each morning the triple-cooing turtle-dove
would probe around our yard
coo-ca-cai? a nag, a hullabaloo
I couldn't help but hear as *cosa fai?*

Mostly summer turned away, tightened
to a knot of roots at river's edge
where earth erodes from a red gum
unable to grip things, strangely exposed.

No use saying it was him not me
or, dispel the senses, repeat: the mind lies.
Even the faintest trails led back to that
weight cradled in the stomach's pit.
What was *it* doing? What did *it* have to say?

for the wake and skeleton dance

the dreamtime Dostoyevskys murmur of a recession in the spirit world
they say,
the night creatures are feeling the pinch
of growing disbelief and western rationality
that the apparitions of black dingos stalk the city night, hungry
their ectoplasm on the sidewalk in a cocktail of vomit and swill
waiting outside the drinking holes of the living
preying on the dwindling souls fenced in by assimilation

the dreamtime Dostoyevskys ponder
as dark riders in the sky signal a movement
for the wake and skeleton dance
it's payback time for the bureaucrats in black skins
and the fratricide troopers before them
with no room to move on a dead man's bed

is it all worth holding onto these memories
amidst the blood-drenched sands?
better to forget?

the dreamtime Dostoyevskys feel the early winter
chilled footsteps walk across their backs in the dark hours,
the white man didn't bring all the evil
some of it was here already
gestating
laughing
intoxicated
untapped
harassing the living
welcoming the tallship leviathans of two centuries ago
that crossed the line drawn in the sand by the Serpent
spilling dark horses from their bowels
and something called the Covenant,
infecting the dreamtime with the ghosts of a million lost entities
merely faces in the crowd at the festival of the dead,
the wake is over
and to the skeleton dance the bonemen smile
open season on chaos theory
and retirement eternal for the dreamtime Dostoyevsky   *2000*

white stucco dreaming

sprinkled in the happy dark of my mind
is early childhood and black humour
white stucco dreaming
and a black labrador
an orange and black panel-van
called the 'black banana'
with twenty blackfellas hanging out the back
blasting through the white stucco umbilical
of a working class tribe
front yards studded with old black tyres
that became mutant swans overnight
attacked with a cane knife and a bad white paint job

white stucco dreaming
and snakes that morphed into nylon hoses at the terror
of Mum's scorn
snakes whose cool venom we sprayed onto the white stucco,
temporarily blushing it pink
amid an atmosphere of Saturday morning grass cuttings
and flirtatious melodies of ice-cream trucks
that echoed through little black minds
and sent the labrador insane
chocolate hand prints like dreamtime fraud
laid across white stucco
and mud cakes on the camp stove
that just made Dad see black
no tree safe from treehouse sprawl
and the police cars that crawled up and down the back streets,
peering into our white stucco cocoon
wishing they were with us   *2000*

the golden skin of cowgirls

at the end of a brief Warrego sojourn
hungry and gravel strung
after searching for days and only finding emptiness
accompanied by road-trains heading for the slaughterhouse

little piggy eyes staring
through the slats of the trailers
with a beige, yet invisible shit-mist that stays up your nose
and gets into everything
and like the classical lion with a thorn in its paw
Brisbane lurks on the other side of those hills,
smooth green monoliths
tickled by the arias of Harold Blair
as they reflect the silky breeze
that sometimes carries the perfume
from the golden skin of cowgirls:
award winning, lightly browned pastry,
best pies and cream-buns this side of the Great Divide
where the road-trains pause
and truckers chow down on sausage rolls and waves of sweet,
darkened milk
letting piggy buy some time
before the boners get the best of him

nothing out here at the moment but crackling radio waves
that deliver piggy his requiem;

Charlie Pride, easy-over-agriculture-blues   2002

NICK RIEMER (b 1972)

The Fence

The fence is there, still the same as itself, it is a line,
it is the fence_____

_____ it blocks things. Everything else
is on the other side, like today now, walking through a park
with ibises flying overhead, other humans
in the long grass making cat noises.

Like, therefore, this exact thought – a ridiculous thought,
really other things, e.g. light, TV, the future,
stupid actions regretted and repeated.

E.g. Ibis Culture, containers, people practising fencing.

        (You'll have to wait, Ken.)

And one question is: why this weight of waiting as the fence
stretches on, on, never giving out, why do you never want
what you've already got, will you never know now?

I ask the fence and the fence asks me. Something's
separating me from the fence. What I know about it
is a separation, this fence is a separation . . .

the most I can say is: there's a separation of some sort somewhere,
between something and something else, it means you can never know,
it means you can only know: there may be things
hidden behind other things, like with that statue I saw today.

What's on the other side? Though mere, it looks quite sheer.
The ibises might know, I can hear them there, sifting through rubbish.
Are they all on the same side? Every ibis
might have its own side, sides everywhere:
                      side
                      side
                      side
                      side
                      side. Which side this is, I wonder?

I wish one of the ibises would accost me. To tell the truth,
I suspect the other side is blank: the fence is
What There Is, I'm convinced there's nothing

except the fence. E.g. novels, air disasters, supermarkets
and supermarket bags, the la-la-landscape. E.g. windows,
fences, middle class tongues, waste, infinity, the crowd.

Is the fence keeping the ibises out or me in?
Quite a dualismo eh, these thoughts on the fence,
while one ibis probably flaps off into the distance,

the fence's white, light fight against the might of the night and above it
the only bright, the bite of a height (shite, right?) that you suspect

might be up there somewhere but can it just stretch off, dividing?
Can the double side divide unbounded fields?

Here is the stop, here is the interruption to,, here is the viion.

Water is on the other side, I can see it but I can't reach it.
It waits glassily, flows into itself. (Don't ask hard questions, Ken).

WHOSE SIDE ARE THE THOUGHTS ON, I ask again, quite suddenly,
are they on a side of the fence or could they be the fence's actual side?
And what about Mr Howard, would he like this poem?

Now, the stars invite the grass to grow,
that sounds nice, but the thing is, the group you're in knows you,
can describe you, even what it doesn't know yet.
Whatever you do it will sweep it up, be able to comment,
as though it's never noticed the fence. Will there always be, the fence?

I will now tell you my PIN number: 7642,
and I could also say *the red sunset from crying*, and in this whole fence
all you have is that you know the fence is really there,
it's what makes things what they are,

it's necessary, just like glass, the soft and unbreakable,
it's what keeps us from being in the right, as I said before,
        now I wish I hadn't,

and if you're talking about my religious experience, well,
apart from believing in the ibises, I started
at the UM and then went on through to the OM and now I'm at the AM,
and I also think what a disgrace about the Popes.
        Why is the Pope called 'Carol'?

        – OK, so I kissed the ticket inspector, Ken

I hope I will be able to probably find a job,
preferably not writing notices like this work was attributed
in the past to a Portuguese artisan because of a claimed similarity
to the work of the school of Nuno Gonzales. Today,
several specialists propose seeing instead the hand of a French

master strongly influenced by Flemish art,
anyway it's all part of the fence
that goes without saying like most things,

        hence, the fence

so, this has all just been about my voice hasn't it
sorry sorry sorry sorry sorry sorry sorry sorry sorry sorry sorry

2005

Parts of the tongue

A predilection for stone fruit
sees a trail of peach
and plum stones in his shadow
You had traced him down
this discreet path to where
his casual touch
                    was six light insect
feet on your forearm

In the magazine you read about
the ten sexiest women
for April; they all live
in suburbs beginning with W
and wear impossible shoes

You hunt for modern equivalents
of *One Hundred Ways with Mince*
and watch his hand become
refined under its wedding ring,
the fingers longer and nails less bitten

He coaxes your shoulders straight,
uncurling them with firm hands
but you were merely bent over
with laughter
Now your tongue forks into four:
one part for being good-natured
        one for lamentation
                    the third part of irony
and the last for an imaginary language

You move to a newly-invented
suburb beginning with X
where you will use the four parts
of the tongue with equilibrium

2007

Storyteller

Hey girl
Who your mob
Where you from

Who's your mother
What's your father's name
You not from around here eh

You must be a long way from home
You look familiar
When you ready we'll talk

But you'll need to listen
'cause you're not ready yet
You talk too much

You need to open your eyes
No more talkin'
Just listen

One day you come back eh
You come back here
You sit on dirt floor of my country

And you listen
You listen to the stars turning at night
They help you, you know

They bring you here
They see everything
That night sky them follow you

They look after you too
Good spirits
They know who your people

You not lost girl
When you ready
You'll be back

You see girl
Today, it's not your time
Our story it waits for you

2008

The Monkey-Seller's Stall

The monkeys in the TV-sized cage at the roadside
have the faces of old men confronting death.
Under their black velvet fur, a pale immanence.

They stare at me with a terrible awe.
I am huge, monstrous, while they are splitting
like cells, like the infinity of mirror images.

Behind my skin there are clouds of smoke,
underground fires and this smothered city.

Through the mirror, I am watching the monkey-seller stalking.
I am watching one monkey in the seizure of screaming,
his voice an emptying.

In his agate-black eyes I am immediate and loss.   1999

Autumn is Everywhere

                                        Even in an explosion
if you have the right shutter-speed: the shards of rock

– projectiles – will become fluttering leaves decorating an icy wind.
Autumn is everywhere. Autumn is your skin flaking,

those shards becoming boulders offered to the eye
of an electron microscope, becoming food for dust-mites,

becoming the conundrum of The Instant:
How can moments, things, have an independent existence?

Yet, if found among the scattered remains of an explosion,
the shards of my canines and molars will prove my existence.

Everywhere I look the avenues of trees are exploding in slow-motion.

                                                    2005

Cemitério da Ajuda

We would expect families to be living in the vaults,
so many are small stone houses with painted doors and curtained windows,
the coffins mirror-smooth and on bunks along two walls,
and there are fewer than have been abandoned
on any street in an actual city. Through one grimy window
I see a shelf like a mantelpiece with framed photos
of a woman as a child and as a teenager and then of her as a bridesmaid.
On the clean floor there's a line of yellow teddy-bears
and in a darkened corner, encircled by fallen petals, a vase of roses.
Why am looking in on this sadness? In another vault,
across from the grey dusty coffins, broken shelves;
and in another, a monochrome studio-portrait of the entire family
as would be hung with pride above a matriarch's bed.
Why am I weeping again as I never do in my adopted country?
Why, as I am wandering the streets of memorial homes and cenotaphs,
hiding in the shade of Cyprus trees charred by the noon sun?
When I cross paths with the three old women bundled in their black,
they don't murmur *Bom dia*. To them I am less than the dead,
not even a curator of remains, not even a ghost-writer - *a tourist.*
I'm sick of this. I can't stop weeping.   2007

PAUL MAGEE (*b 1970*)

Study

The professor of suicide and its sociology
runs a special unit in methodology.
I think of him. And a bit shaky. There's
a ledge in my mind, more literally a
memory of how I leapt over to the other wing
of the hostel and still fly from it.
I might have suicided had I slipped. Fourteen stories
of empty space below
I would have inhabited briefly, each one a
life-time, which is never more than a smattering impression
of love. From such moments we are shaken decades later.

Elegy

Round about this time of the year my father comes back to life.
There are seasons of things and he is one of them.
It's hard to know quite how to talk to him then.
But he was so easy in his nature. I could mention his death
or pretend, it wouldn't matter.

We make coffee in his ritual way, pouring the tiny cups
just so. It's true we don't drink it anymore.
It's obvious he wants to know of my child. When they're
older they'll chat, and I'll leave the floor to them.
That's how it would always have been. It was

one of our childhood mysteries, that ease.
He asks about my travels – the last time we spoke
was on a phone line from Tierra del Fuego.
I can't remember a word we said.
What do you do with their quiet?

BRONWYN LEA (*b 1969*)

The Cairn

Mt Warning, New South Wales

You look to me for answers

but I know nothing. I am simple stone
conscripted with a leaf into a human

sign. I promise you I solve nothing.
I am mere punctuation to alert you
to juncture & entrance. Check yourself:

are you where you should be by now?
Where did you mean to be & how far
have you strayed? I concede to follow me
might bring disaster but can you afford

to ignore my improbable height?
Had a strong wind toppled me
or an animal bungled too close you might
have been saved this interminable doubt

you might have walked blithely to your end
never suspecting the error in your path.
Now here you are mid-point in your journey
questioning a stone of your origins & destination.
Bronwyn, it is not in my make up to pity you.
Make a decision & be on your way.   *2008*

A Place

There is a place I like to go
that is behind language

I like to go there & wobble
like a melon on a table

or a spoon that doesn't care
if it is chosen or not

I also like to come back
& slip into 'myself'

like a pair of silk pyjamas
ornamental & cool to touch.   *2008*

REBECCA EDWARDS (*b 1969*)

Draw a Lion

They said. With a yellow noose I caught one
tassel-tailed, roaring like the sun.

In science we split the caramel eye of an ox
flattened it into charts
which our retinae screened upside down
and our forebrains righted.

Where did yellow begin? On the lips of my father,
in the cave of my ear, or at the point
where speech was pinned by my pencil?
The lion yawned and slipped away.

What is yellow? Is the word I utter
the colour buzzing in your shuttered eye?

Is yellow in the lidded pot
still yellow?

And what do we know of green
if butterflies see more shades in a leaf
than the human mind has language?

And can they see the lion
staring out from their wings?   *1998*

The Mothers

are breathing into my left ear.
Their hands brush my shoulder.
I can smell their hardened palms
they are onion, soap and polish.
Their strong fingers, washing the heads of husbands
holding the spines of husbands desperate from war
smoothing the blood slick from the brow of the first born
I can feel their exhausted fingers.
Their smoky hair spikes the hairs along my arm.
Hair which was leaden with stove grease and nicotine,
which came out on brushes in thickets after the last born
their hair spikes me, ratchety as a cough.
My mothers hug me in the hail of wombs.
Red lips of black mothers releasing golden heads
black bushed desert mothers crowning blue scalps of the cold countries
head through pelvis, through pelvis, to the mothers with soft fur on
        their breasts
and the mothers who rocked us on four firm limbs, who eased us out,
        humming
in their wordless tongue
back to the mama watching plate-eyed
hooking her tail over my ear like a question
her muzzle streaked with marks we remember
in ochre, berry-stain and kohl.
In her womb, the cell-mother, dreaming of mud.
A pearl passed from daughter to daughter
riding in the one who rides my shoulder.
I feel her long loving tongue on my cheek,
smell her musk between my legs.   *2000*

The Young Milton Moon Throws His Pots
into the Brisbane River

Sometimes you get tired of giving it away.
Of lovers expecting gifts of your life's work.
If you were an architect
would they ask you to build them a house?
Not just design, but *build*: scrape each brick out of clay
you scrub pub toilets to afford.

Sunday mornings are good.
Football drunks drop coins into their piss,
stumble off with open flies.
Why are you doing this?
You're almost thirty.
See that derro who won't look you in the eye:
that's you. Just give it time.

It's getting colder.
A skinny girl with goosebumps on her arms jogs by
dragging a panting dog: *'Come on!'*
If you were a dog the other dogs
wouldn't stoop to sniff your arse.

They're not just pots they're vessels into which you've poured your guts;
canopic jars of this country's earth and your own.
Scrub your hands under the tap and walk home.

They're waiting for you, your people, tall as gums,
generous as figs.
They have passed through fire.
No mongrel wanted to buy even one,
and you kept your prices low.

Across at West End a barge claws the river deeper,
more dangerous.
A mean moon snickers as you throw them all in.
They slip under without even a splash
so you smash one on the footpath and chuck in the shards.
No one's getting any more for free.

The Fugitive

When a man is grateful
to a river for his life
she carves her bed in his skin –
her undertows will always
pull him off his course.

It was a dandelion that did him in
when its cluster-head of seed blew up.
He still flinches watching horses
step across a paddock.

His soles map the escape.
Fear sharp as a tamarisk thorn
lodged in the tender arch of a foot;
even now he checks his tracks
for blood on the bitumen.

Inconceivable:
here he can walk for days
in a single direction
without crossing one checkpoint
border control. He walks

and finds himself yet again
at some river's edge, not knowing
what has happened in between
only that the moon has risen
water lapping at his knees.

2004

all the blue rushing through the pinpoint of an iris

all the blue rushing through the pinpoint of an iris
lemon trees alight with yellow yells
butterflies land on my father's bare head
the forces of the ocean gentle its bay shores

lemon trees alight with yellow yells
the breath gentles the body
the forces of the ocean gentle its bay shores
soldiers of sunset stand on the boulevard

the breath gentles the body
we are just clouds caught on fence posts
soldiers of sunset stand on the boulevard
while their motorbikes graze on the asphalt

we are just clouds caught on fence posts
clapping hands, birds fly up to the shot of a gun
while their motorbikes graze on the asphalt
the trenches in my dreams are full of fathers' blood

clapping hands, birds fly up to the shot of a gun
butterflies land on my father's bare head
the trenches in my dreams are full of fathers' blood
all the blue rushing through the pinpoint of an iris   *2006*

The evening is loud with life

Leaning on the language of leaving
and the road a line from a song,
the door smiles open

After the crescendo
the tick of the clock
and a car driving past

Headlights behind her
she is approaching me
moon walk with my daughter   *2006*

Liverpool

liverpool, where is the city? – the grey platforms
glitter/ cigarette butts, sydney headaches & cultural
nooks/& loudspeakers all moving backwards/ as we
pull out from town hall/ & slowly make our way home/
to the grand destination of being –

                            'all stations to
liverpool via granville – first stop central, then
redfern – then all stations to liverpool via
granville'/ all homesick westies board the red
rattlers with elbows & parramatta beanies & scarves
hanging out the windows/

                         at night after the hoyts
& hungry jacks/ adolescent girls stare nervously
through glass doors into rocking train corridors/
into the shaky sway of empty green carriages –

reebok thieves, masturbators & killers/ & vomit
washing beneath the cabin doors of tired train
drivers, trying not to kill the next suicide on
the tracks/

                precious carriages guarded by railway
detectives/ smashing handcuffs against rails/ FEET
OFF THE FUCKING SEATS!/ smashing fists against fare
evaders, seat slashers & train wreckers/ at the end
of the line is liverpool:

                    where joyce maine is queen/
where the man pops up on the tv screen 'up the
road from baulkham hills', & yells 'let me do it
right for you!'/ liverpool, you dump, you hell hole/
you pollen & pollution collector/ you test tube of
heroin, you bucket of liver/

                  liverpool, you supermarket
culture, you checkout chick/ you are responsible for
hair gel & hairdressers like 'antons' & 'classiques'/
& donuts & cake shops & fat legs & summer frocks –
rapraprap gear & tracksuits/

                    liverpool, you sydney
basin basement/ i find the bargains/ i shop at
k-mart & target every day/ liverpool, where 'the
customer is always right', until ripped off/ where

door knockers for the spastic centre get a kick in
the teeth/
        liverpool, city of little sympathy &
violent video/ city of passing western suburbs
heroes in video ezy aisles/ inbetween new releases,
pornography, action & horror/
                      i make eye contact with
an overweight man/hugging toffee apples, diet coke,
hawaiian crunch & popcorn/ in each other we both see,
we will never come together & we will never leave
this city/ arnold schwarzenegger will make it better/

& a house alarm & a gun licence & crook lock/ &
derryn hinch to shuv it up all the small time crims
& give us all some largeness/ & some good old
fashioned morals & justice/ at least in our own
homes/
        'hinchy' nightly at 7.00 & 'maccas' with two
allbeefpattiespecialsaucelettucecheesepicklesonions
onasesameseedbun & choosycheesechoosersalwayssay
cheesepleasewhentheychoosethecheeseonthecheese
burgersatmcdonalds –
                i learnt that mythology ten
years ago, liverpool, i have never forgotten/ & i
have not forgiven you casula high – you concrete
gaol with your grey face to piss on/
                   you detention
centre for growth – with the teachers who fuck the
students & the students who go to prison/ casula in
the cow paddocks behind inghams – an appropriate
backdrop for frozen & suffocated chickens/
                 yep – &
the flannelette shirts & indian skirts/ panel vans,
old holdens & V8s/ & cigarette packets pushed up
beneath the sleeves/ peter jackson's, winfield 25s
& a marijuana earring & what are you smilin' at?/
& why doesn't anybody write poetry about us?/
                 super
aggressive – traffic mongers – tow trucks – insurance
– pink slips, green slips/ slip over in the factory –
fracture your neck – claim compo, pension – sore back
– pay rego/ pay your own way into revesby workers,
into parents without partners/
         & if they overtake

you in the peak hour rush on the hume hwy/ on the
canterbury road thru milperra/ then get out – walk
over – punch 'em thru the window – kick in the
mudguard – it's aluminium/

more carparks than parks,
more sizzlers than books/ & old school friends work
at the pavlova pantry, n.r.m.a./ join the army, the
police force/ or get married in tears in big park
or in the divorce & damnation fires of st lukes/

liverpool, it's good to be home/ dazzled by your
cultural desert/ your childhood, your domestic
violence/ your family victims & survivors/ & the
off yellow glow in suburban backyards/ the starlings,
the sparrows, the hills hoists, the clark rubber
swimming pools/

the guard dogs on chains/ the
thousands of aviary birds/ bull terriers, dobermans
& german shepherds/ overhead wires & telegraph
 poles/ & where is the city?

– the place where
newspaper & tv people come from?/ what is the
aquarius bookshop?/ & how do those people get to sail
on the harbour?/ & should i send my poetry to a
publisher?/

liverpool, you are the shifty hands of
john 'the shoddy mechanic'/ of caryards tuneups &
wreckers/ dyna tune, ultra tune & autoservice/ city
of vacuum cleaner encyclopedia & lawnmower/ & more
liquorlands & TABs than you can lay your damn
pay packet on/

liverpool, city of the damned/ of
lost dreams, tv screens: the unhealthy unwealthy
& unwise of burke's backyard dreaming & the david
jones show/

abusers & losers i'm telling you straight,
 'cos i'm a westie': you gotta be rich to live in
sydney – you gotta be smart to go to uni – & you
gotta be famous to be in the movies/

why it takes
half a day for us just to get to the beach/ & sunday
afternoon on the way home/ one single stream of
summer car metal/ & heavy metal blaring from
metallic blue & purple/

on the road past lucas
heights & deadman's creek & thru the mecarno lights –
& along the hume hwy & canterbury road via the
heathcote turn off/ into no-man's & no-woman's land   1996

DAVID MUSGRAVE (b 1965)

Lagoon

This is where I come from if it's true
to say I come from somewhere not just
anywhere south of the Imagination,
where they came from, ended up,
warty hills of the Monaro
or an Irish quag.
It's Lagoon, with wind-tussocked, wrinkled
hills worn down to a murmur
that claims me.
Flat skied, convict-shaped
earth, the barren sweep
from Tannas Mount knuckled
with Bathurst quartz, small and obedient
noon shadows: this is where justice
jammed them, impatient and impenitent
forebears transported for a brace
of crimes: possession
of a stolen lamb,
highway robbery
and other, nameless filchings.
It's hard to tell exactly where
it was: the lagoon has forgotten
itself, drowned
under Chifley Dam's
green skin brailled by metallic rain,
or a mired bend in Campbell's River
where dragonflies whirr in a spectral frenzy
like solid drops of petrol darting in the sun.
I have inherited their future
born of silent massacres,
patient weathering
of the cold fastness of hills
and endurance of each summer's baked mirages.

They mastered the art of sticking
to the narrow furrows of their lives
whereas I have learnt
only the art of streets,
sailing between their guttered shores
on that new ocean, traffic.
Every trace of them has vanished.
There is a school there now,
where children, yet to learn
that dreams are what make death real,
play in the stark sun.
Horse studs
gather along the creek
and they stand there, fluid
flanks shiny in wintered light
chewing and staring down
impostors in their midst.
Time has stolen it,
evaporated family mysteries
like the slow death of a photograph
of the old farm,
like neap days
pinched of history.

2004

MORGAN YASBINCEK (b 1964)

nineleven

when she was woken, told about the planes
the scenarios would not gather

she realised she had been hit, her collapsed spine televised
from circulating helicopters

she had time for a short call on her mobile before she was:

sucked out of a window, tossed into a livid blue sky

jammed into a stairwell with thousands of hands, hands and smoke

wading through ash and dust, scooping it out of her ears, mouth, eyes,
coughing it onto her clothes

queuing to give blood, lighting candles

digging for three nights without sleep

sitting on the aircraft trying to remember the emergency procedure;
oxygen, life jacket, the toggles, the whistle   *2004*

echo

his was a distraction you could build a house around, he
became a centerpiece in the garden, a sundial of sorts

what compelled her, as she bathed him each day with
hand–made soap scented with sandalwood and pachouli
dried him with a rose–coloured towel and massaged oil
into his withering spine

was a time past, before he'd looked into water, when
he'd looked into her, fascinated, he'd set his arms around her
to hold her just before he caught his reflection in the
birdbath

so there he stood, like a sculpture melting in the heat
of his own longing, a plant drying out, dying upwards, away
from the earth

they had to unhook his hands from the birdbath
in the end, how does a man drown in that much
water, they wanted to know

looking for himself, she answers   *2009*

JOHN KINSELLA (*b 1963*)

Visitant Eclogue

FARMER

Well, I said to the missus that something pretty odd
was happening out here, this being the third night
lights have appeared over the Needlings; and she
said stay clear Ben Rollins, stay clear, don't go
sticking your nose into something you don't understand.

And I said, well it's my place and if anything weird
is up I wanna know about it. And it's just starting
to dry off in these parts, and it's almost a fire risk.
The everlastings will be out soon and they'll dry
until they crinkle like cellophane in the hot
easterlies, and like a blowtorch they'd go up
taking the surrounding paddocks with them.
So here I am, *touched by your presence*, not quite
sure what to make of it but knowing that this
is as big as it gets, that death'll have nothing on it.

VISITANT

radiant inner heart countertracking epicycloidal
windrows and approaching harvest, as if to probe your body
like a contagion that'll never let you go,
corporate body politic, engraving crops
and stooking heretics, this our usufruct,
wickerman serving up the meek & generic
as vegetation names itself and the corpse
fills with a late shower, nomadic
emergent anticipation, toxic cloud of otherness
presence before authentic essay in defence
of time's minor fluctuations,
and we comprehend your gender,
missus as signifier to your gravelled utterance

FARMER

Now keep my missus out of it, she doesn't want
a bar of it – I've already made this clear. Hereabouts
it's mainly grain, though those offerings dotting the fields
in this brooding light are sheep that'll work in trails
down to the dam and struggle for shade or shelter beneath
a single tree. Around here used to be stands of mallee
and York Gum, though I'm not sure what the natives
call it. Yep, they were here before us,
though there's none around now so I can't help you there.

VISITANT

in family structure, as dialect wears out
and you claim ownership – down from the ship
we name and conquer, that's what you'd have us think,
to go your way and validate; scarifiers and hayrakes,

all aftermath and seed drilled to be ellipsed by grains
of superphosphate, expressionist and minimal
all at once, expanding tongues as if a place of worship
might spontaneously erupt, the face of a prophet
frowning in local stone, or grinning out of a piece
of imported fruit – the simplest is most exotic

FARMER

We've always been churchgoers, and I'm proud to say
that I'm an alderman; we've just got new bells
and they ring out through the valley like they're
of another world, and believe it or not, the congregation
has almost doubled in the last few weeks. I say
it's the bells but my wife reckons it's in the air,
that people feel depleted and need something
to absorb the emptiness. When pushed, she can't put
a finger on it. The minister has mentioned it in his sermons.

1999

Yellow

Tim has been filed
in Yellow Faction
at school. He is frustrated
and angry: he wants to be in Red
Faction, especially for the Cross Country,
which even five-year-olds train for in the Bush.
Character building. Robust. Preparatory.
I take him out to the garden
where I have piled the spent broad bean stalks,
grey ropes of pea vines,
dead clumps of wild oats,
for a quick burning-off. We are
making ash for the next generation,
I tell him. The fire whips about in the cold
late autumn easterly. It should cut apart
the flames but incites them. Tim,
analytical as always, notes the colour of flame
and distance of colour from the fuel. The orange
and yellow flames, furthest away, linger longer,
waver. I say: see, yellow is fast,
and yellow is the colour of the sun,

it is the body of the flames, orange
is the colour of the sun, it is the body
of flames. But Tim is also suspicious
of orange. When he hears a slow ballad
sung in French by, say, Piaf he says: I don't
like it, it makes me see orange in my head.
He and I, from a distance, consider
the waverings of orange and yellow. He
interrupts the burn-down – smoke making day
night, and wisps of ash fluttering about
like something good – and says: fire
is red too and red is a great colour.
and the flames closer to what's burning
are almost blue. Blue is the fastest colour.
Inside the sun is the blue of our souls.
All other colours are fed by blue
and it makes us fast.
                    A few days ago,
during a sun shower, Tim said that rain drops
don't let some colours of the spectrum
through. Or even let them exist, like indigo,
which *must* be in the fire too.

ALISON CROGGON (b 1962)

The Elwood Organic Fruit and Vegetable Shop

I will go walking in Elwood with my mind as smooth as a marrow
winking at the unruffled sky throwing its light down for free
letting the gardens exude their well-groomed scents and thinking
    everything good
to the Elwood Organic Fruit and Vegetable Shop:
for the counter is democratically in the centre and everyone smiles
for people go on with the civil business of buying and selling under the
    handwritten notices
for bawling children are solaced with grapes and handled to leave no bruises
for the mangoes are soft yellow thighs and the strawberries are klaxons of
    sweetness
for the mignonette purses its frilly lips and snowpeas pout their
    discreet bellies and the melons hug their quirky shapes under their
    marvellous rinds

for onions ringing their coppery globes and o the silver shallots
    and the hairy trumpets of leeks
for the cabbages folding crisp linens and the broccolis
    blooming in purple tulles and the dense green skirts of lettuces
for peaches like breasts of angels and passionfruits hard and
    dark and bursting with seed in your palm
for the dull gold flesh of pontiacs and knotty umbers of yams
    and new potatoes like the heels of babies
for the tubs of sweet william and heart-lifting freesias and orchids
    damp and beautiful as clitoral kisses
for poignant basil and maiden-haired fennel and prim blue-lipped
    rosemary and o! irrepressible mint!
how they nestle up the vegetables, promising them the fragrance of
    their ardour!
the marriages which await them! the lips that moisten to meet
    them! glorious speech of the earth!

1997

Language

This of course has nothing to do with words which
may be hammered into atoms or dressed in tulle
whatever you like they will do what you say
obediently, biding their time.
They'll outlast you anyway.

How to bud into this world that makes you so lonely.
How to become pitiless enough
to see one singular thing.
How to murder the god in yourself
in order to discover an absence
you might believe in –
those sorts of questions –

and how the grammar of love
depends on the spaces and
those several others
who continually insist on the sky
and today it really is blue and white
and closer than any language.

2002

Ode

We were woken too early, before the moths had died in the streets,
when buds had barely hardened in the frost, when stars are hurtful
and famished. They took us through gardens and past the halls
where once we had lingered, past the houses and doused markets.
Our footsteps echoed back like iron. Of course we were frightened,
that was a given, of course we remembered photographs we had studied
that then had nothing to do with us. The empty light of morning
made anything seem possible, even freedom, even God. We stumbled
on familiar roads, and everything turned away from us,
lamp posts, windows, signs. They weren't ours any longer. Even the air
greeted us differently, pinching our skin to wake us from its dreams.

*

Words of course were beyond us. They were what killed us
to begin with. They were taken away from the mouths that loved them
and given to men who worked their sorceries in distant cities,
who said that difficult things were simple now and that simple things
no longer existed. It was hard to find our way, we understood
the tender magic of hands, we knew the magic of things not spoken,
but this was a trick we couldn't grasp. It lifted the world in a clump of glass
and when everything came back down the streets had vanished.
In their places were shoes and clotting puddles and sparking wires
and holes and bricks and other things that words have no words for
and that silence swelling the noise until you can't hear anything at all.

*

It's said that the dead don't dream, but I dream of flowers.
I could dream so many flowers—lilies like golden snow on water,
hyacinths the colours of summer evenings or those amaranths they call
love-lies-bleeding. I dream of none of those. I dream instead
of wind-blown roses that grew in our shabby yard, of daisies
glimpsed through the kitchen window, of marigolds that glowed
through nets of weed. But most of all, I dream of red anemones
that never grew in my garden. They rise on slender stalks,
their seven-petalled heads bobbing and weaving in the wind.
Wind-flowers, Pliny called them, because they open only in the wind,
and the wind scatters their petals over every waste in the world.

2008

The Tale of Dark Louise

Must there always be some stray, hungry suitor?
I strive and I struggle, I can't keep the wolf.
On the day foretold by the travelling scholar,
I take my hank of flax and ride out.
The herring in the sea fall into a trance,
I put on the dress that brought me this shame.
Fire is never out of my chamber,
and the convent's interdiction falls between.
I'm not beautiful, but my eyes are drunk with music.
I will write whatever I want on your soul.
The vine is heavy again with the sweetest grapes,
and the ale flows, and the cellar drowns.

2002

Pursuit

I have not had fortune but I have seen the resplendent moths
of Daghestan. I have travelled through clusters of their castles
and found them wingless, lain deep, like the oak apple.
And in Angola I have seen hundreds of butterflies grieving.
I have seen butterflies swerve like the fiddle and the bow.
I once heard a boy sing on the deck of a Black Sea steamer,
There is a small and fragile bug!

The respiration,
the pulses of the heart, the beating that bursts the lid of the shell.
In sago I found the weevil itself, and I smelled the perfumes
of the males. Often I've dreamt of the wasp's tumbled journey,
the mosquito's guilt and thrift, how the ant slipped down
to haunt the grass, how the hornet left only the skin of my fruit.
For insects have a beauty that hurts, and that may even darken
the sky. They drum with their bellies upon the twig. They have
learned to cleanse their blood with light. I have seen a mantis
of a delicate mauve impaled on the flea's single spine. I have
known the mere segmented grub, and I have shared the earth
with lice. In the forests of the Congo, I recorded the stickiness
of swarms. O unforgettable flies of Palestine! O cicadas of Spain
in the year I was born!

2002

Headcount (1788)

so far: 1 Governor (Phillip) and his staff
of 9 - 1 surveyor-general - 1 surgeon
(White) and 4 assistants - 1 chaplain
(Johnson) and Mary his spouse - 2
servants - 211 marines their 27 wives
and 19 offspring - 548 male convicts -
187 female convicts - 17 convict kids (4
born on board) - sundry sheep hogs
cats dogs goats poultry (all types) from
England - 1 bull 1 bull-calf 7 cows 1
stallion 3 mares 3 colts 44 sheep 4 goats
28 boars and sows from the Cape of
Good Hope - private stock of officers -
varying numbers of natives (*naked and
saucy with spears and tommyhawks*) -
strange animals - coloured birds - Space
so much I feel *launched into eternity* -
and me.   *1996*

The Fall

People will gasp. They'll point at you in disbelief, but before they can absorb the
reality of what they're witnessing, the miracle will be over.   Paul Auster

She takes a tall building as hers is to be a very long fall.
She was always going to fall, whether she got to the top
Or not. Depression is holy. You have to be called.
She hears the children cheering inside: there is no hope.

She was always going to fall, whether she got to the top
And jumped, or was pushed. It says so in the contract.
She remembers the small print: *There will be no hope:
However, cleanse your heart with prayer before combat.*

She will jump. Or she will be pushed. See contract.
From this height, West 33rd Street has a silent mystique.
Her heart is clean out of prayer: nothing will extract
The dread, the black-dog knowledge it is all a mistake.

From the eighty-sixth floor, West 33rd Street is silent.
There is no consolation for those who cling to the railing
Only dread. She believes this is what the prophet meant.
With her body in her throat, she lets go, and is falling.

There is no consolation for those who cling to the rails.
I don't think I'm lost, but I don't know where I am.
She has let go, hesitated in the air. She has yet to exhale.
Her body hangs over a matrix of chaos and desolation.

She is not lost, but falling like Eve into the Big Apple.
Each year takes a minute, each week a singing second:
Her body hangs over a matrix of chaos, as she topples
Downwards, too fast for those below to comprehend.

In the air, a moment can take on the time centuries span.
She falls through former selves above a thousand heads.
No one looks up. No one looks towards the bright sedan:
Within a handful of time, it will be her crumpled bed.

She falls, self by self, over a crowd of a thousand heads.
Failing always at physics, this falling is her punishment:
In seconds, her crumpled body will lie in its metal bed
Where she shall sleep, no matter what the prophet meant.

Physics having failed her, she falls at the speed of night.
She is spinning through childhood on a taut yo-yo string
Aching for God, and some sleep. She is alone alright:
The playground, the pool. She is the one with no wings.

She spins through a childhood and the cool New York
Night, clutching an orchid in her white-gloved hand.
Wingless, she is tumbling through twenty-three years
Of astonishing despair. She is the Angel of Manhattan.

Clutching an orchid, she flies through the rhyme We All
Fall Down and cannot get up (the pool, the playground).
She is often astonished at the depth of despair in her soul:
Still she tries to find God, endeavours to never look down.

She is falling down, cannot get up, and so goes the rhyme.
Her descent through adolescence with its paintbox of blood
Is final. She leaves her life and her longing for God behind.
If not this flight, then what in heaven can make her good?

She descends through adolescence, obsessed with its paints
And its blood. It feels always like falling (she never flew).
Nothing on earth can make her good, for she is tainted.
See, a stocking is down, she has already lost both her shoes.

Moments are made to be flown through: you climb, and
If you have the courage, leap. She knows this much is true.
Shoes gone, stocking down, orchid clutched in left hand
She hisses by on a seam of light only darkness could pursue.

If you have the courage, leap, the prophet may have said.
Clinging to life like a leaf in the suburbs, she never took
The plunge. But now, how she sings on that hissing thread!
How bright and thin the sound of her whistling rebuke!

She clings like a leaf to the life she never took to, falls
Towards womanhood where things start to look black.
The whistle of her descent becomes a God-awful squall:
In these final few feet, she knows there is no going back.

It is during womanhood that blacknesses start to appear.
Lay your hands upon me: can you feel my broken heart?
There is no going anywhere in these final falling years
No rehearsal, no second chance. This is the lonely part.

A broken heart can make a woman climb, and catapult.
(She flashes on being caught in her father's open arms.)
There is no rehearsal, no second chance, no way to halt
This lunge. She was always going to come to harm.

She falls into her father's arms from various heights:
This was the light that held her darknesses from her.
Now, as she plunges, she invites the harm of night.
Into the smog and the New York noise she is hurled.

Out of the darkness, she blurs into light for a moment.
No one has time to point or scream at the miraculous
Sight. The streetlights and smog receive an angel sent
From the Empire Deck. Those above are still oblivious.

And then the car. No one has time to point or scream:
The word Forgive is already forming on thickening lips
As she curls into metal, perfectly. The Empire is a dream
She always had. She was contracted to climb to the tip.

Her lipsticked mouth is locked around a word, Forgive.
Yes, depression is holy. (Another soul has just been called.)
The orchid is a contract she clutches in one hand: To live
You must climb to the very top, for it is a very long fall.

2003

maximus

a broken autumn may possess a certain crescendo
    esp. when the ear can distinguish between du pré
& yo yo with the elgar played on the same davydo-
    v cello!   but when the former arrives at her encore

(dead as she is)   & the listener happens to be me
    the question beggars hell down in the heart   if a
life is curtailed by   multiple sclerosis   lobotomy
    car crash   overdose   suicide   (or other)   *how far*

can the abovementioned crescendo go?   my soul
    I know has a bad case of rickets & I am a formula
short   but when I sing me a song with words ol'
    fashioned & hymnal for sure   loud!   a cappella!

(to annoy the neighbours) something akin to plenty
invades me   & life no longer seems all that empty   *2009*

DÎPTI SARAVANAMUTTU (*b 1960*)

Anatolian Sonata

Finally to England, where you get
dive-bombed by the relative's
television.
You start to feel like a bird,
whose personality and plumage get
darker as it matures;
leaving your heart open,
still traversing some dry, almost barren
landscape, where the fruit shocks you
with complete and unpredictable sweetness.

Somewhere in a life full of music
you wiped out your possessions.
Refusing any livable
compromise, now face life as abstract
as contours on a map or the view
from an aeroplane.
Back home,
even your silence had been
filled with just her voice,
shaking your (speaking) body
with the clarity of recognition.

While travelling alone
in Turkey, your paranoias multiply
faster than Romeos at the bus depot,
until the trip by sea from Trabzon
to Istanbul, when you're elated to find
that you're sailing to Byzantium

                            again –
and that even captivity,
post the catharsis of travel,
may afford us a song.
Seagulls on the Sea of Marmara
look wasted and happy,
drunk on turquoise water
beyond the debris of the inland shore.

Looming over frailer craft like your
projections for the coming northern winter,
Turkish warships patrol the Dardanelles.   *1993*

Talk of Angels

Yeats' wild swans stare into space
their heads are the shape of desire
and the shards of the end of desire.
And I'm still touched by the absurd
speed of your chemistry, and
I want you to come here
before my perspective smashes, and I long
to complicate all simple things
by wanting them with you.

And I consider the proposal, that
repressed attraction feels as destructive
to the person attracting it, as
thalidomide, and totally not
anyone's idea of fun.
Especially you
who flow in some other direction
from what it takes to be saintly.

But it's what those swans are there for –
they daydream so much
that their days are full
of retrospective meaning. Thinking these
and other things I start to feel
like the Moghul painters who discovered perspective
but not depth. Poets,
you've probably heard
are an incestuous tribe,
conferring recognition by the literal
laying on of hands.

On the sort of day
when metaphors follow you around
and especially drop into your conversations,
it's like a revelation
that Irigaray's work on ethical passion
stumbles on that possibility
(regardless of gender)
about doing it like an Angel;
and shaping all of this into a gesture
as the world turns.   1993

Dingo Trails

An existential vocation after all, being a clown.
Sitting about in windswept places, bits of red dust
and grit making your eyes hurt;
all this shifting chronology, life, worlds,
past the howl of a wild dog and its need to find
a bit of homely earth and lie on it. To breathe.
Occasionally depleted, even brutal,
staring at the garden with an ashy heart.

Write of love and you'll find it, of peace
and it is there. Perhaps we do exist as paradox,
all accidental meanings considered;
asking why, saying it's just your destiny
to stop Charlie Chaplin being chased
permanently out of the room. Not realising
there was even a competition, there's the pity!

It's something like the way what we see
might become us, gentle breadcrumbs scattered
across the front footpath, blue and red rosellas
that sometimes look like accidental gemstones
set within the skeletal parabola of a winter,
and a pear tree, against a darkening silver sky.   *2004*

CATHERINE BATESON (b 1960)

Learning to Swim

Every time we touched each other, we left a fingerprint of sweat,
the grass died back, the hens stopped laying,
and on the fig tree outside my bedroom the figs ripened.
That summer we read girlie magazines spilling beer
on my white sheets and over the pages of *Penthouse*.
His big body was as pale as parsnip, black hairs sprouted
in unlikely places but his hands were like talc and
I loved his unhappiness, his migraines.

I'd always had boys before, stumbling through their paces
lights off and everything, even their knees, strange in the dark.
This was so different, like learning to swim
after years of walking your hands in the shallows
fooling nobody.
Look, now I can backstroke and butterfly,
I can dive from the high tower.

He opened me like an oyster,
like an artichoke. I was brine and undertow when he broke
over me, his hands full of music, each finger
singing a note purer than sainthood.

I swaggered into the year wearing that song
never again so unknowing,
never again so electric.   *2009*

S 21

Of what will they dream?
Which song will they remember? What name
will they want to name – the bones – in their darkness?

Mario Licón Cabrera, *Osario*

The way – ideally – we might remember:
a glass case or a neat Perspex tower
of skulls and thighbones.
Blood and rust melded together
in the springs of an old French style bed base.
An old cartridge case shit can.
Samplers of jumbled DNA,
a room of ragged cast-offs.
How to come away from it,
to photograph it, how long to stay there and stare
at the spattered tiles and the ripped out wiring.
To wonder what endless days
reading an archive of ten thousand 'confessions'
does for the eyes; I'm sick of questions
no-one wants to answer.
A forensic display of bullet wound trauma,
all logic and angles
is somehow a relief.

In the schoolyard recanters stacked up
end on end, queued for each device, machines
no theory committee
could calibrate to perfection.
Lies, half-truths, false leads, endless plot.
To write 'my life is not worth a bullet'
concludes more than narrative.
How to sign off a letter
with terror's salutations – and after that?
'Ahhrgh' perhaps, or a dog's whimper,
or a dragging chain.
Someone who'd been to Belsen
had written 'Justice' in the visitor's book.
But this was a rustic and ham-fisted machine
with no industrial prototype.

I too have to write, wondering where I am
on the chain-link of paranoia
connecting a tyrant to a farmer's son
who was handy with a shovel;
someone like the accountant across the corridor
doing the company's credit/debit sheet –
the guy with *all* the stories, who
knew how to file, the one who said
he'd done his job protecting his nation
with a few blunt instruments
a fountain pen, and a beautiful signature.   *2009*

PHILIP HODGINS (1959-1995)

Apologies

I'm sorry.
Because it's only possible
to think in clichés
when the end is really nigh
there won't be any standing back
to write like no-one else.
Because it's really happening. The symptoms
wouldn't lie. The bruising,
bleeding, swelling, loss of sight:
I'll hate this death
because it gives the meaning back
to words I never thought I'd have to use.
I can't explain. The words
are plain, the images obvious –
'This was the last work. Notice the crows.'

That's the way the symptoms really are –
not the body sending first calls now
and last calls now
but two married people
sitting in a hospital corridor
gazing down the length of sorrow.
Their only child will not bury them.
I must tell them how sorry I am.   *1986*

Shooting the Dogs

There wasn't much else we could do
that final day on the farm.
We couldn't take them with us into town,
no-one round the district needed them
and the new people had their own.
It was one of those things.

You sometimes hear of dogs
who know they're about to be put down
and who look up along the barrel of the rifle
into responsible eyes that never forget
that look and so on,
but our dogs didn't seem to have a clue.

They only stopped for a short while
to look at the Bedford stacked with furniture
not hay
and then cleared off towards the swamp,
plunging through the thick paspalum
noses up, like speedboats.

They weren't without their faults.
The young one liked to terrorize the chooks
and eat the eggs.
Whenever he started doing this
we'd let him have an egg full of chilli paste
and then the chooks would get some peace.

The old one's weakness was rolling in dead sheep.
Sometimes after this he'd sit outside
the kitchen window at dinner time.
The stink would hit us all at once
and we'd grimace like the young dog
discovering what was in the egg.

But basically they were pretty good.
They worked well and added life to the place.
I called them back enthusiastically
and got the old one as he bounded up
and then the young one as he shot off
for his life.

I buried them behind the tool shed.
It was one of the last things I did before
we left.
Each time the gravel slid off the shovel
it sounded like something
trying to hang on by its nails.

1988

The Land Itself

Beyond all arguments there is the land itself,
drying out and cracking at the end of summer
like a vast badly-made ceramic, uneven and powdery,
losing its topsoil and its insect-bodied grass seeds
to the wind's dusty perfumes, that sense of the land,
then soaking up soil-darkening rains and filling out
with the force of renewal at the savoured winter break.
Sheep and cattle are there with their hard split feet.
They loosen topsoils that will wash away or blow away,
punishing the land for being so old and delicate,
and they make walking tracks that run like scars
across the bitten-down paddocks stitched with fences
while the farmers in their cracked and dried-out boots
wait for one good season to make their money green again.
In places where the land has begun to heal itself
there are the younger old cuisines, softer footed,
the emu farms and kangaroo farms, both high-fenced
and nurtured by smart restaurants and tax write-offs.
Further out where the colours are all sun-damaged
and the land is sparse and barely held together
you find the future waiting for its many names.
Company personnel in mobile labs are already there,
taking readings and bouncing lumps of jargon off satellites.
A field geologist sits in an air-conditioned caravan.
She sees in front of her a computer screen of numbers
then through a dust-filtered window the land itself.
She looks back and forth. Something here is unrealized.
It might be an asset. It might be an idea.

1995

Frisky Poem and Risky

Regarding respects I'm fully
purchased within my own
exchanges
Please give my regards to our
God down and above
I would also like more spirits
so the list can be sent
Before receiving your hearing
I had to write to a conference
Sincerely I'm yours against
all evil co-ordinators
I decided from myself stems
a meaning and a creation
The prices I payed in every
eye ear and tongue will
wish they gave the correct addresses
My project have been pulsed
by blacks, and repriced
rejected too personally politically
This document I place, will be
the birth shown
A division by me is true
of knowledge in poetry
I've got history information
My date rave into sane real
I am amended then lended
Are you prepared for the
Nee Nee who died
I anticipated my pissed mind
I wish to withdraw all
my poems from the
building and put in the
open spaces.
As for gardens of me growing
out to another country
I may do honestly
My heart ain't pure love
My brain ain't poison daze

Ngunda Bimiai spoke the message.
All I did was draw this.
All I did was pass on
But one thing they gave me
is my own selfing self.

1995

KATHRYN LOMER (*b 1958*)

Bats

Summer days when we sit on the veranda
in fat old armchairs with built-in glass niches
to hold our beers, watching colour leak from the valley,
letting our neighbours fill us with gossip –
the new school teacher's suspected affair,
the publican (my uncle) drinking more than he sells,
the fire-spotter's wife grown so lonely
she's begun to write poetry –
as if country town leitmotifs might build a symphony
and some beauty be extracted.
In the background the river slurs its downhill song,
washing out alluvial tin the Chinese missed,
while near the coast wallabies graze dusk-dim paddocks bare,
and to the west form the green hop flowers
whose pollen will later burn my skin in the harvest.
And somewhere the girl you will choose over me
experiments with lipstick and high heels.
Above our heads small bats like cut-outs of night
zoom and cluster with mouse-like squeaks and trills,
their soft wingbeats punctuating our conversation
and us oblivious to all that they sense,
as unaware of our futures as they of theirs.
How we go in to bed and make love, giggling,
not self-conscious or anxious or bored,
trusting instincts to guide us through the dark.
Now that I am going back to the valley, I remember.
I picture us there on the veranda,
before our histories, full of hope.

2007

Ngunda   *messenger of God (author's note)*

Olive Grove

On the other side of the dry valley
somebody cultivates shadows.
Who?
Somebody tends an orchard of spectres
I would have missed
but for an opening here on the hill
and a chance light
that shows up pale aqua
against pale brown.

We all nurture a ghost tree
an invisible blue design
in secluded terrain
– a network of what might be.
Oh what a farmer
to maintain so many
so neatly!   *1987*

Navigator

Dusk obscures distance; fades in a ghost gum
which in turn dissolves into shadow.
A spinifex pigeon dashes into the night
leaving just the close-up –
desert grass stitched like lazy-daisy knots to ochre sand.

When like an hourglass
it is all absorbed and the black
has finally come through,
darkness brings to light
half a hemisphere of desert sky:

you, a newcomer no bigger than my thumbnail
inhabiting this flat belly
set your intricate course by the star map.
Seeing you, the night sky offers all,
a galaxy's imprinted on your tiny crown.   *1997*

writer's subject

forgive my paradox
of course it should be so:
step through my door
my myths my skin
(each cell bloody with memory)
as if my birth is not
a miraculous random act

let me steep rose petals for you
halve eggplants   set yoghurt in a cloth
& swing it in a window
let me teach you how to dance
& read you poetry by Tekeyan
let me take you to my mother
bring your questions your curiosity
watch her creased brown hands
work frantic at the patterns in her tablecloth
watch her eyes meet yours
full & brilliant
with the most appalling courage

come bright postmodernist
we are your writer's subject
claim our borders as your own
for what is truth?
you are our turk
exile us again
again
we will march for generations into mesopotamia
our family shod like horses
& let loose

2000

Marathon

At 4am
the service station across the road is bright and still,
the dog sleeps on the other couch &
the breeze through the door is cool and dry.
Sometimes a car hums by.

The specialist thumbed through my file.
I watched his hands work perfectly.
He said my lymphocytes are low and my numbers have halved.
I tried to grasp this arithmetic. It spilled into my lap.
He said there's nothing more to do but shoot me.
I laughed, said something about horses.
He stared back, unsmiling, rubbed his face hard with his
perfectly working hands.

When I was young I saw a film about a dance marathon
in a small American town, some desperate lovers.
Their exhaustion haunted me.
A night bird calls loudly, persistently.
Some nights I hear a train from far away.
If you just sit still, time passes too.
Like this marathon hope.

Tomorrow will be very hot again.   *2008*

ANTHONY LAWRENCE (b 1957)

The Drive

My father could not look at me
as we sat in the back of a white sedan
on our way to the police station.
But I looked at him. He was staring
straight ahead through all the years
his son had disappointed him.

News had come through of the boy
who'd fire-bombed the car outside
the Methodist Church. When the detectives
arrived, I was having a family
portrait taken. I saw the suits and ties
in the window, then the doorbell rang.

I smiled into the flash, ran to the bathroom
and vomited my head off. I wanted to make
the Australian team as a fast bowler.
I wanted Frances Clarke to love me.
But instead I'd struck a match and immolated
the minister's new Valiant, my breath

punched out of my lungs by the boom.
I ran behind the Sunday-school buildings
and confessed to the lawn-raking currawongs.
I watched black smoke like useless prayer
gutter into the Sydney sky.
The sirens were a long time coming.

As we pulled into the station carpark,
dead leaves and the two-way static
sounded like years of thrashings: blue
welts across the backs of my legs like
indelible neon, and my mother's weeping
for the times I nailed her with insults

to the wall. But now, after breakdowns,
divorce and a distance of eighteen years,
we can talk about the sound a belt makes
as it flies in the bathroom; about
the violent spirit of a teenage son.
My mother kisses my eyes to stop

the sadness we've known from breaking
through. My father tells me about his life
instead of brief reports from the office.
I love them, these parents and strangers,
these friends who appear from time to time,
sharing their names, their blood.   1993

Mark and Lars

Wind and rain, and sometimes pigeonshit in your eyes
when Sydney's trains had doors you could wrench open,
with guards taking your false name and telling you
to pull your head in.
                    Going over the harbour,
you had to watch the pylons – they made a whip
of air as they came at you, but Mark slapped one,
tagging grey steel, and left his finger
like a white finch perched on a rivet. At least
that's how I imagined it, walking back with him
over the bridge next morning, a red blur of absence
seeping through the end of his bandage,
but no finger, not even a smear on the pylon
to tell what had happened.

And years later,
older but still reckless, imagination packed it in
when my sad mate Lars lost his head
on the Western Suburbs line, misjudging the space
between two speeding trains – a sound like
a deflated football being booted, and Lars
falling back through the door, the original punk
graffitist, spraying the inside of the carriage.
And drunk, we assisted him, throwing up our guts
and hearts, crying for help and Jesus, spinning
the brake-wheel like we'd always promised,
the sparks and guards leaping out into the dark.
On Toongabbie station I looked through a crowd
of emergency people – Lars was laid out weirdly
in his black duffel-coat, the collar turned up hugely;
mad Lars, who'd have said *Whoever finds my noggin*
they'd better take care of the bastard.   1993

Bait Ball

It can appear and surface anywhere, from cape or bay, to water
so completely open, a sighting of land could be a thunderhead
or slate grey swell that redefines horizons.
    Out here, on the East Australian Current, its only cover
        is cloud, and that's been blown by the presence
of aerial trackers and pelagic hunters, who oversee and under-
write its formation and ruination: shearwaters, gulls, terns,
gannets, seals, tuna, marlin, dolphins.
    From a distance, the water's breaking surface
        and the diving birds responsible for this
contained disturbance are what's obvious: gannets, climbing
for a killing view, angle and then fall away, shutting their wings
a wingspan above the sea, bubble trailing as they dive,
dispersing fish that reform like any swarm, under threat,
from every angle – pilchards, slimy mackerel, and those
whose names are found within the loose phraseology
of phenomenon and its poetry: grinners, scale-shedding
counterfeiters, bell-nosed, sweet-lipped gliders, and anything else
you'd care to imagine, though here they are one tight grouping
of a species filed away under Panic and Numbers and Fear.
Yellowfin tuna and marlin, striped or black and lit up
with the neon of their swift intention, work to keep the baitfish

tight and rolling. Dolphins ultrasound directions to each other
in the way an unseen gesture can send a working mongrel
behind or to ground in a sheep dog trial.
   Whales, arriving like dark consignments of cold fronts
      come adrift, approach and enter this overblown re-
configuration of water-spawned DNA, unslinging the great
blue hinges of their mouths that work like purse seine nets
filtering feathers and sunlight and scales.
What's not visible is still audible out here, where the bait ball,
though diminished, has moved on with the current, away
from the light and aerial bombardment, leaving a slick of oil.
Broadbill swordfish, rising from depths unimaginable and cold,
follow and find this raw invitation to feast.
   In black and white frames, with a soundtrack
      live and non-archival, dorsal fins and bills break
through the exhausted ranks of the ball, and what's revealed,
in the time it takes for a scattering of fish to die, for the moon
to flare and fade, is one large eye, turned upwards, like glass
being blown and fleshed with need.   *2008*

GIG RYAN (*b* 1956)

The Cross/The Bay

She turns blue in the bathroom
Meanwhile the endless parades of Youth and Beauty
recreationally pop in.
She recalls him, fagging out on a higher plane
when their blank eyes met

The visited day lurches forward,
still negative on the blood test, bereft of hope.
The rich embrace a cause
like if you sink, you're guiltless.
He pitches for a fight. The illusion drops.
You leave the car. You leave them all.
The cockroach fidgets on the stove's coil.
In another flat a Spanish lament tilts its stealthy ardour
like crumbs. You wriggle on the grave sea wall.
Weddings drop like flies.
The city looks at itself.   *1990*

The Domesticity of Giraffes

She languorously swings her tongue
like a black leather strap as she chews
and endlessly licks the wire for salt
blown in from the harbour.
Bruised-apple eyed she ruminates
towards the tall buildings
she mistakes for a herd:
her gaze has the loneliness of smoke.

I think of her graceful on her plain –
one long-legged mile after another.
I see her head framed in a leafy bonnet
or balloon-bobbing in trees.
Her hide's a paved garden of orange
against wild bush. In the distance, running
she could be a big slim bird just before flight.

Here, a wire-cripple –
legs stark as telegraph poles
miles from anywhere.
She circles the pen, licks the wire,
mimics a gum-chewing audience
in the stained underwear of her hide.
This shy Miss Marigold rolls out her tongue

like the neck of a dying bird.
I offer her the fresh salt of my hand
and her tongue rolls over it
in sensual agony, as it must
over the wire, hour after bitter hour.
Now, the bull indolently
lets down his penis like a pink gladiolus
drenching the concrete.

She thrusts her tongue under his rich stream
to get moisture for her thousandth chew.   *1987*

Yachts

They are the sound of teacups wheeled off,
of a woolly butt's littlest birds rattling
song-bottles in all its sun-tiered racks.

And if you can imagine brittle bells
fiddled with and shaken, if you can hear
a woman placing her earrings in a pearl

shell, if you can hear the chime from
a lacquered box at the gateway to a Palace,
if you can hear the feet of a bird on tin

shingles in the depth of an agate sky,
then you'll know too the sound of a latch
dropping shut, and you'll know the little

shovelfuls of laughter children scatter
on the grass. You'll know the call
of an oriole on a lakeside walk and how

rain drips from branch to branch in bushes
that have broken out in buds. And you
might even know, some evening when

the weather's calm, the sky still blue,
how a child drops a soupspoon in a dish.
Or you might hear the bird, the one that

calls to whoever sits on the porch on
a summer's night and listens to the tripping
of bells from a bay, having already

struggled up a precipitous pass
and dared difficult, sultry questions
with their face open to the sea.

Maybe you only hear yourself stumble
up a staircase and drop your keys. Maybe
you only hear the sharp strike-notes

of bell-ringers announcing the passing
of another life, or hear your name on
the lips of sailors who sit with spray

on their fingers as they pull in the weights
and chip and chisel into the night.
Perhaps you hear your life winched in

under a dying sun. Or perhaps you hear
a child count stars in the water off a rickety
pier – despite clouds moving in, despite

gulls in the wind just off the masts.   *1996*

Bahadour

The sun stamps his shadow on the wall
and he's left one wheel of his bicycle
spinning. It is dusk, there are a few minutes

before he must pedal his wares through
the streets again. But now, nothing
is more important than his kite working

its way into the wobbly winter sky.
For the time he can live at the summit
of his head without a ticket, he is following

the kite through pastures of snow where
his father calls into the mountains for him,
where his mother weeps his farewell into

the carriages of a five-day train. You can
see so many boys out on the rooftops this
time of day, surrendering diamonds to

the thin blue air, putting their arms up, neither
in answer nor apprehension, but because
the day tenders them a coupon of release.

He does not think about the failing light,
nor of how his legs must mint so many steel
suns from a bicycle's wheels each day,

nor of how his life must drop like a token
into its appropriate slot; not even
of constructing whatever angles would break

the deal that transacted away his childhood –
nor of taking some fairness back to Nepal,
but only of how he can find purchase

with whatever minutes of dusk are left
to raise a diamond, to claim some share
of hope, some acre of sky within a hard-fisted

budget; and of how happy he is, yielding,
his arms up, equivalent now only to himself,
a last spoke in the denominations of light.   *2003*

PETER ROSE *(b 1955)*

Vantage

Hanging out the stained tablecloth
and several monogrammed handkerchiefs
once belonging to my father, I look up.
It is a high wild imperious handsome day.
I had it to myself for an hour,
like an ambivalent character in Conrad,
nautical man alone with his dyspathy.
Now, looking round me, I confront
a universe like an empirical zoo,
everyone watching: a stunned young man
washing up in his hungover way,
a calico cat wedged in its tree,
patient for doves, that elderly
Russian woman leaning from her window,
drying her grey magisterial hair.
Staring, just staring, everybody staring.
Or is this egoism, morning's fine way
of mocking an unshaved transcendentalist?
Today I feel like greeting each of them singly,
Charlestoning across this concrete courtyard,
essaying some ludicrous summery gesture –
though when I venture 'Good morning'
the Russian woman goes on staring,
her mannish mouth ambiguously grave.
Conceivably deaf, incontestably beautiful,
this was someone's Beatrice,

leaning now from a window in a suburb
thousands of miles from the known
and the ardent. What is it you would
have me say? she insinuates,
unravelling her grey magisterial hair
while I stroke the belled calico cat,
admire the republic of verdure canopying
our shared courtyard. Last night
it was a refuge for insolent possums,
maddening my neighbour's Airedale,
forcing an early waking – not unwelcome.
Again I greet my ironic Russian,
sternest of sharers. Again, no answer.
Yes, it is a high wild imperious handsome day.
Upstairs my espresso pot has long boiled dry,
the companionable stock flavours the house
with rosemary and celery and thyme.
In a blind room at the end of the hall
a tender guest, laziest of celebrants,
wakens in my bed, traces the knots
and fjords of my absence. Calling.   1993

PETER KIRKPATRICK (b 1955)

Texas, Queensland

'And that's the school up there.' And you say, 'Ahhh . . .'
It all makes sense. It's all in place. The hills
remote and dark; the square and simple houses;
the bull calf in its paddock; and the dogs
that roar at you like Fascists having fun.
And the people are good people. They can talk
the weather over for an hour. And drink!
The morning after you could spell this place
with XXXX. There's nothing else to do.
The B&S maybe. Go shooting, fishing.
Work. Fight. Dissolve into the distances.
God knows what it's like in summer. In winter
the night-cold cuts like broken glass, and dawn
bites with the smell of someone burning something.   1990

Wally, Wally

He strayed into our lives in middle-age,
still briefly playful till he settled down:
more war-torn uncle than surrogate child.
You called him Puss; I nicknamed him The Digger.

He'd lost most of his teeth; also his balls;
and was so furry that an idiot vet
misdiagnosed him as a girl. For months
we called him Wanda, then we realised.

I made up silly songs about him which
I still sing sometimes, in the car, alone.
I'd like to say I miss him every day,
but that's a lie. I think about him though.

The way he'd pause mid-lick, one hind leg held
aloft, and listen – sometimes with a sniff –
for predators or prey behind the lounge.
We might exchange an *It's a jungle* look.

He slept so calmly it was good to watch.
He'd seek our company to do it, like
a trick. He was so long retired from hunting birds
that roosting doves would peck around his bowl.

Once only did he sort of catch a mouse:
an old, fat, sick one that he walked into
beside the stove. He brought it, twitching, to us
as if to say *Here, thanks for the sardines.*

To my deep shame I kicked him, more than once,
when he was in the way – not hard, but hard
enough. And he forgave, forgot. If there's
a life hereafter he'll be there, not me.

That mouse he caught: each time he passed the stove
he'd glance to see if there were any more,
remembering. We used to laugh at it:
instinct, or something. I do it now myself.

2006

Cancer Poem

Stiletto heel-marks pepper the linoleum
staccato blemishes
through which no single animal can be tracked
beneath the surgically white moon.
In the ceiling where stars should be
the ventilation holes are exact.
The moth-eaten breast repels.
I can understand the story is small
but I have come to the house of white linen
to the strangers luminous as mothers
and need to find the significance here.
It was a birth taking place.
Absurd prayers which spoke to a god she forgot
to the miracle of loaves and sardines
to the expanse of bloody sand between nipples
to the poisoned scalp and the androgynous
line of wheelchairs gambling their gears.
Words can't wait for a precise blade.
Some scissors spill a glistening gut
drench her in wine, cut up the lake
with star-shapes and poignancies.
All the shadows and angles need you to hear.
Need no one. Need words that are
shuffled for comfort, meanings that multiply
defying the rudderless air.   *1995*

Electra

I walk the dirt roads with my cousin.
Boys whistle only at her
but she wants me to walk with her all the time.
She won't go alone to the beach or the shop.

Along Cudmirrah's paths and to the movies
we walk arm in arm
counting the whistles on all her fingers.
I'd prefer to be talking with Moss

in his rattle-trap caravan
about the ships big as black meadows
which, all along the reef, tilt into silt.
I tell Moss that a dog dreams

flat on his back
flat, docile, but sharp in his bones.
Sometimes I sleep like a drowned river,
I say, and sometimes on a precipice

a falling into or away from.
Sometimes I sleep like a one-eyed gull
swooping from a clifftop down
to submarine canyons of fish.

(I can't imagine how bored he was)
but sometimes, I say, I dream
flat on my back, as an animal does, and
hundreds of kingfish swim in fertile pairs

gliding over wrecks where gold coins
dance in the fists of statues
and anchors rust in anonymous caverns.
These are the ballrooms where no rules dance

Moss says, and he calls me Electra.
I tag alongside my cousin
watching the Pointers, the surfing boys circle
her urn-bright nipples, and dream of being older.   *1996*

Museum Flute

Too fragile to be touched, too rare
to be played
love trails the history of all your mouths.

From Norwich, East Anglia
the 12th century whispers its dark air
through your hollowed bird bone.

Christ has had such a long time dying
we must need antiquity
your brooding slits, your silent crying.   *2006*

Fauna of Mirrors

Seven years of luck ago, I smashed the oblong mirror
and the cells trapped inside my body broke through
sharded glass with a clatter of weapons.
     I hunched into anger, so that death and I
were no longer parted–but a colour like any other colour,
a reflection, as any other, an image frozen
in fractures, splinters falling into the day's new light.

     In 18th century Paris, Father Fontecchio began
categorising the uncollected fauna of mirrors, those shifty
shiny, fabulous creatures said to wield the ancient magic
of the Yellow Emperor. They don't grant wishes,
'Can I be thinner?' but show themselves as a flick or fin:
the turned face, feint or glimpse, the umbilicus urging
itself back into the eyrie's womb-blood, love scented.

     Gestures lean towards themselves, a reflection
tongued silver. I write my name in broken steam
each letter learned for the first time, each without hunger,
a form. And sleep, the short bereavement of self sundered
from self; dreams, the parallel tricks that anticipate mourning.
I dreamed of wading through dawn, an anaemic moon
waning from my eyes like a steady deliberate angel.

I dreamed of a god drinking from dry hands,
his image sleeping beside me like a road, his body
stripped bare, pared back to the minimal sign,
to markings cuneiform as the tracks of birds in clay.
     The breast and the belly, the man-wetted thigh:
their fragments and half-promises can't haunt a woman
who has conquered the distance between her eye and the light.

The emptiness of light; the veined beauty of a wrist.
     Changzhuo's face covered in bees, his body
immune to the nettling music of wings.
The mirror drinks our lives; the years in there, sad
as a mother's averted gaze, the sea in there softening beyond
gestation: oyster, phoenix, the shining salmon,
an ancestry passed down the Spanish side to Ireland.

Starlight twists inside the mirror
and an old woman wades barefoot across the moon, later
washing towels of blood to hang between the fibro houses
clutched around a shore. Children there, too, shaking the sand
from polished bones – a bird's skeleton, its stutter raked
by storms, every pit and blemish smoothed, held. What luck
to be confronted, daily, by the mirror's radical memory

its freedom to invent.
Father Fontecchio, shuffling his parchment in the quiet
libraries of France was recording the karyotype's mesh,
the helical pattern of skin and sex.
        Naked, malleable as the soon-another-something-else
of a Borges fable, when I look into the mirror
it receives me less coldly; nothing hovers there, not even breath.

2006

DOROTHY PORTER (1954-2008)

Bull-leaping

Is poetry a strange leftover
of Minoan bull-leaping?

the archaic skill
of flying over the back
of the beast

and gracefully surviving,
making it look easy

the bare sweaty breasts
the gilded loin cloth

the crowd enjoying
your big sexy risk.

Or is this kind of poetry
a forgotten fresco crumbling
under a mound of prose

the pieces glimmering
like snakes scuttling to ground?

1996

The Water

It's the water I remember,
the warm salt-lick silk of it
around my half-grown hand

and the air
crackling with hot holiday smells,
sausages, eucalyptus and Aerogard

was it one moment
on that rocking pontoon
or a thousand?

was it one time
I chanted to myself
remember, remember, remember?

the water. my hand. summer.
my life cooking up a storm.

and my loneliness
electric.   *1996*

KEVIN HART (*b 1954*)

The Calm

There is a cancer fiddling with its cell of blood
A butcher's knife that's frisking lamb for fat
And then there is the Calm.

All over the world numbers fall off the clocks
But still there is the Calm. There is a sound
Of a clock's hands

And then there is the Calm.

Now there are children playing on a beach
Out on the Marshall Islands
With fallout in their hair, a freak snowfall.
There is no Calm

But then there is the Calm.
All night I feel my old loves rotting in my heart
But morning brings the Calm

Or else the afternoon.

Some days I will say yes, and then odd days
It seems that things say yes to me.
And stranger still, there are those times
When I become a yes

(And they are moments of the Calm).   1994

Beneath the Ode

Just there, beneath the ode, a speck of dust.
You flick it with a little finger. No,
        A spot of ink. But wait:
        Now that you look up close,
It is a word. Quick, magnify the thing!

Good Lord, there are two words, no, three or more,
All blowing up like helium balloons.
        And so your hand transcribes,
        And so the glass falls down:
The words all shrivel to a dot again

As though graffitied on a baby's eye.
But who? An angel pausing from the dance?
        You take another book
        And there it is, that spot.
So was it always there but never seen,

Or has it come on just this summer day
Along with letters, clouds, a line of ants?
        It is a strange strange world,
        This one in which we live.
Whom do you call, the cops or cardinals?

Do state police answer the phone these days?
Is there a prefix for the Vatican?
        The questions multiply
        While in each book you own
Each poem edges closer to that dot.   1999

The Bird is Close

Half-dreaming and naked, I am laying dresses over my left arm
    While night blows through our bedroom window:
Here are the easy florals of summer

    And here a velvet gown whose crimson folds I love . . .
How strange a thing in the wee hours
    When the only sound is a flutter of a bird's wings

    And that heard just the once.

A whisper of feathers in a wardrobe near an open window
    And I am handling silk and tulle
For mother,

    And it is 1963, so nothing is ever lost
I tell myself, except

    It is 1989 and I am laying out her clothes
After the funeral and wondering what to do with them.
    Years later, a sound, half-heard, of wings at night,

Is making me go further in the dark
    While my wife sits on our bed in a little lamplight
Feeding our new daughter

    Who startles when I bring down a box.

And I am shivering now in the warm summer night
    For I know the bird is close
With a wing broken perhaps and eyes as wild as mine,

    But there's a final box, with faded maps,
A notebook brimming with sweet days.

                      Inside the wardrobe now,
Crouched down
    And sweating, as if covered in black felt,
I have crossed a line I did not know was there:

    I cannot see my hands
But they are holding the bird, tightly and tenderly,

    Before I touch the bird.

                                  1999

the honey-pit

I

historical:

these are strangers with
their awkward gaze claiming
kinship like an egg
teetering in rough
hands

you signal
– no

II

numerical:

60,000 or
63,000
1915 '16 '17
6
million
40 million (minimum)
****** ***

*** ***

****

III

lyrical:

hyacinth
lily
the first
forget-me-nots

and yesterday
a breath of
jasmine steamed
out to wind

open to a mild
September sun I'm
glad we're all
replaceable

IV

metaphorical:

the brutal sheep-let-loose
flick knives shimmy
a suave gestalt –
fiddlers disappearing faster
than you can count them
always someone
running

(meanwhile, beneath a haystack

V

liturgical:

item: one pr. womens shoes
item: one pr. workboots
item: one pr. mens shoes
item: one pr. womens shoes (evening)
item: one pr. childrens shoes

VI

biographical:

I don't think poetry
can save us   2001

PETER BOYLE (*b 1951*)

Everyday

You go to a restaurant and eat a meal and you choke and die. It
happens like that. You feel horny and visit a sauna, get careless, catch
aids and die. You open a present while straphanging on a tram, miss
your stop, get off in a hurry, don't notice a truck, get hit and die. Or
you breathe the mould of your own body for a lifetime, day after silent
day, and you turn white and die. Or you open your hand and the
lines suddenly go walking off in different directions over the edges
of the world and this puzzles you and you can't understand it and out
of such perplexity you die. One day the face of the sunflower deity
is splattered on the bedsheets and you grow prickly and are never
visited by the bees that carry sweetness in their thighs and from the

hunger for their soft release you die. You construct a house of stone underneath a well of pure skywater and there you bring the pillars of every deity and the offerings for every cult and you crush flowers and the tiny hands of the newborn dead till reincarnating as gesture without body you die.

On a Saturday during the football on an airplane over Antarctica in galoshes in a business suit on the holiday of a lifetime tomorrow and yesterday after five minutes of thinking and a decade of acceptance passionlessly as oxygen from a mask in this room which has grown as small as a child's crib you open your mouth to all that exits and all that rushes in and wanting so much to speak you start to mime the opening of a word

and you begin to understand
how the silence that fills you and the passion for words that overflows
is your own private and chaotic death.   *2001*

Π.O. *(b 1951)*

He:Her
from 24 Hours

He:
    We were
all at this Disco (one
night) – all fuking around, an' Frank
comes up behind me
an' goes: Benny! – Benny! –
Grab 'Roz' so i can grab 'Ang'.
    Yer. Right.
(e!) I tried!
    I go: Come here (Roz) (fuken).
Give me a 'kiss'!
    She goes: 'Nope!'
. . . . an' walks-off!
    Frank comes
back over: Grab Roz IDIOT!
    I go: I TRIED!
He goes: ———TRY AGAIN!

I go: Roz!
Come here fuken – give me a kiss!
     She goes: 'Nope!'
. . . . and walks off!
     I'm standing there
like a FUKEN IDIOT, an' i'm getting
knocked back
               for 'HIM'
     That's FUCKED!
This is FUCKED!
     Every cunt's
turned into a 'statue', an' 'SHE' hates
     my GUTS!

Her/She:
     That's CRAP!
. . . . i didn't want to know him!
     When he came over
and ASKED me, i thought: Oh-my-GOD!
What do i do now??????????'?!
     Cos i liked him!
I was jus' 'embarrassed'!
     An' guys
they're so 'scared' of doing it
     they 'instantly'
think, they've been rejected!
     It doesn't 'occur'
to them, you're SHITTING yourself!
     Thinking: What if
he thinks, i'm a shit kisser or something.
     I know it's 'pathetic'
. . . . but that's what i was thinking.
     I talked to Ang, about it!
I said: Everytime
he gets 'pissed' he . . . notices me!
     She goes:
Don't worry about it.
     Jus' → 'Fuck' him!
Fuck him or something.
     But he
doesn't WANT to 'FUCK' me, i go.

So she goes:
Well. . . . . (jus') 'Fuck him' anyway!
      (You know
what she's like – She doesn't want
      to hear
            all that crap!)

Anyway:

      Nex' day,
we're in this joint (in Chapel
Street), an' they're 'all' standing around
      talking about it
going: 'You're
      a BITCH Roz you "rejected" Benny'
. . . and so on.
      So I go: RIGHT!
That's 'IT'!
      I grabbed him (by tha
back ov tha head) pushed him (back!)
      thru tha door
pushed him out (onto Chapel Street)
      (:belted his head
on a pole, on tha way out) dragged him
      into the middle
of the Tram-tracks, an' said: 'Right!'
      E V E R Y O N E LOOKING*?*?*?*?*?*?*?!
. . . . an' stuck my tongue
      down his throat
                  – FULL ON ! ! ! –
– Right ! –
      Everybody HAPPY (now)??
. . . . and walked back into the shop.
      Benny came back in . . . . . .
going: I.Can't.Believe.You.Just.Did.That!
      I.Can't.Believe.You.Just.Did.That!
But i could tell,
      he liked it!

1996

Alcohol

You are the eighth
and shallowest
of the seven seas,

a shrivelled fragmented ocean
dispersed into bottles, kegs, casks,
warm puddles in lanes behind pubs:
a chain of ponds.

Also a kind of spa,
a very hot spring:
medicinal waters to be taken
before meals, with meals, after meals,
without meals;

chief cure
for gout, dropsy, phlegm,
bad humours, apoplexy, rheumatism
and chief cause of all the same.

At best you make lovely mischief:
wetter of cunts,
drooper of cocks.

At worst you never know when to stop:
wife-beater, mugger of innocents,
chief mitigating circumstance
for half the evil in the world.

All of which I know too well
but choose to ignore,
remembering each night only this advice:
never eat on an empty stomach;

for always you make me a child again –
sentimental, boring
and for one happy hour very happy –
sniffing out my true character like a dog:
my Sea of Tranquillity,
always exactly shallow enough to drown in.   *1988*

Destiny

It was a simple melody on two flutes,
Brief, meagre, somewhat plodding,
Unembellished,
A slight piece, as I thought, concluding
A side of *La Flûte Indienne*. What the notes
Said of it I forget, except its title,
Destino – Destiny. Destiny?
How did that name get itself attached
To a tune with so thin a
Resonance, that offered so little?

Yet, later, those narrow notes, that solemn fluting,
Playing on, played on the mind,
Thin and cold
As Andean air and its barren ground
That offers so little. And an image was competing,
Now recalled and Indian too, a hall
Of mummies, ancestors,
Trussed and rigid, upright underground, marshalled
There, bearing a bleak justice
That could prove perpetual,

Their dead mouths singing, singing, round and stretched,
Two opposite dry lines of O's,
Two hollow ranks
Of flutelike ceaseless crying that rose
Above hearing, and brought to mind the things you've wished
Never to know, what you hear
In lulls, behind all sounds,
Or when the first bird sings and its little chinks
Gather from the morning air
The whole weight of silence.   *1988*

Made to Measure

Impossible to wield
The acreage of the fabric that unfolded,
Slung from his shoulders like a crumpled field:
The distance from one Christmas to the next
When he was only seven
Was aching there; a foreign city flexed
Among the ripples; a face, the star-shocked heaven
About his flailing arms were shrugged and moulded.

Too heavy to outrun,
Too slow to measure what it underwent,
Though gradually the passage of the sun,
Unmanageable in its train of light,
Seemed almost to respond
As he yanked the yards of stuff in like a kite
And gathered the brocade that trailed beyond
His arms' reach to the scale of measurement,

However strange the weave
That writhed about the working of his hands:
The footage too atrocious to believe,
Printed with corpses; Greece; the falls of salmon;
Her upturned silken wrist
He would have torn out history to examine;
His father's final blessing, which he missed.
However far he comes or where he stands,

At last, and limb by limb,
Contour by contour, that unfolded cape
Settles ever more fittingly on him.
His forehead is the line of the sky's vault,
His shoulders trace the ground,
His palms the ways he wandered by default,
And in his gestures those he knew are found.
What shape the day discovers is his shape.   *2009*

They Assume the Survivors are Australian
from Seven Songs for Sydney

You, Carnarvon, at Empire's end
    with your one baker
        baking all night,
you wordless
    under too large a moon,
making sandwiches by the pound.

Some of those women have since died,
    the youngest married long ago,
        some moved interstate
    for the franchises, the chicken farms
coin-laundromats
        & sportsgood stores
    but who hasn't, man or woman, set up
        some urn and trestle and waited
            in aspects, as a line?

All hearts have nourished
                    sworn enemies

And the hatred still wanders
    through scholarship, flares
or ebbs in assiduous pendulation.
    At the pub they are saying,
        'Lynch them.'
        'Lynch their captain.'
And you, Carnarvon, you have to find,
    unlock and expend the last resource;
you only, the smallest town on earth
        must fight into civilisation.

You, stone faced, who pushed out a cup.
You, turning,
to hide your tears from their faces.

1992

Australia

You big ugly. You too empty. You desert with your nothing nothing nothing. You scorched suntanned. Old too quickly. Acres of suburbs watching the telly. You bore me. Freckle silly children. You nothing much. With your big sea. Beach beach beach. I've seen enough already. You dumb dirty city with bar stools. You're ugly. You silly shoppingtown. You copy. You too far everywhere. You laugh at me. When I came this woman gave me a box of biscuits. You try to be friendly but you're not very friendly. You never ask me to your house. You insult me. You don't know how to be with me. Road road tree tree. I came from crowded and many. I came from rich. You have nothing to offer. You're poor and spread thin. You big. So what. I'm small. It's what's in. You silent on Sunday. Nobody on your streets. You dead at night. You go to sleep too early. You don't excite me. You scare me with your hopeless. Asleep when you walk. Too hot to think. You big awful. You don't match me. You burnt out. You too big sky. You make me a dot in the nowhere. You laugh with your big healthy. You want everyone to be the same. You're dumb. You do like anybody else. You engaged Doreen. You big cow. You average average. Cold day at school playing around at lunchtime. Running around for nothing. You never accept me. For your own. You always ask me where I'm from. You always ask me. You tell me I look strange. Different. You don't adopt me. You laugh at the way I speak. You think you're better than me. You don't like me. You don't have any interest in another country. Idiot centre of your own self. You think the rest of the world walks around without shoes or electric light. You don't go anywhere. You stay at home. You like one another. You go crazy on Saturday night. You get drunk. You don't like me and you don't like women. You put your arm around men in bars. You're rough. I can't speak to you. You burly burly. You're just silly to me. You big man. Poor with all your money. You ugly furniture. You ugly house. Relaxed in your summer stupor. All year. Never fully awake. Dull at school. Wait for other people to tell you what to do. Follow the leader. Can't imagine. Work horse. Thick legs. You go to work in the morning. You shiver on a tram.

(1981) 1989

Little Red Riding Hood

I always had such a good time, good time, good time girl. Each
and every day from morning to night. Each and every twenty-four
hours I wanted to wake up, wake up. I was so lively, so livewire
tense, such a highly pitched little. I was red, so red so red. I was
a tomato. I was on the lookout for the wolf. Want some sweeties,
mister? I bought a red dress myself. I bought the wolf. Want some
sweeties, mister? I bought a red dress for myself. I bought a hood
for myself. Get me a hood. I bought a knife.   *1982*

JOHN FORBES (1950-98)

Four Heads & how to do them

The Classical Head

Nature in her wisdom has formed the human head
so it stands at the very top of the body.

The head – or let us say the face – divides into 3,
the seats of wisdom, beauty & goodness respectively.

The eyebrows form a circle around the eyes, as
the semicircles of the ears are the size of the

open mouth & the mouth is one eye length from
the nose, itself the length of the lip & at the top

the nose is as wide as one eye. From the nose
to the ear is the length of the middle finger

and the chin is 2½ times as thick as the finger.
The open hand in turn is as large as the face.

A man is ten faces tall & assuming one leaves out
the head the genitals mark his centre exactly.

The Romantic Head

The Romantic head begins with the hands cupped
under the chin the little fingers resting on the nose
& the thumbs curling up the jaw line towards the ears.

The lips are ripe but pressed together as the eyes
are closed or narrowed, gazing in the direction of
the little fingers. The face as a whole exists to gesture.

The nose while beautiful is like the neck, ignored,
being merely a prop for the brow that is usually
well developed & creased in thought – consider the lines

'the wrinkled sea beneath him crawls' locating the centre
of the Romantic head above the hairline & between the ears;
so the artist must see shapes the normal eye is blind to.

This is achieved at the top of the cranium where the skull
opens to the air, zooms & merges with its own aura.
Here the whole diurnal round passes through. In this way

the dissolution the quivering chin & supported jaw seemed
to fear, as the head longed for, takes place. The head, at
last one with the world, dissolves. The artist changes genre.

The Symbolist Head

No longer begins with even a mention of anatomy,
the approach in fact leaves one with the whole glittering
universe from which only the head has been removed.
One attempts, in the teeth of an obvious fallacy, to find
the shape, colour, smell, to know the 'feel' of the head
without knowing the head at all. And the quarry is elusive!
If the stomach disappears, butterflies are liberated & while
the head teems with ideas who has ever seen one? Equally,
the sound of a head stroked with sponge rubber or the sound
of a head kicked along the street on Anzac Day could be
the sound of a million other things kicked or stroked.
The head leaves no prints in the air & the shape of an
absence baffles even metaphysics. But the body connects
to the head like a visible idea & so has its uses, for
what feeling is aroused by The Winged Victory of Samothrace
but piercing regret for the lost head? And beyond the body,
a landscape is not just our yearning to be a pane of glass
but a web of clues to its centre, the head. And here, like one day
finding a lone wig in the vast rubbish dump devoted to shoes,
the Symbolist head appears, a painting filled with love
for itself, an emotion useless as mirrors without a head.
This art verges on the sentimental. It's called 'Pillow Talk'

The Conceptual Head

1) The breeze moves
   the branches as sleep moves the old man's head:
   neither move the poem.

2) The opening image becomes
   'poetic' only if visualised

3)   but even so `
   the head can't really be
           seen,
           heard,
           touched
           or smelt –
   the Objective Head would be raving nostalgia.

4) Yet the head is not a word
   & the word means 'head'
   only inside the head or its gesture,
           the mouth.
           So the poem can't escape,
           trapped inside its subject
   & longing to be a piece of flesh and blood
   as
           Ten Pounds of Ugly Fat
           versus
           The Immortal Taperecorder
   forever.

5) While anatomy is only a map, sketched
           from an engaging rumour,
   metaphor is the dream
   of its shape –
           from 'head in the stars'
           to 'head of lettuce'

   Between the two
   the poem of the head is endless.

6) Now the world of the head opens
   like the journals of old travellers
           & all your past emotions
   seem tiny, crude simulacra of its beauty.
   & you are totally free

7)   Greater than all Magellans
     you commence an adventure more huge and intricate
     than the complete idea of Mt Everest.
     And this academy can teach you no more.
                         The voyage will branch out,
     seem boring & faraway from the head,
     but nothing can delay you
     for nothing is lost to the head.

8)   Goodbye,

               send me postcards
               and colourful native stamps,
                                        Good luck!

                                                    1976

Speed, a Pastoral

it's fun to take speed
& stay up all night
not writing those reams of poetry
just thinking about is bad for you
                    – instead your feelings
follow your career down the drain
& find they like it there
among an anthology of fine ideas, bound together
by a chemical in your blood
that lets you stare the TV in its vacant face
& cheer, consuming yourself like a mortgage
& when Keats comes to dine, or Flaubert,
you can answer their purities
with your own less negative ones – for example
you know Dransfield's line, that once you become a junkie
you'll never want to be anything else?
               well, I think he died too soon,
as if he thought drugs were an old-fashioned teacher
& he was the teacher's pet, who just put up his hand
                    & said quietly, 'Sir, sir'
               & heroin let him leave the room.

                                                    1988

Love Poem

Spent tracer flecks Baghdad's
bright video game sky

as I curl up with the war
in lieu of you, whose letter

lets me know my poems show
how unhappy I can be. Perhaps.

But what they don't show, until
now, is how at ease I can be

with military technology: e.g.
matching their *feu d'esprit* I classify

the sounds of the Iraqi AA – the
thump of the 85 mil, the throaty

chatter of the quad ZSU 23.
Our precision guided weapons

make the horizon flash & glow
but nothing I can do makes you

want me. Instead I watch the west
do what the west does best

& know, obscurely, as I go to bed
all this is being staged for me.   *1992*

Ode to Karl Marx

Old father of the horrible bride whose
wedding cake has finally collapsed, you

spoke the truth that doesn't set us free –
it's like a lever made of words no one's

learnt to operate. So the machine it once
connected to just accelerates & each new

rap dance video's a perfect image of this,
bodies going faster and faster, still dancing

on the spot. At the moment tho' this set up
works for me, being paid to sit and write &

smoke, thumbing through Adorno like *New Idea*
on a cold working day in Ballarat, where

adult unemployment is 22% & all your grand
schemata of intricate cause and effect

work out like this: take a muscle car &
wire its accelerator to the floor, take out

the brakes, the gears the steering wheel
& let it rip. The dumbest tattooed hoon

– mortal diamond hanging round the Mall –
knows what happens next. It's fun unless

you're strapped inside the car. I'm not,
but the dummies they use for testing are.   *1992*

PHILIP SALOM (*b 1950*)

Driving to Bury his Ashes

Already late. Trying to make up time, worrying
the high revs will eat the oil, or shrink bearings,
but when I slow to eighty kilometres per hour
something in the underworld of cars, odd karma,

starts shaking and won't stop, worse than normal
tremors of the wheel in my fingers, wrists,
even the door is trembling and it only stops
when I accelerate to a hundred and twenty

on the wet road, the tail-spray from other cars
blinding on the windscreen and slow cars
suddenly appearing. Sunlight swoops and flattens
and I squint through water-glare as if

the car's enveloped in a gleaming dress
sheer and wanton from the body of the road,
unsure if I'm staring at the luminous distance
gone from judgement, or the nearness of accident.

I drive with a kind of passion
returning now that death has worn us down,
as if he's gone there first, taken the worst of it
and made it less. He would have hated *this*:

the car pitched like a high note through corners,
the car beating the road down through the rain
and nerve-line over-taking. It's odder than fear
or the held-back yell in the body of a skid—

tyres hit a sheet of water and aquaplane:
the wheel goes smooth, and quiet, time gone
like the moments after he stopped breathing
then began again. I take the long flat speed

of Benger straight, slowing, then stopping at
the cemetery. And turning the engine off.
The first one here.

                    *

It is sealed so well
we do not open the plastic urn
for fear of spilling his ashes
so we lower it into the hole intact.
It is only the size of a present
you might pass to someone at Xmas
and is less real somehow
than the work-face of the spade
worn silver in the shape of a heart
we have dug the hole with.

We stand into the west wind
which is cold and dry now
and buffeting my mother
who is so frail from it all
she has to lean, and I see her
wavering in the strength
the pushing back and letting-go
of loss. And we all know
it was right of her to choose
to bury him here with the son
they lost forty years ago,
the last-born who filled her
life deeply then was gone.

It almost seems sometimes
the dead fall back a generation
to belong. The two of them,
silent and aching on a slope
facing west, over to Benger
farms where she was born,
the coast and the silver ocean,
and where she is next to go.
We stand, free of the awful
shuddering grief, just tears
and the wind and this sudden
clarity, of having buried him.   *2001*

The Composer Shostakovich Orders His Funeral

What is *Negativity* ? What is *Sarcasm*?
If it's anything like 100 proof, I'll drink it.
It patters in my stomach like a snare drum,
yes: the tense skin (psoriasis) the drumstick
allegros which clatter down the wrist.
The minor keys always, the only big beats
(savage) of Stalin's Boots, his banging
up the staircase at 4am (bedwetting time).
Got your little suitcase packed? *Composer?*

My music could end with a single
note: a hole in the back of the neck.
I hear thousands of notes, a symphony
and nothing happens. He grunts once,
and thousands die. Who moves more people?
Who is the Greatest Artist? Composer Stalin!

What kind of citizen does he want?
The Future: a one-size-for-all blow-up doll,
eyes wide open, legs wide open, mouth shut.
Yes, opinions nil. A clean arse.
Paranoia turned out into the snow sets cold.
Don't say anything wrong, or your son
will denounce you. Ah, yes, he has.

The West burnt their red-hot brand
on me, their man who fell from the rack
into detractions, denunciations, post mortems.
What's *A Soviet Artist's Reply to Just Criticism?*
Why is the mighty Ninth, the Beethovean
Romantic Knee-Trembler instead a Knee-Jerk
Dud? Either that or dedicate it in Glory
to the Secretary General Himself – do
my best work for Him? I shit instead.

The Great Puppeteer Himself! Little
Shostakovich is just a click-jointed player
chewing his lips . . . ventriloquism for manic
mixed metaphors: Tragedy is everywhere but
look, listen: everyone is happy, happy,
oh, everyone is well informed, or well-
informed on. Unhappiness is not allowed.

Arh, accused yet again: damned and damned
from Stalin down, from US academics up.
In the West they know everything – that the puppet
is the real me. In the West they just don't kill
their artists like they used to. We do.
Arthur Miller is rightly shaken seeing me.
I am a native of Shaken.

       Even the Age's Seer
after a night of coffee and heavy dossiers
needs an outlet: what a noise he makes
pissing into the water of the toilet.
There! That's Greatness. *That's* music.
Uh uh, too much gravity . . .
General Tractor Anthemist! Blight of Agriculture.
Piss in the snow. Piss in the faces of the damned.
Why won't somebody kill him?

Andante, adagio, standstill.
The window panes are sheets of vodka
but I get sober looking through them.
When I go walking I breathe out
from my note-perfect memory
clouds of absence: poets, peasants, generals,
all killed equally. Is life any easier
because of music? I need a coat and scarf:

I hear silenced gunshots in the snow.
Old women he broke, Party men who
shat their pants every day they met him,
fall down in despair. He is dead. *Dead?*
00 proof. Bastard.
Ah Nikita: and the thaw, the freeze, thaw, freeze.
Ah Brezhnev, grey suits, bleak and buttons,
a frieze of medals. I could hang a whole sonata
in the space between his nose and his lips.

I think I'll die.

KEVIN BROPHY (*b 1949*)

What I believe

I believe the world is round like a ball and spins through space.
This belief helps me get along with neighbours and work colleagues.
Without it I would be mad or sick, I believe.
I believe there are human footprints on the moon.
This belief helps me to bear watching television news.
I believe that money is the shadow of infinity,
that I will die and know nothing about it.
I believe you are like me.
This belief, I believe, makes me a fool or an optimist.
I believe most of us mistake the present for the past,
and that the future is the past;
that what is right is nearly always obvious;
that belief works best as a necessity or a distraction.
I believe the universe is a dangerous place.
I believe that God is an elaborate and mediocre idea;
that panic is our companion,
and travelling through space will be the last of our tasks.
I believe the purpose of all this is the creation of memory.
I believe most beliefs are yet to be discovered.
I believe in what is most fragile and uncertain,
the paragraph, for instance, or clouds; rain; leaves.
I believe death makes love possible,
and that if you do not train them at once your beliefs
    will bark all night.   *2002*

Walking towards sunset

I could have kept going past my front door
all the way to the end of the street and across
the tops of the shops, on over Moonee Ponds Creek
and beyond the hills of Essendon to a stony ledge
where the sky drops to the floor of the galaxy
and bends back up, an infinite dome, over my head.
I would have stood there, toes over the rocky edge,
knowing my eyes were made for looking at this:

the last slant-wise flash of careless brilliance
from that unimaginable bomb in the daily sky,
as silent as a distant war, filling doubt with light;
and from that ledge it would have seemed an answer
to last night's dream. I would have stayed
until the day abandoned me as each one does.   *2002*

MARTIN HARRISON (*b 1949*)

Late Western Thought

There were crested pigeons
whirring up
from the edges of the driveway –

getting lift-off with
their high-pitched wing beats,
like springs rattling in an old car.

So, you couldn't help but notice them.
You took them in
much the same way the piebald horse had started wandering over:

the horse was a fat-bellied shadow ambling through the stillness
where the light was turning.
Nearby, some thistles: beyond them, the mare and pony grazed on the slope.

You'd see none of this clearly till later.
(There would have been your own looking, walking, to account for.)
The pigeons, the horse, the crickets, the dwarf paperbarks were just there,

scarcely visible,
secretly communicative in
every direction like a place where paths, meandering, at last meet.

Sure, a bird had then cried out
as if the moment could go dark with an utter suddenness.
You'd remember that bird as (somewhere) a cuckoo-dove before rain.

(You'd remember it as a whoop, a shout, rather than a call.)
But you would, by then, be walking back down the driveway
oblivious to the clay-coloured light, the pale wisps of grass

and the heaped-up blemish of gravel
which marked some ants-nest, living or abandoned.
Later, you'd say you saw everything. It entered you.

Of course, it remains no more than a story.
About seeing and forgetting, its narrative is the root of compassion,
not least because, afterwards, you must still capture it at one go –

yes, in a single, sharp flame of light –

setting and slanting,
raking deep fire behind the trees (they're black silhouettes on the ridge),
invisibly burning you, invisibly burning itself.

2001

ALAN GOULD (*b 1949*)

The Move from Shelter

Laughing, we raced for the nearest shelter, found
a vast workshop, within which gloom we stood
among the chainblocks, lathes, heavy vices,
all recently abandoned. We breathed
a pungency of motor oil and metal filings.
For half an hour the downpour's roar cocooned us,
its ambient hiss a constancy like
the white noise between television channels.
So that we felt exposed when the storm dwindled,
and we started out, climbing through woods,
the sky tremendous in aftermath, cloudwrack
glimpsed and sunlight liquid, foliage bright
like brass on a lathe, diaphanous in places,
at each slight breeze the canopy dripping,

the whippy branches beside our track flicking
rain in our faces, droplets scintillant,
momentary in the air like a storm
of asteroids against the green tumult of leaves.
Our berets, tunics, were rain-darkened, clung
to the skin as though they were some loose
reptilian skin, our boots rain-sheeny, slippy,
and the cold of our hands, our faces, which neither
the sun nor our movement seemed to warm,
spread throughout our bodies, like the cold
in the tree's heartwood, in the flakes of shale
tumbling from our boots downhill, cold
of the gleaming earth itself and its creatures
easing cramped limbs as they ghosted themselves
deeper into their small hollows.
                              It is . . .
it is this *detail* near the sense, mundane
yet filigreed with such cold beauty that
I cannot disentangle from the mind
as we descend to the little village
and see the evidence report has spoken of,
and call up the helicopters, and zipper
the plastic bags, remarking how the rain
has slimed the different surfaces of all
that has been burnt in this place into
a black paste which fouls our uniforms
and makes it impossible to distinguish
the blackness that brushes us, clings to us,
whether it is charcoal from some roofbeam
or some blackened, suppliant human hand.   *1996*

Intently

From the darkness and audience foot-shuffle
I'm watching this man of instinctive kindness.
He is busy in the wings, arranging props,
intently dabbing lollipops of makeup
on small cheeks. Later, he will glimmer
with hilarity, will guffaw louder than any dad
as the kids come on and do their cute routines.

He's thickset, weathered like an upland farmer,
I can imagine him dressing a lamb carcass,
or present at the birth of a calf. Sometimes with parents
I've watched him listen askance, like one patient
with a foreigner's attempts to be understood.
Yes, here's good-will, as ever in the wings,
but no less a form of imperial rule for that.

And when the corridors seethe, he deals
not with children, but with mass and flux,
yet his eye is there for the one child
enclosed in grief's absolute. It's this astounds,
this overflow of self-possession. It is
charity deep as the gene pool. I note how it dances
across the tenets of dogma, evasive as Puck.

For you have it or you don't, they say,
this knack of living like light at the shifting point
of others' need. Lacking that gift, I watch,
and my envy is disarmed by this,
this intent, thickset man busy with paints
among small faces upturned toward him,
that sway and vie, unconscious as sunflowers.   *1996*

An Interrogator's Opening Remarks

We have no wish to lead you anywhere.
If anything we'd like to do you good.
The facts, of course, will shine like silverware,
but you must feel secure; that's understood.

A good rapport is what we're really after.
By all means keep the things you know concealed.
We know you know, behind the tea and laughter,
your secrets are a gravitational field.

We're falling in toward them very fast.
This happens by your simply being here
subtracted from the household of your past,
naked with what we think you think is dear.

So now let's chat, old son. You're not alone.
Your time is ours. Your choices are your own.   *1996*

Approaching the Edge

Life lies always at some frontier, making sorties into the unknown.

M C Richards

1

What did they suppose, those Age of Discovery mariners,
as they sailed towards the known world's rim?
Were there any atheists on those European ships?
Some knew Pliny had reported tribes whose one leg
doubled as a parasol, men whose nostrils
functioned a mouth and that the Garamantes
were promiscuous, like sailors. Some heard Iambulus had visited
a 'happy isle' where the inhabitants clicked divided tongues
and spoke two ways at once. Some believed Raphael Nonsenso
sailed to Utopia with Vespucci, unaware the Greek
meant 'no place'. Most, I suspect, had glimpsed cow-hide
and vellum maps, the plated backs of serpents
eating their own tails, the script 'terra incognita'
and ink coastlines that started as approximations
and trailed away into the sea. They may have fancied dragons,
giants, men with horns and wings, women with barking heads,
the wondrous beasts that travellers sighted but never
managed to bring home. There would have been a moment
that they couldn't see, a moment when they could have
drawn back, before their ship felt the tug, the current
above a waterfall, and they were swept towards the edge.
Where did this water go? Where was I about to fall?

2

It's only from the air that the western desert paintings
make sense to the European eye – dunes in a dry creek bed,
passages between waterholes, the return of Halley's Comet.
Maps and Dreaming. Is it all known and passed on,
a negotiation and representation of the world
telling the lies that get to truth? To what did they aspire?
Does anyone remember Icarus now, or Daedalus,
the greatest inventor of his age? Who made the axe,
the wedge, the wimble, sails for ships and built the labyrinth.
And the son ... such primitive technology, paper and wax,

and ninety-three million miles to the sun. From Stanwell Tops
we float beneath nylon sails, hang from carbon fibre rods,
all the physics calculated to defy gravity for a while.
But there's only one direction so we must land
and carry our contraptions back up the cliff if we're to fly again.
Aldrin, Armstrong, Collins knew where they were going
better than Magellan whose circumnavigation
took twelve days short of three long years. Their maps were clear,
complete, we watched them all the way, a small step, two hundred
and thirty thousand miles and just four days away.
The footprints they left on the moon will last at least
ten million years. Which is more frightening, to know
exactly where you're going or think you'll never know?

3

Anaximander thought the earth a cylinder suspended
from the vault of heaven and it's been round, rectangular
and oval since. The Mappaemundi depicted earth as flat,
Jerusalem its centre, sea around the clustered land.
There was order in the heavens, astrology unified
terrestrial and celestial realms and even thunderstorms
were humours of the gods. A lawful universe:
sailors set their course by the stars, spirits lived in water
and in fire, were placated by rites and sacrifice.
Without auguries, entrails, Newton could predict the future;
on a piece of paper, calculate the past: a lawful universe,
though his rigid laws of motion were another myth. Matter roams
more or less at random, and we are atoms caught between
too many worlds, undecided where to go, energy created
and destroyed. The further Hubble sees the more we shrink,
yet I blink and Jupiter's moons respond. The universe
may be expanding, might be infinite, might not, could be
curved into a hypersphere without boundary, nowhere
a centre or an edge. Could be doughnut shaped, a labyrinth,
wormholes where we live other lives in a different time
and place, or a Mobius strip so we go round and come back
mirror images of ourselves. There are singularities
from which no traveller has returned. God may not play dice,
but the world's a game of chance and we're high rollers,
shaking our fists, blowing into cupped hands,
murmuring 'seven, seven', shooting snake's eyes.

4

How very different we are and how alike.
On the edge of Pulpit Rock I lie on my back,
look to the sky locked above me like the hatch
of a bathysphere and descend, the pressure equal
and increasing on either side of its tight skin.
Theoretically, travelling near the speed of light,
we could circumnavigate the galaxy in about four years
and return four hundred thousand years after we set out.
Time does not move but we chase our future into the past
and can't hold on to now. You sit with your legs hanging
into the cold air trapped between banks of cliff. Below you
each tree is clear and distinct; across the valley
they run in waves and intermingle until the canopy
is a plum-blue sea. Mist drifts towards the south-west falls.
Magellan took thirty-seven days to cross the straits
that bear his name, a narrow, twisting passage
through mountains clamped in snow; had already
executed one ship's captain – mutiny – and lost one ship
to storm. Another doubting captain took the *San Antonio*
back to Spain. Magellan passed from Atlantic to Pacific seas
but how to separate one drop of water from another
undifferentiated drop? We're sailing different seas and similar,
you and I, looking up or down, seeing monsters.

5

My sails are wanting for the wind. Between their slack canvas
and the water, sun repeats and I shade my eyes to look
to the rudder and a rope hanging from the stern.
I look for your figure on the shore, the creaking fixity
of the pier, the sandstone blocks that make the promenade,
the way the grass grows up towards the rotunda balanced
like a fo'c'sle in drydock for repairs. One Empire Day
we built a bonfire in the park, let off Roman Candles, rockets,
Catherine Wheels and threw bungers between each other's legs.
A match fell into one boy's stash and it blew up,
a revelation that left him shocked to tears: in seconds
the merging of a black hole and a neutron star
expels the energy the sun lets go in ten billion years.
When white light strikes the upper atmosphere
it scatters to create blue sky; at the horizon, the pressure
and greater depth of air deplete the shorter frequencies
and we see red though each colour has its shade of grey.
Low tide grounds a fleet of bluebottles, sails swelling

in the sun. Boys burst them with their feet or pick them up
on sticks and chase their sisters up the beach.
After Magellan had been killed, Juan Sebastian del Cano
assumed command. Shipworm forced him to abandon
the *Conception*, and the leaky *Trinidad* was left behind.
I look towards the far edge of the sea, the straight line
between a double shade of blue, the tinfoil glints
that spark like uncertainty on a radar screen.
My charts are waterproof, I have a radio, dry food,
spare batteries for the beacon should the boat capsize.
I can find no more words to give you, my lips
the hatchway to a locked sentence, my eyes shut tight.
Still the wind does not come and I make no move.

6

Where do I end and you begin? What marks the border between us?
We walked from India to Nepal without knowing,
threw away the dope when we turned to see a watchtower
with a flag. Even this was unmanned so, unwilling to go back,
we went on to find the river was up and there was no way
to get to Kathmandu. Indo-Chinese countries wrap around
each other like sleeping bodies, Vietnam folds both Laos
and Cambodia in its embrace. The Berlin Wall
split the world between east and west. Magellan sailed
to see on which side the Spice Isles lay, in Portugal's domain
or Spain's, but there's no fixed point, just directions
and relationships. He left Seville with five ships, two hundred
and seventy men or thereabouts. Del Cano returned
with just one ship and barely twenty men. When I lie by you,
am I touching another or myself, can we be considered separate
when we interact? Did we choose this small bed
or is our existence here some unlikely chance? There's a tendency
to follow a pre-determined path but deviations do occur
and are significant on a sub-atomic scale. The Greeks,
the church, Newton, all were wrong but the world worked for them –
even for Einstein belief's as powerful as truth.
In the beginning was the bang and the end may be one too –
between the first and last frontiers we walk no-man's-land,
look for cow-hide, vellum, the spoor of unicorns, ask for water,
abandon hope, and wake to hope and fail again. On the border
silence stands guard, its edge suspicious as a customs officer's eye,
each word a possible transgression, a clue to a smuggled heart.

2000

Postscript: like Picasso

A man's just sitting there on the crescent
taking it all in or letting it all pass by,
the traffic, birdcall, the sun that falls
on his bald head polishing it like Picasso's,
all brown and round and shining,
sitting there like a stone or a frog or a Buddha.

He is of it all, even this speeding past,
the wheels that push away contradictions
between the need to grip and the need to
slip away. He must feel the cars pull air after them
in packets, swoosh, swoosh, and another
swoosh, as he sits there in the gaps, persistently.   *2003*

JOHN JENKINS (*b 1949*)

Push This Wall Back

Push this wall as far back as you can.
Now as the bricks fall down, trace
in their dusty trance what you have told yourself,
stories you remember, some of which actually happened.

The story you invent from memory says where you
come from, have been, are finally going.
It says why you! And why not. And how we all fit
into bigger memories called history and culture.

Is civilisation too big a word for little worlds like us
to fill? Is the tiny 'I' excluded? How many voices
must chorus its successive waves before you find
your voice in that receding wave of voices? You hear
you everywhere, and see your face in the profile of an age.

No wonder there are gaps! If we could recall any
hour truthfully, it would take an hour to recall!
A day a day, a year of years to tell all
that detail, shining dust of tears, from the miles
of files, just like the real thing. God's memory perhaps
is like atoms buzzing on, a cosmos beaming
it all back again, out of the big black hole in which time
just disappears! How could we endure it?   *2008*

Six O'clock Swill

Mr Menzies takes me by the hand, glancing at the clocks of
Flinders Street Station. It's ten to six. He eyes the display
of hats at the corner, picturing himself in dove-grey Akubra,
but shakes his head. We cross, and stand outside the doors
of *Young & Jacksons*, unseen by the working men who reel
from every door to leave their pile of steaming sick retched
into the gutter, spit and stagger, then barge a way back in,
through blasts of beer fumes and drinkers pressing forward,
elbow-tight, back to the bar. 'Ahem, young man, this is not a pretty
sight, yet salutary. Do you know that word?' (I nod.) Menzies
melts straight through two big plate-glass doors, and I follow;
his hand is cool in mine. Though we are invisible to it, the crowd
falls back from us. 'Just as well, or they might make a fuss,
seeing their PM in this unseemly den.' The reek of men in singlets
and boots erupts. Summer air, sweet with nausea and foam.
'The sweat of many backs built pyramids,' he notes.
Adrenalin awash with slops, at five minutes to the hour.
Everything floats and erupts at once. The hubbub is immense,
rising like the hands that ferry 'shouts' above a stale gloom,
liquid gold drips down backs, from the jump back to knots
of men with tongues like unrolling carpets, a sip or gulp
to hit the back throat. And one more. And again.
Big hands grab and spill with clunk and clutter
at the glasses, shake in racks and dash them under handles
filled in rows and rows, two minutes left and gulping down.
Mr Menzies frowns. 'This,' he says, 'is the very picture
of insobriety. What is the answer? Encourage savings,
or church leaders might exhort them, good influence
of wives, a thin line between them and complete ruin –
six o'clock! That is when the pubs shut.' (I nod again.)
'My boy, stay away from this. A whisky by your fireside,
or lager on a hot day at the picnic races. But do not blight your life
with intemperance.' The crowd rocks. Suddenly, it's six o'clock.
Then I tell him my idea. 'Why not keep the pubs open, so they
don't swill?' 'Ah, sweet innocence of youth!' His indulgent smile.
'If we did that, these chaps would drink all night. Drink, until they
could not stand, or walk, or work. They would be paralytic.'
I tell Mr Menzies, I don't know that word. 'Ah, *stonkered*!'

2008

Pride of Erin

The public telephone is a cage for the exhibition
    of Chrissie.
She comes from Science to the shop.
Saunters with her friends through a suburb of dogs,
    keeping ahead of evening, just beating it inside.
Smoke from the slow-combustion heaters.
A sun, low in the sky, giving lamplight and no warmth.
A dying star and the domino theory of barking, when
    light starts to fail.
She has trouble with the door; with instructions.
Is afraid of losing her coin; doesn't have another one
    on her right now.
Is afraid of *not at home. Might be round at Greg's.*
And outside, Sharon and Cheryl and Debbie are wearing
    duffle coats, in range.
She is a carrier of nomadic truth.
Wishes commitment.
Knows of energies deep within her, under pressure, that
    she squanders on choir or keeping things clean.
No-one guesses them.
They are efforts of will.
Soldiers win medals with them.
She watches the duffle coats picking at dusk.
Watches the way teenage girls jostle and shift; are
    non-committal, like baboons.
Can't stop herself being like this most times.
Finds herself doing it.
Wonders if noticing things is the essence of growing
    old; and that as we pass some mid-point it falls
    away again, eventually back to nothing.
With difficulty, she comes from the booth into what
    is left of today.
Makes her turn.
Watches her friends move on.
In the darkness they seem to float, like objects
    displacing their own weight in water.

1984

Polka

But the park was in trouble long before the man and his dog arrived. Summer had brought its permanent cushion of drunkards to the benches, and under the knife-wounded tree trunks picnics flourished like bird-baths. The dog was excited. It bounced. It leapt through the hysterical hoops of command. People aren't fond of leaping dogs and advertise them in the paper as being 'good with children'. I first learned to translate classified advertisements when looking for a house to rent. That 'sunny' means a Sahara treelessness, and 'students ok' means contaminated. Once I nearly inspected a house described as 'unusual'. Beneath far-away trees loosely bandaged with newspaper, the man seemed very small – almost the ideal first home. And his dog, still testing some distant trampoline. 'Olympian'. 'Suit conversationalist'. 'Loves height'.

1984

MICHAEL DRANSFIELD (1948-73)

Fix

It is waking in the night,
after the theatres and before the milkman,
alerted by some signal from the golden drug tapeworm
that eats your flesh and drinks your peace;
you reach for the needle and busy yourself
preparing the utopia substance in a blackened
spoon held in candle flame
by now your thumb and finger are leathery
being so often burned this way
it hurts much less than withdrawal and the hand
is needed for little else now anyway.
Then cordon off the arm with a belt,
probe for a vein, send the dream-transfusion out
on a voyage among your body machinery. Hits you like sleep –
sweet, illusory, fast, with a semblance of forever.
For a while the fires die down in you,
until you die down in the fires.
Once you have become a drug addict
you will never want to be anything else.   *1970*

The Escape from Youth

My father's discipline closed me like a box.
A hardness hammered shut the lid.
For fifteen years, no matter what he did,
I was unreachable. Venom sealed the locks.

Neutral beauty kept me company. Walking
through neighbours' cattle, from moving skies and trees
I learnt the slower vaster intimacies.
Avoiding the world of men, I stopped talking,

except intensely to myself. Rumours
of happiness sometimes seeped outside the box.
'Untrue!' I howled, and double-checked the locks.
In the dark, poetry grew like a tumour.

When the poems were big enough to break
their way out, dragging me behind, I saw
my father's face, more bitten than before,
a soft fist eaten by love, impossible to hate.

There is no forgiveness now, nor the need.
Silence bred rich fruits – a known self, those skies –
for which I thank my father. Amnesia lies
behind our peace. Neither of us dares to bleed.   *1989*

Heat

Under aspens with their white flowers falling
silently as snow, a boy and a girl,
maybe seventeen, leaning through stale air towards
each other, across a table in the packed
Athens square where waiters with silver trays
swerve and swoop, bringing beer, ouzo, mezethes.
I love you, says the boy with believable eyes.

Smooth as pebbles in the sea's mouth, one bleached phrase
among endless collisions of speech, his words
flame towards originality, barrel
through the soft mulch of overuse in centuries
of verse, ballads and popular songs, sliding

between bed sheets rancid with rhetoric
to touch down softly in the pit of her stomach.

Evening with its white locks falling open,
a shady Athens square with its girl and boy
like two cauldrons carrying the same hot liquid
dissolving everything – the square, the tables,
their bodies – into one delicious urgency.
In the evening cool they rise and disappear
down a narrow street where, still burning

they knock at my lit door and find it locked.
Laughing, they walk away quickly, choosing
night with its pale flesh slowly opening.   *1989*

ALAN WEARNE (*b 1948*)

*Legend: Jack, the barman, talks to Kim. Saturday,
6 June 1970, 1.15 a.m.*

from The Lovemakers

   Kim, I know what's happening; you better know
what's happening. The manager's suspicious and, since he thinks
I know these things, trust me, I say, Kim's mighty clean.
Doesn't he look it? The manager, of course, knows this
but what's, he asks, what's that boy *do?*
                                  Can I keep you
out of trouble? What do you think!
                                  Instead,
I'll circle to my point. In Melbourne
I've this mate, this silly mate. A few weeks back,
whilst I'm down there, Bernie,
who for his sins is something of a poof at times,
Bernie thinks he's met this kid, your age,
who's horny for him. And he is not.
And I was ringside to it: all the set-up,
all the follow-through and final mess, the blubbering threats,
the being mad enough to phone this boy at home,
start to abuse his dad.
                          It's okay, this tale hardly fits
my kind of line (and even if it did
I'd never turn on diamond-eyes for you, young Lacy)

but I like what I'm seeing and my point is:
we have to get to know each other better
(isn't that what Bernie's tiny tragedy is
telling us?) much better.
            Yes I know a few Americans:
stand back though, look at your actions, look at them again:
we aren't repeat we aren't in Gangland USA.
And even if we were you're no Al Capone.
Courtesy of Dad you're the local semi-rich kid,
thanks to your few plantations (small, discreet)
trying to make the extra quid, liking the idea
of breaking out.
         But the Americans?
Kim cobber, mate, pal, son, old son,
imagine *them* as a more, much more, ridiculous *us*,
and then imagine *us* trying to play at *them*;
ask: where can, when will, such parodies
cease?
      What the Americans are bringing in
they sure aren't bringing out.
           They're certain to like
what you have and,
though the deal's to swap it for something that,
on occasions, kills (I need to tell you, Kim, kills)
the kids love it.
       I won't even look at it:
me who did my stretch ten/ eleven/ twelve
years back, who coped, but hardly needs to do
much of that again.
         Could I keep you out of trouble?
Well there's trouble-trouble and there's
getting-caught trouble. What do you think!
All I can advise is Kim, ask yourself:
how far do I wish to travel; and then take your pick.
    Have *I* killed anyone? Have I *killed* anyone? Have I killed *anyone?*
    We should know each other better.
I find it near impossible to reply:
but there may've been this person, so I'll try.
No, I didn't hate this person, probably loved
this person, but one day I returned from where
I'd been to find out what my trust was worth,
what this person truly, quite and simple,
was, had done. Who never knew how caught

they were. Just once I took this person
behind some building (I was being trusted now) and . . .
left them for dead? Let's say
I haven't seen them since.
                              I've killed?
I doubt it.
          Doubts, though, are never enough.
          I hope not.
          You better know what's happening, Kim.   *2001*

Carrie, Wal

from The Lovemakers

          Part ingenue/part flapper, Carrie could sing *Do do do*
what you done done done before baby
high steppin' in with top hat and tails, kisses,
trilling a quite passable do re mi;
in this, Wal's other world, with all its democracy of hugs,
she could ignore that malicious sneer *Getta life!*

For it was envy which fuelled the getta life
syndrome: if her men were where and when required . . . whacky doo
          There is a certain premium in hugs:
Carrie had often craved them like a baby.
But no use blubbering *Why me?*
Why the woman in the moon!
                              Then though came the kisses.

You could lose your brain with kisses.
And, once they'd evaporated, 'When will I really getta life?'
you asked. 'What went before was hardly *me*:
all that strangers in the night dooby dooby doo
taa ciao see ya round baby.'
          Wal always greeted his friends with hugs,

there was no other way, hugs
were a necessity.
                    'But Carrie,' he confessed, 'the kisses!'
Oooooh baby!'
And Wal, OIC Operation Gettalife,
let forth a Flintstonian *Yabba dabba doo!*
What? Embarrassed? Who? Me?

Wal's friends enjoyed Carrie. 'They know me,'
she felt proud to say, 'know me as safe.' (Though attempting
                anything but hugs
would find her up past the neck in deep doo-doo.)
And if you had to double-take men giving each other kisses
in today's world, well getta life,
get two!
          And if Wal sometimes was one big baby,

thanks for the practice, one day she might produce a baby.
(Since there must be some dimension beyond *Me*,
myself and I name her a better way to getta life.)
      But would that be the final outcome of the hugs,
the total destination of the kisses?
For they could chill her, all the intricate dos

'n' don'ts of hugs 'n' kisses,
and the smug resignation of *It'll do me*
was never Carrie's way.
                'Getta life?' she asked no-one but
                herself '. . . getta baby?'

2004

ALEX SKOVRON (*b 1948*)

The Note

Savaged at the skirts by a terrier toddler
yelping a tongue of rage she alone
translates, she alone, she the one mad lunge
away from public loss, she the one
arbitrary breath from private break,
savaged, cracked, is astonished to detect

a drawn-out half-inhuman howl
filling out like dye the supermarket aisle,
a wail into whose pedalpoint she very slowly
tunes, to claim it as her own.

1999

Some Precepts of Postmodern Mourning

There must be a body, but there needn't be.
The body must be remembered with some fondness:
there must be at least two eulogists, and a third
must have been detained by traffic or a death
and the service must proceed. Sex
must be mentioned, but preferably not, except at the wake
or the seance when most words are permissible again.
On second thought, this precept needn't apply.
But at least one text must be read from,
preferably composed by the body and significant; it
must include expletives, but needn't do so.
Everyone must look dignified and important, or at least
significant; move deliberately but not heavily; smile
but laugh once only. Black must be avoided,
except in socks and sunglasses, which must be worn
during the service as well as outside afterwards.
There must at least be a reference to Celtic poetry
or Jewish ancestry, and both Testaments must be drawn upon.
Someone must remark 'I still can't believe it'
then 'Yes I can', and someone must respond
with a philosophical but solicitous lift of an eyebrow.
One of the mourners must be overheard to whisper,
'I'm surprised she didn't come, though it doesn't
surprise me.' It must be noted that the body
could never suffer fools gladly, and someone
must observe how much he or she is only now learning
about the body. Someone must say at least one Italian thing
either to the mourners or to the body, but a French
or German or Latin or Spanish or Sanskrit thing
will do, or a thing in any other accredited language,
provided the expression is significant. There must be
no public mysticism, though there may be, and coffee
or white wine must be served afterwards. Someone
needs to be squinting tears, preferably a large man
in a double-breasted suit with a crimson kerchief
protruding rudely, coupled with a pallid pusillanimous
niece with a weak chin and beatific smile
nodding with significance. Reincarnation must be accepted
by at least half the mourners, but not mentioned,
though strange omens and premonitions over recent weeks
must be seen as significant in retrospect.

The body must be understood to be pleased with the service,
the simple dignity and grace of the occasion,
the Baroque cantata, the words, the weather. Everything
must be just so. Everything must be significant.
Though in the end it needn't be. Later, this in itself
must be acknowledged as most significant of all,
or at least put down to the quintessential irony of death.

2003

Supper Song

The perfect utterance is not enough
The measured utterance The disembodied face
Baying at the moon
Is not enough You are not
And I am not enough To have been guided
Out of Egypt is not enough
Climbed to the pinnacle
Of ashes or the point of a pin is not enough
To have danced in the storm Danced
Inside the needle's eye Danced upon the tongue
Of a fat flame is not enough
To have stared stared into the eye
Of the needle or curled into its thin comfort
Is not enough The comfort
Of blistering flame The slash
Of blistering ice in the jaws of dawn
Is not enough The knife
Turning gold in its glistening hand
Is not enough And the flung stone And the lamp
At midnight
Sweating a thin song is not enough
                              No song
Is enough without the inconsolable tide No word
Enough without the groan under the earth
The dizzy sudden shock of a plummeting flight
Downward into the well of a dream
Down into the square cell
At the staircase foot No fever No magical flute
Is enough without the shuddering breath
No lie enough without its drunken truth
No life without its death O pathos
Of the spheres

2003

Going down. With no permanence

I'm finding it impossible to begin, as you've ended so little. Last night my heart was a cheap flag waving to the nearest mirror in sight. I couldn't believe anything, seeing you drive away into others' arms. I'm no sweet virgin sock-washer either. So it's a matter of priorities I guess, just who wants to gamble. Talk of loving when there is no goal. Of belief when there is no road. My shoes are off and I'm walking barefoot. Down a long avenue of arms and kisses like knots. I'm getting tired and angry and thinking hell, I'm no sock-washer but there must be some other venue. I say my heart's big enough, it is. Every time it's eaten and collapses like a cough.

Today I'm trying to be reasonable. You're having breakfast with her. And there's no wedding ring, baby, fidelity, photo. No day to week token of what we have, a visible future. Crazy thing, it's happening everywhere. You waft into my room bringing delicious words, eyes, every other love you're still attached to, claim.

'I want all love-rites simultaneously.'

'I don't want to negate anything.'

Yes I understand. Incredible egotist! that one cracked heart is your own, gyrating in its uncertainty. Adoration. Adulation. Your heart seeks to reflect itself. Narcissus in the bath. How many loves do you want? Are you never full, leaky bucket?

And now you turn to your sock-washer reasoning socks are better than none. So you're surrounded again. Pursued and claimed. A shroud of outrage going up. Thinking of numbers and lines. It sharpens your humour. While I love this one the others must love me too. I'll keep my heart spinning. You think you're responding, keeping all the doors open. Yes. Yes.

This is the road my bare feet touch. Going down. The avenue with few affirmatives. Going down. With no permanence. This is the alternative to restrictions. So we assume. Without end.

1973

The country as an answer

Endlessly walking the green hills in wet agitated goloshes,
trees lean outwards . . . they are nothing but leaves,
beautiful, coloured, falling and dying. The hills rise up,
breasts faces hands, their silence is complete.

I sit down and mud falls from my boots.

Cows plod towards a creek.

Not a single person is visible as the landscape flows and
dips . . . invisible dyings . . . no answer but what it is.
I have come a thousand miles to be here.
Peace, they tell me, sending messages from the black city.
This is what peace is? No use for the earth but as a place
to lie down in . . . faceless bodiless . . . passive with
admiration? There is no love or hate here, the contrast is
so subtle.

I feel the mud in my hands, the wet bright grass.

I understand I am meaningless here, merely another presence
. . . the trees do not recognise me, the cows do not remember.

The landscape has absorbed me, giving nothing to be desired.

1973

MARTIN JOHNSTON (1947-90)

The typewriter, considered as a bee-trap,

is no doubt less than perfectly adapted
to its function, just as a bee-trap,
if there are such things, would hardly be the ideal contrivance
for the writing of semi-aleatory poems about
bee-traps and typewriters. Why, in any case,
you are entitled to ask, should I
want to trap bees at all? What do with them
if caught? But there are times, like today,
when bees hover about the typewriter
more frequently than poems, surely knowing best
what best attracts them. And certainly at such times,
considered in terms of function and structure,
the contraption could be argued to be

anything but a typewriter,
the term 'anything' being considered
as including, among all else, bee-traps,
softly multiplying in an ideal world.   *1984*

Esprit de l'escalier
Cyclops Song 1

Good manners, sir, are an infernal machine,
and unjuicing your companions a problem in tact
'at the meeting of two value-systems.' If
you complain, so may I. Sir, I am an ogre
not a structural linguist. Even so I understood,
of course, your ridiculous alias, and I knew
perfectly well what 'Noman is hurting me' meant,
but I played by the rules. So now my face feels like pork-crackling,
looks like it too, I imagine. You've ruled yourself out,
made yourself Noman indeed. But how would you have done
on *my* IQ tests? Did you get my jokes?
Next time around we'll understand each other,
next time I'll ask you round the back.
I, for one, am going to make sure I get it right.   *1984*

The recidivist
Cyclops Song 6

But just consider his subsequent career.
Eight years of gluey fucking, interspersed
with the occasional peeved Please miss I wanna go home.
Then the bullyboy muscleman act – gunning down
every younger better-looking bloke for miles around – 'O man
of many devices!' – Killa Godzilla, more like it.
And a kink about bondage.
                              The thrushes flutter in the greased noose.
And then after all that the stickybeak gods
had to be flown in from Athens or wherever
like a mob of arbitration commissioners. You:
I'm talking about you. But at least,
you bastard, blind as I am, and a hostage
to your stiff-twined cordon of darkness, *I*
am still the one who writes the poems.   *1984*

Lucky for Some
What the Soothsayer Said

Some people, hearing your name, will suppose you have died.
You will be alien no matter what land you live in.

When people meet and you're present, you'll vanish from view.
You will see houses and tombs of your forebears erased.

Those you come to think of as your friends will not recall
what you have lent them or a word that you have said.

You'll find it's lonesome being you.
Your siblings will keep lists of your betrayals.

Women of such beauty that you can't believe it's true
will chop your heart to sausage mince

and tie themselves to worthless men.
You will have a long life to remember all of this.

When you write, your ears will be torn off and nailed to doors
so that the world can have a place to pour its filth.

Your eyes will fill with broken limbs like trees smashed in a gale;
there'll be no time for talk of love.

Your children who are soft as grass before the reaper's blade
have been corrupted while we speak.

Now because you put your trust in words,
for what it's worth, a poem, please.   *2007*

Signs and Wonders

The Motorists Association map records no flower-decked
memorials to those who slipped across into the galaxy
that's parallel to ours – that shifting multiverse of memory

with its variable stars, eclipsing binaries, black holes:
who knows the edge, can gauge the length and breadth
and depth of such a state? The map's no help.

One minute, cruising, then the full-stop to the fable
of a life, and silent trickle out of time,
the premonition they are news they'll never read,

the autos gliding to the church door
where the men in pearl-grey gloves unload the cargo,
move so stately while the gawpers stamp around,

a danse macabre in the cut-grass of the world,
and women wailing for the demon driver, car a pile of scrap,
and workmates saying 'Got the morning off at least'.

The Kylies, Shanes and Daryls, bright as Aztec youths
selected for their prowess and their beauty, to be
idols on their great day, grin from fading snaps

of parties, celebrations, pinned to power poles
and roadside trees and barriers: it's best
not to imagine how they look now in reality

or what we, rushing past as fast as engineering
and the road permit us, might say to them if we could.
What would we ask these demigods?

Their shrines flick by, a via dolorosa: dates and messages
obscured by speed we travel at. No, these are off the map
between each franchised town with signs

of Johnny Beercan's errand in the wilderness:
the empty Fourex, VB, Coopers, Tooheys, Boags,
and Cascade, and the Reschs of time lost,

and other empties, flattened, bloated: magpies, hares,
echidnas, parrots, foxes, wallabies and wombats,
down the Roo Morgue Avenue.

No dot on a chart conveys the detail
of the world the traveller glimpses: tidy parks
cicadas sing in sweet as Bach's perpetual canon,

while a leather ball leaves willow,
and the clouds advance with varied pace
above onlookers tendering the umpire free advice.   *2007*

Dorothy's Skin

At fourteen, my daughter knows why *The Old Couple* on the
      beach, not *The Tiger*
leaps at her from her Christmas gift. She likes Dali. I don't,
      except for one image
that I flip pages for, until I realise they've left it out: *Lifting
      the Skin of the Water*
to See the Dog Sleeping in the Shade of the Sea. Down the road
      from Tamworth,
from Christmas at my mother's, Goonoo Goonoo paddocks
      wear bright, bad toupees.
Surreal colour wraps Wallabadah hills from ridge to
      highway, like an over-packaging
of something subtle. *Look there!* Kath Walker would stop
      you. She'd peel back the veil
of leaves so you'd see the slender swamp orchid growing
      up the paperbark. *Kath*, then,
in the seventies, on my visits to Stradbroke Island –
      Noonuccal land – before she became,
or reclaimed, *Oodgeroo*. I still don't know whether she
      lifted a layer, or added another.

When I met Oodgeroo, I met my mother: not just Dossie's
      poise, eyes and Lindt-like
skin, but the funny-bugger with a steak knife, buried, a
      serrated intensity that
unsettled me – a boy of elocution lessons and an easier ride,
      a man of lighter brown
travelling, whose tab of overt intolerance came in at insults
      and one lost girlfriend.
I wasn't there when indignity did its daily round – rarely
      blunt, rather, a pointed
needling that cut near the core, left wounds that broke their
      stitches every morning
I did know that the sharp steel about Oodgeroo was also
      about my mother. On campus –

UQ – a doctor's daughter from Ingham or Innisfail, some
                    sugar town, told me Queensland
houses on their skyscraper stilts were the perfect metaphor
                    for non-Indigenous Australia's
perch on the land. Then she described the GTO, that
                    seventies model of sexual intimacy
popular where she came from: *Gravy Train On – Wooh-Wooh!!*
                    – the only girl she knew
her age, in her town, that hadn't been gang-raped. I had no
                    reason to disbelieve her.
I thought about targets: when you're a candidate for grief,
                    keep moving. I knew some of
the men's stories: my sister's man, jumping from a moving
                    car on a lonely Tassie road
to miss a bashing; my sister's son, dodging a splintered
                    pool cue in that high-culture
high-altitude, cold and broken town, Orange; but not the
                    women's. When we were kids
mum kept us in motion, in baths and out, to school and
                    back: the devil had a thing about
motors on the idle. Doss draped protective layers on us all:
                    cardigans, scholarships and
singing lessons, and more manners and mannerisms than
                    the middle-class we aped.

I like Queensland houses. I want and don't want to lift the
                    skin of settlement.
If Oodgeroo were alive, I'd take Doss to Straddy. Maybe
                    they wouldn't hit it off – just
fight like the sisters they seem. Yet they might walk
                    alongside each other, an old couple
on the beach. Oodgeroo could lift the skin of sea and land
                    – when, and when not,
to harvest oysters – show mum the swamp orchid, tell her
                    of the Grannies
that walk some nights, stories she's never heard. In the
                    Link-Up office, counsellors talk
to me in supervision of taking clients, their stolen
                    generation clients *home*. Everyone

seems to know just where the fucking place is. Doss Lennis
           from old Newtown, black
with steam-train soot, respect-full *Dot*, from the Ladies
           Auxiliary Tamworth RSL –
mum's many layers peel so slowly. The West Indian cover
           is an old friend. Eighty four
years along – long wait – I hear the word 'Aboriginal'
           creep into a self-descriptive
sentence. Dorothy's skin is so thick and yet so thin. Where
           can I find those red shoes
you simply click to teleport you home?   *2003*

The Up Train

There's no country: Sydney merely thins.
Desperate to get out of town, I lift streets from the soil,
digging for dirt.

To the west, half a rainbow snags clouds. The Egyptians knew
why ibis bend into the waterlogged lanes of Lidcombe Oval
like runners ignoring the gun.

Near Penrith, a hawk flaps angel wings
backwards, black mask round its head, tethered
by a sight line to the need below.

I'm heading where I can hear
crows mourn, watch wag-tails swish their bums
for hours.

The train climbs Linden bush. In the valleys that fall
either side, gum blossom – fluffy as fresh pecorino – sprinkles
whole, wooded ridges. I sit back, happy

as a black cockatoo about to launch its gravity
from a bobbing pine-branch, a baby ape
with a gift pair of wings.   *2003*

The Beginning

God himself
having that day planted a garden
walked through it at evening and knew
that Eden was not nearly complex enough.
And he said:
'Let species swarm like solutes in a colloid.
Let there be ten thousand species of plankton
and to eat them a thousand zooplankton.
Let there be ten phyla of siphoning animals,
one phylum of finned vertebrates, from
white-tipped reef shark to long-beaked coralfish,
and to each his proper niche,
and – no Raphael, I'm not quite finished yet –
you can add seals and sea-turtles & cone-shells & penguins
(if they care) and all the good seabirds your team can devise –
oh yes, and I nearly forgot, I want a special place
for the crabs! And now for parasites to keep
the whole system in balance, let . . .'

'In conclusion, I want,' he said
'ten thousand mixed chains of predation –
none of your simple rabbit and coyote stuff!
This ocean shall have many mouths, many palates. I want,
say, a hundred ways of death, and three thousand of regeneration –
all in technicolor naturally. And oh yes, I nearly forgot,
we can use Eden again for the small coral cay in the center.

'So now Raphael, if you please,
just draw out and marshall these species,
and we'll plant them all out in a twelve-hectare patch.'

For five and a half days God labored
and on the seventh he donned mask and snorkel
and a pair of bright yellow flippers.

And, later, the host all peered wistfully down
through the high safety fence around Heaven
and saw God with his favorites finning slowly over the coral
in the eternal shape of a grey nurse shark,
and they saw that it was very good indeed.   *1976*

The Sun Hunters

In old stories the jungle was busy
eating explorers. Jaguars, pythons,
piranhas, and giant wife-seizing apes –
the rank green bubbled with them.
You used your ten cartridges a day.

The rainforest is really too busy
to feel you passing through.
(Pity the Spanish conquistadors
marching for months in full armor!)
Mammals in a jungle are harmless hangers-on,
though the forest *is* magic. Twenty years will turn
the farmer's pink elapsed porker
to labrador-sized black foraging swine.
The game of strangle-my-neighbour
leaves little time for assaults
on inedible bipeds – the real prize
in a jungle is not white flesh
but a place in the sun.

From above you see only the glorious
Upper Circle, not the slums beneath.
Even parasitic festoons seem gay,
those tons of creeper riding
on strangled boughs. It's like
judging a country by its brochure.
Down below is the gloom of green knives.
Where cedar seeds patter to ground
a thicket of embryos starts the long climb.
Creepers fling lassoes, wrestle them
down to the soil like roped calves.
Promising thrusts to the canopy
are torn up by pigs,
blasted by a half-dozen caterpillars.
(A blue *Ulysses* floats on up
from the sapling it has doomed).
The stillness is of impending death:
wrestlers waiting for neckbones to crack.
The name of this pattern is Balance of Scarceness:
the rarer the tree, the scarcer what eats it –
ichneumon eats caterpillar, eats tree, eats light . . .

The strangler-fig sends out cathedral flanks,
vast in its leafless underworld, composing
a Gothic hall of arc-and-secant roots
around the plundered trunks.
Lianas lace all against the storm
– guy-ropes bracing a miles-square tent,
its poles all slightly suspect.

Master of all is old Python-trunk, the Aristolochia.
Follow him, and you re-live history. Here
he began, spiralling up sheer
through thirty dark metres;
the Indian-rope-trick speaks
of a host-tree, rotted and gone,
whose dimensions show
in the oak-thick swaying coils
like lathe-turnings run to fat.
There, near the river, he surged to the light,
roamed for a decade over the mangroves,
returned to the land.
Here a side-stem has touched soil
and sent out suckers. Fed from rhizomes below,
they twine like smooth cords
leafless until they reach the light.
Some, missing their hold at the canopy
hang the giddy way down.
Others have twined their hopes
up a cycloned-off stump that ends bare
half-way to the sun –
around it the stems mat and dangle,
stranded on a rotting trapeze.

Here his main-stalk straddled a dying white-cedar
and fifty years later fell down in spirals
that hang like the bowels of a gutted pig.
For five years he tried to save himself
festooning the underbrush with coils of flute-edged wood,
till down on his luck he sprawls,
waist-thick, where a sapling snapped.
He rubs on the ground, striking roots, then rises sheer
as a bell-pull, the rope of a cathedral bell,
up into the light to smother a hectare.   1989

Nemargon, the Lightning Grasshopper

To make thunder
says Nemargon the Lightning Man,
strike your axe against rock.
To make lightning
axe on axe
flint-head to flint-head
till the pure spark leaps.
For a Gunumelung storm
you cannot have too many axes, or arms.
The Lightning God wears
a girdle of axe-heads;
he sends out his messenger, the six-armed
lightning grasshopper, proclaiming
reds and orange and the sharp blue
between stricken stones.

The grasshopper chirrups,
in two or three places,
his stridulent song of Nemargon
whetting his stone. One vibrant messenger
to each valley. Pluck him
out of his chosen tussock
– you grasp the cyclone in your hand.   *2000*

ROBERT GRAY (*b 1945*)

Journey: the North Coast

Next thing, I wake up in a swaying bunk,
as though on board a clipper
clambering on the sea,
and it's the train that booms and cracks,
it tears the wind apart.
The man's gone
who had the bunk below me. I swing out,
cover his bed and rattle the sash –
sunlight's rotating
off the drab carpet. And water sways
solidly in its silver basin, so cold
it joins through my hand.

I see, where I'm bowed,
one of those bright crockery days
from so much I recall.
The train's shadow, like a bird's,
flees on the blue and silver paddocks,
over fences that look split from stone,
and banks of fern,
a red clay bank, full of roots,
over dark creeks, where logs are fallen,
and blackened tree trunks.
Down these slopes move, as a nude
descends the stairs,
slender white eucalypts,
and now the country bursts open on the sea —
across a calico beach unfurled,
as from a clothesline, and scattering motes of light
that make the whole compartment whirl.
Shuttering shadows. I rise into the mirror
rested. I'll leave my hair
ruffled a bit, stow the book and wash bag
and city clothes; everything done,
press down the latches
into the case, that for twelve months have been standing out
of a morning above the wardrobe
in a furnished room.   1973

In Departing Light

My mother all of ninety has to be tied up
to her wheelchair, but still she leans far out of it sideways;
she juts there brokenly,
able to cut
with the sight of her someone who is close. She is hung
like her hanging mouth
in the dignity
of her bleariness, and says that she is
perfectly all right. It's impossible to get her to complain
or to register anything
for longer than a moment. She has made Stephen Hawking look healthy.
It's as though
she is being sucked out of existence sideways through a porthole

and we've got hold of her feet.
She's very calm.
If you live long enough it isn't death you fear
but what life can still do. And she appears to know this
somewhere,
even if there's no hope she could speak of it.
Yet she is so remote you think of an immortal – a Tithonus withering
forever on the edge
of life,
although with never a moment's grievance. Taken out to air
my mother seems in a motorcycle race, she
the sidecar passenger
who keeps the machine on the road, trying to lie far over
beyond the wheel.
Seriously, concentrated, she gazes ahead
towards the line,
as we go creeping around and around, through the thick syrups
of a garden, behind the nursing home.

Her mouth is full of chaos.
My mother revolves her loose dentures like marbles ground upon each other,
or idly clatters them,
broken and chipped. Since they won't stay on her gums
she spits them free
with a sudden blurting cough, that seems to have stamped out of her
an ultimate breath.
Her teeth fly into her lap or onto the grass,
breaking the hawsers of spittle.
What we see in such age is for us the premature dissolution of a body
that slips off the bones
and back to protoplasm
before it can be decently hidden away.
And it's as though the synapses were almost all of them broken
between her brain cells
and now they waver about feebly on the draught of my voice
and connect
at random and wrongly
and she has become a surrealist poet.
'How is the sun
on your back?' I ask. 'The sun
is mechanical,' she tells me, matter of fact. Wait
a moment, I think, is she
becoming profound? From nowhere she says, 'The lake gets dusty.' There
is no lake

here, or in her past. 'You'll have to dust the lake.'
It could be
that she is, but then she says, 'The little boy in the star is food,'
or perhaps 'The little boy is the star in food,'
and you think, More likely
this appeals to my kind of superstition – the sleepless, inspiring homunculus.
It is all a tangle and interpretation,
a hearing amiss,
all just the slipperiness
of her descent.

We sit and listen to the bird-song, that is like wandering lines
of wet paint –
is like an abstract expressionist at work, his flourishes, and
then
the touches
barely there,
and that is going on all over the stretched sky.
If I read aloud skimmingly from the newspaper, she immediately falls asleep.
I stroke her face and she wakes
and looking at me intently she says something like, 'That was
a nice parcel.' In our sitting about
she has also said, relevant of nothing, 'The desert is a tongue.'
'A red tongue?'
'That's right, it's a
it's a sort of
you know – it's a – it's a long
motor car.'
When I told her I might be in Cambridge for a time, she told me,
    'Cambridge
is a very old seat of learning. Be sure –'
but it became too much –
'be sure
of the short Christmas flowers.' I get dizzy,
nauseous,
when I try to think about what is happening inside her head. I keep her
out there for hours, propping her
straight, as
she dozes, and drifts into waking; away from the stench and
the screams of the ward. The worst
of all this, to me, is that despite such talk, now is the most peace
I've known her to have. She reminisces,
momentarily, thinking I am one of her long-dead
brothers. 'Didn't we have some fun

on those horses, when we were kids?' she'll say, giving
her thigh a little slap. Alzheimer's
is nirvana, in her case. She never mentions
anything of what troubled her adult God, the evil passages
of the Bible, her own mother's
long, hard dying, my father. Nothing
at all of my father,
and nothing
of her obsession with religion, that he drove her to. She says the
    magpie's song,
that goes on and on, like an Irishman
wheedling to himself,
which I have turned her chair towards,
reminds her of
a cup. A broken cup. I think that the chaos in her mind
is bearable to her because it is revolving
so slowly – slowly
as dust motes in an empty room.
The soul? The soul has long been defeated, and is all but gone. She's only
    productive now
of bristles on the chin, of an odour
like old newspapers on a damp concrete floor, of garbled mutterings, of
some crackling memories, and of a warmth
(it was always there,
the marsupial devotion), of a warmth that is just in the eyes, these days,
    particularly
when I hold her and rock her for a while, as I lift her
back to bed – a folded
package, such as,
I have seen from photographs, was made of the Ice Man. She says 'I like it
when you – when
when
you . . .'
I say to her, 'My brown-eyed girl.' Although she doesn't remember
the record, or me come home
that time, I sing it
to her: 'Sha lala
la la lala . . . And
it's you, it's you,' – she smiles up, into my face – 'it's you, my brown-eyed girl.'

My mother will get lost on the roads after death.
Too lonely a figure
to bear thinking of. As she did once
one time at least, in the new department store
in our town; discovered

hesitant among the aisles; turning around and around, becoming
a still place.
Looking too kind
to reject even a wrong direction,
outrightly. And she caught my eye, watching her
and knew I'd laugh
and grinned. Or else, since many another spirit will be arriving over there,
　　whatever
those are – and all of them clamorous
as seabirds, along the walls of death – she will be pushed aside
easily, again. There are hierarchies in Heaven, we remember; and we know
of its bungled schemes.
Even if 'the last shall be first', as we have been told, she
could not be first. It would not be her.
But why become so fearful?
This is all
of your mother, in your arms. She who now, a moment after your game,
　　has gone;
who is confused
and would like to ask
why she is hanging here. No – she will be safe. She will be safe
in the dry mouth
of this red earth, in the place
she has always been. She
who hasn't survived living, how can we dream that she will survive her death?

2001

DIANE FAHEY (*b 1945*)

Andromeda

She was the first pin-up.
Naked and bejewelled
she was chained to a rock
then thrown by heavy-breathing
winds into wild postures:
at each new angle, lightning
popped like a photographer's flash.

The gold circling her neck
matched her hair, the emeralds
her eyes, the rubies her nipples,
and the amethysts those bruises.

In lulls of wind, she pulled
against iron, stood almost straight.
The sky was a mouth swallowing her,
the sun a glimmering eye.
Lolling in the tide, a sea-dragon
slithered and gurgled like
some vast collective slob.

From afar, Perseus saw her first
as a creature writhing on a rock;
close-up, she was a whirlpool
of rage and terror and shame.
The dragon he changed to stone
with hardly a thought.
But his strength almost failed him
in breaking those chains.

Looking away from her nakedness
he smooths her ankles, wrists.
She waits for the moment
when he will meet her eyes.   *1988*

Dressmaker

As a girl I loved fabrics, stitching, moulding them to fit.
I remember a flared dress, pink roses on white.
Wearing it with my first high heels, I tottered past
neighbourhood louts slung on a verandah; from their transistor
Marty Robbins sang, 'A White Sport Coat and a Pink Carnation.'
As I blushed they eyed the smoky summer air.

At sixteen, a slippery silk dress with whorls of crimson,
pinched in with a cummerbund. With unswerving hips
I passed the greengrocer, an Italian who sighed, whistled, called,
in one sound, his pregnant wife thrusting beans
and tomatoes into paper bags; her look touched mine:
wary, beyond challenge, sisterly.

Ten years of illness next, when I bundled myself
inside coats in summer, wore black as often as not.
Hard to stand straight inside a body so out of kilter.

Since then I have put on the garment of my womanhood.
It marks the curves and leanings of my flesh,
holds in, reveals, what I have come to be,
beyond promise and blight. I know its weight,
its transparency, its rawness, its flawed smoothness.
I wear it now with something close to ease,
with the freedom, almost, of nakedness.   *1990*

Earwigs

Provenance of name unknown – lost in
some entomologist's periwig, or fallen
from his ear-trumpet into an inkwell . . .

When needed one could always be found
in manuscripts, combing the fine print,
leaving, if squashed, a messy signature.

Unlettered bibliophiles, earwigs can feel
secure between the most unnerving thoughts,
subversive quips; are untroubled equally

by the pedestrian and the soaring.
Endowed with wings rarely used, pincers
slow to take the point, they fare best

in the great outdoors, investigating
yellowed pages of Brussels sprouts,
promoting life's general raggedness.

To hold or behold them may not be pleasant
yet they are quite unexceptional –
forked tails curled up in meaningless threat.

Should they create a society, build
cities of fragments, promenade their young,
we might find them interesting, endearing.

But what they like is to bore small holes
in things. Still, they know patience;
make devoted mothers: woven,

as we are, into the world's substance.   *1993*

Solitude

It's something they carry with them
               – explorers   night shifts   seaman –
like a good pair of binoculars
or a camera case
          perfectly and deeply compartmented.
It has a quiet patina
that both absorbs and reflects
        like a valuable instrument
              you have to sign for
– contract with alone –
       and at the end of the voyage
             you get to keep.
Sometimes it's very far away.
Sometimes so close
       at first you think the person next to you
is picking up putting down
          a personal cup
           a book in another language
before you realise what
– when talk has moved off
        leaning its arms
           on someone else's table –
is being
handed to you.   *1996*

ROBERT ADAMSON (*b 1943*)

Into Forest

My face the long grey fish drifts above
the soft floor over the leaves
returning to their previous lives

it looks into the centre of spores
clustered under the tree fern fronds with eyes
trying to forget

High above where I have never lived

a thornbill jets through the twigs
and the rufus whistlers begin their territorial
alarms – So I am finally here
watching my face searching for the next mask

In the house my wife is moving behind
sheets of glass holding the pages of sleep
I can't read – she awaits

the time we have been trying for
the moments without wings we can never own
she looks out at my face

It is a life I am unable to recall or imagine

In the house among the spotted gums
my face has been up all night talking to itself
speaking in tongues

crashing about in the living room
a bowerbird caged-in growing weak
in panic howling

Here in the bush it makes no sound
the eyes join the moving sky
and the mouth draws in more air for its lies

the black tongue a broken wing
and the beaked nose a dorsal before the chin's bristle

I try to remember a face in a language
we speak trees in   1982

Canticle for the Bicentennial Dead

They are talking, in their cedar-benched rooms
on French-polished chairs, and they talk
in reasonable tones, in the great stone buildings
they are talking firmly, in the half-light
and they mention at times the drinking of alcohol,
the sweet blood-coloured wine the young drink,
the beer they share in the riverless river-beds
and the back-streets, and in the main street –

in government-coloured parks, drinking
the sweet blood in recreation patches, campsites.
They talk, the clean-handed ones, as they gather
strange facts; and as they talk
collecting words, they sweat under nylon wigs.
Men in blue uniforms are finding the bodies,
the uniforms are finding the dead: young hunters
who have lost their hunting, singers who
would sing of fish are now found hung –
crumpled in night-rags in the public's corners;
discovered there broken, lit by stripes
of regulated sunlight beneath the whispering
rolling cell window bars. Their bodies
found in postures of human-shaped effigies,
hunched in the dank sour urinated atmosphere
near the bed-board, beside cracked lavatory bowls,
slumped on the thousand grooved, fingernailed walls
of your local police station's cell –
bodies of the street's larrikin Koories
suspended above concrete in the phenyl-thick air.
Meanwhile outside, the count continues: on radio,
on TV, the news – the faces
of mothers torn across the screens –
and the poets write no elegies, our artists
cannot describe their grief though
the clean-handed ones paginate dossiers
and court reporters' hands move over the papers.   *1989*

The Language of Oysters

Charles Olson sat back in his oyster-shed
working with words – 'mostly in a great
sweat of being, seeking to bind in speed' –

looked at his sheaf of pages, each word
an oyster, culled from the fattening grounds
of talk. They were nurtured from day one,

from the spat-fields to their shucking,
words, oysters plump with life. On Mooney Creek
the men stalk the tides for corruption.

They spend nights in tin shacks
that open at dawn onto our great brown river.
On the right tide they ride out

into the light in their punts, battered slabs
of aluminium with hundred-horse Yamahas on the stern
hammering tightly away, padded by hi-tech –

sucking mud into the cooling systems,
the motors leave a jet of hot piss in their wakes.
These power-heads indicate

the quality of the morning's hum.
The new boys don't wake from dreams
where clinkers crack, where mud sucks them under,

their grandfather's hands fumbling
accurately, loosening the knots. Back
at the bunker the hessian sacks are packed ready

and the shells grow into sliding white foothills.
A freezing mist clenches your fingers,
the brown stream now cold as fire:

plunge in and wash away last night's grog,
in the middle morning, stinging and wanting
the week to fold away until payday.

On the bank, spur-winged plovers stroll in pairs,
their beak-wattle chipped by frost,
each day blinking at the crack of sun.

Stalking for corruption? Signs.
Blue algae drifts through your brother's dream
of Gold Coasts, golf courses. The first settlement.   *1997*

The Goldfinches of Baghdad

These finches are kept in gold cages
or boxes covered in wire mesh;
they are used by falcon trainers as lures,
and rich patriarchs choose these living ornaments
to sing to them on their deathbeds. Their song is pure
and melodious. A goldfinch with a slashed throat
was the subject of a masterpiece painted in the

sixteenth century on the back of a highly
polished mother-of-pearl shell – it burns
tonight in Baghdad, along with the living,
caged birds. Flesh and feathers, hands
and wings. Sirens wail, but the tongues
of poets and the beaks of goldfinches burn.
Those who cannot speak burn along with the
articulate – creatures oblivious to prayer burn
along with those who lament to their god.
Falcons on the silver chains, the children
of the falcon trainer, smother in the smoke
of burning feathers and human flesh.
We sing or die, singing death
as our songs feed the flames.   *2006*

JOHN TRANTER (*b 1943*)

from *The Alphabet Murders*

23

We could point to the poem and say 'that map',
the heart's geography, and words enact
the muscly parable of exploration: on your right
Maugham's club foot which tromps the clay of life into
a lovely chorus line of English prose; on your left
the dead Romantics, gone into that same earth
that took their tears and all their unforgivable
syntactical mistakes. The land is cruel
with existentialists, though lyric poets
wander through like crippled birds. . . but this map
is false and crazy – here the Doppler shifts
convert to analogue then back to pulse-code modulation
information full of news and noise, so the heart's
continent abandons form and drifts out into the night sky
full of parachutes, and we feel the mind's mountains
bumping against our head like knobs,
for the little 'heart' grows 'dark' at night
and lacking infra-red photometry and radar
we rave down along the flare path looking like
an anxious moth, don't we? In the flight plan?

But there you go again, plotted out of your simple wit
and this is the second-level problem: observers
without the keys to fit their own responses
so that a poem is merely rhyme and meaning, or a gift
of gaudy trash, and nothing else. So we slog on
to navigate the fading resonance of our capacities
and find the luminescent map of armies
burning on the plain.   *1976*

Voodoo

From his rushing-away, from his
ever-receding throne, under a rainy
canopy of trees and scraps of cloud
that topple back, shrink and disappear,
embalmed behind his rear window in a nest of
crushed velvet plush, the flash wog's nodding dog
blinks out his witless approval to the vehicles
that shadow him forever.

His twin the dipping bird sips and sips,
tilts back, cools off, dries out,
dries out utterly, totters weakly
on the lip of philosophy
then dips again.

These two critics teach us how to live,
rehearsing the gap between the no-no
and the drink-again. Their motto? Every day
I will get better at embroidering the lingo
of the tongue-tied doctors of letters; every night,
in the lack of light, I will get better
and better at the negative virtues, telling
girls to piss off, who needs them,
swimming off the edge of the rock
ledge into the plunging broth of deeper waters,
soaring up to the stratosphere, bothering the angels
and yarning with God. My left hand does it,
my right hand tells me that it's right.

In the pre-dawn rack and bash of winter peak hour
traffic on the Sydney Harbour Bridge you notice them
hefted up over the city like ju-ju dolls

in the trance of a terrible gift. You note
the man with gauntlets and the goggled girl
on motorbikes, the nurses' giggles
in the fogged-up Mini Moke, an ambulance weaving
and howling in the rear-view mirror, the tablets
rattling in the Emergency Bucket, the icy rain
furious and seething on the road, and Noddy
and his loopy brother brooding on it all
for our sake, so that we can see it whole.   *1988*

Fine Arts

Beyond their exhausting vanity and their hatreds
the Old Masters agreed in the small hours:
a work of art, they said, collectively,
    lies in a kind of mud:

gossip, bad faith, someone else's
wife, phone bills, a little happiness. And so we
go on, they said, doing what we can; while
across a horizon full of exasperating detail
    a headache piles up.

And yet the swimming pools are full of children
laughing in that deafening sun, and the barbecue
gets assembled. In the long afternoon one marries,
    one plans a divorce.

Are the Old Men right to maunder, taking young love
as a sketch for heaven on earth? The hot spring
fevers burn away the bossy mannerisms, bringing
complex couplings: some in beds, some on the telephone,
but mostly delirious: is this possible?
    Is that right?

An emotion as perfect as a painting hangs over Sydney.
In the shadowy cave an apprentice, humming
quietly, colours in a background of traffic
while the Master stares through the bright doorway
    lost in the visible world.

                                              1988

Lavender Ink

Look, there she is: Miss Bliss, dozing
in the shade of a Campari umbrella. Beside her
a book – something brilliant: Callimachus,
let's say, printed in an elegant Venetian type –
half-read, with the most alarming
                    metaphors to come,

and a glass of gin, a cool dew
blooming on the crystal, the air
                    kissing her skin
and the neighbour's hi-fi playing
'I Can't Get Started' in a distant
                    corner of the afternoon.

The yachts on the water.
                    The tinkle of ice.

I'm thinking of you reading this,
reinventing Sydney
a thousand years from now, and not
getting it quite right: missing the
delicate hangover, the distant murmur
of the city, the scent of this ink
                    drying on the page.   *2001*

ROGER McDONALD (*b* 1941)

Two summers in Moravia

That soldier with a machinegun bolted
to his motorcycle, I was going to say
ambled down to the pond to take
what geese he wanted; but he didn't.

This was whole days before the horizon trembled.

In the farmyard all the soldier did
was ask for eggs and milk.
He and the daughter (mother sweeping)
stood silent, the sky rounded
like a blue dish.

This was a day
when little happened,
though inch by inch everything changed.
A load of hay narrowly crossed the bridge,
the boy caught a fish underneath in shade,
and ducks quarreled in the reeds.
Surrounded by wheat, everyone heard the wind
whisper, at evening, as though grain already threshed
was poured from hand to hand.

This was a day possible to locate, years later,
on a similar occasion; geese alive,
the sky uncracked like a new dish,
even the wheat hissing with rumour.
I was going to say unchanged
completely, but somewhere behind
the soldier had tugged his cap,
kicked the motor to harsh life
and swayed off,
the nose of the machinegun tilted up.   *1975*

JULIAN CROFT (*b 1941*)

Sandworm

Beach worms are spade-headed
        with wharfies' hooks around the mouth.
They scent the stockinged stink
        trussed like a ham in a nylon net
as it slides across the bar-top smooth
        of watered sand. They come out
of the ground like death through the swing
        doors of a hospital ward – urgent,
to grab a rotten limb before it's pinched
        by interfering fingers. You've
got to be quick, quicker than it, thumb
        and forefinger round its throat
and out it comes, blood-red tube
        from its silver yellow winding sheet,
feet and feet of it into a bucket.
        Strung out and slack, it waits
to be used, lure and line, hook and bait,
        death tied in knots about itself.   *2006*

Labour and Capital

I worked with a man who could hardly breathe:
a chest like a forty-four gallon drum,
shoulders three pick-handles across.

Used to being a big man his voice was now two sizes too small,
and his body hung like a droughty scarecrow's –
they had put him in charge of the sweepers.

He told me. Wheezing. Coughing. Eyes watering
like it was the first morning smoke. About relining
the blast furnace with high temperature bricks.

Good news for the share-holders, down-time
got less and less (a pause for air) as the boss
found ways of getting back into the furnace sooner.

Two sugar bags, fore and aft, dripping wet,
a steaming sandwich-board
as soon as you stepped in the oven,

your breath cooled from dry lime-kiln white
into scalding fog. He hawked the memory from his lungs.
And then you laid red-hot bricks with leather gloves.

The smell of burning hide as you picked out bricks
told you what your feet knew through your boots,
this is what sunday school had promised,

and now you were in it even though you hadn't
broken any commandment except covet
your neighbour's new fridge and car:

five minutes before you were relieved,
though that went up to seven when
the credit squeeze was on, and ten off,

for four hours, then a break, and back
into it, week after week, all through
the prosperous fifties when all was well.   *2006*

Seascape with Young Girl

The heat seethes dragonflies,
their sheen, the exact colour of flight;
pink orchids stretch on wispy stems
not-quite rope tricks.

She pauses for a moment on the path
where tangled tea-trees shine
with Old Man's Beard;
two skinks glissando through her hands
and a stumpy-tail, lichen-patched, in the sun,
recognizes her with a long Jurassic gaze.

She thuds at any hidden snake
and a pair of blue wrens split the air,
splice it up, disappear.

At last — a spill of sand,
the first steep slope, a slap of wind
and before her the smiling sea.
Left and right, the dunes loll
lion-colour. Below,
the light bleeds silver on water;
a rainbow sail windsurfs the inshore green
and cries of gulls and children thin into air,
pure as the notes of a pipe.

Suddenly on the next knoll, in one quick leap,
there's a boy — slanting eyes, curly hair —
capering, he slings a stone,
whistles and swoops and rolls and will be seen.

Her eyes fine to horizons,
the line of her throat and chin
is smooth as the headland and as remote;
she will not notice him.
And just as suddenly he's gone.
Her neck acknowledges an absence.

The rainbow sail is down;
wavelets fawn, bright-fanged, on the beach:
the day's a haze of white noise,

tinnitus of tomorrow.
Everything's far away,
is within reach.   1986

The Kiss

I love the way
a Pole will take your hand
in both of his
and straighten with the merest hint
of a military click
and bow his head
and tighten his grip
and press his moist and fervent lips
to your skin,
also the gentle after-caress
of his moustache.
Most, I love the dark
and frankly soulful look
(still holding your hand)
he'll fix you with
for exactly three seconds after:
the look that says
this, we understand, means nothing
and everything –
    you are a stranger I salute
across the eternal silence of this space,
    you are Baila, my first love,
in her blue cotton dress,
    you are my mother
holding back her tears,
    you are garrulous Mrs Zukowski
who gave us eggs,
    you are all our grandmothers
waving after the train,
    you are woman,
we may never meet again.   1994

Horizon

is gentle geometry, the ghost of Euclid.
Not quite time or place, it boasts no deity,
is democratic but elusive,
we never see our own.
What of tomorrow and all your line?
The margin moves as they sail in –
the least mast tip's all you'll discern
for it's round as second chance
but holds none.
Even dreams embrace no final rim,
waking is just meniscus.
But the stranger's smile returned
is a shared border, a lifting of tariffs.
Some wear their threshold like a cloak
or suck it dry.
Some turn theory edge-on
and push their people over:
Argentina's beaten silver,
Rwanda, Srebrenica, ploughed under,
Cambodia's stacked-up grins.   *2008*

Freesias

Two sceptics at odds may cancel out
like minus signs, to say Why doubt?

See where I've planted the Snowdon corms
between the stones. Too shallowly: the leaves
splay out, bent to a world of wind,
we tread the green flames unawares.
September will turn us – Ah! Japanese,
the air round their creamy cups spreading a covenant,
Sadness-Joy. Like wind chimes touching the edge of song,
or a small high window's mouthful of sky.
Breathe in their fragrance now,
the rush of yes but, if, maybe,

till the ghostly sacs of the lungs swell out
and airiest Other floods the brain. You too, Martin,
come back into the sun, I have picked you a percept, here –

a straggly bouquet of Being, quite unconcealed,
and it knows you, bronchiole and cell,
it is soothing the labyrinth to a safety net,
calming the rivers of blood as they leave and arrive.
Would you say it's beyond the play of beyond,
this scent – the hint of a universe drifting apart
like philosophy's fine dissolve?

Almost unbearable sweetness anyway.
Almost thought.   *2008*

Port Lincoln

The endless white ah-ah-ing of the sea
is the sound of forgetting
and the touch of it too:
the sea-line laps our footprints back
to the clear broth of first being,
the littoral of find and lose that is
the moment remembering itself and letting go.

Here, in six clear feet of water below the dock,
starfish dozens, such kindergarten creatures,
stud the sand with random rivets,
anchor earth itself with gravity clamps,
imaging their element as blue-gold heaven.
Each pliant clutch spreads wide its private pink.
That one – so fixed! And yet it moves.

Its flow is a sort of flight,
a placid hydraulics with every direction forward
following any cosmic compass point
it signifies and is – five fingery feet
fringing a mouth in search of the other,
a ruthless purity that stretches and contracts,
elongates to a manikin secreted in a crack,

or pulls food in to centre's firm conviction.
Somewhere right now someone may be
sliding a fine soup under glass,
tracing this cell stuff to an essence
recalling tomorrow as genome,
the future tense of yes:
a circular shortcut, like the sea's

great mirror of hope, star looking back at star.
Symmetry seems safe – like question and response,
the way that axon leans to axon,
coaxing metaphysics by caress.
Lucky the atom has its own world view,
so a starfish is at finest resolution
electrostatic No respecting difference.

As I watched Lachlan watch one on his palm
it stretched and curled
and struck a questioning pose –
was his hand sea or sky or sand?
Later, rolling plasticene to five-armed orange blobs,
he sank so starfish-deep within himself,
the making remembered him.   *2008*

GEOFFREY LEHMANN (*b 1940*)

The Two Travellers

A girl was picking parsley near a church,
An old man fished the summer stream for perch,

There was a pear tree; but we had to ride
Through heath and furze and up a mountainside . . .

We crossed the snowline, lit a fire and sang
That night and the deserted valley rang.

We slew a dragon, travelled up the pass,
Went through a town of broken boards and glass.

Dead spirits swarmed across a sandy plain.
Dry lightning, and a blind man gasped for rain.

Years later in a stream we washed our hair
And swam one night, then slept beneath a pear.

A parsley field and church shone in the sun,
The girl was there. We diced and my friend won.   *1972*

The Old Rifle

In the long school holidays in summer
I'd be out in the orchard
with an old rifle Mr Long fixed up,
shooting at rosellas
that were raiding fruit.
As each bird fell I'd watch
where the blue and red flickered down,
then I'd drop the rifle and run.
That way I stocked my aviary
with broken-winged rosellas,
And somewhere in my childhood
I dropped and forgot that rifle.

A year of grass grew over it.
Men were working in the orchard one day,
and my brother, the dentist, four years old,
was playing in the grass and found the rifle,
rusted all over – a wreck –
as though it had lain there for years.
My brother knew how to hold a gun
and pointing it at Jim Long, said,
'I'll shoot you Mr Long.'

He said, 'Oh don't shoot me, Barry –
shoot Bill over there.'
Barry pointed the gun at Bill.
'I'll shoot you Uncle Bill.'
'Don't shoot me, Barry,' Bill said,
'Shoot Ted here.' And Ted said,
'Why not shoot Jip?'

Jip was a good sort of dog,
my black and white fox terrier cross,
who was racing around the orchard,
looking for rabbits.
Barry dropped to one knee and squinting took aim.
Jip dropped dead on the spot.
They buried him, telling no one,
but in their haste
made the hole too shallow,
and a few days later the story came out
when the fowls scratched him up.

'You know, Barry's quite a fair shot,'
Mr Long said,
out in the bush with Barry and me.
'My word I am,' said Barry.
'I can hit anything.'
'Can you, Barry, well – see what you can do.'
Barry took the rifle,
went down on one knee
and aimed at Mr Long's billy hanging
from a distant branch.
He fired,
and a stream of brown tea came spurting out.   1976

Parenthood

I have held what I hoped would become the best minds of a generation
Over the gutter outside an Italian coffee shop watching the small
Warm urine splatter on the asphalt – impatient to rejoin
An almond torta and a capuccino at a formica table.
I have been a single parent with three children at a Chinese restaurant
The eldest five years old and each in turn demanding
My company as they fussed in toilets and my pork saté went cold.
They rarely went all at once; each child required an individual
Moment of inspiration – and when their toilet pilgrimage was ended
I have tried to eat the remnants of my meal with twisting children
Beneath the table, screaming and grabbing in a scrimmage.
I have been wiping clean the fold between young buttocks as a pizza
I hoped to finish was cleared from a red and white checked table cloth.
I have been pouring wine for women I was hoping to impress
When a daughter ran for help through guests urgently holding out
Her gift, a potty, which I took with the same courtesy
As she gave it, grateful to dispose of its contents so simply
In a flurry of water released by the pushing of a button.
I have been butted by heads which have told me to go away and I have
    done so,
My mouth has been wrenched by small hands wanting to reach down to
    my tonsils
As I lay in bed on Sunday mornings and the sun shone through the slats
Of dusty blinds. I have helpfully carried dilly-dalliers up steps
Who indignantly ran straight down and walked up by themselves.
My arms have become exhausted, bouncing young animals until they
    fell asleep

In my lap listening to Buxtehude. 'Too cold,' I have been told,
As I handed a piece of fruit from the refrigerator, and for weeks had
    to warm
Refrigerated apples in the microwave so milk teeth cutting green
Carbohydrate did not chill. I have pleasurably smacked small bottoms
Which have climbed up and arched themselves on my lap wanting
    the report
And tingle of my palm. I have known large round heads that bumped
And rubbed themselves against my forehead, and affectionate noses
That loved to displace inconvenient snot from themselves onto me.
The demands of their bodies have taken me to unfamiliar geographies.
I have explored the white tiles and stainless steel benches of restaurant
    kitchens
And guided short legs across rinsed floors smelling of detergent
Past men in white with heads lowered and cleavers dissecting and
    assembling
Mounds of sparkling pink flesh – and located the remote dark shrine
Of a toilet behind boxes of coarse green vegetables and long white radishes.
I have badgered half-asleep children along backstreets at night, carrying
Whom I could to my van. I have stumbled with them sleeping in my arms
Up concrete steps on winter nights after eating in Greek restaurants,
Counting each body, then slamming the door of my van and taking
My own body, the last of my tasks, to a cold bed free of arguments.
I have lived in the extreme latitudes of child rearing, the blizzard
Of the temper tantrum and my own not always wise or honourable
    response,
The midnight sun of the child calling for attention late at night,
And have longed for the white courtyards and mediterranean calm
    of middle age.
Now these small bodies are becoming civilised people claiming they are not
Ashamed of a parent's overgrown garden and unpainted ceilings
Which a new arrival, with an infant's forthrightness, complains are 'old'.
And the father of this tribe sleeps in a bed which is warm with arguments.
Their bones elongate and put on weight and they draw away into space.
Their faces lengthen with responsibility and their own concerns.
I could clutch as they recede and fret for the push of miniature persons.
And claim them as children of my flesh – but my own
    body is where I must live.

1990

Adulterers

After that first urgent
kissing at the door
and all the prearrangements

whispered down the phone
and all that splendid
disarray of clothes,

the interplay of skins and liquids,
the short delirium of smells
and all such pure

antiphonal delights
the cigarettes are lit at last . . .
and sprawled there in a

twist of sweat
a conversation comes to life:
obsessions of the absent husband,

shortfalls of the absent wife.   *2001*

The Poem That You Haven't Seen

The poem that you haven't seen
and someone should by now have written

concerns the sub K219
holed and damaged off Bermuda,

its death chutes locked on Washington
New York and Boston, its power plant sliding

into meltdown. It tells of how
with no remote, two Russians wound

all four reactor rods to safety.
The poem that you haven't seen

revives how Sergei Preminin,
apprentice seaman, just on twenty,

and First Lieutenant Belikov
between them in that cancelled air

cranked by hand the death rods down
through 65 degrees of heat

wreathed with gas and radiation.
The poem tells of how the first

and then the other man passed out
and in his turn was dragged aside

and how Sergei went stumbling back
to fix the rod that saved the cities

and how the exit hatch slammed shut
and how the captain heard that death

gasping on the intercom.
The poem that has not been written

would also show the less dramatic
efforts made to tow and salvage

before the submarine in silence
sank slowly through 6,000 metres.

The poem that has not been written
restores to us the morning traffic

in Washington, New York and Boston
and has a grab of Gorbachev

with Reagan stooped at Reykjavik
five days later over papers.

The poem that has not been written
ends with Sergei Preminin –

and the sub K219
corroding on the ocean floor,

its missiles undelivered.   *2001*

Hats

'Hats off in the Mess!' was the cry of the drill-
    instructor, when he'd brought our bunch
of air-cadets to a ragged halt. And where
    are you, now, Sergeant Retallack –
eighty-something or out of time? For years
    I've tried to keep on taking my hat
off in the mess, less from deference than
    in a kind of defiant celebration;
the hats wear out, the mess goes on, my arm's
    less dexterous in salute. We never
knew what brought your tanned and seamy face,
    your chopped form and chesty bellow
to put the fear of God and the Air Force into
    our balky ways. Perhaps you were born
where we found you daily, stamping the red dirt
    of the Bullring out at Pearce Station,
profiled against the black Neptune bombers,
    their million-candlepower spotlights
hooded, their radar pods dozing. I thought
    of you this morning, Sergeant, seeing
in The New York Times a shot of a man in a field
    in Sarajevo. He was bowed
in a way you probably wouldn't approve, the spine
    gone out of him as he prayed by the grave
of one of his bunch dug in at the stadium.
    His hat alas is still on, with
a bulked jacket, castoff snow, dozens
    of plank markers, and as you
would say, Sergeant, from force of habit, the mess.   *1999*

Dreaming the Bridge

after Claude Oscar Monet, Bridge Over a Pool of Water Lilies, 1899

This way the light is all gone and a velvet abyss
    opens, you hope, for solace. Darkness
teems with darkness. Something has bundled place
    for time to hold, and sent it away.
        You cannot remember your name.

A voice confides that we live in a rainbow of chaos,
      its arc a wave in a lost sea:
and you think that you think of words on a warrior's gate –
      'The world is a bridge: pass over it,
                  but never build a house.'

There was a time when mammoths crossed the Seine
      as though to pace by Notre Dame
and take the Rue Saint-Jacques: a time for Xerxes
      to clog the Hellespont with ships
                  and span a way to death:

time for the Roman engineers to fling
      arch over arch in the Pont du Gard,
holding a cup to the lips of thirsty Nimes:
      time for 'When your enemy flees,
                  build him a silver bridge.'

None of them lingers now. Only Monet's
      Japanese bridge, itself the match
of lilied water, air in green array,
      earth's rondure, and for gift
                  the mind's dark fire.   2003

Word

from A Mass for Anglesea

Hand on hilt was the way to listen once,
smoke from the burning spice around you,
the Good News brushing mail, and you its minder.

Later, a placeman, chic in SS black,
could lodge for an hour in the high Dom,
denying Christ the star his mother gave him.

'By the words of the Gospel blot out all our sins' –
the book kissed, an old yearning
up like crocus out of the blank of snow;

or, as it might be, a curlicue of tendril,
greening its inches across a branch
of mother-vine, a partisan of life.

Outside, a bronzewing's foraging in the shrubs,
chestnut and cinnamon feather-deep,
and a flame skipper's backing and filling in air,

printed again and again on the ocean's page.
As John tells it, Christ is word
and vine both, meaning and fruit displayed

on the world's lattice, if only the light will hold.
The rumouring leaf is frail with use,
but the tale's there, as once black on papyrus,

or lit by gold and lapis on the clipped skins;
so, blind at best to much about me,
I try once more for a touch of the word's Braille.   *2008*

AILEEN KELLY (*b 1939*)

Encounters with my mother's ghost

I met her
in the kitchen. She was shouting.
No man or child answered.
The floor was slippery with botched
cooking none of us had eaten which she had
thrown down of her power.
Power we had not noticed
when she walled a war out of her house
where every pastry rose to our clean fingers
and nothing was ever allowed to be broken.

I met her
in the church. She was shouting
her name not her nickname nor
the mouthful her parents gave her but
the name only God ever called her
when she was too given to know herself called.
And I could not hear what syllables
she shouted. Only
the truth of it plucking the strung rafters
to sound the hollow air vaulted in stone.

I met her in the street.
She was revving
the little red sports car she sometimes
joked about but never found the right to buy.
No neighbour frowned or tutted
but the hard desire of her anger shut
out their good-day smiles
and claimed the thundering scandal
her careful quiet was busy to deny
all her careful life.   1994

They flee from me

A copper copter after midnight
coarse-grinds shreds of what-who fear
into the chamber between thought and paper
where I was silent not to spook
whatever life on naked foot
might edge towards the familiar scent of crumble
to take bread any moment now
from my stilled hand.

Less than a thought-fox, merely
a laicised churchmouse – some small wildness
unafraid as that first-flight thornbill,
nest-fluff still tangled on his head
beside my window poised to watch me,
openmouthed for food not shock,
till his father came to fluster innocence
and drive him second flight
to a further tree.

One inhumane propeller
skeins out from my childhood
the sky full of a wounded bomber
and us wide-eyed beneath.
The kids next door know only in dream or game
the need for bulletproofed sharp-seers
boldly going
roughly getting somewhere
over our mundane city open to view.

On task.
Grinding away beyond my suburb.   2006

honesty-stones

The land between us
had grown so bare
the landscape so denuded –
all we had left was what we knew –
just the rocks and the shade they cast –
your eyes my eyes across them.

We did not need to speak, to talk.
Everything was in the rocks.
It had been said before.

We could not live there.   1971

wind painting

lake birds in wind
ride a bucking
saddle of water

afghan dogs
float in the wind
their tresses laid back
like the hair of the willow

they are dancing under

the wind's water

like a film of themselves-
in-slow-motion

the wind buckets
the lake's surface

slops tilt
over the brim

the coots
ride it out on the slant
sliding & riding
in the sunblack light

which pinks the skin
of the pelican's
beak membrane round
the lump
of the frog he is swallowing
– there – in the lee by the willow –

hawk makes the high hill
over the tossing pine trees
spire of his hunting site
& the redbrowed finches & little birds
evanesce in the short grass
blown on screams of panic
thin as grass seeds

entering the invisible

there is one fat gold
dandelion for van gogh
tethered by its own sap
in the black damp shade
by the clump of horseshit   1985

JOHN WATSON (b 1939)

from *Montale*

   At the Grotto Double Pool

The future arrives with just such a flooding wave:
A small child was carried by a swell, a hastening
Exceptional wisdom of water,
         as safe as Moses out of one

Pool into another like a startling enjambment
Serendipitously avoiding sea wall, jutting
Rock, rail and stanchions
                  so that

In a moment carried like a leaf or Eeyore stick
Executing the down swerve of a sine curve
         she represented, she declared
Modulation, involuntary action, protective love.

From His Parapet

From his parapet he looked down. Even as
He heard a faint musical scale
A large wave entered the pool

And swept the little girl
Over a stone wall
And under a hand rail

Into a second pool
While avoiding every obstacle
Cliff rock, plinth, stone sail.

She looked as untroubled as a pearl
Just taken from its shell;
She still had the same smile.

In Tidal Baths

A small girl
Stood in the waveless pool
A large wave
Cried out from somewhere.
On the wave's back
Like Mazeppa, she rode
Over the sea wall
Under the railing
Missing a stanchion
Into the lower pool
Without freckle of fear
Or frown of surprise.
In the conjecture
Of the lower shallows
She looked round:
Transposed like someone
Transported in time
Laughing but unharmed.

2006

Once in a Lifetime, Snow

Winters at home brought wind,
black frost and raw
grey rain in barbed-wire fields,
but never more

until the day my uncle
rose at dawn
and stepped outside – to find
his paddocks gone,

his cattle to their hocks
in ghostly ground
and unaccustomed light
for miles around.

And he stopped short, and gazed
lit from below,
and half his wrinkles vanished
murmuring *Snow.*

A man of farm and fact
he stared to see
the facts of weather raised
to a mystery

white on the world he knew
and all he owned.
Snow? Here? he mused. I see.
High time I learned.

Here, guessing what he meant
had much to do
with that black earth dread old men
are given to,

he stooped to break the sheer
crust with delight
at finding the cold unknown
so deeply bright,

at feeling it take his prints
so softly deep,
as if it thought he knew
enough to sleep,

or else so little he
might seek to shift
its weight of wintry light
by a single drift,

perceiving this much, he scuffed
his slippered feet
and scooped a handful up
to taste, and eat

in memory of the fact
that even he
might not have seen the end
of reality . . .

Then, turning, he tiptoed in
to a bedroom, smiled,
and wakened a murmuring child
and another child.   *1969*

The Broad Bean Sermon

Beanstalks, in any breeze, are a slack church parade
without belief, saying *trespass against us* in unison,
recruits in mint Air Force dacron, with unbuttoned leaves.

Upright with water like men, square in stem-section
they grow to great lengths, drink rain, keel over all ways,
kink down and grow up afresh, with proffered new greenstuff.

Above the cat-and-mouse floor of a thin bean forest
snails hang rapt in their food, ants hurry through several dimensions:
spiders tense and sag like little black flags in their cordage.

Going out to pick beans with the sun high as fence-tops, you find
plenty, and fetch them. An hour or a cloud later
you find shirtfulls more. At every hour of daylight

appear more that you missed: ripe, knobbly ones, fleshy-sided,
thin-straight, thin-crescent, frown-shaped, bird-shouldered,
    boat-keeled ones,
beans knuckled and single-bulged, minute green dolphins at suck,
beans upright like lecturing, outstretched like blessing fingers
in the incident light, and more still, oblique to your notice
that the noon glare or cloud-light or afternoon slants will uncover

till you ask yourself Could I have overlooked so many, or
do they form in an hour? unfolding into reality
like templates for subtly broad grins, like unique caught expressions,

like edible meanings, each sealed around with a string
and affixed to its moment, an unceasing colloquial assembly,
the portly, the stiff, and those lolling in pointed green slippers . . .

Wondering who'll take the spare bagfulls, you grin with happiness
– it is your health – you vow to pick them all
even the last few, weeks off yet, misshapen as toes.   *1977*

The Future

There is nothing about it. Much science fiction is set there
but is not about it. Prophecy is not about it.
It sways no yarrow stalks. And crystal is a mirror.
Even the man we nailed on a tree for a lookout
said little about it; he told us evil would come.
We see, by convention, a small living distance into it
but even that's a projection. And all our projections
fail to curve where it curves.
                              It is the black hole
out of which no radiation escapes to us.
The commonplace and magnificent roads of our lives
go on some way through cityscape and landscape
or steeply sloping, or scree, into that sheer fall
where everything will be that we have ever sent there,
compacted, spinning – except perhaps us, to see it.
It is said we see the start.
                              But, from here, there's a blindness.
The side-heaped chasm that will swallow all our present
blinds us to the normal sun that may be imagined
shining calmly away on the far side of it, for others
in their ordinary day. A day to which all our portraits,

ideals, revolutions, denim and deshabille
are quaintly heartrending. To see those people is impossible,
to greet them, mawkish. Nonetheless, I begin:
'When I was alive –'
                 and I am turned around
to find myself looking at a cheerful picnic party,
the women decently legless, in muslin and gloves,
the men in beards and weskits, with the long
cheroots and duck trousers of the better sort,
relaxing on a stone verandah. Ceylon, or Sydney.
And as I look, I know they are utterly gone,
each one on his day, with pillow, small bottles, mist,
with all the futures they dreamed or dealt in, going
down to that engulfment everything approaches;
with the man on the tree, they have vanished into the Future.

1977

The Dream of Wearing Shorts Forever

To go home and wear shorts forever
in the enormous paddocks, in that warm climate,
adding a sweater when winter soaks the grass,

to camp out along the river bends
for good, wearing shorts, with a pocketknife,
a fishing line and matches,

or there where the hills are all down, below the plain,
to sit around in shorts at evening
on the plank verandah –

If the cardinal points of costume
are Robes, Tat, Rig and Scunge,
where are shorts in this compass?

They are never Robes
as other bareleg outfits have been:
the toga, the kilt, the lava-lava
the Mahatma's cotton dhoti;

archbishops and field marshals
at their ceremonies never wear shorts.
The very word
means underpants in North America.

Shorts can be Tat,
Land-Rovering bush-environmental tat,
socio-political ripped-and-metal-stapled tat,
solidarity-with-the -Third-World tat tvam asi,

likewise track-and-field shorts worn to parties
and the further humid, modelling negligée
of the Kingdom of Flaunt,
that unchallenged aristocracy.

More plainly climatic, shorts
are farmers' rig leathery with salt and bonemeal,
are sailors' and branch bankers' rig,
the crisp golfing style
of our youngest male National Costume.

Mostly loosely, they are Scunge,
ancient Bengal bloomers or moth-eaten hot pants
worn with a former shirt,
feet, beach sand, hair
and a paucity of signals.

Scunge, which is real negligée
housework in a swimsuit, pyjamas worn all day,
is holiday, is freedom from ambition.
Scunge makes you invisible
to the world and yourself.

The entropy of costume,
scunge can get you conquered by more vigorous cultures
and help you to notice it less.

Satisfied ambition, defeat, true unconcern,
the wish and the knack for self-forgetfulness
all fall within the scunge ambit
wearing board shorts or similar;
it is a kind of weightlessness.

Unlike public nakedness, which in Westerners
is deeply circumstantial, relaxed as exam time,
artless and equal as the corsetry of a hussar regiment,

shorts and their plain like
are an angelic nudity,
spirituality with pockets!
A double updraft as you drop from branch to pool!

Ideal for getting served last
in shops of the temperate zone
they are also ideal for going home, into space,
into time, to farm the mind's Sabine acres
for product or subsistence.

Now that everyone who yearned to wear long pants
has essentially achieved them,
long pants, which have themselves been underwear
repeatedly, and underground more than once,
it is time perhaps to cherish the culture of shorts,

to moderate grim vigour
with the knobble of bare knees,
to cool bareknuckle feet in inland water,
slapping flies with a book on solar wind
or a patient bare hand, beneath the cadjiput trees,

to be walking meditatively
among green timber, through the grassy forest
towards a calm sea
and looking across to more of that great island
and the further topics.   *1987*

It Allows a Portrait in Line-Scan at Fifteen

He retains a slight 'Martian' accent, from the years of single phrases.
He no longer hugs to disarm. It is gradually allowing him affection.
It does not allow proportion. Distress is absolute, shrieking, and runs him
    at frantic speed through crashing doors.
He likes cyborgs. Their taciturn power, with his intonation.
It still runs him around the house, alone in the dark, cooing and laughing.
He can read about soils, populations and New Zealand. On neutral
    topics he's illiterate.
Arnie Schwarzenegger is an actor. He isn't a cyborg really, is he, Dad?
He lives on forty acres, with animals and trees, and used to draw it
    continually.
He knows the map of Earth's fertile soils, and can draw it freehand.
He can only lie in a panicked shout *SorrySorryIdidn'tdoit!* warding off
    conflict with others and himself.
When he ran away constantly it was to the greengrocers to worship
    stacked fruit.
His favourite country was the Ukraine: it is nearly all deep fertile soil.

Giggling, he climbed all over the dim Freudian psychiatrist who told us
    how autism resulted from 'refrigerator' parents.
When asked to smile, he photographs a rictus-smile on his face.
It long forbade all naturalistic films. They were Adult movies.
If they (that is, he) *are bad the police will put them in hospital.*
He sometimes drew the farm amid Chinese or Balinese rice terraces.
When a runaway, he made uproar in the police station, playing at three
    times adult speed.
Only animated films were proper. *Who Framed Roger Rabbit* then
    authorised the rest.
Phrases spoken to him he would take as teaching, and repeat.
When he worshipped fruit, he screamed as if poisoned when it was fed
    to him.
A one-word first conversation: *Blane. – Yes! Plane, that's right, baby! – Blane.*
He has forgotten nothing, and remembers the precise quality of
    experiences.
It requires rulings: Is *stealing very playing up, as bad as murder?*
He counts at a glance, not looking. And he has never been lost.
When he ate only nuts and dried fruit, words were for dire emergencies.
He knows all the breeds of fowls, and the counties of Ireland.
He'd begun to talk, then resumed to babble, then silence. It withdrew
    speech for years.
When he took your hand, it was to work it, as a multi-purpose tool.
He is anger's mirror, and magnifies any near him, raging it down.
It still won't allow him fresh fruit, or orange juice with bits in it.
He swam in the midwinter dam at night. It had no rules about cold.
He was terrified of thunder and finally cried as if in explanation *It – angry!*
He grilled an egg he'd broken into bread. Exchanges of soil-knowledge are
    called landtalking.
He lives in objectivity. I was sure Bell's palsy would leave my face only
    when he said it had begun to.
Don't say word! when he was eight forbade the word 'autistic' in his presence.
Bantering questions about girlfriends cause a terrified look and blocked
    ears.
He sometimes centred the farm in a furrowed American Midwest.
Eye contact, Mum! means he truly wants attention. It dislikes I-contact.
He is equitable and kind, and only ever a little jealous. It was a relief
    when that little arrived.
He surfs, bowls, walks for miles. For many years he hasn't trailed his left arm
    while running.
I gotta get smart! looking terrified into the years. *I gotta get smart!*

                                                                    1996

The Last Hellos

Don't die, Dad –
but they die.

This last year he was wandery:
took off a new chainsaw blade
and cobbled a spare from bits.
Perhaps if I lay down
my head'll come better again.
His left shoulder kept rising
higher in his cardigan.

He could see death in a face.
Family used to call him in
to look at sick ones and say.
At his own time, he was told.

The knob found in his head
was duck-egg size. Never hurt.
Two to six months, Cecil.

I'll be right, he boomed
to his poor sister on the phone
I'll do that when I finish dyin.

                    *

Don't die, Cecil.
But they do.

Going for last drives
in the bush, odd massive
board-slotted stumps bony white
in whipstick second growth.
I could chop all day.

*I could always cash
a cheque, in Sydney or anywhere.
Any of the shops.*

Eating, still at the head
of the table, he now missed
food on his knife side.

Sorry, Dad, but like
have you forgiven your enemies?
Your father and all of them?
All his lifetime of hurt.

I must have (grin). *I don't*
think about that now.

      *

People can't say goodbye
any more. They say last hellos.

Going fast, over Christmas,
he'd still stumble out
of his room, where his photos
hang over the other furniture,
and play host to his mourners.

The courage of his bluster,
firm big voice of his confusion.

Two last days in the hospital:
his long forearms were still
red mahogany. His hands
gripped steel frame. *I'm dyin.*

On the second day:
You're bustin to talk but
I'm too busy dyin.

      *

Grief ended when he died,
the widower like soldiers who
won't live life their mates missed.

Good boy Cecil! No more Bluey dog.
No more cowtime. No more stories.
We're still using your imagination,
it was stronger than all ours.

Your grave's got littler
somehow, in the three months.
More pointy as the clay's shrivelled,
like a stuck zip in a coat.

Your cricket boots are in
the State museum! Odd letters
still come. Two more's died since you:
Annie, and Stewart. Old Stewart.

On your day there was a good crowd,
family, and people from away.
But of course a lot had gone
to their own funerals first.

Snobs mind us off religion
nowadays, if they can.
Fuck thém. I wish you God.   *1996*

The Instrument

Who reads poetry? Not our intellectuals;
they want to control it. Not lovers, not the combative,
not examinees. They too skim it for bouquets
and magic trump cards. Not poor schoolkids
furtively farting as they get immunized against it.

Poetry is read by the lovers of poetry
and heard by some more they coax to the cafe
or the district library for a bifocal reading.
Lovers of poetry may total a million people
on the whole planet. Fewer than the players of *skat*.

What gives them delight is a never-murderous skim
distilled, to verse mainly, and suspended in rapt
calm on the surface of paper. The rest of poetry
to which this was once integral still rules
the continents, as it always did. But on condition now

that its true name is never spoken: constructs, feral poetry,
the opposite but also the secret of the rational,
And who reads that? Ah, the lovers, the schoolkids,
debaters, generals, crime-lords, everybody reads it:
Porsche, lift-off, Gaia, Cool, patriarchy.

Among the feral stanzas are many that demand your flesh
to embody themselves. Only completed art
free of obedience to its time can pirouette you
through and athwart the larger poems you are in.
Being outside all poetry is an unreachable void.

Why write poetry? For the weird unemployment.
For the painless headaches, that must be tapped to strike
down along your writing arm at the accumulated moment.
For the adjustments after, aligning facets in a verb
before the trance leaves you. For working always beyond

your own intelligence. For not needing to rise
and betray the poor to do it. For a non-devouring fame.
Little in politics resembles it: perhaps
the Australian colonists' re-inventing of the snide
far-adopted secret ballot, in which deflation could hide

and, as a welfare bringer, shame the mass-grave Revolutions,
so axe-edged, so lictor-y.
Was that moral cowardice's one shining world victory?
Breathing in dream-rhythm when awake and far from bed
evinces the gift. Being tragic with a book on your head.

1999

On the North Coast Line

The train coming on up the Coast
fitting like a snake into water
is fleeing the sacrificial crust
of suburbs built into fire forest.
Today, smoke towers above there.

We've winged along sills of the sea
we've traversed the Welsh and Geordie
placenames where pickaxe coughing
won coal from miners' crystal lungs.
No one aboard looks wealthy:

wives, non-drivers, Aborigines,
sun-crackled workers. The style
of country trains isn't lifestyle.
River levees round old chain-gang towns
fall away behind our run of windows.

By cuttings like hangars filled with rock
to Stroud Road, and Stratford on the Avon,
both named by Robert Dawson, who ordered
convicts hung for drowning Native children
but the Governor stopped him. God

help especially the underdogs of underdogs
and the country now is spread hide
harnessed with sparse human things
and miles ahead, dawning into mind
under its approaching cobalt-inked

Chinese scroll of drapefold mountains
waits Dawson's homesick Gloucester
where Catholics weren't allowed to live.
There people crowd out onto the platform
to blow smoke like a regiment, before windows

carry them on, as ivory phantoms
who might not quip, or sue,
between the haunches of the hills
where the pioneer Isabella Mary Kelly
(*She poisons flour! Sleeps with bushrangers!*

She flogs her convicts herself!)
refusing any man's protection
rode with pocket pistols. Which
on this coast, made her the Kelly
whom slander forced to bear the whole guilt,

when it was real, of European settlement.
Now her name gets misremembered:
Kelly's crossing, Kate Kelly's Crossing
and few battlers on this train
think they live in a European settlement

and on a platform down the first
subtropic river, patched velvet girls
get met by their mothers' lovers,
lawn bowlers step down clutching their nuclei
and a walking frame is hoisted yea! like swords.

2003

The mudcrab-eaters

Nothing lovers in their forties do together
    that they don't, you'd say, repeat.
    But then, this day, what others here
    so feast, rising on the lean threat
    of the night apart? Or so taste
    and toast their exquisite lot?

    Who else at Gambaro's is happy?
    With dolphin glances serving
    each other, the lovers sit, sea-delight
    lightening air. And though
they night and morning years-long sat down to mudcrab,
    they have never eaten mudcrab before.   *1980*

In-flight note

Kitten, writes the mousy boy in his neat
fawn casuals sitting beside me on the flight,
neatly, *I can't give up everything just like that.*
Everything, how much was it? and just like what?
Did she cool it or walk out? loosen her hand from his tight
white-knuckled hand, or not meet him, just as he thought
*You mean far too much to me. I can't forget
the four months we've known each other.* No, he won't eat,
finally he pays – pale, careful, distraught –
for a beer, turns over the pad on the page he wrote
and sleeps a bit. Or dreams of his Sydney cat.
The pad cost one dollar twenty. He wakes to write
It's naive to think we could be just good friends.
Pages and pages. And so the whole world ends.   *1988*

The Land's Meaning

for Sidney Nolan

The love of man is a weed of the waste places.
One may think of it as the spinifex of dry souls.

I have not, it is true, made the trek to the difficult country
where it is said to grow; but signs come back,
reports come back, of continuing exploration
in that terrain. And certain of our young men,
who turned in despair from the bar, upsetting a glass,
and swore: 'No more' (for the tin rooms stank of flyspray)
are sending word that the mastery of silence
alone is empire. What is God, they say,
but a man unwounded in his loneliness?

And the question (applauded, derided) falls like dust
on veranda and bar; and in pauses, when thinking ceases,
the footprints of the recently departed
march to the mind's horizons, and endure.

And often enough as we turn again, and laugh,
cloud, hide away the tracks with an acid word,
there is one or more gone past the door to stand
(wondering, debating) in the iron street,
and toss a coin, and pass, to the township's end,
where one-eyed 'Mat, eternal dealer in camels,
grins in his dusty yard like a split fruit.

But one who has returned, his eyes blurred maps
of landscapes still unmapped, gives this account:

'The third day, cockatoos dropped dead in the air.
Then the crows turned back, the camels knelt down and stayed there,
and a skin-coloured surf of sandhills jumped the horizon
and swamped me. I was bushed for forty years.

'And I came to a bloke all alone like a kurrajong tree.
And I said to him: "Mate—I don't need to know your name —
Let me camp in your shade, let me sleep, till the sun goes down."'

1962

Ruins of the City of Hay

The wind has scattered my city to the sheep.
Capeweed and lovely lupins choke the street
where the wind wanders in great gaunt chimneys of hay
and straws cry out like keyholes.

Our yellow Petra of the fields: alas!
I walk the ruins of forum and capitol,
through quiet squares, by the temples of tranquillity.
Wisps of the metropolis brush my hair.
I become invisible in tears.

This was no ratbags' Eden: these were true haystacks.
Golden, but functional, our mansions sprang from dreams
of architects in love (*O my meadow queen!*).
No need for fires to be lit on the yellow hearthstones;
our walls were warmer than flesh, more sure than igloos.
On winter nights we squatted naked as Esquimaux,
chanting our sagas of innocent chauvinism.

In the street no vehicle passed. No telephone,
doorbell or till was heard in the canyons of hay.
No stir, no sound, but the sickle and the loom,
and the comments of emus begging by kitchen doors
in the moonlike silence of morning.

Though the neighbour states (said Lao Tse) lie in sight of the city
and their cocks wake and their watchdogs warn the inhabitants
the men of the city of hay will never go there
all the days of their lives.

But the wind of the world descended on lovely Petra
and the spires of the towers and the statues and belfries fell.
The bones of my brothers broke in the breaking columns.
The bones of my sisters, clasping their broken children,
cracked on the hearthstones, under the rooftrees of hay.
I alone mourn in the temples, by broken altars
bowered in black nightshade and mauve salvation-jane.

And the cocks of the neighbour nations scratch in the straw.
And their dogs rejoice in the bones of all my brethren.

1962

Those who have seen visions

Those who have seen visions do not smile.
They speak. They take a ripe peach and bite
straight through the furzy skin to the juice. They shit
as the body directs. They have seen visions while
at just such functional tasks. You cannot tell
and yet you tell at once. Is it an absence of light
or a presence? It is a burden. Even the night
cannot ease knowledge. There is no escape at all.

On an obscure wall with quick strokes on wet plaster
Piero della Francesca painted Christ
lifting his heavy torso, released at last
into vision. The painter was concentrating his cluster
of geometric tokens to clamp like a bite
against the neck of absence. We flinch alright.

1983

Australian Horizons

The strangled high voices of Australian men
again and again remind me of barbed wire
and the wind twanging for distance. Then
I remember the eyes of Australians squinting
as they might be, say, behind windscreens or in traffic
with sun glare and sun mirage in their eyes.

Distance is hard to get out of Australian eyes.
Even in cities there's a bit of dust on the tongue, and men
keep a bit of silence under the armpit. Sometimes in traffic
there's the old childhood, twanging like wire:
and even city kids know the sense of paddocks squinting:
Australia's a burr that itches right into you, then.

High voices are for distance. You yell out, and then
you listen and wait. There is dust in your eyes
as well as on your tongue. The threat of silence squinting
still pinches to treble the voices of Australian men.
Memory is tight as the vibrations of fencing wire
even in Sydney with its high whine of endless traffic.

4 p.m. in the Public Bar, and it's busy traffic
alright. The itch mounts. It is getting higher. Then
memory clicks. This is beyond Sydney, the sound hits wire
back in the haze of distance and you squint your eyes
as if you had just walked in. Like iron filings, men
are drawn to the magnet of habit. They're squinting.

Once in Venice near the Grand Canal I caught the squinting
high male voices of Australians, dusty in the traffic
of foreign pedestrians. They herded together, six men
and their wives. I felt the sweat of their armpits and then
the way they bunched tighter. There were gates in their eyes
and their defensive silence was taut as barbed wire.

Their women dived for shops, picked up glass and wire
souvenirs, went further afield. They peered then returned squinting
to the Tourist Menu outside the Trattoria. The blokes kept their eyes
narrow as a field of seeds or the dotted lines in traffic.
They clung and were defensive. Their distance then
was absolute and inflexible. There were burrs in those men

and their voices were tight. They'd not left home at all but were men
rolling pellets of dust under the tongue to become wire
high pitched in empty paddocks, blinking and squinting.

2000

The City of Empty Rooms

Once, when it was a village,
Its natural walls were the long beach
Energised by the surf and the repetition of surf,
And behind the sand hills, the river
Sodden with mangroves and scuttle of crustaceans.
A few fishermen, then a dirt road
And the first hotel. The rest is history.

The river is a puzzle of canals
And bridges. The fibro sheds
Were like seed-pods: the sandy soil
Is now a forest of towers.
                              Instead of foliage
There are lights in every room
Instead of flowers there are balconies and glass.
At night, in the city of empty rooms

Like small plagues of hairy caterpillars
Cars move in dense processions
Of set patterns.
Three a.m. Four a.m. In some of the forest towers
Not even one light sets out signals.
Ten a.m. In all of the thousand bedrooms
If one figure moves it is an event:
Like a spouting whale, or like a lone sea eagle.   *2006*

DAVID MALOUF (*b 1934*)

Confessions of an Only Child
for my sister

Two years five days between us, and my nose
(or rather, grandfather's)
put firmly out of joint. Then half the length
of a pool over the hundred-metres dash
to my masculinity. You were like father, I like mother,
a happy compromise – though we were seldom on speaking terms
and scrapped like tigers mostly. I wrote you out
of my childhood, preferring
afternoons without you, a moony child practising thunder
by Czerny, Clementi,
to our closetings together through chicken pox, slow wet weeks
at the beach-house playing euchre for film star swaps.
My afternoons in fact
were yours. The poems are also yours, and empty
without you. Now there are deaths
between us, and a marriage, three hectic stars
you've captured from the dark. They flare, they plunge away, go flying
down the wet beach. We are left
alone as in our earliest photograph: a stack of ruined sandcastles
between us, behind
the last patch of scrub, grey ring-barked trunks in winter sunlight; ahead
a night of carbide lamps. Like stars on brilliant claws battalions
of soldiers crabs death-rattle
and wheel across the zodiac, sand granules
pour through my fist. The Pacific poised
on a day late in the 'thirties rolls its thunder
towards us, pulled awry
by the moon. Our faces gather

their lines, their light, we grow like one another, the high cheekbones
of parents and other strangers
rise under the skin. We might be twins at last, with nothing
between us, no time at all. Burned to a blackness
we smile into the sun.   *1974*

Into the Blue

Voyages

Jangling in my head the blue night-music
        of the Bay. Our limbs
emerged out of its salt.

When the moon blazed a track
        across it we were tempted. Only
our breath, only our need

for the next breath constrained us.
        It was our other selves
that tried it,

in sleep. And arrived
        safely. And never did
get back.

Stars

Its licking round our knees a shy demand
        for closeness. When we looked
        up, the sleepy stretch and dazzle of it
        took us
out and further out than thought could reach.

First apprehension
        of distance: the far, the near.
        When night came on
        in the wet sand instant
galaxies – look! – stamped out under our feet.

Rockpools

Glass you could put a fist through
    unbloodied. Red velvet
    mouths, skirts ruffled, claws, their sideways dart
and pause a stop start tango.

Distant rooms. When they fall still,
    in the underwater
    look that looks back at us the shock
of family likeness.

The Catch

Ribbons of drowned sunlight under the smoky
    flow. Boneless
    ghosts that flutter free of
our lists. They
    are the ones, the only ones
    we want on our lines.

Always the mystery of other
    flesh and occasions,
    creatures floating
clear of their future –
    us – and the slow
    ache of transformation.

Pinprick starry
    bubbles where feathers sprout.
    At six o'clock,
warm on a plate,
    the named ones, the catch.
    What we famish

for are the un-named
    others. Dropped lines trawl
    our veins for a colour –
blue, the blue of blue
    skies to collect
    our thoughts in as the first

planets clock in,
    and the Bay, that salt mouthful

of the sea's unsounded
silence,
    yawns and takes up
    our story   *2007*

CHRIS WALLACE-CRABBE *(b 1934)*

Melbourne

Not on the ocean, on a muted bay
Where the broad rays drift slowly over mud
And flathead loll on sand, a city bloats
Between the plains of water and of loam.
If surf beats, it is faint and far away;
If slogans blow around, we stay at home.

And, like the bay, our blood flows easily,
Not warm, not cold (in all things moderate),
Following our familiar tides. Elsewhere
Victims are bleeding, sun is beating down
On patriot, guerrilla, refugee.
We see the newsreels when we dine in town.

Ideas are grown in other gardens while
This chocolate soil throws up its harvest of
Imported and deciduous platitudes,
None of them flowering boldly or for long;
And we, the gardeners, securely smile
Humming a bar or two of rusty song.

Old tunes are good enough if sing we must;
Old images, re-vamped *ad nauseam*,
Will sate the burgher's eye and keep him quiet
As the great wheels run on. And should he seek
Variety, there's wind, there's heat, there's frost
To feed his conversation all the week.

Highway by highway, the remorseless cars
Strangle the city, put it out of pain,
Its limbs still kicking feebly on the hills.
Nobody cares. The artists sail at dawn
For brisker ports, or rot in public bars.
Though much has died here, little has been born.   *1963*

Other People

In the First World War they . . .
Who were *they?* Who cares anymore? . . .
Killed four of my uncles,
So I was told one day.

There were only four on that side of the family
And all swept away in a few bad years
In a war the historians tell us now
Was fought over nothing at all.

Four uncles, as one might say
A dozen apples or seven tons of dirt,
Swept away by the luck of history,
Closed off. Full stop.

Four is a lot for uncles,
A lot for lives, I should say.
Their chalk was wiped clean off the slate,
The War meant nothing at all.

War needs a lot of uncles,
And husbands, and brothers, and so on:
Someone must *want* to kill them,
Somebody needs them dead.

Who is it, I wonder. Me?
Or is it you there, reading away,
Or a chap with a small-arms factory?
Or is it only *they?*   1971

There

At the bottom of consciousness there is a clear lake
The waters of which throb ever so lightly
(Like the bodies of lovers after their spasm ends)
Throwing dimpled distortion across the rocky bed,
Greenish round rocks, the size of a grapefruit, say,
And through these cold waters fish are swimming
Seeming quite continuous with their medium
As sexual love flows directly through God.
Here water moves the slubbing barabble of language,
Gust and pith, cacophony, glossolalia,
Gift of the gab and purple rhetoric,

Moaning in rut, scream, snicker and the rip
That is sheer pain.
                           Yes, these are of language
But not yet *it*. They are the pool,
Its diamonds and yabbies, ripple and scale,
Insatiable glittering . . .
               I'm afraid I don't know what paths
Lead up from the pool to where I think and talk;
By what stony track with landslip and synapse
Distracted everywhere, choked with scrubby thorns
We got to where we are. Conscious.
                                    Aren't we?
Oh hell, we seem to think we understand:
When I ask at the ticket-box they sell me a ticket
But I do not know what the recently dead will ask us
When they walk through the scrub again like sunbeams.   1988

Genius Loci

When I can't sleep and prove
a pain in the neck to myself
I will sneak downstairs, dress up warmly
and squeeze into whelming darkness
or piccaninny daylight, where
I may just glimpse at a corner
one of the Jika Jika slipping away
lapped in a possumskin rug.

I will hurry like steam to the corner,
ever so much wanting to say,
'Hey, wait. I have so much that I . . .'
But there will only be
broad street, creamy houses, dew
and a silence of black shrubs.

Maybe if I got up
a little more smartly next time,
got out on the road quick,
I could sneak up closer
on that dark tribesman in his furry cloak
and ask him . . .
                    oh, something really deep:

something off the planet.   1988

The Bush

for Seamus Heaney

Overture:
               violins:
it is all scraggy,
wideawake,
               ironical,
decked out
               in denim fatigues.
Witty and welcoming,
               leathery-evergreen,
bemedalled with beercans,
cowpat and wallaby-dung,
flap,
     nub,
          hinge,
               node,
blindeye quartzite,
               wafery sandstone,
bright as a button
subtle for mile on mile
far from vulgarity
               (far from sleek Europe)
in its array of
               furniture tonings
sheeted by sunglaze
               lovingly dusted,
wispy and splintery,
tussocky,
               corduroy,
all of its idiom
dry as a thesis
to moist outsiders:
wonderfully eloquent
               on its home ground,
branchful of adverbs,
lovingly
               wombat-hued,
dreamily
               sheeptoned,
fluted with scalloping surf
and every step a quip.

1990

Good Friday Seder at Separation Creek

The moon has a flat face,
yellow Moses peering over the chine
of our neighbourhood mountain. Growl,
goes the rough surf. Our backstage mopoke
may have guessed that we lack
shinbone and bitter herbs for the occasion
while nuggety Joshua, gleeful as ever,
nicks off to his bedroom in order to find
the tucked-away afikomen. His brother
is all tricked out in Liverpool strip,
as red as Karl Marx but much fitter.

Braggart moon floats loftier now,
a white queen dragging the tides along
like a cloak of crushed velvet.
No rest for the wicked: surfers are camped,
or shacked, all the way from Pisgah to Sinai.
If they read, it is airport novels
with titles embossed in gold, but not the scriptures,
not crazy Nietzsche, certainly not Oscar Wilde
who shrugged and scribbled, 'what comes of all this
is a curious mixture of ardour and indifference,'
and believed all art is entirely useless,

or said, or thought, or wrote, that he believed it,
a plump serious chap who lived
beyond religion on the Plains of Art.
Now, over a varnished tabletop
we recite the special dealings that a people
had with He-who-is while quitting Egypt,
but it does feel quaint to have this on Good Friday,
a day whose very name has the kids
wondering if the language was taken ill
at its coining. Those big waves barge home
out of a Matthew Arnold metaphor

while the grained beach stands in for Zion,
offering peace of mind. No sweat
this evening, with our salt stars sailing
through the black text of pinetree branches
and that mopoke murmuring its bafflement
in the very face of the Torah,

sitting on the shoulder of mortality.
It's a gorgeous night. And there we go:
Diana of the fibros cannot show us that
history is a polychrome figure,
thorned, gassed and smeared with blood

1993

Erstwhile

Your girlfriend rang me up today,
your former girlfriend,
                       no, that isn't right,
the present friend of all that once was you,
your fetch or
what remains in the little photographs:
a boy in black-and-white
riding a horse into the scrub
or, freckled, reading out of doors,
both times T-shirted,
your hair a thick, dark bowl-cut,
                         my erstwhile son.

Oh yes, she rang today,
had taken somebody out to see your grave
near the forked white trunk,
and we were sad together
on the phone, for a hard while
thinking of you, long gone now. Hence.
Where? Where are you?
In poor fact I can never come to grasp
the meaning of it all, supposing
that to be what religion's all about.
The loss remains behind
                     like never being well.

1998

from *Modern Times*

X

The time comes when you have to start again;
Rewriting Western Civ is a bed of nails.
The great surrealists turned out to be
Inventors of a tin, toy, painted train
Which choofs around its figure-eightish tracks
Yet again, once every generation. Whoopee!
Now it's comfy ackers who've taken on
The engine-driving of the avant-garde,

Pretending, in their salaries and jeans
To be the saltimbanques who cycle round
The edge of a volcano (boop-a-doop!)
Vertiginously. Their superannuation
Cushions the cutting edge; it's pretty tough
To be a PoMo shithead jacking off.

XIV

Van Gogh said misery would never end,
Teeth of pain sunk deep in our common neck,
His own art as rich as a dearest friend,
Bright love in every smear and dab and speck.
How he would have doted on this view
Of bluegums, terracotta, golden wattle:
A south far deeper than he ever knew
Or called to mind after a second bottle

With the not-quite-reliable aid of God.
He could feel Spirit in cornfields or the hay,
Down a dark line of cypresses, maybe
Or in some fiercely flowering almond tree,
But only if he managed a really good day.
Otherwise he grimly trod – and trod.   *2001*

It Sounds Different Today

How far can it matter to 'god' or to
the human race, let alone this planet

whether you notice how far the dry valley has
turned silvery when you opened your sunned eyes;

again, if you noticed that fade-red MG, or
how accurately words can set down the sight

of a digging wombat hurling up brown clods
of burrow-earth? We must have been set down

here to do something or other well, but then
who or what is ever going to remember that,

you ask yourself, taking an epicurean nap.
No deadlines this week, nothing to do for

odd students, nor for the undulating network
family means; next in the scale would come the

Persian carpet of history, in which there just
might be a dint or digit that remembered your

being here – for say a century, or several
until the whole circus had been burned off

the road, costumes, clown and performing bears
including the human race, as it might have been.

Come to that, when you take good note
of the way plural midday sunlight glances back

brassily from the upper leaves of those spotted gums
or jot down the names you most frequently forget,

it is absurdly being done for some project which
we may as well name god: ironically put together

from the Ikea kits of personal consciousness,
those private dillybags that could well include

cataracts, PMT, envy, Protestantism and all.
You pick up your old box of coloured pencils and start again.

2008

Surfers

Far out, down heaving green glass hills
The surfers ride the summer seas.
Their taut brown bodies, arms upraised,
Slide through an Egyptian frieze.

High and dry upon the beach,
Pinned to my rug by a glaring sun
I sit among the picnic things,
Alone and fat and forty-one.

And idly through the memory's hand
Stream visions of a Cornish day
When effervescent waves and air
Sparkled into glinting play.

The breakers crash, a board flies up.
A boy runs laughing on the land,
Then, turning, wades to ride again.
I close the fingers of my hand.   1980

Grandchild

Early this morning, when workmen were switching on lights
in chilly kitchens, packing their lunch boxes
into their Gladstone bags, starting their utes in the cold
and driving down quiet streets under misty lamps,
my daughter bore a son. Nurses sponged him clean
as the glittering shingle of suburbs beside the river
waned to a scattered glimmer of pale cubes.
We met at half-past twelve in a ward crowded
with people busy with parcels and extra chairs.
A bunch of flowers fell on the floor. We passed
the baby round. His dark head lay in my hand
like a fruit. He seemed to be dwelling on something
half-remembered, puckering his brow, occasionally
flexing fingers thin and soft as snippets of mauve string.
Far below in the street lunch-time crowds flowed out
among the traffic. Girls went arm in arm on high
heels. An ambulance nosed into a ground-floor bay.

A clerk strode in the wind with a streaming tie.
Beyond the office blocks and the estuary, in Santa Fe,
Northampton or the other side of town, a young man
may be gripping a girl's hand as they climb upstairs.
She is wearing a cotton dress. Her sandals slip
on metal treads. She laughs, embarrassed, excited
at being desired so urgently in the
minutes before this grandchild's wife is conceived.
And his best friend, whose parents quarrel all day
about leaving Greece, is lying perhaps in his cot
on a balcony, watching his fat pink hands and woolly sleeves
swatting at puffs of cloud in the airy blue.
News he may break to our boy in some passage-way
in a house we've never seen is breeding now
in the minds of pensive children queuing by Red Cross
trucks, or curled like foetuses deep under warm quilts
as the long ship-wrecking roar of the distant sea
slides to the coming of night and fades away.   *1988*

JENNIFER STRAUSS (*b 1933*)

Tending the Graves

There are days when the dead will have nothing to do with us –
In summer mostly, when a dry wind from the north
Gusts up just as you enter the cemetery gates
And the roses are overblown, the gum trees stripping,
And you know the flowers you've brought will wither fast
And are besides the wrong size for the holder
And you've forgotten scissors, and something to carry water.

It's not reproach. They have no need to tell us 'You
Have given away my books, taken another lover into my bed,
Made of my children something I do not approve' – all that
We can say for ourselves. It is absolute absence.
They are so engrossed by death they refuse even to haunt us.
We must tend the grave and walk away; unrewarded,
Unreproached, unforgiven; our feet heavy with life.

1988

Wife to Horatio

You didn't know Horatio had a wife?
Of course he did. To marry is the fate
Of ordinary men. And his wife says:
'No interviews! They are forbidden.
My husband is a private citizen,
And ill. You think I'd let vultures like you
Rip open that old wound? Why would you want
To dig up all that buried agony?
Hamlet's skull whitens like Yorick's now
And on those walls where once the dead king stalked
The sturdy sons of Fortinbras play ball.
His rule is well enough. Was it surprising
That he grew restive hearing Hamlet praised
Perpetually? Not that I'd criticize
My husband's friend; I'm told that friendship's noble,
Ophelia was my friend – we laughed a lot.
I know that Hamlet had great difficulties,
And when the great have problems, we all know,
It is the ordinary lives that pay.
Ophelia was my friend – but she was dead,
And the live child in my belly jumped
When the king frowned. I found that I had wits
(My family too was not uninfluential):
We sought permission to withdraw from court.
It came readily, and as a bonus
Horatio was appointed (a neat move)
To write the official life of the late Prince –
Oh yes, the work's in progress. There came too
The settlement of this estate. The king
Is not ungenerous. He sent birth gifts,
The boy a handsome set of fencing foils,
My daughter pearls. Yes, that's Ophelia
Playing by the river. Aren't we afraid?
Not more than ordinary parents are.
Horatio, it's true, was rather anxious.
And no, we didn't talk it out. Come, come,
You've lived in Denmark, surely you must know
What miseries breed from talk. We needed
Action. There'll be no drowning here.
I've seen to it that she knows how to swim.'

1988

Tiananmen Square June 4, 1989

Karl Marx, take your time,
looming over Highgate on your plinth.
Snow's falling on your beard,
exiled, huge, hairy, genderless.
Terminally angry, piss-poor,
stuffed on utopias and cold,
cold as iron.

I'm thinking of your loving wife,
your desperate children and your grandchild
dead behind the barred enclosure of your brain.
Men's ideas the product, not the cause
of history, you said?

The snow has killed the lilacs.
Whose idea?
The air is frozen with theory.

What can the man be doing all day
in that cold place?
What can he be writing?
What can he be reading?
What big eyes you have, mama!
Next year, child, we will eat.

I'm thinking of my middle-class German grandmother
soft as a pigeon, who wept
when Chamberlain declared a war.
Why are you crying, grandma?
It's only the big bad wolf, my dear.
It's only a story.

There's no end to it.
The wolves have come again.
What shall I tell my grandchildren?

No end to the requiems, the burning trains,
the guns, the shouting in the streets,
the outraged stars, the anguished face
of terror under ragged headbands
soaked in death's calligraphy.

Don't turn your back, I'll say.
Look hard.
Move into that frozen swarming screen.
How far can you run with a bullet in your brain?

And forgive, if you can, the safety of a poem
sharpened on a grieving night.

A story has to start somewhere.   *1990*

Letting Go

Tell the truth of experience
they say they also
say you must let
go learn to let go
let your children
go

and they go
and you stay
letting them go
because you are obedient and
respect everyone's freedom
to go and you stay

and you want to tell the truth
because you are yours truly
its obedient servant
but you can't because
you're feeling what you're not
supposed to feel you have
let them go and go and

you can't say what you feel
because they might read
this poem and feel guilty
and some post-modern hack
will back them up
and make you feel guilty
and stop feeling which is
post-modern and what
you're meant to feel

so you don't write a poem
you line up words in prose

inside a journal trapped
like a scorpion in a locked
drawer to be opened by
your children let go
after lived life and all the time
a great wave bursting
howls and rears and

you have to let go
or you're gone you're
gone gasping you
let go
till the next wave
towers crumbles
shreds you to lace –

When you wake
your spine is twisted
like a sea-bird
inspecting the sky,
stripped by lightning.   1992

The Witnesses

This morning, stirred beneath the agitation of the rain
came three white-collar magpies to my lawn.
Jehovah's Witness-like they knocked
they knocked upon my window pane,
stood black demanding entrance. I held my ground
but they were smart and oh-so-keen,
so upright, firm they pushed their song at me,
surprised my shrinking soul.

'Spare my breath,' I said, 'you've fangled
on my lawn all night. Enough's enough.
What more have you to tell?'
'O foolish pale and puny earthling,
save your wit – our glamorous warbling
has unlocked the last old secrets of the soul.
Go warm your winters fast against the
rising dark, the setting sun,
the climbing moon, the mourning grasses
and the chill of dusk.'

The Soldier's Reward

I'm Gerry Ivan James Chickenmar Grantling
I'm five foot four or is it three?
Joined the forces as a private
Weren't no blue-arsed flies on me!
Worked as stockman on a station
Always earnt me meat 'n bread
I'm as good as any whiteman
Yet I'm here stone cold and dead
In the stinkin' cell at Condo
I was drunk and I was brash
Bought meself some plonk an' devon
Staggered up the street . . . then crash!
Local sergeant and constable
Read the riot act out loud
Law said Abos can't have liquor
I was doin' what's not allowed.
They forget that I'm a Private
Fought for freedom – two great wars –
They threw me on the cold stone cell floor
Broke me neck – the rotten whores!   *1978*

'Consultation'

Me, mate?
You'll get no views from me!
Where did I ever go?
Who did I ever meet?
What did I ever see?
Nothin' just the old river, the gumtree
The mission. Me seven kids, four grandkids
Blacks gamblin' drunk, fightin', laughin', cryin'
Mostly gamblin'. Playin' 'pups' wild deuces game
Doin' it, risking their twenty cents to try to win thirty
Price of bread, you know. You know, life ain't too bad here
No runnin' water, no fireplaces, huh, no houses even
Jus' the kerosene tin and hessian bag humpies.
They say there's 'welfare' for Blacks these days
But the mission looks the same to me. Seven I got

An' another one in the barrel – put there by the 'manager'
'Cause his wife cut him short or somethin'
Nothin' changes. I don't ever see nothin' much
An' no-one asked me my view before.   *1978*

VIVIAN SMITH (*b 1933*)

For My Daughter

Made from nothing, bud and rose,
kisses, water, mystery,
you who grew inside our need
run, in your discovery,

out of the garden's folded light.
out of the green, the fountain's spray,
past the shrubs, the dew-lit ferns,
out to the noise, the street, the day,

and stand, in your astonishment,
beneath the hanging heavy limes
(O my child, O my darling daughter,
summer was full of wars and crimes)

to see the foal, the clown, the doll,
the circus and procession band
march up the street and march away . . .
And so you turn and take my hand.   *1967*

Night Life

Disturbed at 2 a.m. I hear a claw
scratching the window, tapping at the pane,
and then I realise, a broken branch,
and yet I can't turn back to sleep again.

Slowly, not to wake you, I get up,
thinking of food, perhaps a quiet read.
A cockroach runs across the kitchen floor,
its lacquered shell as quick and dry as seed.

Outside the chalice lily lifts its cup
in adoration to the mirrored moon,
full of purpose as it trembles there,
collecting drops of moisture on its spoon.

Noises of the night, it's all alive,
birds shifting in the steady trees,
slugs and snails eating fallen flowers,
a moth freighted with fragilities.

Nocturnal life, the other side of things,
proceeding whether we observe or not,
like rows and rows of brown coastal ants
transporting food from here to another spot.   *2006*

EVAN JONES (*b 1931*)

Generations

I go to see my parents,
we chew the rag a bit;
I turn the telly on
and sit and look at it.

Not much gets said:
there doesn't seem much point.
but still they like to have
me hanging round the joint.

I go to see my son,
I'm like a Santa Claus:
he couldn't like me more;
mad about him, of course.

Still years before he learns
to judge, condemn, dismiss.
I stand against the light
and bleed for both of us.   *1967*

Eurydice Remembered

The shadows of your cheek
deepened and were defined
under your cloud of hair:
I called you into being out of air
because you filled my mind;
I almost made you speak.

I sang, and there you stood;
I stopped, and you were still:
in that that echoing cave
I played and sang with all the craft I have
to bring you to my will,
to wake your frozen blood.

We trod a winding path,
my music led your feet.
And then I failed: I turned
to speak, not sing: and all at once you burned
to air. Now I must meet
all women in their wrath.

1967

Him

Why does he never sleep, when sleep is healing?
All night while I lie still, not feeling feeling,
He walks the networks of my little city,
Swinging his lantern, crying out the time.

Later and later. When I swing awake
I try to trace his movements, but he goes
Always by back ways and the hidden places,
Fugitive, cautious, undiscernible.

Persistently I strive to meet him, whether,
When he at last obtrudes on my short sight,
He prove dog-faced or radiant, standing in
Insanity, or on the shores of light.

1967

Nursing Home

Incontinence, and the mind going. Where?
The place is all it should be. Not enough.
She's had such spirit. *No more advice, thank you!*
And she'd slam down the receiver. Hated drudging:
The house is crawling away with dirt, but I'm
Going out to garden. Thwarted, self-thwarted:
Gave up the piano when her marriage failed,
Should have had a career. Instead she moved:
Twenty houses in forty years. And always
Well, dear son, at last we've found the right one.
Never. And now, this one room, to be shared
With a woman still as a stonefish.

                           Sunday morning:
Outside, the trees wrestle with spring wind.
She sits here in her chair beating her tray:
Sister sister sister sister sister!
Clenches her lips, hums against them. And again
Sister sister sister sister sister!
High, scratched voice: *Behind me behind me behind me!*
What is, Mother? A pause. *I don't know.*
And again the drumming: *Sister sister sister!*

      *

The mind going, and coming back, and going.
Each ebb, a little further. She says one evening
A bit flat today. Long pause, and then
I don't like this place. (What is *this* place?)
And slowly: *All that way along that wall!*
Too far to go.

                 I stand smoothing her forehead,
Her child's become her parent, saying with her
The night prayers. She's growing peaceful now.
I'm drawn to the edge of a mystery. The mind
I cannot know, what does it know? She seems
Listening. As a remote landscape listens
To its river in a circle of hills. As a boat
Far out may heed the current beneath,
Bearing it further. What sounds? To us, silence.   *1982*

Drifters

One day soon he'll tell her it's time to start packing.
and the kids will yell 'Truly?' and act wildly excited for no reason,
and the brown kelpie pup will start dashing about, tripping everyone up,
and she'll go out to the vegetable-patch and pick all the green tomatoes from
    the vines,
and notice how the oldest girl is close to tears because she was happy here,
and how the youngest girl is beaming because she wasn't.
And the first thing she'll put on the trailer will be the bottling-set she never
    unpacked from Grovedale,
and when the loaded ute bumps down the drive past the blackberry-canes
    with their last shrivelled fruit,
she won't even ask why they're leaving this time, or where they're heading for
– she'll only remember how, when they came here,
she held out her hands bright with berries,
the first of the season, and said:
'Make a wish, Tom, make a wish.'   *1968*

Homecoming

All day, day after day, they're bringing them home,
they're picking them up, those they can find, and bringing them home,
they're bringing them in, piled on the hulls of tanks, in medevacs, in convoys,
they're zipping them up in green plastic bags,
they're tagging them now in Saigon, in the mortuary coolness
they're giving them names, they're rolling them out of
the deep-freeze lockers – on the tarmac at Tan Son Nhut
the noble jets are whining like hounds,
they are bringing them home
– curly-heads, kinky-hairs, crew-cuts, balding non-coms
– they're high, now, high and higher, over the land, the steaming *chow mein*
their shadows are tracing the blue curve of the Pacific
with sorrowful quick fingers, heading south, heading east,
home, home, *home* – and the coasts swing upward, the old
    ridiculous curvatures
of earth, the knuckled hills, the mangrove-swamps, the desert emptiness . . .
in their sterile housing they tilt towards these like skiers
– taxiing in, on the long runways, the howl of their homecoming rises
surrounding them like their last moments (the mash, the splendour)
then fading at length as they move

on to small towns where dogs in the frozen sunset
raise muzzles in mute salute,
and on to cities in whose wide web of suburbs
telegrams tremble like leaves from a wintering tree
and the spider grief swings in his bitter geometry
– they're bringing them home, now, too late, too early.

1969

Going

for my Mother-in-Law, Gladys

Mum, you would have loved the way you went!
One moment, at a barbeque in the garden
– the next, falling out of your chair,
hamburger in one hand,
and a grandson yelling.

Zipp! The heart's roller blind
rattling up, and you, in an old dress,
quite still, flown already from your dearly loved
Lyndon, leaving only a bruise like a blue kiss
on the side of your face, the seed beds incredibly tidy,
grass daunted by drought.

You'd have loved it, Mum, you big spender! The relatives,
eyes narrowed with grief, swelling the rooms
with their clumsiness, the reverberations of tears, the endless
cuppas and groups revolving blinded as moths.

The joy of your going! The laughing reminiscences
snagged on the pruned roses
in the bright blowing day!

1974

Betrayers

Why, in this strange and beautiful land,
do we feel like betrayers?
In the midst of the family,
watching the circular agonies of cat and mouse
on the family screen
and knowing that nothing ever dies, neither Tom nor Jerry,
why do we sense Gethsemane?

In the still watches of the night,
with the family abed and a half-dozen half-read books
open on the floor by our chair,
why do we suddenly go out and breathe in
the absolution of starlight streaming
from beyond history?
In the flotsam of days passing and past,
washed up on the shores of our lawns, our rooms,
in the broken prams, old photos, play-houses, toys,
why should the nervous noise of the waves
mutter of past betrayals
– and why do the shells in its fingers sound like coins clinking
    disconsolately together?   1978

Doctor to Patient

Please sit down. I'm afraid I have some
rather bad news for you: you are now seventeen
and you have contracted an occupational disease called
unemployment. Like others similarly afflicted
you will experience feelings of
shock, disbelief, injustice, guilt, apathy, and aggression
(although not necessarily in that order)
and you'll no doubt be urged to try the various
recommended anodynes: editorials in newspapers,
voluntary unpaid work for local charities, booze,
other compulsive mind-destroyers, prayer, comforting
talks with increasingly less-interested friends.
It is small comfort to know that the disease
is universal and can accommodate
the middle-aged and thirtyish and strikes down
those in camps in Kompong Sam and Warsaw.
However you will discover, as time passes,
that your presence in itself will make others
obviously uncomfortable. Try not to let
your shadow, at this stage,
fall across your neighbour's plate; eat
with the right hand only; do not touch
others in public (this can be easily
misconstrued); keep always
down-wind, if possible. Please remember
you have now become our common vulnerability

personified. Oh yes, and, by the way,
you will be relieved to know the disease
is only in a minority of cases terminal.

Most, that is, survive. Next, please.   1986

A Park in the Balkans

Aerial photographs have revealed newly bulldozed areas believed to be the
massacre site of some 6000 Muslim males taken away after the fall of Srebenica.
The question of their fate has not significantly impeded the 'search for peace' in Bosnia.

A policy was walking in a park,
Three governments went jogging slowly by:
One turned and made a rather blurred remark,
The other two said nothing but looked sly.

A speech was feeding pigeons on the lawn,
Crumbling moral precepts in one hand.
A speaker (circling patiently since dawn)
Still sought official clearances to land.

Leaf conferred with leaf on every tree
– None sought the honour of being first to fall,
The natural chlorophyll of sophistry
Worked its chemistry in the veins of all . . .

Park visitors at noon were the usual crowd:
Some threats, a solemn warning, and a plea.
History passed over them like a cloud
(A dream of empire winced rheumatically).

An embargo sat blinking in the sun.
The sky was beret-blue and impotent.
Harsh resolutions flew off, one by one,
And most of them were most sincerely meant.

All through that long, long summer afternoon
Traumas lay like lovers on the grass.
A guilty silence deepened; all too soon
What no one could prevent had come to pass . . .   1997

The Sadness of the Creatures

We live in a third floor flat
among gentle predators
and our food comes often
frozen but in its own shape
(for we hate euphemisms
as you would expect) and our cat's
food comes in tins, other than
scraps of the real thing and she
like a clever cat makes milk
of it for her kittens: we shout
of course but it's electric
like those phantom storms
in the tropics and we think of
the neighbours – I'm not writing
this to say how guilty
we are like some well-paid
theologian at an American
College on a lake
or even to congratulate
the greedy kittens who have
found their mittens and are up
to their eyes in pie. – I know
lots of ways of upsetting
God's syllogisms, real
seminar-shakers some of them,
but I'm an historical cat
and I run on rails and so
I don't frame those little poems
which take three lines to
get under your feet –
you know the kind of thing –
The water I boiled the lobster in
is cool enough to top
up the chrysanthemums.
No, I'm acquisitive and have
one hundred and seven Bach
Cantatas at the last count,
but these are things of the spirit
and my wife and our children

and I are animals (biologically
speaking) which is how the world
talks to us, moving on the billiard
table of green London, the sun's
red eye and the cat's green eye
focusing for an end. I know
and you know and we all know
that the certain end of each of us
could be the end of all of us,
but if you asked me what
frightened me most, I wouldn't
say the total bang or even
the circling clot in the red drains
but the picture of a lit room
where two people not disposed
to quarrel have met so
oblique a slant of the dark
they can find no words for
their appalled hurt but only
ride the rearing greyness:
there is convalescence from this,
jokes and love and reassurance,
but never enough and never
convincing and when the cats
come brushing for food their soft
aggression is hateful;
the trees rob the earth and the earth
sucks the rain and the children
burgeon in a time of invalids –
it seems a trio sonata
is playing from a bullock's
skull and the God of Man
is born in a tub of entrails;
all man's regret is no more
than Attila with a cold
and no Saviour here or
in Science Fiction will come
without a Massacre of the Innocents
and a Rape of El Dorado.   *1970*

Non Piangere, Liù

A card comes to tell you
you should report
to have your eyes tested.

But your eyes melted in the fire
and the only tears, which soon dried,
fell in the chapel.

Other things still come –
invoices, subscription renewals,
shiny plastic cards promising credit –
not much for a life spent
in the service of reality.

You need answer none of them.
Nor my asking you for one drop
of succour in my own hell.

Do not cry, I tell myself,
the whole thing is a comedy
and comedies end happily.

The fire will come out of the sun
and I shall look in the heart of it.   *1978*

An Exequy

In wet May, in the months of change,
In a country you wouldn't visit, strange
Dreams pursue me in my sleep,
Black creatures of the upper deep –
Though you are five months dead, I see
You in guilt's iconography,
Dear Wife, lost beast, beleaguered child,
The stranded monster with the mild
Appearance, whom small waves tease,
(Andromeda upon her knees
In orthodox deliverance)
And you alone of pure substance,

Non Piangere, Liù   *Don't cry, Liù: Puccini,* Turandot.
An Exequy *alludes in form and subject to 'The Exequy', by Henry King (1592-1669).*

The unformed form of life, the earth
Which Piero's brushes brought to birth
For all to greet as myth, a thing
Out of the box of imagining.

This introduction serves to sing
Your mortal death as Bishop King
Once hymned in tetrametric rhyme
His young wife, lost before her time;
Though he lived on for many years
His poem each day fed new tears
To that unreaching spot, her grave,
His lines a baroque architrave
The Sunday poor with bottled flowers
Would by-pass in their mourning hours,
Esteeming ragged natural life
('Most dearly loved, most gentle wife'),
Yet, looking back when at the gate
And seeing grief in formal state
Upon a sculpted angel group,
Were glad that men of god could stoop
To give the dead a public stance
And freeze them in their mortal dance.

The words and faces proper to
My misery are private – you
Would never share your heart with those
Whose only talent's to suppose,
Nor from your final childish bed
Raise a remote confessing head –
The channels of our lives are blocked,
The hand is stopped upon the clock,
No one can say why hearts will break
And marriages are all opaque:
A map of loss, some posted cards,
The living house reduced to shards,
The abstract hell of memory,
The pointlessness of poetry –
These are the instances which tell
Of something which I know full well,
I owe a death to you – one day
The time will come for me to pay
When your slim shape from photographs
Stands at my door and gently asks

If I have any work to do
Or will I come to bed with you.
O scala enigmatica,
I'll climb up to that attic where
The curtain of your life was drawn
Some time between despair and dawn –
I'll never know with what halt steps
You mounted to this plain eclipse
But each stair now will station me
A black responsibility
And point me to that shut-down room,
'This be your due appointed tomb.'

I think of us in Italy:
Gin-and-chianti-fuelled, we
Move in a trance through Paradise
Feeding at last our starving eyes,
Two people of the English blindness
Doing each masterpiece the kindness
Of discovering it – from Baldovinetti
To Venice's most obscure jetty.
A true unfortunate traveller, I
Depend upon your nurse's eye
To pick the altars where no Grinner
Puts us off our tourists' dinner
And in hotels to bandy words
With Genevan girls and talking birds,
To wear your feet out following me
To night's end and true amity,
And call my rational fear of flying
A paradigm of Holy Dying –
And, oh my love, I wish you were
Once more with me, at night somewhere
In narrow streets applauding wines,
The moon above the Apennines
As large as logic and the stars,
Most middle-aged of avatars,
As bright as when they shone for truth
Upon untried and avid youth.

The rooms and days we wandered through
Shrink in my mind to one – there you
Lie quite absorbed by peace – the calm
Which life could not provide is balm

In death. Unseen by me, you look
Past bed and stairs and half-read book
Eternally upon your home,
The end of pain, the left alone.
I have no friend, or intercessor,
No psychopomp or true confessor
But only you who know my heart
In every cramped and devious part –
Then take my hand and lead me out,
The sky is overcast by doubt,
The time has come, I listen for
Your words of comfort at the door,
O guide me through the shoals of fear –
'Fürchte dich nicht, ich bin bei dir.'   *1978*

How Important is Sex?

Not very. Even if it plays a not
Inconsiderable part in misery,
You can be unhappy without reference
To its intervention or its absence.

Our researchers have discovered even
Species whose reproductive processes
Are quite unsexual – and usually these
Are the more efficient and uncomplicated.

But, says the man waiting for a letter
And trying to read an article in a liberated
Magazine, I haven't been able to keep
My mind off sex since I was seven.

Others' minds go further back. Perhaps
Our evolution took the one track
(As the mind has it) into love and found
That those innovatory machines

The genitals, once in place, wouldn't
Be denied their significance. The sight
Of mummy's hair puts us on the spot,
A cave more mysterious than the mouth.

Fürchte . . . *Fear not, I am with you: J. S. Bach*, Motet No. 4

Now flow from it plays and operas
And the horrible spoutings of rancid
Kitchens: a world of novels awaits
The boy taught things by his jokey schoolmates.

But you are talking about love, you'll say.
Yes, and I know the difference,
Taking down a wank magazine,
Then a note more fingered than any photo.

Nevertheless, I am a respecter
Of power, having seen a skinny girl
Screaming in the playground, oblivious
Of boys, wake to her hormonal clock

As Juliana or as Mélisande –
Even the great gods and captains
Might relax with a plaything
As bold and changeable as this.   *1981*

Basta Sangue

In the National Gallery of Victoria
Is a nineteenth-century genre painting
Showing a ewe on guard beside the body
Of her dead lamb while all around her sin-
black crows stand silent in the snow. Each time
I pass the picture I find I shudder twice –
Once because good taste is now endemic
And I cannot let the sentimental go
Unsneered at – I have gone to the trouble of
Acquiring words like 'genre' and will call
Them to my aid – but secondly I know
I've been that ewe and soon will be that lamb,
That there's no way to love mankind but on
The improvised coordinates of death,
Death which rules the snow, the crows, the sheep,
The painter and the drifting connoisseur.

Enough of blood, but Abraham's raised knife
Is seldom halted and any place for God
(Even if he didn't give the orders)
Will be outside the frame. A melody
Can gong the executioner's axe awake,
A painting take away our appetite
For lunch, and mother-love still walk all night
To lull a baby quiet. Whatever gathers
Overleaf is murderous: we move
On through the gallery praising Art which keeps
The types of horror constant so that we
May go about our business and forget.   *1999*

Both Ends Against the Middle

Deep inside the Imperial War Museum
Where children are surprised by undreamt dreams
            Destruction's most impartial theorem,
The Rolls-Royce Merlin Aircraft Engine, gleams.

It seems just lowered by Donatello's tackle:
He would have known why copper pipes entwine
            So murderous a tabernacle
And where control and fate might share a line.

Would we be right to look for innocence
Or guess that need to kill has shaped such grace?
            Here uncompanionable Science
Is linked to everything that is the case.

In similar mode the sculptor's brilliant carving
Regains in bronze a living massacre.
            Death eats, the vivid world is starving,
Each holocaust become a shepherd's star.

The Spitfire's engine's once kinetic fury
And Donatello's layered appetite
            Are Humanism's judge and jury,
The Alpha and Omega of delight.   *1999*

from *Anima*

XIII

We lived on the Quadrant behind Government House
in what had been a doctor's dispensary,
one room with huge windows looking out
on harbour views and the ubiquitous cranes
over a run-wild garden full of feral
cats who used to climb and fight in trees,
falling shrieking to the earth as some
unused footage in a Tarzan film.
We watched them fascinatedly go about
their awesome lives: kitchens paraded before
a hulking tom reclining on the asphalt
above the garden's rim, grabbing and raping
a hapless infant tabby as a matter of course.
We wondered at its applicability
to the human condition, gave it up and settled
for a wide view of the harbour and the cranes.
Then I was trying to construct a partial
aesthetic based on Stevens' poetry,
his ideas of Ideas of Order,
of how to write a poem not about
poems but the way a building's front
meant so much to the image of the street,
the street to the vaguely ambiguous landscape,
the landscape to the country and the world
just like the motto children put in the front
of school exercise books. I wrote a dozen
poems. You were encouragement personified.
The impulse departed and a lack remained
not big enough to make me unconscious of
the quality of life you'd brought to me.
In our strange room top-heavy with views we celebrated
all we had found and lost and found again.
Then back to the remaining months of the year
and my first, slimmest of volumes, sky-blue covered
with a welcoming acclamation from a Sydney
critic, so long ago 'the sense faints picturing them'.
We came back to Sydney in a blaze of summer
heat one half a life and more ago.

was it lives or moments had kept us apart
one seemed the other in those well-nigh impossible
times of times   it always came together
out of spaces apart in times of unbeing alone
the very memory of each or most
of our meetings spins my head like a
flipped coin   fool's gold caught from the air
tossed between strangers always on the verge
of intimacy   of really meeting this once at last
I'll bide our times together in dream
of now and here waking again together   *1994*

Something for the Birds

Two muezzin magpies from pine minarets
call up the sun and every worshipper
of it and every Allah in this world
and past it to the very stars and planets,
bouncing their raucous callings that recur
from every pine and Moreton fig unfurled
in fruit or acrid and inedible leafage,
concerting even the currawong's wolf-whistling,
the mynah's noisy double-talk and jazz
of technicoloured lorikeets that swing
in every which way upside down and sing
out loud, far wider in their equipoise
than struttings of those sulphur crested sinners,
white cockatoos, roof battering, crop-devouring.
The muslin magpies call above and carol
in and out of the same recurrent day
over the human lives that hardly matter
in worlds of wings and envelopes of air.   *2005*

Stroke

I

In the faint blue light
We are both strangers; so I'm forced to note
His stare that comes moulded from deep bone,
The full mouth pinched in too far, one hand
Climbing an aluminium bar.
Put, as though for the first time,
In a cot from which only a hand escapes,
He grasps at opposites, knowing
This room's a caricature of childhood.
'I'm done for.'

'They're treating you all right?'
We talk from the corners of our mouths
Like old lags, while his body strains
To notice me, before he goes on watching
At the bed's foot
His flickering familiars,
Skehan, Wilson, Ellis, dead men, faces,
Bodies, paused in the aluminium light,
Submits his answer to his memories,
'Yes, I'm all right. But still it's terrible.'

Words like a fever bring
The pillar of cloud, pillar of fire
Travelling the desert of the mind and face.
The deep-set, momentarily cunning eyes
Keep trying for a way to come
Through the bed's bars to his first home.
And almost find it. Going out I hear
Voices calling requiem, where the cars
Search out the fog and gritty snow,
Hushing its breathing under steady wheels.
Night shakes the seasonable ground.

II

Decorous for the dying's sake
The living talk with eyes and hands
Of football, operations, work;
The pussyfooting nurses take
Their ritual peep; the rule demands

I stand there with a stiff face
Ready, at a word or gleam,
To conjure off the drops of sweat.
So small a licit breathing-space
Brings each inside the other's dream.

Across the bright unechoing floors
The trolleys and attendants rove;
On tiptoe shine, by scoured walls,
The nearly speechless visitors
Skirt the precipice of love.

III

Oaks, pines, the willows with their quiet
Terror; the quiet terror of my age;
The seven-year-old bookworm sitting out
At night, in the intense cold, the horse
Tethered, the stars almost moving,
The cows encroaching on the night grass.
The frost stung my lips; my knees burned;
Darkness alone was homely. The hawthorn tree
Glimmered as though frost had turned to language
And language into sharp massy blossoms.
Once, I even scraped my father's hand
And glimpsed the white underside of poplars
That, moving, almost touched the flashing stars.
Squat, steep-browed, the Methodist Church nestled
Halfway between the distant police station
And the near barn; a whole world
Gave neither words nor heat, but merely
A geometry of the awakening sight.
I had forgotten that night, or nights;
And if I think back, there's nothing mythical:
A cross-legged kid with a brooding nose
His hands were too chilled to wipe,

A book whose pages he could hardly turn,
A silent father he had hardly learned
To touch; cold he could bear,
Though chill-blooded; the dark heat of words.
A life neither calm nor animal.
Now, in the deeper quiet of my age,
I feel thirty years
Turning my blood inwards; neither trees nor stars,
But a hush and start of traffic; spasms of sound
Loosening tram rails, bluestone foundations,
Manuscripts, memories; too many tasks;
A body shrinking round its own
Corruption, though a long way from dying.
We suit our memories to our sufferings.

IV

Every clod reveals an ancestor.
They, the spirit hot in their bodies,
Burned to ash in their own thoughts; could not
Find enough water; rode in a straight line
Twenty miles across country
For hatred jumping every wire fence;
With uillean pipes taunted the air
Ferociously that taunted them;
Spoke with rancour, but with double meanings;
Proud of muscle, hated the bone beneath;
Married to gain forty acres
And a family of bond servants; died bound.
I, their grandson, do not love straight lines,
And talk with a measured voice – in double meanings –
Remembering always, when I think of death,
The grandfather, small, loveless, sinister,
   ('The most terrible man I ever seen',
   Said Joe, who died thin as rice paper)
Horse-breaker, heart-breaker, whose foot scorches,
Fifty years after, the green earth of Kilmore.
It's his heat that lifts my father's frame
Crazily from the wheel-chair, fumbles knots,
Twists in the bed at night,
Considers every help a cruelty.

V

Indoors and out, weather and winds keep up
Time's passion: paddocks white for burning.
As usual, by his bed, I spend my time
Not in talk, but restless noticing:
If pain dulls, grief coarsens.
Each night we come and, voyeurs of decay,
Stare for minutes over the bed's foot,
Imagining, if we think at all,
The body turning ash, the near insane
Knowledge when, in the small hours,
Alone under the cold ceiling, above
The floor where the heating system keeps its pulse,
He grows accustomed to his own sweat
And sweats with helplessness, remembering
How, every day, at eight o'clock
The Polish nurse kisses him goodnight.
His arms are bent like twigs; his eyes
Are blown to the door after her; his tears
Are squeezed out not even for himself.
Where is the green that swells against the blade
Or sways in sap to the high boughs? To the root
He is dry wood, and in his sideways
Falling brings down lights. Our breath
Mingles,
Stirs the green air of the laurel tree.

VI

The roofs are lit with rain.
Winter. In that dark glow,
Now, as three months ago,
I pray that he'll die sane.

On tiles or concrete path
The old wheeling the old,
For whom, in this last world,
Hope is an aftermath,

And the damp trees extend
Branch and thorn. We live
As much as we believe.
All things covet an end.

Once, on the Kerrie road,
I drove with him through fire.
Now, in the burnt cold year,
He drains off piss and blood,

His wounded face tube-fed,
His arm strapped to a bed.

VII

At the merest handshake I feel his blood
Move with the ebb-tide chill. Who can revive
A body settled in its final mood?
To whom, on what tide, can we move, and live?

Later I wheel him out to see the trees:
Willows and oaks, the small plants he mistakes
For rose bushes; and there
In the front, looming, light green, cypresses.
His pulse no stronger than the pulse of air.

Dying, he grows more tender, learns to teach
Himself the mysteries I am left to trace.
As I bend to say 'Till next time', I search
For signs of resurrection in his face.   *1966*

Give me time and I'll tell you

O how they opened the gates for me,
and the birds stood on the earth and waited for me,
and behind the barbed wire hard air
noticed we were coming. So give me
time and I'll tell you

how I nearly died for my country
and failed to: last of the big survivors.

Survival is a game at which
the incurious are best;
if they have to walk past corpses, they'll do it
with a frown of concentration.

And I was curiously incurious.
Volunteering, called up, getting the times wrong,
I ended up walking to glory between two MPs,
chiacking, my Trotskyist rag in my pocket,

innocent, cocky, doomed,
like a conman.

O sentries, will you guard the frosty river
patrolling the acres of harsh grass, so midnight
can settle into the water? I wasn't good
at sentry-go. They caught me
in the Rec. Hut, my cap over my ear,
stirring the hot coals with my bayonet.

On the parade-ground, where heavy
sun and the heavier rifle-stock
seemed slapping always on bare flesh,
I learned again the body is a fever;
my shoulders split black like figs.

For two weeks, both knees in plaster,
I was the parody of an airman
(but that was in another city)
Each day, as I shuffle-marched
into his lift, the lift-driver said,
what've they been doing to you,
eh, Curl?

playing Rugby with me, actually,
Curl.

Or deafened by a stray grenade
that rolled more nervously than usual
or falling to water-logged lungs
from the commando-rope's
sad height, or with wrist smashed by an iron hoop,

we might all have said, Eh,
what've you been doing to yourself,
Tich, Tiger, eh, Darky, Curl?

and it would have meant nothing. Then, I was healthy,
breathing the clear day of promises,
sleeping on earth or in luggage-racks,
able to bear my body's occasions.

But, later,
a pin of fire screwed every joint.
Once, when they were short-handed,
the self-conscious Wing-Commander medico
poised the needle, and missed the big vein,
and hurried off, embarrassed by blood.
Seldom have moustaches suffered so.

My veins were full of silt.
If I bent my elbow
it was like earth shifting in a tube.
I reached out, poetry drew me
like a death in the desert. I was
nearly choked, as with an evil spirit
choking with love.

When I was invalided out, I was
six stone of lightly stooped bones,
too thin to button my blue belted uniform jacket
my feet were tender as a new club-foot.

It was wartime. Yet these were the violences
of dull chance, normality, peace
follies made for the timidest of men.   *1976*

from *Golden Builders:*

I

The hammers of iron glow down Faraday.
Lygon and Drummond shift under their resonance.
Saws and hammers drawn across the bending air
shuttling like a bow; the saw trembles
the hammers are molten, they flow with quick light
striking; the flush spreads and deepens on the stone.
The drills call the streets together
stretching hall to lecture-room to hospital.

But prop old walls with battens of old wood.

Saturday work. Sabbath work. *On this day
we laid this stone
to open this Sabbath School. Feed My Lambs.*

The sun dies half-glowing in the floating brickdust,
suspended between red and saffron.
The colours resonate like a noise; the muscles of mouth
neck shoulders loins arm themselves against it.
Pavements clink like steel; the air soft,
palpable as cork, lets the stone cornices
gasp into it. Pelham surrenders, Grattan
runs leading forward, seeking the garden's breadth, the fearful
edge of green on which the sexes lay.

We have built this Sabbath School. Feed My Lambs.

Evening wanders through my hands and feet
my mouth is cool as the air that now thins
twitching the lights on down winding paths. Everything
leans on this bright cold. In gaps of lanes, in tingling
shabby squares, I hear the crying of the machines.

O Cardigan, Queensberry, Elgin: names of their lordships.
Cardigan, Elgin, Lygon: Shall I find here my Lord's grave?

　　　XIX

How soon will some self-turning
find me caught
in that ultimate stance of the poet,
the Montale watcher-figure,
brown-faced, cinematic,
half-hidden in the salt air,
hands bent in his pockets.

Shall I at will recall you

as you went past me
the hair moved on your shoulders
the straight waist hardly walking

bring you to mind
as you stand　　　and you are one line
from nape to ankle
your foot pivots
a dancer's movement on the stone.

Shall I catch back
the bobble of fuchsia-red
that almost touched you
swings now once or twice   and you stand
keeping its movement in you

        as in the soundproof room
        you begin to hear
        the still air flowing

It should be hot today
the sun quivering
the wind flat on the magnolia,
every ounce of the earth rising   1976

A Tincture of Budapest

I have lived for thirty years
with a tincture of Budapest,
the reddish hills of Buda, whose long bridges
filled squares with the living, then with the dead,
the burning factories caught in the water,
the brown bodies held fast

in their skin, in a photograph
of almost winter. I learned Csépél,
Kilian, to set beside Kossuth,
and saw the plumbing of war stretched across
Petöfi Square, Bem Square, Republic Square,
with the gun barrels burnt at their corners.

I learned the unconscious of maps
in those photos; their waters broke in my dreams
of a city wound on to a river
like a great fabric on a spool. I learned Györ,
Pecs, the call signs of free radios,
I learned borders, entries and exits.

I learned that no killings give me pleasure;
the AVO grouped by the wall for execution
lean together, their eyes squeezed so thin
it looks as if the wind blows their faces.
Next they are seen sprawling on the ground.
Next, it is said, laughing at café tables.

The camera is deadlier than the gun.
The freedom fighters in their long thin coats and armbands
fell too. They lay crushed like flags
on the buckled tram lines. There time will drench them
and the text books will make them faint and drab,
and only the poet as historian will discern them.

And yet how useless poets are, how feeble
their anecdotes and promises.
History leaves them staring resentfully
at cities they'd farewelled, now long rebuilt.
If they are needed it's only as a town
needs bells; or as a bell needs echoes.

It's just that each of us has a lost language,
to be cherished and built back,
piece by piece, into the mind.
Like Cornish. Kernow. Whose very name
became its myth, so that it can't be spoken
without a spine chill. Mine is Hungary.   *1991*

Small Brown Poem for Grania Buckley

Paleface, small fume of fire,
flame that burns nobody,
each time you come into the room
you compose a new colour.

You have mastered the trick
of hovering in doorways
with the fury of the eavesdropper,
peacemaker, magpie at nesting,

Your cardigan worn like an argument,
your runner's legs in straight trousers,
as you stand there, being praised,
as if your whole figure had just been brushed.

Even in the rashness of the close
night, you ask questions about space,
as we watch the black spread like lava
and the stars keep their grip on it
in the pale, pale cold of Kildare.   *1991*

Morgan's Country

This is Morgan's country: now steady, Bill.
(Stunted and grey, hunted and murderous.)
Squeeze for the first pressure. Shoot to kill.

Five: a star dozing in its cold cavern.
Six: first shuffle of boards in the cold house.
And the sun lagging on seven.

The grey wolf at his breakfast. He cannot think
Why he must make haste, unless because their eyes
Are poison at every well where he might drink.

Unless because their gabbling voices force
The doors of his grandeur – first terror, then only hate.
Now terror again. Dust swarms under the doors.

Ashes drift on the dead-sea shadow of his plate.
Why should he heed them? What to do but kill
When his angel howls, when the sounds reverberate

In the last grey pipe of his brain? At the window sill
A blowfly strums on two strings of air:
Ambush and slaughter tingle against the lull.

But the Cave, his mother, is close beside his chair,
Her sunless face scribbled with cobwebs, bones
Rattling in her throat when she speaks. And there

The stone Look-out, his towering father, leans
Like a splinter from the seamed palm of the plain.
Their counsel of thunder arms him. A threat of rain.

Seven: and a blaze fiercer than the sun.
The wind struggles in the arms of the starved tree,
The temple breaks on a threadbare mat of grass.

Eight: even under the sun's trajectory
This country looks grey, hunted and murderous.

1952

Morgan   *Daniel Morgan (c.1830-1865): a bushranger*
in south-central New South Wales and Victoria

Five Days Old

for Christopher John

Christmas is in the air.
You are given into my hands
Out of quietest, loneliest lands.
My trembling is all my prayer.
To blown straw was given
All the fullness of Heaven.

The tiny, not the immense,
Will teach our groping eyes.
So the absorbed skies
Bleed stars of innocence.
So cloud-voice in war and trouble
Is at last Christ in the stable.

Now wonderingly engrossed
In your fearless delicacies,
I am launched upon sacred seas,
Humbly and utterly lost
In the mystery of creation,
Bells, bells of ocean.

Too pure for my tongue to praise,
That sober, exquisite yawn
Or the gradual, generous dawn
At an eyelid, maker of days:
To shrive my thought for perfection
I must breathe old tempests of action

For the snowflake and face of love,
Windfall and word of truth,
Honour close to death.
O eternal truthfulness, Dove,
Tell me what I hold –
Myrrh? Frankincense? Gold?

If this is man, then the danger
And fear are as lights of the inn,
Faint and remote as sin
Out here by the manger.
In the sleeping, weeping weather
We shall all kneel down together.

1961

Back Street in Calcutta

I have walked among you sorriest skeletons,
Observed that pain is a vacuum – nothing good,
Crevasses in the flesh, emergence of bones;
A little guiltily I shall take my food,
I shall sit playing Bruckner, have his tones
Awaken some pain and anger, then relax,
Or dim sad concepts of order fill my veins:
Of beauty I'll sing to you silent on your backs.

In all your agonies O spare compassion
For me, the well lined and articulate fool
Who knows he tears you, stretched so still, to live.
Tormented flesh that is my flesh, forgive!
And lap around my deathbed like a pool
That starving I may make a true, final confession.   *1964*

Harry

It's the day for writing that letter, if one is able,
And so the striped institutional shirt is wedged
Between this holy holy chair and table.
He has purloined paper, he has begged and cadged
The bent institutional pen,
The ink. And our droll old men
Are darting constantly where he weaves his sacrament.

Sacrifice? Propitiation? All are blent
In the moron's painstaking fingers – so painstaking.
His vestments our giddy yarns of the firmament,
Women, gods, electric trains, and our remaking
Of all known worlds – but not yet
Has our giddy alphabet
Perplexed his priestcraft and spilled the cruet of innocence.

We have been plucked from the world of commonsense,
Fondling between our hands some shining loot,
Wife, mother, beach, fisticuffs, eloquence,
As the lank tree cherishes every distorted shoot.

'Harry', 'Old Timer', 'A Man' and 'The Old Women' *are from* 'Ward Two', *an eight-poem series from Webb's stay in Parramatta Psychiatric Hospital in 1960–61*

What queer shards we could steal
Shaped him, realer than the Real:
But it is no goddess of ours guiding the fingers and the thumb.

She cries: *Ab aeterno ordinata sum.*
He writes to the woman, this lad who will never marry.
One vowel and the thousand laborious serifs will come
To this pudgy Christ, and the old shape of Mary.
Before seasonal pelts and the thin
Soft tactile underskin
Of air were stretched across earth, they have sported and are one.

Was it then at this altar-stone the mind was begun?
The image besieges our Troy. Consider the sick
Convulsions of movement, and the featureless baldy sun
Insensible – sparing that compulsive nervous tic.
Before life, the fantastic succession,
An imbecile makes his confession,
Is filled with the Word unwritten, has almost genuflected.

Because the wise world has for ever and ever rejected
Him and because your children would scream at the sight
Of his mongol mouth stained with food, he has resurrected
The spontaneous thought retarded and infantile Light.
Transfigured with him we stand
Among walls of the no-man's-land
While he licks the soiled envelope with lover's caress

Directing it to the House of no known address.   *1964*

Old Timer

I have observed even among us the virus
Eating its way, lipping, complaining
In a multitude of cozening wheedling voices:
O Being is tender and succulent and porous:
Erect your four paternal walls of stone
(Gauleiters with burnished window badges, no faces):
Checkmate the sun, the cloud, the burning, the raining,
Let deferential stars peep in one by one:
Sit, feed, sleep, have done.

Ab aeterno ordinata sum   *I was set up from everlasting (Proverbs 8:23):*
Christian liturgy applies these words to Mary.

Isolate the Identity, clasp its dwindling head.
Your birth was again the birth of the All,
The Enemy: he treads roads, lumbers through pastures,
Musters the squeaking horde of the countless dead.
To guard your spark borrow the jungle art
Of this hospital yard, stamp calico vestures
For HM Government, for your funeral;
And in this moment of beads let nothing start
Old rages leaping in the dying heart.

So we become daily more noncommittal:
This small grey mendicant man must lean
Against his block of wall, old eyes rehearsing time
Whose hanged face he is. I take my fatal vital
Steps to the meal, the toilet, in worse than derision
Of his pipe craving a fill, of his monologue and rhyme:
Children who loved him, Bathurst, Orange, of green
Neighbourlinesses, of the silken and stony vision:
His faith-healing, his compassion.

But some little while ago it was all appalling.
He knew my footstep, even the pipe
Between blackened teeth hissed in its comeliness
As an exotic snake poising itself for the falling
Of heart's-blood, tobacco; an ancient iron of unrest
Melted before his hopeful word of address.
Christ, how I melted! for healing and faith were ripe
As Bathurst opening the gigantic West
Or Orange golden as the breast.   1964

A Man

He can hardly walk these days, buckling at the knees,
Wrestling with consonants, in raggedy khakis
Faded from ancient solar festivities,
He loiters, shuffles, fingering solid wall:
    Away down, the roots, away down,
    Who said Let there be light?

The clock in its tower of worked baroque stone
Holds at three o'clock and has always done.
Nothing else shuffles, works, is ended, begun,
There is only the solid air, the solid wall.
    Away down, the roots, away down,
    Who said Let there be light?

Three weeks under the indigent paid-off clock:
He pulls from his photograph album the heavy chock,
Squats like a king behind a heavy lock,
Niched in and almost part of solid wall.
    Away down, the roots, away down,
    Who said Let there be light?

Canaries silent as spiders, caged in laws,
Shuffle and teeter, begging a First Cause
That they may tear It open with their claws
And have It hanging in pain from solid wall.
    Away down, the roots, away down,
    Who said Let there be light?

His King's Cup for swimming, the shimmering girl,
The photogenic light aircraft spin and whirl
Out of the loam, stained by all weathers, hurl
Their petty weight against a solid wall.
    Away down, the roots, away down,
    Who said Let there be light?

The great goldfish hangs mouthing his glass box
And élite of weeds, like an old cunning fox
Or red-bronze gadfly, hangs in contentment, mocks
All that is cast in air or solid wall.
    Away down, the roots, away down,
    Who said Let there be light?

But his Cup glitters, the light monoplane bucks
Into the head-wind, girls in panel trucks
Arrive like flowers, and the dry mouth sucks
Deeply, puffs into flesh behind solid wall.
    Away down, the roots, away down,
    Who said Let there be light?   *1964*

The Old Women

From social ellipses, from actual weight and mass
They are disembarking, from age and weight and sex,
Floating among us this Sunday afternoon,
Ugly, vague, tiny as the vagrant island of gas
Embracing, nosing certain unthinkable wrecks,
Sunken faces like the face of the cretin moon.
Son, husband, lover, have spun out of orbit; this place
Holds the fugitive vessel to be kissed; and the rest is space.

They wait in the visitors' room: archaic clothing,
Reading-glass, patois of tin, rigmarole hair.
Men like meteorites enter their atmosphere:
The bombast, the wake of fire, the joy, the nothing,
Known strata of repartee unveiled with care,
Ice Age of the cherished calculated fear.
Gravity bends to an earlier law in this place:
Comes a lifting of heads among grazing herds of space.

The grazing herds are all for a foundering
Old planet borne in the omnibus of the sun
Patchy and coughing in all its wheels and wild
About the roof. They watch her blundering
While gravity pauses, down to clipped hedges, mown
Grasses, ferrying pastries for her child.
So this is earth, the worn stockings in this place.
They are chewing and swishing, the startled herds of space.

They have missed her absurd mimesis of cosmic war;
Her rain of trivial shapely missiles; the pimple
Of the megaton explosion upon her brow;
Her deaths by the spadeful; her dancing orator.
Missed the man punchdrunk, grappling with a simple
Colour or stone or song that might disavow
His midget mother tumbling in metre, displace
The ancient entente between earth and space and space.

Giggling, squinting, with laundry, confectioneries,
Old women bear fodder for the universe, add their spark
To a train of time that blows open the infinite.
It is blackness about them discloses our galaxies.
Look on these faces: now look out at the dark:
It was always and must be always the stuff of light.
The decrepit persistent folly within this place
Will sow with itself the last paddock of space.

1964

Living With Aunts

1

Passed to two maiden aunts, the quiet child
absorbed the trinity of their beliefs;
only in adolescence she learned to cry
and later, much later, to analyse her griefs.

Her thoughts were tracts they never visited:
the child became myself, always unknown
but present, obedient, silent. I watched them eat
slowly, talk slowly, and the seeds were sown

of the divinity of the *Sydney Morning Herald*,
the British Empire, and the ABC:
I was always told how fortunate I was
as though my needs were met by literacy.

My aunt once saw reviewed in her Saturday *Herald*
The Rise and Fall of the British Empire. She
read it to us in helpless disbelief.
(It wasn't mentioned on the ABC)

2

I'd always thought Soames Forsyte was a cousin,
I'd heard so much about him. One aunt read
all of the Saga, the other had poor eyesight
so she and I both painstakingly were fed

news of the Forsytes slowly at the table.
I knew Soames better than I knew my father
whose death I learned about in secret from
a *Herald* clipping. I was the child left over.

3

I was always a bother to them, and they'd say
You're not a proper Hellyer, not with brown eyes
(as though it were a crime). I was the wrong
dreamer of wrong dreams, was the wrong size,

never came first in the class for them nor brandished
my energy for causes they considered noble.
But the British Empire after all had fallen
too while they ate so slowly at the table.

1981

Grave Fairytale

I sat in my tower, the seasons whirled,
the sky changed, the river grew
and dwindled to a pool.
The black Witch, light as an eel,
laddered up my hair
to straddle the window-sill.

She was there when I woke, blocking the light,
or in the night, humming, trying on my clothes.
I grew accustomed to her; she was as much a part of me
as my own self; sometimes I thought, 'She is myself!'
a posturing blackness, savage as a cuckoo.

There was no mirror in the tower.

Each time the voice screamed from the thorny garden
I'd rise and pensively undo the coil,
I felt it switch the ground, the earth tugged at it,
once it returned to me knotted with dead warm birds,
once wrapped itself three times around the tower –
                              the tower quaked.
Framed in the window, whirling the countryside
with my great net of hair I'd catch a hawk,
                              a bird, and once a bear.
One night I woke, the horse pawed at the walls,
the cell was full of light, all my stone house
suffused, the voice called from the calm white garden,
                              'Rapunzel'.
I leant across the sill, my plait hissed out
                              and spun like hail;
he climbed, slow as a heartbeat, up the stony side,
we dropped together as he loosed my hair,
his foraging hands tore me from neck to heels:
the witch jumped up my back and beat me to the wall.

Crouched in a corner I perceived it all,
the thighs jack-knifed apart, the dangling sword
                              thrust home,
pinned like a specimen – to scream with joy.

I watched all night the beasts unsatisfied
roll in their sweat, their guttural cries
made the night thick with sound.
Their shadows gambolled, hunchbacked, hairy-arsed,
and as she ran four-pawed across the light,
the female dropped coined blood spots on the floor.

When morning came he put his armour on,
kissing farewell like angels swung on hair.
I heard the metal shoes trample the round earth
                              about my tower.
Three times I lent my hair to the glowing prince,
hand over hand he climbed, my roots ached,
the blood dribbled on the stone sill.
Each time I saw the framed-faced bully boy
                              sick with his triumph.

The third time I hid the shears,
a stab of black ice dripping in my dress.
He rose, his armour glistened in my tears,
the convex scissors snapped,
the glittering coil hissed, and slipped
                              through air to undergrowth.

His mouth, like a round O, gaped at his end,
his finger-nails ripped out, he clawed through space.
His horse ran off flank-deep in blown thistles.
Three seasons he stank at the tower's base.
A hawk plucked out his eyes, the ants busied his brain,
the mud-weed filled his mouth, his great sword rotted,
his tattered flesh-flags hung on bushes for the birds.

Bald as a collaborator I sit walled
                              in the thumb-nosed tower,
wound round three times with ropes of autumn leaves.
And the witch . . . sometimes I idly kick
a little heap of rags across the floor.
I notice it grows smaller every year.   *1975*

The Runner

I never ran so fast as I run now
through the long meadows of sleep
brushing through the lucerne crop
planted out on the river flats
blooming blue & yellow
dazzled with white butterflies,

I never ran so fast as I do now
down the long dark beaches
with the moonlight touching the swell
the suck of the tide going out
& in softening the wet sand.

I can run fast as a dog
or a runaway horse
dodging the low branches
the foam from its jaws
wetting its rough breast
as it gasps through the forest.

All this running I do
in my bed under the window
while the stars burn ice-cold
& the chained dog howls
on the other side of the cutting
where am I running to all night
I wonder   I don't know
am I just running
for the memory of it?

I think of my son at 42
running 15 miles every morning
down the long chalk roads on the island
believing he has the body of a twenty year old
he springs a muscle and has to lie
on the verge for hours
crippled useless   waiting for a car
to come by   we are all puzzled by age
how quickly it comes on striking us down
until we are lying at night
moon-struck with swollen knees
under a window running away.

2001

Old Hardware Store, Melbourne

Being un-organic, non-macrobiotic, lazy
I do not wish to return to the honest names
Or the slow, outmoded, heavy, intractable objects
As: mincers, mangles, mowers, mattocks, hames;
Collars and saddles of horsehair-padded leather;
Pots of cast and enamelled iron; hones
For sharpening blades of shares, shears, scythes and sickles;
Hafted axes; burrs and grinding stones.
    But I value verbs: to mill, till, harrow, harvest, burnish,
Hew, strip, beat, toss, tether, render, comb,
Roast, brew, knead, prove dough – one returns to bread,
To meat, to bellies and bowels, to prick and womb –
To bear, be born, to suck, piss, shit, to cry,
To work, sweat, live, sing, love, pray, die.   *1977*

Olympus

One hundred and eighty degrees is the view from up there.
The windows are hooded, as eagles hood their eyes,
to shield the gods in colloquy from glare.

The boardroom table is wired for sound because
some gods are ageing and don't hear terribly well,
and some of them, after lunch, do nod and drowse.

Being born at the end of an era of hassock and steeple
I used to marvel that the Greeks, who invented reason,
could worship those commonplace Olympian people.

And here I am! The time is a quarter to one.
Amiable Zeus says: 'Ten minutes more, then lunch.'
Lovely Athena, wise in her Parthenon,

classic in logic, sums up the morning prayer:
petitions accepted, dismissed. Through all its degrees
how distant, yet sparkling close, is the view from up here.   *1977*

The Return

The war's been over now for forty years
and you've still to take the enemy off the wire.
Who opened up his back so that his lungs hung out
from behind? Haven't you tired of his shallow moans
in a whole lifetime? I sent you word to empty out
the bucket with the arm and other bits,
to stop up all the cracks. The house
stinks like a shambles. You haven't even sealed
the holes in the cellar and who knows what
might suddenly creep out on us? I don't like
this weather at all. Already my sleep is taking
water, and there are tentacles stretching out,
feeling in the dark. I'm sorry to tell you,
brother, but I'm not spending summer here.
At our age some caution is called for.   *1983*

The Rain

A wind rose early in the morning
and went level and taut through the pines
till noon. Then it brought livid cloud
and shreds of rushing sky. Towards dusk
the birds were blown about like rags.
The rain began later, sudden with thunder.
The lights went off.

                    And so it was
that the mains of heaven, by candlelight
and slow turns, opened to their full extent
and poured down on us a cataclysm
for long hours as we lay cowering,
fearing to leave our bed, and made love
more bitter than before. Whine and grunt
mingled with far tumbling noises, vague
lowing of cattle and shrill, torn calls
whipped by the wind against the panes
that bent under the pressure inwards
like liquid glass, screening monstrosities

that seldom leave the pages of books:
octopus-shaped faces, pregnant and serpent-
handed bodies and knots of creatures
streaked with rain and vanishing to come
again reshaped, recoloured in the dimness
of the diminished candle.

                Groping for words
in the darkened room we prayed for sleep
when I heard a tattered, far cock's crow
borne on the crest of a squall. I spoke loud
then, I said listen, the day's at hand.
I've had enough of this, I'm moving back
to the harbour. Then I heard her voice,
slow and hoarse. The bird, she said,
must have misjudged its timing.
This rain's for ever. Then she fell silent.
But after a space her voice came again,
now stiff with thorns. Please make no plans
in the dark, she said. Your harbour's not
on any map. And it was indeed further along
the night, as I lay pondering her words,
that the bird's call, sure-footed now,
came through the dying storm and dawn,
lead-fingered dawn, crept up the ashen sky.
We slept.

          Till suddenly the sun
reached the dividing cloud and crashed
bright cymbals of alarm. Summoned,
I sprang to the window and there witnessed
the devastation. The valley rolled
like a yellow river down to the shore
where no roof showed, no belfry nor mast
above the mud that spread out to sea
like an atlas region shaded for disaster.
I shall make some coffee, she said, prepare
the shopping list. But late that evening,
after the dinner and the wine and through
the smoke from chewed-on cigars I thought
I glimpsed the beacon at the Head, the ship
at its anchorage and the lighted wharves
under a sky that looked like rain.

                  1998

Learning all the Words in the World

Walking accomplished, so much energy
goes into words. Each object named
with glee, each name a part of object,
each object recollectable by name
for her admiring listeners.

She sits on the edge of conversation,
practising. 'Shattered', she says, and 'Tipsy',
'Wild goose chase', 'Naïve'. The talkers
glance at her and stop their talk of rape,
rummaging in memory for paradigms
of infant apperception. One recalls
fear, of a gaggle of geese, the other, blame,
defiance, ashes in the mouth.

They cease to scold, sweetening their words, but soon
they're back to what's more natural to them,
rapping the world from pot to politics.
The child turns pages carefully, intoning,
'Apple: fish: jaguar: peacock: unicorn'.
Studious, prim, 'Nuclear war', she says.   *1984*

Moonlighting

After the children are grown and gone,
long nights of love,
the house once more their own.

And now there seems no measure
to love's artfulness,
no limits to their pleasure.

The honeyed fruit hangs low,
plucked, infant-innocent,
its taste sophisticate.

They had no inklings of such late-won rapture
and no words for it,
only their joyous laughter.   *1993*

The Bystander

I am the one who looks the other way,
In any painting you may see me stand
Rapt at the sky, a bird, an angel's wing,
While others kneel, present the myrrh, receive
The benediction from the radiant hand.

I hold the horses while the knights dismount
And draw their swords to fight the battle out;
Or else in dim perspective you may see
My distant figure on the mountain road
When in the plains the hosts are put to rout.

I am the silly soul who looks too late,
The dullard dreaming, second from the right.
I hang upon the crowd, but do not mark
(Cap over eyes) the slaughtered Innocents,
Or Icarus, his downward-plunging flight.

Once in a Garden – back view only there –
How well the painter placed me, stroke on stroke,
Yet scarcely seen among the flowers and grass –
I heard a voice say, 'Eat,' and would have turned –
I often wonder who it was that spoke.   1955

Cock Crow

Wanting to be myself, alone,
Between the lit house and the town
I took the road, and at the bridge
Turned back and walked the way I'd come.

Three times I took that lonely stretch,
Three times the dark trees closed me round,
The night absolved me of my bonds
Only my footsteps held the ground.

My mother and my daughter slept,
One life behind and one before,
And I that stood between denied
Their needs in shutting-to the door.

And walking up and down the road
Knew myself, separate and alone,
Cut off from human cries, from pain,
And love that grows about the bone.

Too brief illusion! Thrice for me
I heard the cock crow on the hill
And turned the handle of the door
Thinking I knew his meaning well.   *1965*

The Rape of Europa

Beautiful Europa, while the billy boils
Underneath the she-oaks, underneath the willows,
Underneath the sky like a bent bow of silver,
Like the arms of a god embracing a mortal –
Beautiful Europa has set out a picnic.

All her father's paddocks that slope to the water
Are singing with runnels and freshets of crystal
And the voice of the river is loud as it plunges
By boulders of granite and shouldering basalt –
On a spit of white sand she is boiling the billy.

The cattle come down to the sand by the river,
Europa is plaiting green willows and buttercups,
Daisies and water-weeds: mocking, she crowns them
With wreaths and festoons, with dripping green garlands,
And climbs to the back of the dark one, the leader.

Europa, Europa, the billy is boiling,
Down from the woolsheds your brothers come riding.
There's a splash in the shallows, a swirl, a commotion,
He has leapt, he is swept in the rush of the current,
And the riders draw rein on the hillside, astounded.

Oh wave to Europa for far she is faring
Past farmyard and homestead, past township and jetty,
And many will say that they saw them go riding,
The girl and the bull on the back of the river
Down to the harbour and over the ocean.

And distant indeed are the coasts of that country
Where the god was revealed in splendour and ardour.
Europa, Europa, as you lay quiet
In sunshine and shadow, under a plane-tree,
Did you remember the river, the she-oaks?   *1965*

Folding the Sheets

You and I will fold the sheets
Advancing towards each other
From Burma, from Lapland,

From India where the sheets have been washed in the river
And pounded upon stones:
Together we will match the corners.

From China where women on either side of the river
Have washed their pale cloth in the White Stone Shallows
'Under the shining moon'.

We meet as though in the formal steps of a dance
To fold the sheets together, put them to air
In wind, in sun over bushes, or by the fire.

We stretch and pull from one side and then the other –
Your turn. Now mine.
We fold them and put them away until they are needed.

A wish for all people when they lie down in bed –
Smooth linen, cool cotton, the fragrance and stir of herbs
And the faint but perceptible scent of sweet clear water.

1984

In the Park

She sits in the park. Her clothes are out of date.
Two children whine and bicker, tug her skirt.
A third draws aimless patterns in the dirt.
Someone she loved once passes by – too late

to feign indifference to that casual nod.
'How nice,' *et cetera.* 'Time holds great surprises.'
From his neat head unquestionably rises
a small balloon . . . 'but for the grace of God . . .'

They stand a while in flickering light, rehearsing
the children's names and birthdays. 'It's so sweet
to hear their chatter, watch them grow and thrive,'
she says to his departing smile. Then, nursing
the youngest child, sits staring at her feet.
To the wind she says, 'They have eaten me alive.'   *1963*

Carnal Knowledge I

Roll back, you fabulous animal
be human, sleep. I'll call you up
from water's dazzle, wheat-blond hills,
clear light and open-hearted roses,
this day's extravagance of blue
stored like a pulsebeat in the skull.

Content to be your love, your fool,
your creature tender and obscene
I'll bite sleep's innocence away
and wake the flesh my fingers cup
to build a world from what's to hand,
new energies of light and space

wings for blue distance, fins to sweep
the obscure caverns of your heart,
a tongue to lift your sweetness close
leaf-speech against the window-glass
a memory of chaos weeping
mute forces hammering for shape

sea-strip and sky-strip held apart
for earth to form its hills and roses
its landscape from our blind caresses,
blue air, horizon, water-flow,
bone to my bone I grasp the world.
But what you are I do not know.   1975

Oyster Cove

Dreams drip to stone. Barracks and salt marsh blaze
opal beneath a crackling glaze of frost.
Boot-black, in graceless Christian rags, a lost
race breathes out cold. Parting the milky haze
on mudflats, seabirds, clean and separate, wade.
Mother, Husband and Child: stars which forecast
fine weather, all are set. The long night's past
and the long day begins. God's creatures, made
woodcutters' whores, sick drunks, watch the sun prise
their life apart: flesh, memory, language all
split open, featureless, to feed the wild
hunger of history. A woman lies
coughing her life out. There's still blood to fall,
but all blood's spilt that could have made a child.   1975

Night Thoughts: Baby & Demon

Baby I'm sick. 1 need
nursing. Give me your breast.
My orifices bleed.
I cannot sleep. My chest
shakes like a window. Light
guts me. My head's not right.

Demon, we're old, old chap.
Born under the same sign
after some classic rape.
Gemini. Yours is mine.
Sickness and health. We'll share
the end of this affair.

Baby, I'm sick to death.
But I can't die. You do

the songs, you've got the breath.
Give them the old soft shoe.
Put on a lovely show.
Put on your wig, and go.

The service station flags, denticulate
plastic, snap in the wind. Hunched seabirds wait

for light to quench the unmeaning lights of town.
This day will bring the fabulous summer down.

Weather no memory can match will fade
to memory, leaf-drift in the pines' thick shade

All night salt water stroked and shaped the sand.
All night I heard it. Your bravura hand

chimed me to shores beyond time's rocking swell.
The last cars leave the shabby beach motel.

Lovers and drunks unroofed in sobering air
disperse, ghost-coloured in the streetlight-glare.

> Rock-a-bye Baby
> > in the motel
> Baby will kiss
> > and Demon will tell.

One candle lights us. Night's cool airs begin
to lick the luminous edges of our skin.

> When the bough bends
> > the apple will fall
> Baby knows nothing
> > Demon knows all.

Draw up the voluptuously crumpled sheet.
In rose-dark silence gentle tongues repeat
the body's triumph through its grand eclipse.
I feel your pulsebeat through my fingertips.

> Baby's a rocker
> > lost on the shore.
> Demon's a mocker.
> > Baby's a whore.

World of the happy, innocent and whole:
the body's the best picture of the soul
couched like an animal in savage grace.
Ghost after ghost obscures your sleeping face.

My baby's like a bird of day
  that flutters from my side,
my baby's like an empty beach
  that's ravished by the tide.

So fair are you, my bonny lass,
  so sick and strange am I,
that I must lie with all your loves
  and suck your sweetness dry.

And drink your juices dry, my dear,
  and grind your bones to sand,
then I will walk the empty shore
  and sift you through my hand.

And sift you through my hand, my dear,
  and find you grain by grain,
and build your body bone by bone
  and flesh those bones again,

with flesh from all your loves, my love,
  while tides and seasons stream,
until you wake by candle-light
  from your midsummer dream,

and like some gentle creature meet
  the huntsman's murderous eye,
and know you never shall escape
  however fast you fly.

Unhoused I'll shout my drunken songs
  and through the streets I'll go
compelling all I meet to toast
  the bride they do not know.

Till all your tears are dry, my love,
  and your ghosts fade in the sun.
Be sure I'll have your heart, my love,
  when all your loving's done.

1975

An Impromptu for Ann Jennings

Sing, memory, sing those seasons in the freezing
      suburb of Fern Tree, a rock-shaded place
with tree ferns, gullies, snowfalls and eye-pleasing
      prospects from paths along the mountain-face.

Nursing our babies by huge fires of wattle,
      or pushing them in prams when it was fine.
exchanging views on diet, or Aristotle,
      discussing Dr Spock or Wittgenstein,

cleaning up infants and the floors they muddied,
      bandaging, making ends and tempers meet –
sometimes I'd mind your children while you studied,
      or you'd take mine when I felt near defeat;

keeping our balance somehow through the squalling
      disorder, or with anguish running wild
when sickness, a sick joke from some appalling
      orifice of the nightwatch, touched a child;

think of it, woman: each of us gave birth to
      four children, our new lords whose beautiful
tyrannic kingdom might restore the earth to
      that fullness we thought lost beyond recall

when, in the midst of life, we could not name it,
      when spirit cried in darkness, 'I will have ...'
but what? have what? There was no word to frame it
      though spirit beat at flesh as in a grave

from which it could not rise. But we have risen.
      Caesar's we were, and wild, though we seemed tame.
Now we move where we will. Age is no prison
      to hinder those whose joy has found its name.

We are our own. All Caesar's debts are rendered
      in full to Caesar. Time has given again
a hundredfold those lives that we surrendered,
      the love, the fruitfulness; but not the pain.

Dr Spock   *Benjamin Spock, writer of influential books on child-rearing,
and an activist in the USA against the Vietnam War*

Before the last great fires we two went climbing
    like gods or blessed spirits in summer light
with the quiet pulse of mountain water chiming
    as if twenty years were one long dreaming night,

above the leafy dazzle of the streams
    to fractured rock, where water had its birth,
and stood in silence, at the roots of dreams,
    content to know: our children walk the earth.   *1975*

The Sea Anemones

Grey mountains, sea and sky. Even the misty
seawind is grey. I walk on lichened rock
in a kind of late assessment, call it peace.
Then the anemones, scarlet, gouts of blood.
There is a word I need, and earth was speaking.
I cannot hear. These seaflowers are too bright.
Kneeling on rock, I touch them through cold water.
My fingers meet some hungering gentleness.
A newborn child's lips moved so at my breast.
I woke, once, with my palm across your mouth.
    The word is: *ever*. Why add salt to salt?
    Blood drop by drop among the rocks they shine.
    Anemos, wind. The spirit, where it will.
Not flowers, no, animals that must eat or die.   *1981*

Death Has No Features of His Own

Death has no features of his own.
He'll take a young eye bathed in brightness
and the raging cheekbones of a raddled queen.
Misery's cured by his appalling taste.
His house is without issue. He appears
garlanded with lovebirds, hearts and flowers.
Anything, everything.
                    He'll wear my face and yours.
Not as we were, thank God. As we shall be
when we let go of the world, late ripe fruit falling.
What we are is beyond him utterly.   *1981*

A Simple Story

A visiting conductor
        when I was seventeen,
took me back to his hotel room
        to cover the music scene.

I'd written a composition.
        Would wonders never cease –
here was a real musician
        prepared to hold my piece.

He spread my score on the counterpane
        with classic casualness,
and put one hand on the manuscript
        and the other down my dress.

It was hot as hell in The Windsor.
        I said I'd like a drink.
We talked across gin and grapefruit,
        and I heard the ice go clink

as I gazed at the lofty forehead
        of one who led the band,
and guessed at the hoarded sorrows
        no wife could understand.

I dreamed of a soaring passion
        as an egg might dream of flight,
while he read my crude sonata.
        If he'd said, 'That bar's not right,'

or, 'Have you thought of a coda?'
        or, 'Watch that first repeat,'
or, 'Modulate to the dominant,'
        he'd have had me at his feet.

But he shuffled it all together,
        and said, 'That's *lovely*, dear,'
as he put it down on the washstand
        in a way that made it clear

that I was no composer.
     And I being young and vain,
removed my lovely body
     from one who'd scorned my brain.

I swept off like Miss Virtue
     down dusty Roma Street,
and heard the goods trains whistle
     WHO? WHOOOOOO? in aching heat.   *1981*

The Twins

Three years old when their mother died
in what my grandmother called
accouchement, my father labour,
they heard the neighbours intone
'A mercy the child went with her.'

Their father raised them somehow.
No one could tell them apart.
At seven they sat in school
in their rightful place, at the top
of the class, the first to respond
with raised arm and finger-flick.

When one gave the answer, her sister
repeated it under her breath.
An inspector accused them of cheating,
but later, in front of the class,
declared himself sorry, and taught us
a marvellous word: *telepathic*.

On Fridays, the story went,
they slept in the shed, barred in
from their father's rage as he drank
his dead wife back to his house.
For the rest of the week he was sober
and proud. My grandmother gave them
a basket of fruit. He returned it.
'We manage. We don't need help.'

They could wash their own hair, skin rabbits,
milk the cow, make porridge, clean boots.

Unlike most of the class I had shoes,
clean handkerchiefs, ribbons, a toothbrush.
We all shared the schoolsores and nits
and the language I learned to forget
at the gate of my welcoming home.

One day as I sat on the fence
my pinafore goffered, my hair
still crisp from the curlers, the twins
came by. I scuttled away
so I should not have to share
my Saturday sweets. My mother
saw me, and slapped me, and offered
the bag to the twins, who replied
one aloud and one sotto voce,
'No thank you. We don't like lollies.'

They lied in their greenish teeth
as they knew, and we knew.
                              Good angel
give me that morning again
and let me share, and spare me
the shame of my parents' rebuke.

If there are multiple worlds
then let there be one with an ending
quite other than theirs: leaving school
too early and coming to grief.

Or if this is our one life's sentence,
hold them in innocence, writing
Our Father which art in Heaven
in copperplate, or drawing
(their work being done) the same picture
on the backs of their slates: a foursquare
house where a smiling woman
winged like an angel welcomes
two children home from school.   *1988*

Oodgeroo of the tribe Noonuccal (1920-93)

Municipal Gum

Gumtree in the city street,
Hard bitumen around your feet,
Rather you should be
In the cool world of leafy forest halls
And wild bird calls.
Here you seem to me
Like that poor cart-horse
Castrated, broken, a thing wronged,
Strapped and buckled, its hell prolonged,
Whose hung head and listless mien express
Its hopelessness.
Municipal gum, it is dolorous
To see you thus
Set in your black grass of bitumen –
O fellow citizen,
What have they done to us?   1966

Gifts

'I will bring you love,' said the young lover,
'A glad light to dance in your dark eye.
Pendants I will bring of the white bone,
And gay parrot feathers to deck your hair.'

But she only shook her head.

'I will put a child in your arms,' he said,
'Will be a great headman, great rain-maker.
I will make remembered songs about you
That all the tribes in all the wandering camps
Will sing for ever.'

But she was not impressed.

'I will bring you the still moonlight on the lagoon,
And steal for you the singing of all the birds;
I will bring down the stars of heaven to you,
And put the bright rainbow into your hand.'

'No,' she said, 'bring me tree-grubs.'   1966

Ballad of the Totems

My father was Noonuccal man and kept old tribal way,
His totem was the Carpet Snake, whom none must ever slay;
But mother was of Peewee clan, and loudly she expressed
The daring view that carpet snakes were nothing but a pest.

Now one lived right inside with us in full immunity,
For no one dared to interfere with father's stern decree:
A mighty fellow ten feet long, and as we lay in bed
We kids could watch him round a beam not far above our head.

Only the dog was scared of him, we'd hear its whines and growls,
But mother fiercely hated him because he took her fowls.
You should have heard her diatribes that flowed in angry torrents
With words you never see in print, except in D. H. Lawrence.

'I kill that robber,' she would scream, fierce as a spotted cat;
'You see that bulge inside of him? My speckly hen make that!'
But father's loud and strict command made even mother quake;
I think he'd sooner kill a man than kill a carpet snake.

That reptile was a greedy-guts, and as each bulge digested
He'd come down on the hunt at night as appetite suggested.
We heard his stealthy slithering sound across the earthen floor,
While the dog gave a startled yelp and bolted out the door.

Then over in the chicken-yard hysterical fowls gave tongue,
Loud frantic squawks accompanied by the barking of the mung,
Until at last the racket passed, and then to solve the riddle,
Next morning he was back up there with a new bulge in his middle.

When father died we wailed and cried, our grief was deep and sore,
And strange to say from that sad day the snake was seen no more.
The wise old men explained to us: 'It was his tribal brother,
And that is why it done a guy'– but some looked hard at mother.

She seemed to have a secret smile, her eyes were smug and wary,
She looked as innocent as the cat that ate the pet canary.
We never knew, but anyhow (to end this tragic rhyme)
I think we all had snake for tea one day about that time.

1966

No More Boomerang

No more boomerang
No more spear;
Now all civilized –
Colour bar and beer.

No more corroboree,
Gay dance and din.
Now we got movies,
And pay to go in.

No more sharing
What the hunter brings.
Now we work for money,
Then pay it back for things.

Now we track bosses
To catch a few bob,
Now we go walkabout
On bus to the job.

One time naked,
Who never knew shame;
Now we put clothes on
To hide whatsaname.

No more gunya,
Now bungalow,
Paid by higher purchase
In twenty year or so.

Lay down the stone axe,
Take up the steel,
And work like a nigger
For a white man meal.

No more firesticks
That made the whites scoff.
Now all electric,
And no better off.

Bunyip he finish,
Now got instead
White fella Bunyip,

Call him Red.
Abstract picture now –
What they coming at?
Cripes, in our caves we
Did better than that.

Black hunted wallaby,
White hunt dollar;
White fella witch-doctor
Wear dog-collar.

No more message-stick;
Lubras and lads
Got television now,
Mostly ads.

Lay down the woomera,
Lay down the waddy.
Now we got atom-bomb.
End *everybody*.

1966

Biami

'Mother, what is that one sea,
Sometimes blue or green or yellow?'
'That Biami's waterhole.
He big fellow.'

'Mother, what make sunset fire,
Every night the big red glare?'
'Biami's gunya out that way,
That his camp fire over there.'

'How come great wide river here,
Where we swim and fish with spear?'
'Biami dug him.
You see big hills all about?
They the stuff that he chuck out.'

1966

Among white people Biami is the best known of the great Aboriginal Ancestors who made the world and men. They were not gods, not worshipped, but were highly venerated. (author's note)

The Love Fight

Spring is a waft, an outcry
of raw green, and the sun's hand
on the small of the back saying
Remember this ache? . . . it is birth.

Then the shock of starlings fighting
with savagery in the sweet morning.
An outrage that these who were newly
feathered in fire for the season
and oiled with the tints of dew
should be victim and conqueror spun
staggering like spent shuttlecocks
pivoted queerly on round heads . . .
until I saw that they were joined.

He changed grip, gagging her beak to her bosom,
and crippling the legs with a spare claw
shuffled her, swept her on the hard stones
glued to his breast as a freak twin,
to fail locked in the round grating
of a drain, and in that unlovely bed
he got her, got her properly with prolonged
repetitive impact counted
by the rhythmic spasm of a wing,
as she, undone, succumbed
totally unbirdlike, soft as a woman.
They were silent, there was no cry.

The whole act was hushed in feather,
shone with the stringent fitness of a wing
to denote the urge of life, and held
me ravished, curious as a child
under the old bland wink of spring that quickens
the viscid sappy vitriol of love.   1972

The White Spider

Something white scuttled
into this black hole
the body soft as a blob of pus,
the legs rapidly working.

This is a creature without camouflage,
its only weapon
being that it is impossible to kill
because of the squash,
so deep a revulsion shakes us
when something white scuttles
into a black hole.

It is a ghost of horror,
so small but of great power,
and horror terror horror terror
go its legs rapidly working.   1976

JACK DAVIS (1917-2000)

Camped in the Bush

Wind in the hair
Of a sleeping child
And the tree-tops wavering,
The starlight mild.

The moon's first peep
On the sand-p1ain rise,
And the fox in the shadows
With flashing eyes.

Over the campfire
The bat cries shrill
And a 'semi' snarls
On the Ten Mile Hill.

And the lonely whistle
Of the train at night,
Where my kingdom melted
In the city's light.   1983

John Pat

John Pat was a 16-year-old Aboriginal boy who died of head injuries alleged to have been
caused in a disturbance between police and Aborigines in Roebourne, WA, in 1983. Four
police were charged with manslaughter over the incident. They were acquitted.

Write of life
the pious said
forget the past
the past is dead.
But all I see
in front of me
is a concrete floor
a cell door
and John Pat.

Agh! tear out the page
forget his age
thin skull they cried
that's why he died!
But I can't forget
the silhouette
of a concrete floor
a cell door
and John Pat.

The end product
of Guddia law
is a viaduct
for fang and claw,
and a place to dwell
like Roebourne's hell
of a concrete floor
a cell door
and John Pat.

He's there – where?
there in their minds now
deep within,
there to prance
a sidelong glance
a silly grin
to remind them all
of a Guddia wall

Guddia   *Kimberley term for white man (author's note)*

a concrete floor
a cell door
and John Pat.   *1988*

NANCY CATO (1917-2000)

The Dead Swagman

His rusted billy left beside the tree;
Under a root, most carefully tucked away,
His steel-rimmed glasses folded in their case
Of mildewed purple velvet; there he lies
In the sunny afternoon, and takes his ease,
Curled like a possum within the hollow trunk.

He came one winter evening when the tree
Hunched its broad back against the rain, and made
His camp, and slept, and did not wake again.
Now white ants make a home within his skull:
His old friend Fire has walked across the hill
And blackened the old tree and the old man
And buried him half in ashes, where he lay.

It might be called a lonely death: the tree
Led its own alien life beneath the sun,
Yet both belonged to the Bush, and now are one:
The roots and bones lie close among the soil,
And he ascends in leaves towards the sky.   *1957*

Great-aunt Ada

Great-aunt Ada never seen till now
You gaze at me across the gulf of years
The hat you hated, stiff with veils and flowers,
Held at your knee, and buttoned to the chin
Your velvet jerkin primly holding in
Corseted waist and wildly beating heart.
I note your lively hair, well plastered down,
Escaping in one curl the straight part
And smooth, tight bun; and in your eyes a glimpse
Of something bound, and fretting to be free.

Your father Captain William loved the sea
And ran away from home when only ten
To join a sailer bound for far Peru.
Brought back, he simply ran away again
Until they let him go . . . Poor Ada, caught
In the pattern of your sex, six children lie
All uncreated yet, and somewhere wait
For you, the future Mrs Algernon Pye
(And Algernon was good to you, no doubt;
You 'settled down' to domesticity.)

You lean impatiently upon the chair
Before the painted backdrop, misty trees
And unreal sky, your vision fixed on far
Exotic lands and other, unknown seas.
Dark brows, small head, a face so like my own
I stare back with incredulous surprise.
What did they do to you, Time and dead convention?
A laughing rebel looks out of your eyes.
With sad post-knowledge I salute you there:
My other self, *mon semblable, ma soeur.*   1965

JAMES MCAULEY (1917-76)

Celebration of Love

All things announce her coming and her praise:
The evening sun, awake in bright dry air;
The invisible patterns of the wind, that fade
To stillness and then faintly reappear,
Alternate as my hope; the gradual shade
That moves across the lucerne-flats; the sheer
Cloud-shapes, leaning on the stony sill
Of distant ranges folded in blue haze;
The river, gliding smoothly as my will
Beneath the solitary heron's gaze;
The trees upon the hill: the living day's
External presences attend and bless
Her coming with an inward happiness.

Wild creatures to our meeting-hour respond
With new alacrity: the sudden flocks
Of parrots hanging in the summer trees
Scatter with loud cries; shy wallabies
Peer out like secret selves among the rocks;
A clod of earth moves, and becomes a rabbit,
Which races madly round the pond
That glottal frogs inhabit;
Magpies fly up from the grass; and even
Those sober citizens of Sweet Content,
Koalas, feel the tug of the event
And look down from their sleepy galleries
In grave astonishment.

Chance, as if in fear that we may lose
The tensions that invigorate our love,
Draws us continually apart, to prove
That by our distant and opposing motions
The many-stranded cord is twisted stronger.
We were not separate, touching no longer,
Nor lonely, though alone:
Until we made life new I had not known
What force lies in our being to defeat
The emptiness that seems an active power
Assimilating life. But we have grown
So full of being that we can complete
The gap in things where time and fear devour.

Now from her eastern road the moon sets sail
To voyage on the summer map of stars
Between Canopus and the Whale.
Let that celestial mood prevail
In us, that we may set our course
For new discovery, and find the source
Of gleaming intimations that have come
Like meteors from elysium,
As driftwood once foretold American shores.
The continent that we infer
Awaits a bold devout discoverer
And why not we,
Who fear no shipwreck and no mutiny?

Cosmography is infinite for love:
The contours change at every step we move.

Always the eager spirit can explore
Beyond the Wallace line of known delight
To an unmapped premonitory shore.
Our meeting makes this summer night
A new world, with new species, and new dangers;
And we are made new in each other's sight.
For by continual growth love keeps us strangers,
Despite the recognitions that descend
From sense into the soul, and there
Are stored against famine, exile, and despair.

Jupiter himself had no such scope
As man, when his inconstant passions range.
For seven days I could be
Married to a mountain or a tree,
In love with swan, or cat, or antelope;
No love of man is strange.
Besides which, it emerges from the deep
Anterior caverns where it raged, before
It found one chosen object to adore.
How is it then that you can keep
All of my lust contained, unless you be
Akin to bird, beast, mountain, tree,
Of wide creation an epitome?

Yet you are more, being yourself; not merely
A script of symbols where my heart can read
Secrets of its nature and its need
And know itself more clearly.
You are yourself; and when we touch
We understand the joy of being two,
Not seeking to annihilate
Distinction, as self-lovers do. The soul
Is born a solitary; others come
With foreign gestures to it, which it must
Learn patiently by heart, or be unjust.
The god has been a child since men began
To worship him; he must become a man.

Imperfect in imperfect, love
Grows within music. Worlds rejoice
To find their lost identities restored
To morning brightness by a clear voice
Recovering the creative word.
Now with uplifted heart, at light's increase,

I praise in you the stars and waterfalls,
The slow ascent of trees, swiftness of birds,
The innocence and order, the wild calls:
The glowing Ithacan web of faithful earth
Coming to luminous rebirth
In the configurations that belong
To silence, when, dark years of waiting by,
Her gaze is lighted by futurity
And all her secret fountains flow in song.

And touched by sunlight, my words change back
Into the daily acts of life.
– Song, you are too late by many years
To be the epithalamion
That I have owed her; say in my excuse
You are the best of many songs begun.
Fear not to be looked at in the sun,
Your meaning is too plain to be discerned;
And few of those that read you will have learned
That every living fruit the soul can bear
Is born of patience and despair.
Heed none of them; your praises lie elsewhere,
And are not given, but are truly earned.

(written 1945) 1946

Pietà

A year ago you came
Early into the light.
You lived a day and night,
Then died; no-one to blame.

Once only, with one hand,
Your mother in farewell
Touched you. I cannot tell,
I cannot understand

A thing so dark and deep,
So physical a loss:
One touch, and that was all

She had of you to keep.
Clean wounds, but terrible,
Are those made with the Cross.

1969

Because

My father and my mother never quarrelled.
They were united in a kind of love
As daily as the *Sydney Morning Herald*,
Rather than like the eagle or the dove.

I never saw them casually touch,
Or show a moment's joy in one another.
Why should this matter to me now so much?
I think it bore more hardly on my mother,

Who had more generous feelings to express.
My father had dammed up his Irish blood
Against all drinking praying fecklessness,
And stiffened into stone and creaking wood.

His lips would make a switching sound, as though
Spontaneous impulse must be kept at bay.
That it was mainly weakness I see now,
But then my feelings curled back in dismay.

Small things can pit the memory like a cyst:
Having seen other fathers greet their sons,
I put my childish face up to be kissed
After an absence. The rebuff still stuns

My blood. The poor man's curt embarrassment
At such a delicate proffer of affection
Cut like a saw. But home the lesson went:
My tenderness thenceforth escaped detection.

My mother sang *Because*, and *Annie Laurie*,
White Wings, and other songs; her voice was sweet.
I never gave enough, and I am sorry;
But we were all closed in the same defeat.

People do what they can; they were good people,
They cared for us and loved us. Once they stood
Tall in my childhood as the school, the steeple.
How can I judge without ingratitude?

Judgment is simply trying to reject
A part of what we are because it hurts.
The living cannot call the dead collect:
They won't accept the charge, and it reverts.

It's my own judgment day that I draw near,
Descending in the past, without a clue,
Down to that central deadness: the despair
Older than any hope I ever knew.

1969

Childhood Morning – Homebush

The half-moon is a muted lamp
Motionless behind a veil.
As the eastern sky grows pale,
I hear the slow-train's puffing stamp

Gathering speed. A bulbul sings,
Raiding persimmon and fig.
The rooster in full glossy rig
Crows triumph at the state of things.

I make no comment; I don't know;
I hear that every answer's No,
But can't believe it can be so.

1971

The Hazard and the Gift
In honour of John Shaw Neilson

How many more times will the silver birch-tree
Change its green fortune into thin gold pieces
And squander them, *pair-impair*, across the lawn?

How many winters, white bark in the moonlight
Gashed with black wounds, will it entangle stars
In a tracery of tassel and delicate spur?

Something implacable, a rasp of terror,
A beauty pointing past itself, the folded
Gift of an impossibility . . .

It isn't ever found, it's only given;
But given only if we try to find;
And even then it's very rarely given.

1971

Petit Testament

In the twenty-fifth year of my age
I find myself to be a dromedary
That has run short of water between
One oasis and the next mirage
And having despaired of ever
Making my obsessions intelligible
I am content at last to be
The sole clerk of my metamorphoses.
Begin here:

In the year 1943
I resigned to the living all collateral images
Reserving to myself a man's
Inalienable right to be sad
At his own funeral.
(Here the peacock blinks the eyes
Of his multipennate tail.)
In the same year
I said to my love (who is living)
Dear we shall never be that verb
Perched on the sole Arabian Tree
Not having learnt in our green age to forget
The sins that flow between the hands and feet
(Here the Tree weeps gum tears
Which are also real: I tell you
These things are real)
So I forced a parting
Scrubbing my few dingy words to brightness.

Where I have lived
The bed-bug sleeps in the seam, the cockroach
Inhabits the crack and the careful spider
Spins his aphorisms in the corner.
I have heard them shout in the streets
The chiliasms of the Socialist Reich
And in the magazines I have read
The Popular Front-to-Back.
But where I have lived
Spain weeps in the gutters of Footscray
Guernica is the ticking of the clock

The nightmare has become real, not as belief
But in the scrub-typhus of Mubo.

It is something to be at last speaking
Though in this No-Man's-language appropriate
Only to No-Man's-Land.
Set this down too:
I have pursued rhyme, image, and metre,
Known all the clefts in which the foot may stick,
Stumbled often, stammered,
But in time the fading voice grows wise
And seizing the co-ordinates of all existence
Traces the inevitable graph
And in conclusion:
There is a moment when the pelvis
Explodes like a grenade. I
Who have lived in the shadow that each act
Casts on the next act now emerge
As loyal as the thistle that in session
Puffs its full seed upon the indicative air.
I have split the infinitive. Beyond is anything.

1944

JUDITH WRIGHT (1915-2000)

Woman to Man

The eyeless labourer in the night,
the selfless, shapeless seed I hold,
builds for its resurrection day –
silent and swift and deep from sight
foresees the unimagined light.

This is no child with a child's face;
this has no name to name it by:
yet you and I have known it well.
This is our hunter and our chase,
the third who lay in our embrace.

This is the strength that your arm knows,
the arc of flesh that is my breast,
the precise crystals of our eyes.
This is the blood's wild tree that grows
the intricate and folded rose.

This is the maker and the made;
this is the question and reply;
the blind head butting at the dark,
the blaze of light along the blade.
Oh hold me, for I am afraid.

1949

Woman to Child

You who were darkness warmed my flesh
where out of darkness rose the seed.
Then all a world I made in me;
all the world you hear and see
hung upon my dreaming blood.

There moved the multitudinous stars,
and coloured birds and fishes moved.
There swam the sliding continents.
All time lay rolled in me, and sense,
and love that knew not its beloved.

O node and focus of the world;
I hold you deep within that well
you shall escape and not escape –
that mirrors still your sleeping shape
that nurtures still your crescent cell.

I wither and you break from me;
yet though you dance in living light
I am the earth, I am the root,
I am the stem that fed the fruit,
the link that joins you to the night.

1949

Train Journey

Glassed with cold sleep and dazzled by the moon,
out of the confused hammering dark of the train
I looked and saw under the moon's cold sheet
your delicate dry breasts, country that built my heart;

and the small trees on their uncoloured slope
like poetry moved, articulate and sharp
and purposeful under the great dry flight of air,
under the crosswise currents of wind and star.

Clench down your strength, box-tree and ironbark.
Break with your violent root the virgin rock.
Draw from the flying dark its breath of dew
till the unliving come to life in you.

Be over the blind rock a skin of sense,
under the barren height a slender dance . . .

I woke and saw the dark small trees that burn
suddenly into flowers more lovely than the white moon.

1953

At Cooloolah

The blue crane fishing in Cooloolah's twilight
has fished there longer than our centuries.
He is the certain heir of lake and evening,
and he will wear their colour till he dies,

but I'm a stranger, come of a conquering people.
I cannot share his calm, who watch his lake,
being unloved by all my eyes delight in,
and made uneasy, for an old murder's sake.

Those dark-skinned people who once named Cooloolah
knew that no land is lost or won by wars,
for earth is spirit: the invader's feet will tangle
in nets there and his blood be thinned by fears.

Riding at noon and ninety years ago,
my grandfather was beckoned by a ghost –
a black accoutred warrior armed for fighting,
who sank into bare plain, as now into time past.

White shores of sand, plumed reed and paperbark,
clear heavenly levels frequented by crane and swan –
I know that we are justified only by love,
but oppressed by arrogant guilt, have room for none.

And walking on clean sand among the prints
of bird and animal, I am challenged by a driftwood spear
thrust from the water; and, like my grandfather,
must quiet a heart accused by its own fear.   1955

Request to a Year

If the year is meditating a suitable gift,
I should like it to be the attitude
of my great-great-grandmother,
legendary devotee of the arts,

who, having had eight children
and little opportunity for painting pictures,
sat one day on a high rock
beside a river in Switzerland

and from a difficult distance viewed
her second son, balanced on a small ice-floe,
drift down the current towards a waterfall
that struck rock-bottom eighty feet below,

while her second daughter, impeded,
no doubt, by the petticoats of the day,
stretched out a last-hope alpenstock
(which luckily later caught him on his way).

Nothing, it was evident, could be done;
and with the artist's isolating eye
my great-great-grandmother hastily sketched the scene.
The sketch survives to prove the story by.

Year, if you have no Mother's day present planned;
reach back and bring me the firmness of her hand.   1955

A Document

'Sign there.' I signed, but still uneasily.
I sold the coachwood forest in my name.
Both had been given me; but all the same
remember that I signed uneasily.

Ceratopetalum, Scented Satinwood:
a tree attaining seventy feet in height.
The pale-red calyces like sunset light
burned in my mind. A flesh-pink pliant wood

used in coachbuilding. Difficult of access
(those slopes were steep). But it was World War Two.
Their wood went into bomber-planes. They grew
hundreds of years to meet those hurried axes.

Under our socio-legal dispensation
both name and woodland had been given me.
I was much younger then than any tree
matured for timber. But to help the nation

I signed the document. The stand was pure
(eight hundred trees perhaps). Uneasily
(the bark smells sweetly when you wound the tree)
I set upon this land my signature.   *1966*

To Another Housewife

Do you remember how we went,
on duty bound, to feed the crowd
of hungry dogs your father kept
as rabbit-hunters? Lean and loud,
half-starved and furious, how they leapt
against their chains, as though they meant
in mindless rage for being fed,
to tear our childish hands instead!

With tomahawk and knife we hacked
the flyblown tatters of old meat,
gagged at their carcass-smell, and threw
the scraps and watched the hungry eat.
Then turning faint, we made a pact
(two greensick girls), crossed hearts and swore
to touch no meat forever more.

How many cuts of choice and prime
our housewife hands have dressed since then –
these hands with love and blood imbrued –
for daughters, sons, and hungry men!
How many creatures bred for food
we've raised and fattened for the time
they met at last the steaming knife
that serves the feast of death-in-life!

And as the evening meal is served
we hear the turned-down radio
begin to tell the evening news
just as the family joint is carved.
O murder, famine, pious wars . . .
Our children shrink to see us so,
in sudden meditation, stand
with knife and fork in either hand.   *1966*

Australia 1970

Die, wild country, like the eaglehawk,
dangerous till the last breath's gone,
clawing and striking. Die
cursing your captor through a raging eye.

Die like the tigersnake
that hisses such pure hatred from its pain
as fills the killer's dreams
with fear like suicide's invading stain.

Suffer, wild country, like the ironwood
that gaps the dozer-blade.
I see your living soil ebb with the tree
to naked poverty.

Die like the soldier-ant
mindless and faithful to your million years.
Though we corrupt you with our torturing mind.
stay obstinate; stay blind.

For we are conquerors and self-poisoners
more than scorpion or snake
and dying of the venoms that we make
even while you die of us.

I praise the scoring drought, the flying dust,
the drying creek, the furious animal,
that they oppose us still;
that we are ruined by the thing we kill.   *1971*

Lament for Passenger Pigeons

Don't ask for the meaning, ask for the use. Wittgenstein

The voice of water as it flows and falls
the noise air makes against earth-surfaces
have changed; are changing to the tunes we choose.

What wooed and echoed in the pigeon's voice?
We have not heard the bird. How reinvent
that passenger, its million wings and hues,

when we have lost the bird, the thing itself,
the sheen of life on flashing long migrations?
Might human musics hold it, could we hear?

Trapped in the fouling nests of time and space,
we turn the music on; but it is man,
and it is man who leans a deafening ear.

And it is man we eat and man we drink
man who thickens round us like a stain.
Ice at the polar axis smells of me.

A word, a class, a formula, a use:
that is the rhythm, the cycle we impose.
The sirens sang us to the ends of sea,

and changed to us; their voices were our own,
jug jug to dirty ears in dirtied brine.
Pigeons and angels sang us to the sky

and turned to metal and a dirty need.
The height of sky, the depth of sea we are,
sick with a yellow stain, a fouling dye.

Whatever Being is, that formula,
it dies as we pursue it past the word.
We have not asked the meaning, but the use.

What is the use of water when it dims?
The use of air that whines of emptiness?
The use of glass-eyed pigeons caged in glass?

We listen to the sea, that old machine,
to air that hoarsens on earth-surfaces
and has no angel, no migrating cry.

What is the being and the end of man?
Blank surfaces reverb a human voice
whose echo tells us that we choose to die:

or else, against the blank of everything,
to reinvent that passenger, that bird-
siren-and-angel image we contain
essential in a constellating word.
To sing of Being, its escaping wing,
to utter absence in a human chord
and recreate the meaning as we sing.   *1973*

For a Pastoral Family

   i   *To my brothers*

Over the years, horses have changed to land-rovers.
Grown old, you travel your thousands of acres
deploring change and the wickedness of cities
and the cities' politics; hoping to pass to your sons
a kind of life you inherited in your generation.
Some actions of those you vote for stick in your throats.
There are corruptions one cannot quite endorse;
but if they are in our interests, then of course . . .

Well, there are luxuries still,
including pastoral silence, miles of slope and hill,
the cautious politeness of bankers. These are owed
to the forerunners, men and women
who took over as if by right a century and a half
in an ancient difficult bush. And after all
the previous owners put up little fight,
did not believe in ownership, and so were scarcely human.

Our people who gnawed at the fringe
of the edible leaf of this country
left you a margin of action, a rural security,
and left to me
what serves as a base for poetry,
a doubtful song that has a dying fall.

ii   *To my generation*

A certain consensus of echo, a sanctioning sound,
supported our childhood lives. We stepped
on sure and conceded ground.
A whole society
extended a comforting cover of legality.
The really deplorable deeds
had happened out of our sight, allowing us innocence.
We were not born, or there was silence kept.

If now there are landslides, if our field of reference
much eroded, our hands show little blood.
We enter a plea: Not Guilty.
For the good of the Old Country,
the land was taken; the Empire had loyal service.
Would any convict us?
Our plea has been endorsed by every appropriate jury.

If my poetic style, your pastoral produce,
are challenged by shifts in the market
or a change of taste, at least we can go down smiling
with enough left in our pockets
to be noted in literary or local histories.

iii   *For today*

We were always part of a process. It has expanded.
What swells over us now is a logical spread
from the small horizons we made –
the heave of the great corporations
whose bellies are never full.
What sort of takeover bid
could you knock back now if the miners,
the junk-food firms or their processors want your land?
Or worse, leave you alone to hoe
small beans in a dwindling row?

The fears of our great-grandfathers –
apart from a fall in the English market –
were of spearwood, stone axes. Sleeping
they sprang awake at the crack

of frost on the roof, the yawn and stretching
of a slab wall. We turn on the radio
for news from the U.S.A. and U.S.S.R.
against which no comfort or hope
might come from the cattle prizes at the Show.

     iv   *Pastoral lives*

Yet a marginal sort of grace
as I remember it, softened our arrogant clan.
We were fairly kind to horses
and to people not too different from ourselves.
Kipling and A. A. Milne were our favourite authors
but Shelley, Tennyson, Shakespeare stood on our shelves –
suitable reading for women,
to whom, after all, the amenities had to be left.

An undiscursive lot (discourse is for the city)
one of us helped to found a university.
We respected wit in others,
though we kept our own for weddings,
unsure of the bona fides of the witty.

In England, we called on relatives,
assuming welcome for the sake of a shared bloodline,
but kept our independence.
We would entertain them equally, if they came
and with equal hospitality –
blood being thicker than thousands of miles of waters –
for the sake of Great-aunt Charlotte and old letters.

At church, the truncate, inarticulate
Anglican half-confession
'there is no health in us'
made us gag a little. We knew we had no betters
though too many were worse.
We passed on the collection-plate
adding a reasonable donation.

That God approved us was obvious.
Most of our ventures were prosperous.
As for the *Dies Irae*
we would deal with that when we came to it.

Dies Irae   *Day of wrath: Title of a Latin hymn on the Last Judgement*

v   *Change*

At best, the men of our clan
have been, or might have been,
like Yeats' fisherman.
A small stream, narrow but clean,

running apart from the world.
Those hills might keep them so,
granite, gentle and cold.
But hills erode, streams go

through settlement and town
darkened by chemical silt.
Dams hold and slow them down,
trade thickens them like guilt.

All men grow evil with trade
all roads lead to the city.
Willie Yeats would have said,
perhaps, the more the pity.

But how can we be sure?
Wasn't his chosen man
as ignorant as pure?
Keep out? Stay clean? Who can?

vi   *Kinship*

Blue early mist in the valley. Apricots
bowing the orchard trees, flushed red with summer,
loading bronze-plaqued branches;
our teeth in those sweet buttock-curves. Remember
the horses swinging to the yards, the smell
of cattle, sweat and saddle-leather?
Blue ranges underlined the sky. In any weather
it was well, being young and simple,
letting the horses canter home together.

All those sights, smells and sounds we shared
trailing behind grey sheep, red cattle,
from Two-rail or Ponds Creek
through tawny pastures breathing pennyroyal.
In winter, sleety winds bit hands and locked
fingers round reins. In spring, the wattle.

With so much past in common,
on the whole we forgive each other
or the ways in which we differ –
two old men, one older woman.
When one of us falls ill,
the others may think less
of today's person, the lined and guarding face,

than of a barefoot child running careless through
long grass where snakes lie, or forgetting
to watch in the paddocks for the black Jersey bull.
Divisions and gulfs deepen
daily, the world over
more dangerously than now between us three.
Which is why, while there is time (though not our form at all)
I put the memories into poetry.   1985

DOROTHY AUCHTERLONIE (1915-91)

Night at the Opera

The sail appears: Isolde tells her tale
Of death and longing, through the rich dark wail
Of horns, and expiates all lovers' sins
In the vicarious orgasm of violins.

What could she do but die on Tristan's breast?
Maison à trois, or Tristan as a guest,
A spell of domesticity when force prevailed?
They'd tried them all in turn and all had failed.
Theirs was an age without the neat resources
Our science offers and our creed endorses;
Their death-in-love at least was swift and sure,
And what they had they held and kept secure.
   (The audience sighed and cleared its throat and rose,
   And here and there a lady blew her nose,
   Or bent to catch a program as it fell,
   And wiped her eyes. The husband murmured: 'Well,
   A cup of coffee and a cigarette, I think;
   Perhaps it's not too late to have a drink,
   I really need a whisky after that;
   Come back to supper with us at the flat . . .')

Lovers since then, of course, have grown more wise:
Love is quite nice, it's true, but compromise
Is necessary now, if we'd survive
In perfect comfort, while we're still alive.
Iseult, you must admit, is in a fix:
Love is a luxury when you're twenty-six,
And what's the passion which the poets sung
Beside the comfort of a mod. brick bung.?
All her former school-friends, one by one,
At last gave in, liked what they got; alone
She sits and dreams all will come right,
Until, waking from sleep, in a long night,
She sees the cold face of solitude
Mocking her truth. Her old despair renewed,
She bids farewell to her high, imperial quest,
Accepts the bird-in-hand and waives the rest.
And in the dark, at first, give her what's due,
She hardly knows the false Tristan from the true.

Tristan is pleased enough: he needs a mate
To calm his blood, so he can concentrate
On getting on; a nice, efficient wife
Gives a good man a solid start in life;
The right clothes, the right guests to entertain,
Church connections – marriage is pure gain
From every practical business point of view,
(With any luck, it might be pleasant too)
And married men, he hastened to reflect,
Carried more weight, commanded more respect
In conferences; and, he'd often noted,
The married men were earliest promoted.
The managing-directorship's his quest,
He'll take the cash in hand, and grab the rest.
His trustiest weapon is his fountain-pen,
His cheque-book is his shield 'gainst other men,
And the white hands of Iseult clasp the cheque
With far more passion than her Tristan's neck.
The fortress they have built to keep out fear
Is a brand-new triple-fronted brick veneer,
With clean oil-heating (wood-fires make a mess,
And slow-combustion heaters not much less;
And their electric blankets, after a fashion,
Warm the twin beds faster than Tristan's passion)

With Swedish furniture and plastic flowers,
And television to while away the hours
Between the evening meal and going to sleep;
The rising young executive must keep
To schedule to succeed in his career:
Sex is for Sundays, Saturday for beer
With the boys, a round of golf, or fishing,
The flicks sometimes, to keep Iseult from wishing
She'd stayed at work, or that the kids were grown,
Or that the horns would blow for her alone . . .
She knows within her heart they never will,
That the true Isolde waits upon the hill,
Ready to put to sea should Tristan call;
The echo of wind and waves far off is all
She ever hears of the heart's long dream;
The sail stays furled above the forward beam.

    Tristan is on committees now three times a week,
He's been elected to the club; is sleek,
Discreetly-suited and wears English shoes,
And has his picture in the social news
Beside his wife, wearing her new mink stole
And the face of one who sees at last her goal
In sight: the long-awaited sublimation
Of a genuine Vice-regal invitation.
    (The violins sound their dark orgasmic tune . . .)
Iseult's dispensing tea this afternoon
To help the Spastic Centre; though she's never been
To see it yet, she's really very keen
To work at some deserving charity,
And spends much time and trouble serving tea
Or having coffee-parties, organising balls,
Writing official letters, paying calls.
Her family keeps her busy, too, it's true;
She has the routine four, two girls and two
Boys, one exactly like his father,
At boarding-school, of course, although she'd rather
Have them at home; still what is one to do?
Their father went, and so the boys must too.
Tristan, she sighs, has joined the club committee,
Four times a week now he stays in the city;
But pottery at night keeps doubts at bay,
And Yoga classes help to fill her day.

She sees him long enough to say 'Good morning',
Reminds him sometimes of the doctor's warning
To take things easy; his coronary occlusion
Didn't surprise her, it seemed a fit conclusion –
The final status symbol of success.
She missed him at first, of course, but rather less
Than she had thought she would. Her son returned
From school, stayed home awhile and learned
The business, acquired a girl and married
Most suitably: three children (one miscarried).
Iseult is busier than ever baby-sitting,
And pottery's abandoned now for knitting.
Both daughters married well; her only pain
Is the problem of her younger son again.
A married woman! Think of the disgrace!
What would his father say? She hides her face
In her once-white hands, looks up again and spies
Her ancient longing in her young son's eyes,
And turns her gaze, compelled against her will,
To where Isolde waits upon the hill,
Hears the waves crash and the true Tristan call,
Sees the white sail flying over all,
And through the thundering surf, the anguished foam,
The horns begin to rise, summoning her home.   *1967*

DAVID CAMPBELL (1915-79)

Ariel

Frost and snow, frost and snow:
The old ram scratches with a frozen toe
At silver tussocks in the payable mist
And stuffs his belly like a treasure chest.

His tracks run green up the mountainside
Where he throws a shadow like a storm-cloud's hide;
He has tossed the sun in a fire of thorns,
And a little bird whistles between his horns.

'Sweet-pretty-creature!' sings the matchstick bird,
And on height and in chasm his voice is heard;
Like a bell of ice or the crack of the frost
It rings in the ears of his grazing host.

'Sweet-pretty-creature!' While all is as still
As the bird on the ram on the frozen hill,
O the wagtail warms to his tiny art
And glaciers move through the great beast's heart.   *1956*

Windy Gap

As I was going through Windy Gap
A hawk and a cloud hung over the map.

The land lay bare and the wind blew loud
And the hawk cried out from the heart of the cloud,

'Before I fold my wings in sleep
I'll pick the bones of your travelling sheep,

'For the leaves blow back and the wintry sun
Shows the tree's white skeleton.'

A magpie sat in the tree's high top
Singing a song on Windy Gap

That streamed far down to the plain below
Like a shaft of light from a high window.

From the bending tree he sang aloud,
And the sun shone out of the heart of the cloud

And it seemed to me as we travelled through
That my sheep were the notes that trumpet blew.

And so I sing this song of praise
For travelling sheep and blowing days.   *1956*

On Frosty Days

On frosty days, when I was young
I rode out early with the men
And mustered cattle till their long
Blue shadows covered half the plain;

And when we turned our horses round,
Only the homestead's point of light,
Men's voices, and the bridles' sound,
Were left in the enormous night.

And now again the sun has set
All yellow and a greening sky
Sucks up the colour from the wheat –
And here's my horse, my dog and I.

1962

We Took the Storms to Bed

We took the storms to bed at night
When first we loved. A spark
Sprang outward from our loins to light
Like genesis the dark.

On other things our minds were bent,
We did not hear the Word,
But locked like Sarah in her tent
The listening belly heard.

And though we wept, she laughed aloud
And fattened on her mirth:
As strange as creatures from a cloud
Our children walk the earth.

1962

The Australian Dream

The doorbell buzzed. It was past three o'clock.
The steeple-of-Saint-Andrew's weathercock
Cried silently to darkness, and my head
Was bronze with claret as I rolled from bed
To ricochet from furniture. Light! Light
Blinded the stairs, the hatstand sprang upright,
I fumbled with the lock, and on the porch
Stood the Royal Family with a wavering torch.

'We hope,' the Queen said, 'we do not intrude.
The pubs were full, most of our subjects rude.
We came before our time. It seems the Queen's
Command brings only, "Tell the dead marines!"
We've come to you.' I must admit I'd half
Expected just this visit. With a laugh
That put them at their ease, I bowed my head.
'My Majesty is most welcome here,' I said.

'My home is yours. There is a little bed
Downstairs, a boiler-room, might suit the Duke.'
He thanked me gravely for it and he took
Himself off with a wave. 'Then the Queen Mother?'
'She'd best bed down with you. There is no other
But my wide bed. I'll curl up in a chair.'
The Queen looked thoughtful. She brushed out her hair
And folded up *The Garter* on a pouf.
'Distress was the first commoner, and as proof
That queens bow to the times,' she said, 'we three
Shall share the double bed. Please follow me.'

I waited for the ladies to undress –
A sense of fitness, even in distress,
Is always with me. They had tucked away
Their state robes in the lowboy; gold crowns lay
Upon the bedside tables; ropes of pearls
Lassoed the plastic lampshade; their soft curls
Were spread out on the pillows and they smiled.
'Hop in,' said the Queen Mother. In I piled
Between them to lie like a stick of wood.
I couldn't find a thing to say. My blood
Beat, but like rollers at the ebb of tide.
I hope your Majesties sleep well,' I lied.
A hand touched mine and the Queen said, 'I am
Most grateful to you, Jock. Please call me Ma'am.'   *1968*

Snake

The tiger snake moves
Like slow lightning. Like
A yard of creek water
It flows over rocks
Carving the grass.

Where have you gone,
Long fellow, cold brother,
Like a lopped limb or
Truth that we shy from
Leaving a cast skin?

Snakes are like a line
Of poetry: a chill
Wind in the noon,
A slalom in the spine
Setting ears back, hair on end.

'Some people will not live
With a snake in the house.'
Mice make off. Look
Under your chair; worse
Take down a book:

A line like an icicle!   1975

JOHN MANIFOLD (1915-85)

The Tomb of Lt John Learmonth, AIF

'At the end on Crete he took to the hills, and said he'd fight it out with only a
revolver. He was a great soldier . . .'   One of his men in a letter

This is not sorrow, this is work: I build
A cairn of words over a silent man,
My friend John Learmonth whom the Germans killed.

There was no word of hero in his plan;
Verse should have been his love and peace his trade,
But history turned him to a partisan.

Far from the battle as his bones are laid
Crete will remember him. Remember well,
Mountains of Crete, the Second Field Brigade!

Say Crete, and there is little more to tell
Of muddle tall as treachery, despair
And black defeat resounding like a bell;

But bring the magnifying focus near
And in contempt of muddle and defeat
The old heroic virtues still appear.

Australian blood where hot and icy meet
(James Hogg and Lermontov were of his kin)
Lie still and fertilise the fields of Crete.

            *

Schoolboy, I watched his ballading begin:
Billy and bullocky and billabong,
Our properties of childhood, all were in.

I heard the air though not the undersong,
The fierceness and resolve; but all the same
They're the tradition, and tradition's strong.

Swagman and bushranger die hard, die game,
Die fighting, like that wild colonial boy –
Jack Dowling, says the ballad, was his name.

He also spun his pistol like a toy,
Turned to the hills like wolf or kangaroo,
And faced destruction with a bitter joy.

His freedom gave him nothing else to do
But set his back against his family tree
And fight the better for the fact he knew

He was as good as dead. Because the sea
Was closed and the air dark and the land lost,
'They'll never capture me alive,' said he.

　　　　*

That's courage chemically pure, uncrossed
With sacrifice or duty or career,
Which counts and pays in ready coin the cost

Of holding course. Armies are not its sphere
Where all's contrived to achieve its counterfeit;
It swears with discipline, it's volunteer.

I could as hardly make a moral fit
Around it as around a lightning flash.
There is no moral, that's the point of it,

No moral. But I'm glad of this panache
That sparkles, as from flint, from us and steel,
True to no crown nor presidential sash

Nor flag nor fame. Let others mourn and feel
He died for nothing: nothings have their place.
While thus the kind and civilised conceal

This spring of unsuspected inward grace
And look on death as equals, I am filled
With queer affection for the human race.

1946

Making Contact

Crazy as hell and typical of us:
The blackout bus-light stippling the passengers' shoulders,
Rumbling through darkness, and a whistling behind me smoulders
Into recognition – 'Comrade' – like that, in the bus.

So that minutes later I am talking across a table
At a tall girl laughing with friendliness and relief –
Soldier with pickup? Not likely. Nothing so brief.
I have found my footing, that's all; I am standing stable.

Oh, I was hungry for this! I needed reminding
What countless comrades are mine for the seeking and finding.
The numbness of isolation falls off me like sleep,

Something a light wind or a word could abolish;
And the girl comrade smiles, disclaiming the knowledge
That at any moment I could put my head in her lap and weep.

1946

Incognito

Every station in the country keeps a pony that was sent
    Late at night to fetch a doctor or a priest,
And has lived the life of Riley since that faraway event,
    But the stories don't impress me in the least;

For I once owned Incognito – what a jewel of a horse!
    He was vastly better bred than many men!
But they handicapped so savagely on every local course
    I was forced to dye him piebald now and then.

For I needed all the money that a sporting life entails,
    Having found the cost of living rather dear,
And my wife, the very sweetest little girl in New South Wales,
    Was presenting me with children every year.

We were spreading superphosphate one October afternoon
    When the missus said she felt a little sick:
We were not expecting Septimus (or Septima) so soon,
    But I thought I'd better fetch the doctor quick,

So I started for the homestead with the minimum delay,
    Where I changed, and put pomade on my moustache;
But before I reached the sliprails Incognito was away,
    And was heading for the township like a flash.

First he swam a flooded river, then he climbed a craggy range,
    And they tell me, though I haven't any proof,
That he galloped thro' the township to the telephone exchange
    Where he dialled the doctor's number with his hoof.

Yes, he notified the doctor, and the midwife, and the vet,
    And he led them up the mountain to my door
Where he planted, panting, pondering, in a rivulet of sweat,
    Till he plainly recollected something more.

Then he stretched his muzzle towards me. He had something in his teeth,
    Which he dropped with circumspection in my hand;
And I recognised his offering as a contraceptive sheath,
    So I shot him. It was more than I could stand.

But I've bitterly repented that rash act of injured pride –
    It was not the way a sportsman should behave!
So I'm making my arrangements to be buried at his side,
    And to share poor Incognito's lonely grave.   *1971*

JOHN BLIGHT (1913-95)

Pearl Perch

There are those fish that swim ever in the dim
recesses of the reef. A visit near
the surface means their swift demise. They can rise,
but never high as flying-fish that skim
across the seas, fleeing from deeper fear.

Yet I have ever marvelled at their eyes
when I have hauled a specimen aboard,
upon the deck have seen their gaze despise
our meaner air, and stigmatise our skies
by dying; seeing nothing to accord
with their deep consciousness – no Lord,
no Saviour? No Saviour! Have I, too, seen amiss
the airy vacuum of heaven where
these eyes at last leak out their dying stare?   *1968*

Down from the Country

When we came down from the country, we were strangers to the sea
The rise and fall of waters without rain,
the lunglike breathing of the estuary
caused our amazement ; and the white stain
of salt on the rocks, when the tide receded,
where we were used to dark mud that a flood leaves behind,
held us enthralled; and we needed
some mental adjustment which people noticed. When the mind
is confronted by such magnitudes of sight and sound
there is no mask for refuge in frown or grimace;
but the face looks blank, as if it were dragged up, drowned.

How much loneliness is there in a different place
out of one's shell, out of all knowledge, to be caught
out of the dullness of self by such alien thought?   *1975*

DOUGLAS STEWART (1913-85)

Two Englishmen

Far, far from home they rode on their excursions
And looked with much amusement and compassion
On Indians and Africans and Persians,
People indeed of any foreign nation
Who milled in mobs completely uninhibited
In the peculiar lands that they inhabited.

But in their own small island crowded thickly,
Each with his pride of self and race and caste,
They could not help but be a little prickly
And in their wisdom they evolved at last
This simple code to save them from destruction –
One did not speak without an introduction.

So naturally when Kinglake on his camel,
Mounted aloft to see the world or take it,
Saw faint against the sky's hard blue enamel
A solar topee, then a shooting jacket,
Then all too clear an Englishman appearing
He found the prospect anything but cheering.

Merely because the distances were wider
One could not speak with every Dick or Harry,
For all he knew some absolute outsider,
Who trotted up upon his dromedary,
And yet he felt, alone and unprotected
On these bare sands some talk might be expected.

Of course, he thought, with spirits briefly lightened,
Though ten to one he did not know the fellow
He might be quite all right; but then he mightn't;
And on he came by sandy hill and hollow –
It was a bit too thick thus to arrive at
The desert's core and then not find it private.

For if for one's own reasons one had ridden
By camel through the empty wastes to Cairo
From Gaza in the distance back there hidden
One did not do the thing to play the hero
Or have some chap come dropping from the sky
To ask what one was doing there, and why.

The sweat lay on his camel dank and soapy
And Kinglake too broke out in perspiration
For close and closer in his solar topee
The stranger came with steady undulation;
One could not hide, for shelter there was none,
Nor yet, however tempting, cut and run.

No, if they met, as meet it seemed they must,
Though heartily he wished him at the devil,
Kinglake decided, halting in the dust,
That if the fellow spoke he must be civil;
But then observed, in ultimate dismay,
He could not think of anything to say.

But he, as it fell out, need not have worried.
It was an English military man
Long years in Burma boiled, in India curried,
Who riding home on some deep private plan
Now sat his camel equally embarrassed
To find himself thus hunted out and harassed;

And while their Arab servants rushed together
With leaps and yells to suit the glad occasion
Each Englishman gazed coolly at the other

And briefly touched his hat in salutation
And so passed by, erect, superb, absurd,
Across the desert sands without a word.

But when they'd passed, one gesture yet endures;
Each turned and waved his hand as if to say,
'Well, help yourself to Egypt'– 'India's yours,'
And so continued grandly on his way;
And as they went, one feels that, truth to tell,
They understood each other pretty well.   *1967*

KENNETH MACKENZIE (1913-55)

The Snake

Withdrawing from the amorous grasses
from the warm and luscious water
the snake is soul untouched by both
nor does the fire of day through which it passes
mark it or cling. Immaculate navigator
it carries death within its mouth.

Soul is the snake that moves at will
through all the nets of circumstance
like the wind that nothing stops,
immortal movement in a world held still
by rigid anchors of intent or chance
and ropes of fear and stays of hopes.

It is the source of all dispassion
the voiceless life above communion
secret as the spring of wind
nor does it know the shames of self-confession
the weakness that enjoys love's coarse dominion
or the betrayals of the mind.

Soul is the snake the cool viator
sprung from a shadow on the grass
quick and intractable as breath
gone as it came like the everlasting water
reflecting god in immeasurable space –
and in its mouth it carries death.

                          (written 1951) 1972

Two Trinities

Are you ready? soul said again
smiling deep in the dark
where mind and I live passionately
grain rasping across grain
in a strangled question-mark
– or so we have lived lately.

I looked through the hollow keyhole
at my wife not young any more
with my signature on her forehead
and her spirit hers and whole
unsigned by me – as before
we knew each other, and wed.

I looked at my grown daughter
cool and contained as a flower
whose bees I shall not be among –
vivid as white spring water
full of womanish power
like the first phrases of a song.

I looked at my son, and wept
in my mouth's cave to see
the seed ready for sowing
and the harvest unready to be reaped –
green fruit shocked from the tree,
the bird killed on the wing.

Well? soul said and I said,
Mind and I are at one
to go with you now – finally
joined now to be led –
for our place here is gone:
we are not among those three.

Soul said, *Now come with me.*

(written 1952) 1972

The Dancers

I reached that waterhole, its mud designed
by tracks of egret, finch and jabiru,
while in the coming night the moon declined:
a feather floating from a cockatoo.

Ten paces more and there, in painted mime,
against the mountain like a stone-axe dropped,
the spirit-trees stood stricken from the time
the song-sticks, songmen, and the drone-pipe stopped.

Some thrust their arms and hands out in the air,
and some were struck, contorted, on their knees,
and deep and still the leaves like unbound hair
lay over limbs and torsos of those trees.

Over their limbs their night-still tresses slept;
faint in the stars a wandering night-bird creaked.
Then, as towards their company I stepped,
the whole misshapen tribe awoke and shrieked.

And, beating from their limbs and leaves, white birds,
like spirits in a terror of strange birth,
streamed out with harsh and inarticulate words
above the mountains, trees and plains of earth.   1962

The Two Sisters

Related by Manoowa from Milingimbi

On the Island of the Spirits of the Dead,
one of two sisters talks.
'We must make a canoe and follow the way
the sun walks.'

They've filled the canoe with sacred
rannga things,
and paddled away into the night
singing ritual songs.

'Sister, look back!' the first sister calls.
'Do you see the morning star?'
Her sister looks out along their wake.
'Nothing. Nothing's there.'

The little sister has fallen asleep.
Again her sister calls,
'Sister, look back for the morning star.'
'Nothing. Nothing at all.'

A spear of light is thrown across
the sea and lies far
ahead upon the sisters' course.
'Sister, the morning star.'

The sun comes up and walks the sky.
A fish with whiskers swims
ahead, and leaps out of the sea,
while the sisters sing.

Day and night, and day and night,
the sisters are gone
with the morning star and the leaping fish
and the sky-walking sun.

The sisters, hoar with dried salt spray,
the semen of the sea,
make landfall where parrots scream
from paperbark trees.

The sisters beach the bark canoe,
unload the *rannga* things.
They thrust one in the earth. From there
the first goanna comes.

They've gone inland. Their digging sticks
make sacred springs.
They leave behind them *rannga* forms
for all living things.

Out gathering food, the sisters have hung
their dilly-bags in a tree.
While they're away, men come and steal
their sacred ceremonies.

The sisters hear men singing and
song-sticks' 'tjong-tjong'.
'Cover your ears. We cannot hear
the sacred song.'

'O, all our sacred ceremonies
belong now to the men.
We must gather food, and bear
and rear children.'   *1970*

Mapooram

Related by Fred Biggs, Ngeamba tribe, Lake Carjelligo

Go out and camp somewhere. You're lying down.
A wind comes, and you hear this *Mapooram*.
'What's that?' you say. Why, that's a *Mapooram*.
You go and find that tree rubbing itself.
It makes all sorts of noises in the wind.
It might be like a sheep, or like a cat
or like a baby crying, or someone calling,
a sort of whistling-calling when the wind
comes and swings and rubs two boughs like that.

A *wirreengun*, a clever-feller, sings
that tree. He hums a song, a *Mapooram*:
a song to close things up, or bring things out,
a song to bring a girl, a woman from that tree.
She's got long hair, it falls right down her back.
He's got her for himself. He'll keep her now.

One evening, it was sort of rainy-dark,
they built a mia-mia, stripping bark.
You've been out in the bush sometime and seen
them old dry pines with loose bark coming off.
You get a lot of bark from those old dry pines,
before they rot and go too far, you know.
That woman from the tree, she pulled that bark.
It tore off, up and up the tree. It pulled
her up, into the tree, up, up into the sky.
Well, she was gone. That was the end of it.
No more that *wirreengun* could call her back.

'Mapooram. Mapooram.' 'What's that?' you say.
Why, that's two tree boughs rubbing in the wind.   *1970*

Billy Bamboo

Related by Billy Bamboo, Wallaga Lake

This wild cherry tree makes a good shade.
I lie down under it and go to sleep.
By and by I hear a roaring sound.
'Oh, thunder storm coming up. I'll soon
fix him.' I break a branch off this tree
and burn it. The smoke goes straight up
into the sky. Those big rolling clouds
divide, one cloud goes one way, one cloud
the other way. You hear thunder rolling
down the sky.

This is our sacred tree.
It belongs to all the blackfellers. You're a bit
of a blackfeller, you try it. You'll say,
'That's true what old Billy Bamboo says.'

Well, my tribe got shot up. A white man found
a baby near the camp and took it back
to the station on his horse. That baby grew up
to be my father.

A Victorian tribe fought
the Wallaga Lake tribe. An old man and his wife
were running away along a path, carrying
a baby with them.
They saw a big log hollowed out
by fire. They put the baby inside the log
and ran on.

A white man was riding his horse.
He heard a baby crying in the bush.
He came to the big log and listened.
He saw the pale feet of the baby sticking out.
He took the child and reared it and gave it
his name. And that baby was my mother.

Me? I'm Billy Bamboo. Anyone will tell you.
The buckjump rider, the bare knuckle fighter.
We used to stand toe to toe. We'd go down
to the creek and wash the blood off our faces
and come back and into it again. I was a flash
young feller in jodhpurs, riding boots and hat.

No, I can't see as well as I used to,
and I have to get about with this stick now.
You should have seen the old people. They would
have told you what the emu told the kangaroo.
Those old people are all gone from this mission.
They're all ghosts walking around in this place.   *1970*

WILLIAM HART-SMITH (1911-90)

Baiamai's Never-failing Stream

Then he made of the stars, in my mind,
pebbles and clear water running over them,
linking most strangely feelings of im-
measurable remoteness with intimacy,

So that at one and the same time I
not only saw a far white mist of stars
there, far up there, but had my fingers
dabbling among those cold stones.   *1945*

Relativity

The main reason why dogs
love to sit in cars
is because
when a dog's inside
a car doesn't move

When the doors
of the small intimate room
with master and mistress in it
close

the room bucks
and barks and makes
most unusual noises
and odours

then houses get up and run
trees get up and run
posts get up and run
and telegraph poles

in fact everything does

With his nose thrust out
bang in the eye of the galloping wind
his right ear streaming
like a strip of rag in a gale

he for a change can sit still
chin on the window-sill

and let the world do all the running about   *1985*

ELIZABETH RIDDELL (1910-98)

The Letter

I take my pen in hand
            there was a meadow
beside a field of oats, beside a wood,
beside a road, beside a day spread out
green at the edges, yellow at the heart.
The dust lifted a little, a finger's breadth;
the word of the wood pigeon travelled slow,
slow half pace behind the tick of time.

To tell you I am well and thinking of you
and of the walk through the meadow, and of another walk
along the neat piled ruin of the town
under a pale heaven empty of all but death
and rain beginning. The river ran beside.

It has been a long time since I wrote. I have no news.
I put my head between my hands and hope
my heart will choke me. I put out my hand
to touch you and touch air. I turn to sleep
and find a nightmare, hollowness and fear.

And by the way, I have had no letter now
For eight weeks, it must be
a long eight weeks
because you have nothing to say, nothing at all,
not even to record your emptiness
or guess what's to become of you, without love.

I know that you have cares
ashes to shovel, broken glass to mend
and many a cloth to patch before the sunset.

Write to me soon and tell me how you are
if you still tremble, sweat and glower, still stretch
a hand for me at dusk, play me the tune,
show me the leaves and towers, the lamb, the rose.

Because I always wish to hear of you
and feel my heart swell and the blood run out
at the ungraceful syllable of your name
said through the scent of stocks, the little snore of fire,
the shoreless waves of symphony, the murmuring night.

I will end this letter now. I am yours with love.
Always with love, with love.   1948

The Children March

The children of the world are on the march
From the dangerous cots, the nurseries ringed with fire,
The poisoned toys, the playgrounds pitted
With bomb craters and shrapnel strewn about;
From the whips, the iron bars, the guns' great shout,
The malevolent teachers and the lethal sports
Played on the ruined fields fenced by red wires.

The children of the world are on the march
With the doll and the school-bag to safe quarters,
The temporary haven, the impermanent home;
Nightly turning their thoughts to the forsaken hearth,
The wandering, wondering children of the world
March on the sea and land and crowded air –
The unsmiling sons, the sad bewildered daughters.   1961

Australia

A Nation of trees, drab green and desolate grey
In the field uniform of modern wars,
Darkens her hills, those endless, outstretched paws
Of Sphinx demolished or stone lion worn away.

They call her a young country, but they lie:
She is the last of lands, the emptiest,
A woman beyond her change of life, a breast
Still tender but within the womb is dry.

Without songs, architecture, history:
The emotions and superstitions of younger lands,
Her rivers of water drown among inland sands,
The river of her immense stupidity

Floods her monotonous tribes from Cairns to Perth.
In them at last the ultimate men arrive
Whose boast is not: 'we live' but 'we survive',
A type who will inhabit the dying earth.

And her five cities, like five teeming sores,
Each drains her: a vast parasite robber-state
Where second-hand Europeans pullulate
Timidly on the edge of alien shores.

Yet there are some like me turn gladly home
From the lush jungle of modern thought, to find
The Arabian desert of the human mind,
Hoping, if still from the deserts the prophets come,

Such savage and scarlet as no green hills dare
Springs in that waste, some spirit which escapes
'The learned doubt, the chatter of cultured apes
Which is called civilization over there.

(written 1939) 1960

Ascent into Hell

Little Henry, too, had a great notion of singing. History of the Fairchild family

I, too, at the mid-point, in a well-lit wood
Of second-rate purpose and mediocre success,
Explore in dreams the never-never of childhood,
Groping in daylight for the key of darkness;

Revisit, among the morning archipelagoes,
Tasmania, my receding childish island;
Unchanged my prehistoric flora grows
Within me, marsupial territories extend:

There is the land-locked valley and the river,
The Western Tiers make distance an emotion,
The gum trees roar in the gale, the poplars shiver
At twilight, the church pines imitate an ocean.

There, in the clear night, still I listen, waking
To a crunch of sulky wheels on the distant road;
The marsh of stars reflects a starry croaking;
I hear in the pillow the sobbing of my blood

As the panic of unknown footsteps marching nearer,
Till the door opens, the inner world of panic
Nightmares that woke me to unawakening terror
Birthward resume their still inscrutable traffic.

Memory no more the backward, solid continent,
From island to island of despairing dream
I follow the dwindling soul in its ascent;
The bayonets and the pickelhauben gleam

Among the leaves, as, in the poplar tree,
They find him hiding. With an axe he stands
Above the German soldiers, hopelessly
Chopping the fingers from the climbing hands.

Or, in the well-known house, a secret door
Opens on empty rooms from which a stair
Leads down to a grey, dusty corridor,
Room after room, ominous, still and bare.

He cannot turn back, a lurking horror beckons
Round the next corner; beyond each further door.

Sweating with nameless anguish then he wakens;
Finds the familiar walls blank as before.

Chased by wild bulls, his legs stick fast with terror.
He reaches the fence at last – the fence falls flat.
Choking, he runs, the trees he climbs will totter
Or the cruel horns, like telescopes, shoot out.

At his fourth year the waking life turns inward.
Here on his Easter Island the stone faces
Rear meaningless monuments of hate and dread.
Dreamlike within the dream real names and places

Survive. His mother comforts him with her body
Against the nightmare of the lions and tigers.
Again he is standing in his father's study
Lying about his lie, is whipped, and hears

His scream of outrage, valid to this day.
In bed, he fingers his stump of sex, invents
How he took off his clothes and ran away,
Slit up his belly with various instruments;

To brood on this was a deep abdominal joy
Still recognized as a feeling at the core
Of love – and the last genuine memory
Is singing 'Jesus Loves Me' – then, no more!

Beyond is a lost country and in vain
I enter that mysterious territory.
Lit by faint hints of memory lies the plain
Where from its Null took shape this conscious I

Which backward scans the dark – But at my side
The unrecognized Other Voice speaks in my ear,
The voice of my fear, the voice of my unseen guide;
'Who are we, stranger? What are we doing here?'

And through the uncertain gloom, sudden I see
Beyond remembered time the imagined entry,
The enormous Birth-gate whispering, 'per me,
per me si va tra la perduta gente.'   (written 1943-44) 1955

---

per me . . .   through me the way among the lost people: Dante, Inferno

Imperial Adam

Imperial Adam, naked in the dew,
Felt his brown flanks and found the rib was gone.
Puzzled he turned and saw where, two and two,
The mighty spoor of Jahweh marked the lawn.

Then he remembered through mysterious sleep
The surgeon fingers probing at the bone,
The voice so far away, so rich and deep:
'It is not good for him to live alone.'

Turning once more he found Man's counterpart
In tender parody breathing at his side.
He knew her at first sight, he knew by heart
Her allegory of sense unsatisfied.

The pawpaw drooped its golden breasts above
Less generous than the honey of her flesh;
The innocent sunlight showed the place of love;
The dew on its dark hairs winked crisp and fresh.

This plump gourd severed from his virile root,
She promised on the turf of Paradise
Delicious pulp of the forbidden fruit;
Sly as the snake she loosed her sinuous thighs,

And waking, smiled up at him from the grass;
Her breasts rose softly and he heard her sigh –
From all the beasts whose pleasant task it was
In Eden to increase and multiply

Adam had learned the jolly deed of kind:
He took her in his arms and there and then,
Like the clean beasts, embracing from behind,
Began in joy to found the breed of men.

Then from the spurt of seed within her broke
Her terrible and triumphant female cry,
Split upward by the sexual lightning stroke.
It was the beasts now who stood watching by:

The gravid elephant, the calving hind,
The breeding bitch, the she-ape big with young
Were the first gentle midwives of mankind;
The teeming lioness rasped her with her tongue;

The proud vicuña nuzzled her as she slept
Lax on the grass; and Adam watching too
Saw how her dumb breasts at their ripening wept,
The great pod of her belly swelled and grew,

And saw its water break, and saw, in fear,
Its quaking muscles in the act of birth,
Between her legs a pygmy face appear,
And the first murderer lay upon the earth.   (*written 1952*) *1955*

Crossing the Frontier

Crossing the frontier they were stopped in time,
Told, quite politely, they would have to wait:
Passports in order, nothing to declare,
And surely holding hands was not a crime;
Until they saw how, ranged across the gate,
All their most formidable friends were there.

Wearing his conscience like a crucifix,
Her father, rampant, nursed the Family Shame;
And, armed with their old-fashioned dinner-gong,
His aunt, who even when they both were six,
Had just to glance towards a childish game
To make them feel that they were doing wrong.

And both their mothers, simply weeping floods,
Her head-mistress, his boss, the parish priest,
And the bank manager who cashed their cheques;
The man who sold him his first rubber-goods;
Dog Fido, from whose love-life, shameless beast,
She first observed the basic facts of sex.

They looked as though they had stood there for hours;
For years; perhaps for ever. In the trees
Two furtive birds stopped courting and flew off;
While in the grass beside the road the flowers
Kept up their guilty traffic with the bees.
Nobody stirred. Nobody risked a cough.

Nobody spoke. The minutes ticked away;
The dog scratched idly. Then, as parson bent
And whispered to a guard who hurried in,
The customs-house loudspeakers with a bray
Of raucous and triumphant argument
Broke out the wedding march from *Lohengrin*.

He switched the engine off: 'We must turn back.'
She heard his voice break, though he had to shout
Against a din that made their senses reel,
And felt his hand, so tense in hers, go slack.
But suddenly she laughed and said: 'Get out!
Change seats! Be quick!' and slid behind the wheel.

And drove the car straight at them with a harsh,
Dry crunch that showered both with scraps and chips,
Drove through them; barriers rising let them pass;
Drove through and on and on, with Dad's moustache
Beside her twitching still round waxen lips
And Mother's tears still streaming down the glass.

(written 1963) 1966

On an Engraving by Casserius

Set on this bubble of dead stone and sand,
Lapped by its frail balloon of lifeless air,
Alone in the inanimate void, they stand,
These clots of thinking molecules who stare
Into the night of nescience and death,
And, whirled about with their terrestrial ball,
Ask of all being its motion and its frame:
This of all human images takes my breath;
Of all the joys in being a man at all,
This folds my spirit in its quickening flame.

Turning the leaves of this majestic book
My thoughts are with those great cosmographers,
Surgeon adventurers who undertook
To probe and chart time's other universe.
This one engraving holds me with its theme:
More than all maps made in that century
Which set true bearings for each cape and star,
De Quiros' vision or Newton's cosmic dream,
This reaches towards the central mystery
Of whence our being draws and what we are.

Casserius *Giulio Casserio (c.1552–1616), along with others named in the third stanza here, was a part of 'the great school in Pedua' which advanced the science of anatomy. Fabrica (1543), by Versalius, was a pioneer work on the subject. Spiegel's Tabulae Anatomicae (1627) posthumously incorporated copperplate engravings by Casserius.*

It came from that great school in Padua:
Casserio and Spiegel made this page.
Vesalius, who designed the *Fabrica,*
There strove, but burned his book at last in rage;
Fallopius by its discipline laid bare
The elements of this humanity,
Without which none knows that which treats the soul;
Fabricius talked with Galileo there:
Did those rare spirits in their colloquy
Divine in their two skills the single goal?

'One force that moves the atom and the star,'
Says Galileo; 'one basic law beneath
All change!' 'Would light from Achernar
Reveal how embryon forms within its sheath?'
Fabricius asks, and smiles. Talk such as this,
Ranging the bounds of our whole universe,
Could William Harvey once have heard? And once
Hearing, strike out that strange hypothesis,
Which in *De Motu Cordis* twice recurs,
Coupling the heart's impulsion with the sun's?

Did Thomas Browne at Padua, too, in youth
Hear of their talk of universal law
And form that notion of particular truth
Framed to correct a science they foresaw,
That darker science of which he used to speak
In later years and called the Crooked Way
Of Providence? Did *he* foresee perhaps
An age in which all sense of the unique
And singular dissolves, like ours today,
In diagrams, statistics, tables, maps?

Not here! The graver's tool in this design
Aims still to give not general truth alone,
Blue-print of science or data's formal line:
Here in its singularity he has shown
The image of an individual soul;
Bodied in this one woman, he makes us see
The shadow of his anatomical laws.
An artist's vision animates the whole,
Shines through the scientist's detailed scrutiny
And links the person and the abstract cause.

Such were the charts of those who pressed beyond
Vesalius their master, year by year
Tracing each bone, each muscle, every frond
Of nerve until the whole design lay bare.
Thinking of this dissection, I descry
The tiers of faces, their teacher in his place,
The talk at the cadaver carried in:
'A woman – with child!'; I hear the master's dry
Voice as he lifts a scalpel from its case:
'With each new step in science, we begin.'

Who was she? Though they never knew her name,
Dragged from the river, found in some alley at dawn,
This corpse none cared, or dared perhaps, to claim,
The dead child in her belly still unborn,
Might have passed, momentary as a shooting star,
Quenched like the misery of her personal life,
Had not the foremost surgeon of Italy,
Giulio Casserio of Padua,
Bought her for science, questioned her with his knife,
And drawn her for his great *Anatomy*;

Where still in the abundance of her grace,
She stands among the monuments of time
And with a feminine delicacy displays
Her elegant dissection: the sublime
Shaft of her body opens like a flower
Whose petals, folded back expose the womb,
Cord and placenta and the sleeping child,
Like instruments of music in a room
Left when her grieving Orpheus left his tower
Forever, for the desert and the wild.

Naked she waits against a tideless shore,
A sibylline stance, a noble human frame
Such as those old anatomists loved to draw.
She turns her head as though in trouble or shame,
Yet with a dancer's gesture holds the fruit
Plucked, though not tasted, of the Fatal Tree.
Something of the first Eve is in this pose
And something of the second in the mute
Offering of her child in death to be
Love's victim and her flesh its mystic rose.

No figure with wings of fire and back-swept hair
Swoops with his: Blessed among Women!; no sword
Of the spirit cleaves or quickens her; yet there
She too was overshadowed by the Word,
Was chosen, and by her humble gift of death
The lowly and the poor in heart give tongue,
Wisdom puts down the mighty from their seat;
The vile rejoice and rising, hear beneath
Scalpel and forceps, tortured into song,
Her body utter their magnificat.

Four hundred years since first that cry rang out:
Four hundred years, the patient, probing knife
Cut towards its answer – yet we stand in doubt:
Living, we cannot tell the source of life.
Old science, old certainties that lit our way
Shrink to poor guesses, dwindle to a myth.
Today's truths teach us how we were beguiled;
Tomorrow's how blind our vision of today.
The universals we thought to conjure with
Pass: there remain the mother and the child.

Lodestone, lodestar, alike to each new age,
There at the crux of time they stand and scan,
Past every scrutiny of prophet or sage,
Still unguessed prospects in this venture of Man.
To generations, which we leave behind,
They taught a difficult, selfless skill: to show
The mask beyond the mask beyond the mask;
To ours another vista, where the mind
No longer asks for answers, but to know:
What questions are there which we fail to ask?

Who knows, but to the age to come they speak
Words that our own is still unapt to hear:
'These are the limits of all you sought and seek;
More our yet unborn nature cannot bear.
Learn now that all man's intellectual quest
Was but the stirrings of a foetal sleep;
The birth you cannot haste and cannot stay
Nears its appointed time; turn now and rest
Till that new nature ripens, till the deep
Dawns with that unimaginable day.'

(written 1967) 1969

[A. D. Hope] **299**

Moschus Moschiferus

A Song for St Cecilia's Day

In the high jungle where Assam meets Tibet
The small Kastura, most archaic of deer,
Were driven in herds to cram the hunters' net
And slaughtered for the musk-pods which they bear;

But in those thickets of rhododendron and birch
The tiny creatures now grow hard to find.
Fewer and fewer survive each year. The search
Employs new means, more exquisite and refined:

The hunters now set out by two or three;
Each carries a bow and one a slender flute.
Deep in the forest the archers choose a tree
And climb; the piper squats against the root.

And there they wait until all trace of man
And rumour of his passage dies away.
They melt into the leaves and, while they scan
The glade below, their comrade starts to play.

Through those vast listening woods a tremulous skein
Of melody wavers, delicate and shrill:
Now dancing and now pensive, now a rain
Of pure, bright drops of sound and now the still,

Sad wailing of lament; from tune to tune
It winds and modulates without a pause;
The hunters hold their breath; the trance of noon
Grows tense; with its full power the music draws

A shadow from a juniper's darker shade;
Bright-eyed, with quivering muzzle and pricked ear,
The little musk-deer slips into the glade
Led by an ecstasy that conquers fear.

A wild enchantment lures him, step by step,
Into its net of crystalline sound, until
The leaves stir overhead, the bowstrings snap
And poisoned shafts bite sharp into the kill.

St. Cecilia *is the patron saint of music.*

Then, as the victim shudders, leaps and falls,
The music soars to a delicious peak,
And on and on its silvery piping calls
Fresh spoil for the rewards the hunters seek.

But when the woods are emptied and the dusk
Draws in, the men climb down and count their prey,
Cut out the little glands that hold the musk
And leave the carcasses to rot away.

A hundred thousand or so are killed each year;
Cause and effect are very simply linked:
Rich scents demand the musk, and so the deer,
Its source, must soon, they say, become extinct.

Divine Cecilia, there is no more to say!
Of all who praised the power of music, few
Knew of these things. In honour of your day
Accept this song I too have made for you.

(written 1967) 1969

Inscription for a War

Stranger, go tell the Spartans
we died here obedient to their commands.   Inscription at Thermopylae

Linger not, stranger; shed no tear;
Go back to those who sent us here.

We are the young they drafted out
To wars their folly brought about.

Go tell those old men, safe in bed,
We took their orders and are dead.   *1981*

The Mayan Books

Diego de Landa, archbishop of Yucatan
– The curse of God upon his pious soul –
Placed all their Devil's picture-books under ban
And, piling them in one sin-heap, burned the whole;

But took the trouble to keep the calendar
By which the Devil had taught them to count time.

The impious creatures had tallied back as far
As ninety million years before Eve's crime.

That was enough: they burned the Mayan books,
Saved souls and kept their own in proper trim.
Diego de Landa in heaven always looks
Towards God: God never looks at him.   *1991*

ROBERT D. FITZGERALD (1902-87)

The Face of the Waters

Once again the scurry of feet – those myriads
crossing the black granite; and again
laughter cruelly in pursuit; and then
the twang like a harpstring or the spring of a trap,
and the swerve on the polished surface: the soft little pads
sidling and skidding and avoiding; but soon caught up
in the hand of laughter and put back . . .

There is no release from the rack
of darkness for the unformed shape,
the unexisting thought
stretched half-and-half
in the shadow of beginning and that denser black
under the imminence of huge pylons –
the deeper nought;
but neither is there anything to escape,
or to laugh,
or to twang that string which is not a string but silence
plucked at the heart of silence.

Nor can there be a floor to the bottomless;
except in so far as conjecture must arrive,
lungs cracking, at the depth of its dive;
where downward further is further distress
with no change in it; as if a mile and an inch
are equally squeezed into a pinch,
and retreating limits of cold mind
frozen, smoothed, defined.
Out of the tension of silence (the twanged string);
from the agony of not being (that terrible laughter

tortured by darkness); out of it all
once again the tentative migration; once again
a universe on the edge of being born:
feet running fearfully out of nothing
at the core of nothing:
colour, light, life, fearfully
becoming eyes and understanding: sound becoming ears . . .

For eternity is not space reaching
on without end to it; not time without end to it,
nor infinity working round in a circle;
but a placeless dot enclosing nothing,
the pre-time pinpoint of impossible beginning,
enclosed by nothing, not even by emptiness –
impossible: so wholly at odds with possibilities
that, always emergent and wrestling and interlinking
they shatter it and return to it, are all of it and part of it.
It is your hand stretched out to touch your neighbour's,
and feet running through the dark, directionless like darkness.

Worlds that were spun adrift re-enter
that intolerable centre;
indeed the widest-looping comet
never departed from it;
it alone exists.
And though, opposing it, there persists
the enormous structure of forces, laws,
as background for other coming and going,
that's but a pattern, a phase, no pause,
of ever-being-erected, ever-growing
ideas unphysically alternative
to nothing, which is the quick. You may say hills live,
or life's the imperfect aspect of a flowing
that sorts itself as hills; much as thoughts wind
selectively through mind.

The egg-shell collapses
in the fist of the eternal instant;
all is what it was before.
Yet is that eternal instant
the pinpoint bursting into reality,
the possibilities and perhaps,
the feet scurrying on the floor.

It is the suspense also
with which the outward thrust
holds the inward surrender –
the stresses in the shell before it buckles under:
the struggle to magpie-morning and all life's clamour and lust;
the part breaking through the whole;
light and the clear day and so simple a goal.   *(written 1944) 1953*

In Personal Vein

Speaking from the heart, rather than with that heed
for accuracy, reason (cowardice, veiled),
which somewhat the years have taught me, somewhat failed
in teaching, I would say there is certain need
even at this hour to remember that men bleed
much the same blood, attackers and assailed;
that shattered dams pour death; that those discs nailed
flush to the earth were cities, whether the deed
were guilt or the judgement on it. This heart's-word
I would not match against logic; there's no doubt
only the one-eyed man walks straight through his brain,
and some considerations are better deferred
ten years, twenty years hence; but, in personal vein,
it is well that the heart sees and still speaks out.

(written 1945) 1953

The Wind at your Door

My ancestor was called on to go out –
a medical man, and one such must by law
wait in attendance on the pampered knout
and lend his countenance to what he saw,
lest the pet, patting with too bared a claw,
be judged a clumsy pussy. Bitter and hard,
see, as I see him, in that jailhouse yard.

Or see my thought of him: though time may keep
elsewhere tradition or a portrait still,
I would not feel under his cloak of sleep
if beard there or smooth chin, just to fulfil
some canon of precision. Good or ill
his blood's my own; and scratching in his grave
could find me more than I might wish to have.

Let him then be much of the middle style
of height and colouring; let his hair be dark
and his eyes green; and for that slit, the smile
that seemed inhuman, have it cruel and stark,
but grant it could be too the ironic mark
of all caught in the system – who the most,
the doctor or the flesh twined round that post?

There was a high wind blowing on that day;
for one who would not watch, but looked aside,
said that when twice he turned it blew his way
splashes of blood and strips of human hide
shaken out from the lashes that were plied
by one right-handed, one left-handed tough,
sweating at this paid task, and skilled enough.

That wind blows to your door down all these years.
Have you not known it when some breath you drew
tasted of blood? Your comfort is in arrears
of just thanks to a savagery tamed in you
only as subtler fears may serve in lieu
of thong and noose – old savagery which has built
your world and laws out of the lives it spilt.

For what was jailyard widens and takes in
my country. Fifty paces of stamped earth
stretch; and grey walls retreat and grow so thin
that towns show through and clearings – new raw birth
which burst from handcuffs – and free hands go forth
to win tomorrow's harvest from a vast
ploughland – the fifty paces of that past.

But see it through a window barred across
from cells this side, facing the outer gate
which shuts on freedom, opens on its loss
in a flat wall. Look left now through the grate
at buildings like more walls, roofed with grey slate
or hollowed in the thickness of laid stone
each side the court where the crowd stands this noon.

One there with the officials, thick of build,
not stout, say burly (so this obstinate man
ghosts in the eyes) is he whom enemies killed
(as I was taught) because the monopolist clan
found him a grit in their smooth-turning plan,

too loyally active on behalf of Bligh.
So he got lost; and history passed him by.

But now he buttons his long coat against
the biting gusts, or as a gesture of mind,
habitual; as if to keep him fenced
from stabs of slander sticking him from behind,
sped by the schemers never far to find
in faction, where approval from one source
damns in another clubroom as of course.

This man had Hunter's confidence, King's praise;
and settlers on the starving Hawkesbury banks
recalled through twilight drifting across their days
the doctor's fee of little more than thanks
so often; and how sent by their squeezed ranks
he put their case in London. I find I lack
the hateful paint to daub him wholly black.

Perhaps my life replies to his too much
through veiling generations dropped between.
My weakness here, resentments there, may touch
old motives and explain them, till I lean
to the forgiveness I must hope may clean
my own shortcomings; since no man can live
in his own sight if it will not forgive.

Certainly I must own him whether or not
it be my will. I was made understand
this much when once, marking a freehold lot,
my papers suddenly told me it was land
granted to Martin Mason. I felt his hand
heavily on my shoulder and knew what coil
binds life to life through bodies, and soul to soil.

There, over to one corner, a bony group
of prisoners waits; and each shall be in turn
tied by his own arms in a human loop
about the post, with his back bared to learn
the price of seeking freedom. So they earn
three hundred rippling stripes apiece, as set
by the law's mathematics against the debt.

These are the Irish batch of Castle Hill,
rebels and mutineers, my countrymen

twice over: first, because of those to till
my birthplace first, hack roads, raise roofs; and then
because their older land time and again
enrolls me through my forbears; and I claim
as origin that threshold whence we came.

One sufferer had my surname, and thereto
'Maurice', which added up to history once;
an ignorant dolt, no doubt, for all that crew
was tenantry. The breed of clod and dunce
makes patriots and true men: could I announce
that Maurice as my kin I say aloud
I'd take his irons as heraldry, and be proud.

Maurice is at the post. Its music lulls,
one hundred lashes done. If backbone shows
then play the tune on buttocks! But feel his pulse;
that's what a doctor's for; and if it goes
lamely, then dose it with these purging blows –
which have not made him moan; though, writhing there,
'Let my neck be,' he says, 'and flog me fair.'

One hundred lashes more, then rest the flail.
What says the doctor now? 'This dog won't yelp;
he'll tire you out before you'll see him fail;
here's strength to spare; go on!' Ay, pound to pulp;
yet when you've done he'll walk without your help,
and knock down guards who'd carry him being bid,
and sing no song of where the pikes are hid.

It would be well if I could find, removed
through generations back – who knows how far? –
more than a surname's thickness as a proved
bridge with that man's foundations. I need some star
of courage from his firmament, a bar
against surrenders: faith. All trials are less
than rain-blacked wind tells of that old distress.

Yet I can live with Mason. What is told
and what my heart knows of his heart, can sort
much truth from falsehood, much there that I hold
good clearly or good clouded by report;
and for things bad, ill grows where ills resort:
they were bad times. None know what in his place
they might have done. I've my own faults to face.

1959

Nuremberg

So quiet it was in that high, sun-steeped room,
So warm and still, that sometimes with the light
Through the great windows, bright with bottle-panes,
There'd float a chime from clock-jacks out of sight,
    Clapping iron mallets on green copper gongs.

But only in blown music from the town's
Quaint horologe could Time intrude . . . you'd say
Clocks had been bolted out, the flux of years
Defied, and that high chamber sealed away
    From earthly change by some old alchemist.

And, oh, those thousand towers of Nuremberg
Flowering like leaden trees outside the panes:
Those gabled roofs with smoking cowls, and those
Encrusted spires of stone, those golden vanes
    On shining housetops paved with scarlet tiles!

And all day nine wrought-pewter manticores
Blinked from their spouting faucets, not five steps
Across the cobbled street, or, peering through
The rounds of glass, espied that sun-flushed room
    With Dürer graving at intaglios.

O happy nine, spouting your dew all day
In green-scaled rows of metal, whilst the town
Moves peacefully below in quiet joy . . .
O happy gargoyles to be gazing down
    On Albrecht Dürer and his plates of iron!   *1924*

The Night-Ride

Gas flaring on the yellow platform; voices running up and down;
Milk-tins in cold dented silver; half-awake I stare,
Pull up the blind, blink out – all sounds are drugged;
The slow blowing of passengers asleep;
Engines yawning; water in heavy drips;
Black, sinister travellers, lumbering up the station,
One moment in the window, hooked over bags;

Hurrying, unknown faces – boxes with strange labels –
All groping clumsily to mysterious ends,
Out of the gaslight, dragged by private Fates.
Their echoes die. The dark train shakes and plunges;
Bells cry out; the night-ride starts again.
Soon I shall look out into nothing but blackness,
Pale, windy fields. The old roar and knock of the rails
Melts in dull fury. Pull down the blind. Sleep. Sleep.
Nothing but grey, rushing rivers of bush outside.
Gaslight and milk-cans. Of Rapptown I recall nothing else.

1926

Country Towns

Country towns, with your willows and squares,
And farmers bouncing on barrel mares
To public-houses of yellow wood
With '1860' over their doors,
And that mysterious race of Hogans
Which always keeps General Stores . . .

At the School of Arts, a broadsheet lies
Sprayed with the sarcasm of flies:
'The Great Golightly Family
Of Entertainers Here To-night' –
Dated a year and a half ago,
But left there, less from carelessness
Than from a wish to seem polite.

Verandas baked with musky sleep,
Mulberry faces dozing deep,
And dogs that lick the sunlight up
Like paste of gold – or, roused in vain
By far, mysterious buggy-wheels,
Lower their ears, and drowse again . . .

Country towns with your schooner bees,
And locusts burnt in the pepper-trees,
Drown me with syrups, arch your boughs,
Find me a bench, and let me snore,
Till, charged with ale and unconcern,
I'll think it's noon at half-past four!

1932

Captain Dobbin

Captain Dobbin, having retired from the South Seas
In the dumb tides of 1900, with a handful of shells,
A few poisoned arrows, a cask of pearls,
And five thousand pounds in the colonial funds,
Now sails the street in a brick villa, 'Laburnum Villa',
In whose blank windows the harbour hangs
Like a fog against the glass,
Golden and smoky, or stoned with a white glitter,
And boats go by, suspended in the pane,
Blue Funnel, Red Funnel, Messageries Maritimes,
Lugged down the port like sea-beasts taken alive
That scrape their bellies on sharp sands,
Of which particulars Captain Dobbin keeps
A ledger sticky with ink,
Entries of time and weather, state of the moon,
Nature of cargo and captains name,
For some mysterious and awful purpose
Never divulged.
For at night, when the stars mock themselves with lanterns,
So late the chimes blow loud and faint
Like a hand shutting and unshutting over the bells,
Captain Dobbin, having observed from bed
The lights, like a great fiery snake, of the *Comorin*
Going to sea, will note the hour
For subsequent recording in his gazette.

But the sea is really closer to him than this,
Closer to him than a dead, lovely woman,
For he keeps bits of it, like old letters,
Salt tied up in bundles
Or pressed flat,
What you might call a lock of the sea's hair,
So Captain Dobbin keeps his dwarfed memento,
His urn-burial, a chest of mummied waves,
Gales fixed in print, and the sweet dangerous countries
Of shark and casuarina-tree,
Stolen and put in coloured maps,
Like a flask of seawater, or a bottled ship,
A schooner caught in a glass bottle;
But Captain Dobbin keeps them in books,
Crags of varnished leather

Pimply with gilt, by learned mariners
And masters of hydrostatics, or the childish tales
Of simple heroes, taken by Turks or dropsy.
So nightly he sails from shelf to shelf
Or to the quadrants, dangling with rusty screws,
Or the hanging-gardens of old charts,
So old they bear the authentic protractor-lines,
Traced in faint ink, as fine as Chinese hairs.

Over the flat and painted atlas-leaves
His reading-glass would tremble,
Over the fathoms, pricked in tiny rows,
Water shelving to the coast.
Quietly the bone-rimmed lens would float
Till, through the glass, he felt the barbéd rush
Of bubbles foaming, spied the albicores,
The blue-finned admirals, heard the wind-swallowed cries
Of planters running on the beach
Who filched their swags of yams and ambergris,
Birds' nests and sandalwood, from pastures numbed
By the sun's yellow, too meek for honest theft;
But he, less delicate robber, climbed the walls,
Broke into dozing houses
Crammed with black bottles, marish wine
Crusty and salt-corroded, fading prints,
Sparkle-daubed almanacs and playing cards,
With rusty cannon, left by the French outside,
Half-buried in sand,
Even to the castle of Queen Pomaree
In the Yankee's footsteps, and found her throne-room piled
With golden candelabras, mildewed swords,
Guitars and fowling-pieces, tossed in heaps
With greasy cakes and flung-down calabashes.

Then Captain Dobbin's eye,
That eye of wild and wispy scudding blue,
Voluptuously prying, would light up
Like mica scratched by gully-suns,
And he would be fearful to look upon
And shattering in his conversation;
Nor would he tolerate the harmless chanty,
No 'Shenandoah', or the dainty mew
That landsmen offer in a silver dish
To Neptune, sung to pianos in candlelight.

Of these he spoke in scorn,
For there was but one way of singing 'Stormalong',
He said, and that was not really singing,
But howling, rather – shrieked in the wind's jaws
By furious men, not tinkled in drawing-rooms
By lap-dogs in clean shirts.
And, at these words,
The galleries of photographs, men with rich beards,
Pea-jackets and brass buttons, with folded arms,
Would scowl approval, for they were shipmates, too,
Companions of no cruise by reading-glass,
But fellows of storm and honey from the past –
'The Charlotte, Java, '93,'
'Knuckle and Fred at Port au Prince,'
'William in his New Rig,'
Even that notorious scoundrel, Captain Baggs,
Who, as all knew, owed Dobbin Twenty Pounds
Lost at fair cribbage, but he never paid,
Or paid 'with the slack of the tops'l sheets'
As Captain Dobbin frequently expressed it.

There were their faces, grilled a trifle now,
Cigar-hued in various spots
By the brown breath of sodium-eating years,
On quarter-decks long burnt to the water's edge,
A resurrection of the dead by chemicals.
And the voyages they had made,
Their labours in a country of water,
Were they not marked by inadequate lines
On charts tied up like skins in a rack?
Or his own Odysseys, his lonely travels,
His trading days, an autobiography
Of angles and triangles and lozenges
Ruled tack by tack across the sheet,
That with a single scratch expressed the stars,
Merak and Alamak and Alpherat,
The wind, the moon, the sun, the clambering sea,
Sails bleached with light, salt in the eyes,
Bamboos and Tahiti oranges,
From some forgotten countless day,
One foundered day from a forgotten month,
A year sucked quietly from the blood,
Dead with the rest, remembered by no more

Than a scratch on a dry chart –
Or when the return grew too choking bitter-sweet
And laburnum-berries manifestly tossed
Beyond the window, not the fabulous leaves
Of Hotoo or canoe-tree or palmetto,
There were the wanderings of other keels,
Magellan, Bougainville and Cook,
Who found no greater a memorial
Than footprints over a lithograph.

For Cook he worshipped, that captain with the sad
And fine white face, who never lost a man
Or flinched a peril, and of Bougainville
He spoke with graceful courtesy, as a rival
To whom the honours of the hunting-field
Must be accorded. Not so with the Spaniard,
Sebastian Juan del Cano, at whom he sneered
Openly, calling him a fool of fortune
Blown to a sailors' abbey by chance winds
And blindfold currents, who slept in a fine cabin,
Blundered through five degrees of latitude,
Was bullied by mutineers a hundred more,
And woke and found himself across the world.

Coldly in the window,
Like a fog rubbed up and down the glass
The harbour, bony with mist
And ropes of water, glittered, and the blind tide
That crawls it knows not where, nor for what gain,
Pushed its drowned shoulders against the wheel,
Against the wheel of the mill.
Flowers rocked far down
And white, dead bodies that were anchored there
In marshes of spent light.
Blue Funnel, Red Funnel,
The ships went over them, and bells in engine-rooms
Cried to their bowels of flaring oil,
And stokers groaned and sweated with burnt skins,
Clawed to their shovels.
But quietly in his room,
In his little cemetery of sweet essences
With fond memorial-stones and lines of grace,
Captain Dobbin went on reading about the sea.   *1932*

South Country

After the whey-faced anonymity
Of river-gums and scribbly-gums and bush,
After the rubbing and the hit of brush,
You come to the South Country

As if the argument of trees were done,
The doubts and quarrelling, the plots and pains,
All ended by these clear and gliding planes
Like an abrupt solution.

And over the flat earth of empty farms
The monstrous continent of air floats back
Coloured with rotting sunlight and the black,
Bruised flesh of thunderstorms:

Air arched, enormous, pounding the bony ridge,
Ditches and hutches, with a drench of light,
So huge, from such infinities of height,
You walk on the sky's beach

While even the dwindled hills are small and bare,
As if, rebellious, buried, pitiful,
Something below pushed up a knob of skull,
Feeling its way to air.   *1939*

Out of Time

I

I saw Time flowing like the hundred yachts
That fly behind the daylight, foxed with air;
Or piercing, like the quince-bright, bitter slats
Of sun gone thrusting under Harbour's hair.

So Time, the wave, enfolds me in its bed,
Or Time, the bony knife, it runs me through.
'Skulker, take heart,' I thought my own heart said,
'The flood, the blade, go by – Time flows, not you!'

Vilely, continuously, stupidly,
Time takes me, drills me, drives through bone and vein,
So water bends the seaweeds in the sea,
The tide goes over, but the weeds remain.

Time, you must cry farewell, take up the track,
And leave this lovely moment at your back!

II

Time leaves the lovely moment at his back,
Eager to quench and ripen, kiss or kill;
To-morrow begs him, breathless for his lack,
Or beauty dead entreats him to be still.

His fate pursues him; he must open doors,
Or close them, for that pale and faceless host
Without a flag, whose agony implores
Birth, to be flesh, or funeral, to be ghost.

Out of all reckoning, out of dark and light,
Over the edges of dead Nows and Heres,
Blindly and softly, as a mistress might,
He keeps appointments with a million years.

I and the moment laugh, and let him go,
Leaning against his golden undertow.

III

Leaning against the golden undertow,
Backward, I saw the birds begin to climb
With bodies hailstone-clear, and shadows flow,
Fixed in a sweet meniscus, out of Time,

Out of the torrent, like the fainter land
Lensed in a bubble's ghostly camera,
The lighted beach, the sharp and china sand,
Glitters and waters and peninsula –

The moment's world, it was; and I was part,
Fleshless and ageless, changeless and made free.
'Fool, would you leave this country?' cried my heart,
But I was taken by the suck of sea.

The gulls go down, the body dies and rots,
And Time flows past them like a hundred yachts.   *1939*

Five Bells

Time that is moved by little fidget wheels
Is not my Time, the flood that does not flow.
Between the double and the single bell
Of a ship's hour, between a round of bells
From the dark warship riding there below,
I have lived many lives, and this one life
Of Joe, long dead, who lives between five bells.

Deep and dissolving verticals of light
Ferry the falls of moonshine down. Five bells
Coldly rung out in a machine's voice. Night and water
Pour to one rip of darkness, the Harbour floats
In air, the Cross hangs upside-down in water.

Why do I think of you, dead man, why thieve
These profitless lodgings from the flukes of thought
Anchored in Time? You have gone from earth,
Gone even from the meaning of a name;
Yet something's there, yet something forms its lips
And hits and cries against the ports of space,
Beating their sides to make its fury heard.

Are you shouting at me, dead man, squeezing your face
In agonies of speech on speechless panes?
Cry louder, beat the windows, bawl your name!

But I hear nothing, nothing . . . only bells,
Five bells, the bumpkin calculus of Time.
Your echoes die, your voice is dowsed by Life,
There's not a mouth can fly the pygmy strait –
Nothing except the memory of some bones
Long shoved away, and sucked away, in mud;
And unimportant things you might have done,
Or once I thought you did; but you forgot,
And all have now forgotten – looks and words
And slops of beer; your coat with buttons off,
Your gaunt chin and pricked eye, and raging tales
Of Irish kings and English perfidy,
And dirtier perfidy of publicans
Groaning to God from Darlinghurst.
                                        Five bells.

Five Bells   *ship's signal for ten-thirty*

Then I saw the road, I heard the thunder
Tumble, and felt the talons of the rain
The night we came to Moorebank in slab-dark,
So dark you bore no body, had no face,
But a sheer voice that rattled out of air
(As now you'd cry if I could break the glass),
A voice that spoke beside me in the bush,
Loud for a breath or bitten off by wind,
Of Milton, melons, and the Rights of Man,
And blowing flutes, and how Tahitian girls
Are brown and angry-tongued, and Sydney girls
Are white and angry-tongued, or so you'd found.
But all I heard was words that didn't join
So Milton became melons, melons girls,
And fifty mouths, it seemed, were out that night,
And in each tree an Ear was bending down,
Or something had just run, gone behind grass,
When, blank and bone-white, like a maniac's thought,
The naphtha-flash of lightning slit the sky,
Knifing the dark with deathly photographs.
There's not so many with so poor a purse
Or fierce a need, must fare by night like that,
Five miles in darkness on a country track,
But when you do, that's what you think.

                                        Five bells.

In Melbourne, your appetite had gone,
Your angers too; they had been leeched away
By the soft archery of summer rains
And the sponge-paws of wetness, the slow damp
That stuck the leaves of living, snailed the mind,
And showed your bones, that had been sharp with rage,
The sodden ecstasies of rectitude.
I thought of what you'd written in faint ink,
Your journal with the sawn-off lock, that stayed behind
With other things you left, all without use,
All without meaning now, except a sign
That someone had been living who now was dead:
'At Labassa. Room 6 x 8
On top of the tower; because of this, very dark
And cold in winter. Everything has been stowed
Into this room – 500 books all shapes
And colours, dealt across the floor

And over sills and on the laps of chairs;
Guns, photoes of many differant things
And differant curioes that I obtained . . .'

In Sydney, by the spent aquarium-flare
Of penny gaslight on pink wallpaper,
We argued about blowing up the world,
But you were living backward, so each night
You crept a moment closer to the breast,
And they were living, all of them, those frames
And shapes of flesh that had perplexed your youth,
And most your father, the old man gone blind,
With fingers always round a fiddle's neck,
That graveyard mason whose fair monuments
And tablets cut with dreams of piety
Rest on the bosoms of a thousand men
Staked bone by bone, in quiet astonishment
At cargoes they had never thought to bear,
These funeral-cakes of sweet and sculptured stone.

Where have you gone? The tide is over you,
The turn of midnight water's over you,
As Time is over you, and mystery,
And memory, the flood that does not flow.
You have no suburb, like those easier dead
In private berths of dissolution laid –
The tide goes over, the waves ride over you
And let their shadows down like shining hair,
But they are Water; and the sea-pinks bend
Like lilies in your teeth, but they are Weed;
And you are only part of an Idea.
I felt the wet push its black thumb-balls in,
The night you died, I felt your eardrums crack,
And the short agony, the longer dream,
The Nothing that was neither long nor short;
But I was bound, and could not go that way,
But I was blind, and could not feel your hand.
If could find an answer, could only find
Your meaning, or could say why you were here
Who now are gone, what purpose gave you breath
Or seized it back, might I not hear your voice?

I looked out of my window in the dark
At waves with diamond quills and combs of light
That arched their mackerel-backs and smacked the sand
In the moon's drench, that straight enormous glaze,
And ships far off asleep, and Harbour-buoys
Tossing their fireballs wearily each to each,
And tried to hear your voice, but all I heard
Was a boat's whistle, and the scraping squeal
Of seabirds' voices far away, and bells,
Five bells. Five bells coldly ringing out.

Five bells.

1939

Beach Burial

Softly and humbly to the Gulf of Arabs
The convoys of dead sailors come;
At night they sway and wander in the waters far under,
But morning rolls them in the foam.

Between the sob and clubbing of the gunfire
Someone, it seems, has time for this,
To pluck them from the shallows and bury them in burrows
And tread the sand upon their nakedness;

And each cross, the driven stake of tidewood,
Bears the last signature of men,
Written with such perplexity, with such bewildered pity,
The words choke as they begin –

'*Unknown seaman*' – the ghostly pencil
Wavers and fades, the purple drips,
The breath of the wet season has washed their inscriptions
As blue as drowned men's lips,

Dead seamen, gone in search of the same landfall,
Whether as enemies they fought,
Or fought with us, or neither; the sand joins them together,
Enlisted on the other front.

El Alamein   (1944) 1957

A Night Attack

Be still. The bleeding night is in suspense
   Of watchful agony and coloured thought,
And every beating vein and trembling sense
   Long-tired with time, is pitched and overwrought.
And for the eye, the darkness holds strange forms,
   Soft movements in the leaves, and wicked glows
That wait and peer. The whole black landscape swarms
   With shapes of white and grey that no one knows;
And for the ear, a sound, a pause, a breath,
   A distant hurried footstep moving fast.
The hand has touched the slimy face of death.
   The mind is raking at the ragged past.
. . . A sound of rifles rattles from the south,
And startled orders move from mouth to mouth.

May 24, 1915   *1917*

The Last to Leave

The guns were silent, and the silent hills
   Had bowed their grasses to a gentle breeze.
I gazed upon the vales and on the rills,
   And whispered, 'What of these?' and 'What of these?'
'These long-forgotten dead with sunken graves,
   Some crossless, with unwritten memories;
Their only mourners are the moaning waves;
   Their only minstrels are the singing trees.'
And thus I mused and sorrowed wistfully.
   I watched the place where they had scaled the height,
That height whereon they bled so bitterly
   Throughout each day and through each blistered night.
I sat there long, and listened – all things listened too.
   I heard the epics of a thousand trees;
A thousand waves I heard, and then I knew
   The waves were very old, the trees were wise:
The dead would be remembered evermore –
   The valiant dead that gazed upon the skies,
And slept in great battalions by the shore.

January, 1916   *1917*

House-mates

Because his soup was cold, he needs must sulk
From dusk till dark, and never speak to her;
And all the time she heard his heavy bulk
Blunder about the house, making a stir
In this room and in that. She heard him mutter
His foolish breathless noises, snarling and thick.
She knew the very words he first would utter;
He always said them, and they made her sick –
Those awkward efforts at a gracious peace
And kindly patronage of high-forgiving.
She knew these quarrelling calms would never cease
As long as she could keep his body living;
And so she lay and felt the hours creep by,
Wondering lazily upon her bed,
How cold the world would be if he should die
And leave her weeping for her stupid dead.   *1919*

LESBIA HARFORD (1891-1927)

Do you remember still the little song

Do you remember still the little song
I mumbled on the hill at Aura, how
I told you it was made for Katie's sake
When I was fresh from school and loving her
With all the strength of girlhood? And you said
You liked my song, although I didn't know
How it began at first and gabbled then
In a half-voice, because I was too shy
To speak aloud, much less to speak them out –
Words I had joined myself – in the full voice
And with the lilt of proper poetry.
You could have hardly heard me. Here's the girl.
The little girl from school you never knew.
She made this song. Read what you couldn't hear.

How bright the windows are
When the dear sun shineth.
They strive to reflect the sun,
To be bright like the sun,

To give heat like the sun.
My heart too has its chosen one
And so to shine designeth.

The windows on the opposite hill that day
Shone bright at sunset too and made me think
Of the old patter I had half forgot,
Do you remember? I remind you now,
Who wandered yesterday for half an hour
Into St Francis, where I thought of you
And how I would be glad to love you well
If I but knew the way. The rhyme came back
Teasing me till I knew I hated it.
I couldn't take that way of loving you.
That was the girl's way. Hear the woman now.
Out of my thinking in the lonely church
And the day's labour in a friendly room
Tumbled a song this morning you will like.

I love my love
But I could not be
Good for his sake.
That frightens me.

Nor could I do
Such things as I should
Just for the sake
Of being good.

Deeds are too great
To serve my whim,
Be ways of loving
Myself or him.

Whether my deeds
Are good or ill
They're done for their own,
Not love's sake, still.

I didn't know it till the song was done
But that's Ramiro in a nutshell, eh,
With his contempt for individual souls
And setting of the deed above the man.
Perhaps I like him better than I thought,

Or would like, if he'd give me leave to scorn
Chameleon, adjectival good and ill
And set the deed so far above the man
As to be out of reach of morals too.
There you and I join issue once again.

(written October 1912) 1941

I can't feel the sunshine

I can't feel the sunshine
Or see the stars aright
For thinking of her beauty
And her kisses bright.

She would let me kiss her
Once and not again.
Deeming soul essential,
Sense doth she disdain.

If I should once kiss her,
I would never rest
Till I had lain hour long
Pillowed on her breast.

Lying so, I'd tell her
Many a secret thing
God has whispered to me
When my soul took wing.

Would that I were Sappho,
Greece my land, not this!
There the noblest women,
When they loved, would kiss.

(written 1915) 1985

Closing Time – Public Library

At ten o'clock the great gong sounds the dread
Prelude to splendour. I push back my chair,
And all the people leave their books. We flock,
Still acquiescent, down the marble stair
Into the dark where we can't read. And thought
Swoops down insatiate through the starry air.

(written 1917) 1941

[Lesbia Harford] 323

I'm like all lovers, wanting love to be

I'm like all lovers, wanting love to be
A very mighty thing for you and me.

In certain moods your love should be a fire
That burnt your very life up in desire.

The only kind of love then to my mind
Would make you kiss my shadow on the blind

And walk seven miles each night to see it there,
Myself within, serene and unaware.

But you're as bad. You'd have me watch the clock
And count your coming while I mend your sock.

You'd have my mind devoted day and night
To you, and care for you and your delight.

Poor fools, who each would have the other give
What spirit must withhold if it would live.

You're not my slave, I wish you not to be.
I love yourself and not your love for me,

The self that goes ten thousand miles away
And loses thought of me for many a day.

And you love me for loving much beside
But now you want a woman for your bride.

Oh, make no woman of me, you who can,
Or I will make a husband of a man.

By my unwomanly love that sets you free
Love all myself, but least the woman in me.

(written 1917) 1941

A Prayer to Saint Rosa

When I am so worn out I cannot sleep
And yet I know I have to work next day
Or lose my job, I sometimes have recourse
To one long dead, who listens when I pray.

I ask Saint Rose of Lima for the sleep
She went without, three hundred years ago
When, lying on thorns and heaps of broken sherd,
She talked with God and made a heaven so.

Then speedily that most compassionate Saint
Comes with her gift of deep oblivious hours,
Treasured for centuries in nocturnal space
And heavy with the scent of Lima's flowers.

(written 1927) 1985

ZORA CROSS (1890-1964)

from *Love Sonnets*

III

When first I whispered in your wondering ear,
'I worship you,' God smiled through all His skies,
Flinging a starry challenge in surprise,
'Wilt thou have Heaven or him?' . . . 'O, holy Seer,'
I answered, 'give me him.' Then, tier on tier,
The cherub-choir that sang above the rise
Of amber air beneath our Father's eyes,
Shouted a song of praise down all the sphere.

For there is neither Death nor Life in love.
And God, whose finger guides eternity,
Lights Paradise with parapets of fire
O'er which He leans His vasty form above,
And, looking through His hills on you and me,
Feeds Heaven upon the flame of our desire.

XLIX

In me there is a vast and lonely place
Where none, not even you, have walked in sight.
A wide, still vale of solitude and light,
Where Silence echoes into ebbing space.
And there I creep at times and hide my face,
While in myself I fathom wrong and right,
And all the timeless ages of the night
That sacred silence of my soul I pace.

And when from there I come to you, love-swift,
My mouth hot-edged with kisses fresh as wine,
Often I find your longings all asleep
And unresponsive from my grasp you drift.
Ah, Love, you, too, seek solitude like mine,
And soul from soul the secret seems to keep.   *1918*

DOROTHEA MACKELLAR (1885-1968)

My Country

The love of field and coppice
    Of green and shaded lanes,
Of ordered woods and gardens
    Is running in your veins.
Strong love of grey-blue distance
    Brown streams and soft, dim skies –
I know but cannot share it,
    My love is otherwise.

I love a sunburnt country,
    A land of sweeping plains,
Of ragged mountain ranges,
    Of droughts and flooding rains.
I love her far horizons,
    I love her jewel-sea,
Her beauty and her terror –
    The wide brown land for me!

The stark white ring-barked forests,
    All tragic to the moon,
The sapphire-misted mountains,
    The hot gold hush of noon.
Green tangle of the brushes,
    Where lithe lianas coil,
And orchids deck the tree tops
    And ferns the warm dark soil.

Core of my heart, my country!
    Her pitiless blue sky,
When sick at heart, around us,
    We see the cattle die –

But then the grey clouds gather,
    And we can bless again
The drumming of an army,
    The steady, soaking rain.

Core of my heart, my country!
    Land of the Rainbow Gold,
For flood and fire and famine,
    She pays us back three-fold.
Over the thirsty paddocks,
    Watch, after many days,
The filmy veil of greenness
    That thickens as we gaze . . .

An opal-hearted country,
    A wilful, lavish land –
All you who have not loved her,
    You will not understand –
Though earth holds many splendours,
    Wherever I may die,
I know to what brown country
    My homing thoughts will fly.   1911

Heritage

Though on the day your hard blue eyes met mine
I did not know I had a heart to keep,
    All the dead women in my soul
Stirred in their shrouded sleep.

There were strange pulses beating in my throat;
I had no thought of love: I was a child:
    But the dead lovers in my soul
Awoke and flushed and smiled;

And it was years before I understood
Why I had been so happy at your side
    With the dead women in my soul
Teaching me what to hide.

For it was not the springtime that had come,
Only one strong flower thrusting through the snows,
    But the dead women in my soul
Knew all that summer knows.   1923

'FURNLEY MAURICE' (FRANK WILMOT) (1881-1942)

Echoes of wheels and singing lashes

Echoes of wheels and singing lashes
    Wake on the morning air;
Out of the kitchen a youngster dashes,
    Giving the ducks a scare.
Three jiffs from house to gully,
    And over the bridge to the gate;
And then a panting little boy
    Climbs on the rails to wait.

For there is long-whipped cursing Bill
    With four enormous logs,
Behind a team with the white-nosed leader's
    Feet in the sucking bogs.
Oh it was great to see them stuck,
    And grand to see them strain,
Until the magical language of Bill
    Had got them out again!

I foxed them to the shoulder turn,
    I saw him work them round,
And die into the secret bush,
    Leaving only sound.

And it isn't bullocks I recall,
    Nor waggons my memory sees;
But in the scented bush a track
    Turning among the trees.

Not forests of lean towering gums,
    Nor notes of birds and bees,
Do I remember so well as a track
    Turning among the trees.

Oh track where the brown leaves fall
    In dust to our very knees!
And it isn't the wattle that I recall,
Nor the sound of the bullocky's singing lash,
When cloven hoofs in the puddles splash;
But the rumble of an unseen load,
Swallowed along the hidden road
    Turning among the trees!

1913

They've builded wooden timber tracks

They've builded wooden timber tracks,
    And a trolly with screaming brakes
Noses into the secret bush,
Into the birdless brooding bush,
    And the tall old gums it takes.

And down in the sunny valley,
    The snorting saw screams slow;
Oh bush that nursed my people,
Oh bush that cursed my people,
That flayed and made my people,
    I weep to watch you go.

1913

Nursery Rhyme

One year, two year, three year, four,
Comes a khaki gentleman knocking at the door;
Any little boys at home? Send them out to me,
To train them and brain them in battles yet to be.
Five year, six year, seven year, eight,
Hurry up, you little chaps, the captain's at the gate.

When a little boy is born, feed him, train him, so;
Put him in a cattle pen and wait for him to grow;
When he's nice and plump and dear, sensible and sweet,
Throw him in the trenches for the grey rats to eat;
Toss him in the cannon's mouth, cannons fancy best
Tender little boy flesh, that's easy to digest.

One year, two year, three year, four,
Listen to the generals singing out for more!
Soon he'll be a soldier-boy, won't he be a toff,
Pretty little soldier, with his head blown off!

Mother rears her family on two pounds a week,
Teaches them to wash themselves, teaches them to speak,
Rears them with a heart's love, rears them to be men,
Grinds her fingers to the bone – then, what then?

One year, two year, three year, four,
Comes a khaki gentleman knocking at the door;

Little boys are wanted now very much indeed,
Hear the bugles blowing when the cannons want a feed!
Fowl-food, horse-food, man-food are dear,
Cannon fodder's always cheap, conscript or volunteer.

When the guns grow rarer, and money's in a fix,
Tax the mother's wages down to twenty-nine and six;
Blood cost, money cost, cost of years of stress,
Heart cost, food cost, cost of all the mess.
Captains draw their wages with a penny in the slot,
But big bills and little bills, mother pays the lot.

Parents who must rear the boys the cannons love to slay
Also pay for cannons that blow other boys away!
Parsons tell them that their sons have just been blown to bits,
Patriotic parents must all laugh like fits!
Raise the boys for honest men, send them out to die,
Where's the coward father who would dare to raise a cry?
Any gentleman's aware folk rear their children for
Blunderers and plunderers to mangle in a war!

One year, two year, three year, four,
Comes a khaki gentleman knocking at the door.
Any little boys at home? Send them out for me
To train them and brain them in battles yet to be!
Five year, six year, seven year, eight,
Hurry up, you little chaps, the captain cannot wait!   1920

JOHN SHAW NEILSON (1872-1942)

You, and Yellow Air

I dream of an old kissing-time
    And the flowered follies there;
In the dim place of cherry-trees,
    Of you, and yellow air.

It was an age of babbling,
    When the players would play
Mad with the wine and miracles
    Of a charmed holiday.

Bewildered was the warm earth
　　With whistling and sighs,
And a young foal spoke all his heart
　　With diamonds for eyes.

You were of Love's own colour
　　In eyes and heart and hair;
In the dim place of cherry-trees
　　Ridden by yellow air.

It was the time when red lovers
　　With the red fevers burn;
A time of bells and silver seeds
　　And cherries on the turn.

Children looked into tall trees
　　And old eyes looked behind;
God in His glad October
　　No sullen man could find.

Out of your eyes a magic
　　Fell lazily as dew,
And every lad with lad's eyes
　　Made summer love to you.

It was a reign of roses,
　　Of blue flowers for the eye,
And the rustling of green girls
　　Under a white sky.

I dream of an old kissing-time
　　And the flowered follies there,
In the dim place of cherry-trees,
　　Of you, and yellow air.

(written 1909) 1919

The Orange Tree

The young girl stood beside me. I
　　Saw not what her young eyes could see:
– A light, she said, not of the sky
　　Lives somewhere in the Orange Tree.

– Is it, I said, of east or west?
   The heartbeat of a luminous boy
Who with his faltering flute confessed
   Only the edges of his joy?

Was he, I said, borne to the blue
   In a mad escapade of Spring
Ere he could make a fond adieu
   To his love in the blossoming?

– Listen! the young girl said. There calls
   No voice, no music beats on me;
But it is almost sound: it falls
   This evening on the Orange Tree.

– Does he, I said, so fear the Spring
   Ere the white sap too far can climb?
See in the full gold evening
   All happenings of the olden time?

Is he so goaded by the green?
   Does the compulsion of the dew
Make him unknowable but keen
   Asking with beauty of the blue?

– Listen! the young girl said. For all
   Your hapless talk you fail to see
There is a light, a step, a call
   This evening on the Orange Tree.

– Is it, I said, a waste of love
   Imperishably old in pain,
Moving as an affrighted dove
   Under the sunlight or the rain?

Is it a fluttering heart that gave
   Too willingly and was reviled?
Is it the stammering at a grave,
   The last word of a little child?

– Silence! the young girl said. Oh, why,
   Why will you talk to weary me?
Plague me no longer now, for I
   Am listening like the Orange Tree.

(written 1916-19) 1934

Schoolgirls Hastening

Fear it has faded and the night:
   The bells all peal the hour of nine:
The schoolgirls hastening through the light
   Touch the unknowable Divine.

What leavening in my heart would bide!
   Full dreams a thousand deep are there:
All luminants succumb beside
   The unbound melody of hair.

Joy the long timorous takes the flute:
   Valiant with colour songs are born:
Love the impatient absolute
   Lives as a Saviour in the morn.

Get thou behind me Shadow-Death!
   Oh ye Eternities delay!
Morning is with me and the breath
   Of schoolgirls hastening down the way.

(written 1922) 1934

To the Red Lory

At the full face of the forest lies our little town:
Do thou from thy lookout to heaven, O lory, come down!

Come, charge with thy challenge of colour our thoughts cool and thin;
Descend with the blood of the sunlight – O lory, come in!

The clouds are away, 'tis October, the glees have begun;
Thy breast has the valour of music, O passionate one!

The rhythm is thine, the beloved, the unreason of Spring.
How royal thy raiment! No sorrow is under thy wing.

Oh thou of intrepid apparel, thy song is thy gown;
Translate thy proud speech of the sunlight – O lory, come down!

(written 1924) 1947

The Moon Was Seven Days Down

'Peter!' she said, 'the clock has struck
    At one and two and three;
You sleep so sound, and the lonesome hours
    They seem so black to me.
I suffered long, and I suffered sore:
    – What else can I think upon?
I fear no evil; but, oh! – the moon!
    She is seven days gone.'

'Peter!' she said, 'the night is long:
    The hours will not go by:
The moon is calm; but she meets her death
    Bitter as women die.
I think too much of the flowers. I dreamed
    I walked in a wedding gown,
Or was it a shroud? The moon! the moon!
    She is seven days down.'

'Woman!' he said, 'my ears could stand
    Much noise when I was young;
But year by year you have wearied me:
    Can you never stop your tongue?
Here am I, with my broken rest,
    To be up at the break of day:
– So much to do; and the sheep not shorn,
    And the lambs not yet away.'

'Peter!' she said, 'your tongue is rude;
    You have ever spoken so:
My aches and ills, they trouble you not
    This many a year, I know:
You talk of your lambs and sheep and wool:
    – 'Tis all that you think upon:
I fear no evil; but, oh! the moon!
    She is seven days gone.'

'Peter!' she said, 'the children went:
    My children would not stay:
By the hard word and the hard work
    You have driven them far away.
I suffered, back in the ten years
    That I never saw a town:
– Oh! the moon is over her full glory!
    She is seven days down!'

'Woman!' he said, 'I want my rest.
    'Tis the worst time of the year:
The weeds are thick in the top fallow,
    And the hay will soon be here.
A man is a man, and a child a child:
    From a daughter or a son
Or a man or woman I want no talk
    For anything I have done.'

'Peter!' she said, "twas told to me,
    Long back, in a happy year,
That I should die in the turning time
    When the wheat was in the ear;
That I should go in a plain coffin
    And lie in a plain gown
When the moon had taken her full glory
    And was seven days down.'

Peter, he rose and lit the lamp
    At the first touch of the day:
His mind was full of the top fallow,
    And the ripening of the hay.
He said, 'She sleeps,' – but the second look
    He knew how the dead can stare:
And there came a dance of last beauty
    That none of the living share.

How cool and straight and steady he was:
    He said, 'She seems so young!
Her face is fine – it was always fine –
    But, oh, by God! her tongue!
She always thought as the children thought:
    Her mind was made for a town.'
– And the moon was out in the pale sky:
    She was seven days down.

He sauntered out to the neighbour's place
    As the daylight came in clear:
'The wheat,' he said, 'it is filling well,'
    And he stopped at a heavy ear.
He said, 'A good strong plain coffin
    Is the one I am thinking on.'
– And the moon was over his shoulder:
    She was seven days gone.   *(written 1925)* 1927

The Crane Is My Neighbour

The bird is my neighbour, a whimsical fellow and dim;
There is in the lake a nobility falling on him.

The bird is a noble, he turns to the sky for a theme,
And the ripples are thoughts coming out to the edge of a dream.

The bird is both ancient and excellent, sober and wise,
But he never could spend all the love that is sent for his eyes.

He bleats no instruction, he is not an arrogant drummer;
His gown is simplicity – blue as the smoke of the summer.

How patient he is as he puts out his wings for the blue!
His eyes arc as old as the twilight, and calm as the dew.

The bird is my neighbour, he leaves not a claim for a sigh,
He moves as the guest of the sunlight – he roams in the sky.

The bird is a noble, he turns to the sky for a theme,
And the ripples are thoughts coming out to the edge of a dream.

(written 1934) *1938*

You Cannot Go Down to the Spring

The song will deceive you, the scent will incite you to sing;
You clutch but you cannot discover: you cannot go down to the Spring.

The day will be painted with summer, the heat and the gold
Will give you no key to the blossom: the music is old.

It is at the edge of a promise, a far-away thing;
The green is the nest of all riddles: you cannot go down to the Spring.

The truth is too close to the sorrow; the song you would sing,
It cannot go into the fever: you cannot go down to the Spring.

1947

Say This for Love

Say this for love, when the great summer time
Is gone, and only winter wisdoms blow:
Fiercely he burned, like some imperious rhyme,
Burned, and he burned, but would not let me go.

Say this, his ominous riddlings were so deep
I could not see, I knew not where he trod.
He did from out a thousand centuries creep,
As some insurgent enemy of God.

Say this for love: You who did smite to kill,
And you did lie, it was my soul to soil;
Dressed as a hatred you did flog me still,
Chained to the last insanities in toil.

Say this for love: For all the ills in him
I give forgiveness for the lies he told;
Say this for love when both the eyes are dim,
And darkness leaves you whimpering in the cold.

(written 1941) 1970

'E' (MARY E. FULLERTON) (1868-1946)

The Selector's Wife

The quick compunction cannot serve;
She saw the flash
Ere he had bent with busy hand
And drooping lash.

She saw him mark for the first time,
With critic eye,
What five years' heavy toil had done
'Neath roof and sky.

And always now so sensitive
Her poor heart is,
That moment will push in between
His kindest kiss.

The moment when he realised
Her girlhood done
The truth her glass had long revealed
Of beauty gone.

Until some future gracious flash
Shall let each know
That that which drew and holds him yet
Shall never go.

1921

Body

We fend for this poor thing,
Wash, dress, and give it food,
Love it before all men
Through each vicissitude.

Give it whate'er it ask,
Shield it from heat and cold,
And croon above its pains
When time has made it old.

It is but house and home
That for no term we rent;
We seldom talk with Him –
Its mighty resident.

Body's the easy one,
That lets the mortal be,
As though the pretty shell
Were the essential He.

Sometimes in hardihood,
We touch the inner door –
Two entities in one
Visited and visitor.

Oh, Tenant of my flesh,
I knock, and turn, and fly,
Afraid of the appraisement
Within that solemn eye.

1942

A Man's Sliding Mood

Ardent in love and cold in charity,
Loud in the market, timid in debate:
Scornful of foe unbuckled in the dust,
At whimper of a child compassionate,

A man's a sliding mood from hour to hour,
Rage, and a singing forest of bright birds,
Laughter with lovely friends, and loneliness,
Woe with her heavy horn of unspoke words.

What is he then this heir of heart and mind?
Is this the man with his conflicting moods,
Or is there in a deeper dwelling place
Some stilly shaping thing that bides and broods?   *1946*

Emus

My annals have it so:
A thing my mother saw,
Nigh eighty years ago,
With happiness and awe.

Along a level hill –
A clearing in wild space.
And night's last tardy chill
Yet damp on morning's face.

Sight never to forget:
Solemn against the sky
In stately silhouette
Ten emus walking by.

One after one they went
In line, and without haste:
On their unknown intent,
Ten emus grandly paced.

She, used to hedged-in fields
Watched them go filing past
Into the great Bush Wilds
Silent and vast.

Sudden that hour she knew
That this far place was good,
This mighty land and new
For the soul's hardihood.

For hearts that love the strange,
That carry wonder;
The Bush, the hills, the range,
And the dark flats under.   *1946*

Eve-Song

I span and Eve span
A thread to bind the heart of man;
But the heart of man was a wandering thing
That came and went with little to bring:
Nothing he minded that we made
As here he loitered and there he stayed.

I span and Eve span
A thread to bind the heart of man;
But the more we span the more we found
It wasn't his heart but ours we bound!
For children gathered about our knees:
The thread was a chain that stole our ease.
And one of us learned in our children's eyes
That more than man was love and prize.
But deep in the heart of one of us lay
A root of loss and hidden dismay.

He said he was strong. He had no strength
But that which comes of breadth and length.
He said he was fond. But his fondness proved
The flame of an hour when he was moved.
He said he was true. His truth was but
A door that winds could open and shut.

And yet, and yet, as he came back,
Wandering in from the outward track,
We held our arms, and gave him our breast
As a pillowing place for his head to rest.
I span and Eve span,
A thread to bind the heart of man!   1918

The Hunter of the Black

Softly footed as a myall, silently he walked,
All the methods of his calling learned from men he stalked;
Tall he was, and deeply chested, eagle-eyed and still,
Every muscle in his body subject to his will.

Dark and swarthy was his colour; somewhere Hampshire born;
Knew no pity for the hunted, weakness met his scorn;
Asked no friendship, shunned no meetings, took what life might bring;
Came and went among his fellows something like a king;

Paid each debt with strict exactness, what the debt might be;
Called no man employed him master; master's equal, he;
Yet there was not one who sought him, none who held his hand;
Never father calling, bid him join the family band.

Tales and tales were told about him, how, from dawn till dark,
Noiselessly he trailed his quarry, never missed a mark,
How the twigs beneath his footstep 'moved but never broke',
How the very fires he kindled 'never made a smoke'.

Men would tell with puzzled wonder, marked on voice and brow,
How he'd stand a moment talking, leave, and none knew how;
'He was there!' and then had vanished, going as he came,
Like the passing of a shadow, like a falling flame.

Once (I heard it when it happened,) word was sent to him,
Of a lone black on Mimosa – O the hunting grim!
Through three days and nights he tracked him, never asking sleep;
Shot, for him who stole the country, him who killed a sheep.

Tomahawk in belt, as only adults needed shot,
No man knew how many notches totalled up his lot;
But old stockmen striking tallies, rough and ready made,
Reckoned on at least a thousand, naming camps decayed.

Time passed on, and years forgotten whitened with the dust;
He whose hands were red with slaughter sat among the just,
Kissed the children of his children, honoured in his place,
Turned and laid him down in quiet, asking God his grace.

1930

The Yarran-tree

The Lady of the Yarran-tree,
    She built herself a house,
And, happy in it, there she lived
    As tidy as a mouse;
She set a stool against the fire,
    And hung the broom beside,
And yet, although she sat alone,
    The door was open wide.

And she beside the Yarran-tree
      Was busy as could be;
She kept her sheep, she carded wool,
      Her bleach was white to see;
She baked her bread from wheat she grew,
      She tanned the good ox-hide;
And still, for all she sat alone,
      Her door was open wide.

The Lady of the Yarran-tree
      Looked out, one night, and saw
The dark hand of a stranger reach
      To lay on her his law;
She rose and drew the curtain close,
      Her little lamp to hide –
And yet, for all she was alone,
      The door stood open wide.

I asked her if she didn't know
      The fears of woman-kind,
That, though by day they come and go,
      Are still within the mind.
She looked at me and slowly said,
      'Such fears in me abide!'
And yet I knew she sat alone,
      The door left open wide.

The Yarran-tree against the spring
      Put on its amber green,
Like golden berries, on each twig,
      Its blossoms all were seen;
I saw the stranger watch the tree,
      The woman there inside –
And still, although she sat alone,
      The door was open wide.

To her beside the Yarran-tree,
      I said, 'Go buy a ring,
A ring of silver laced with steel,
      From which a shot may sing
Then, when the stranger hears the song,
      As winds shall bear it wide,
It will be safe to sit alone,
      The house-door open wide.'

Then she beside the Yarran-tree,
  She turned and looked at me,
She laid the spinning from her hand,
  And spake as still could be;
'Go you,' she said, 'and make the ring,
  And make of it your pride;
That I may safely sit alone,
  The door set open wide.'

I took the woman at her word,
  And straitly there I made
A ring of silver laced with steel,
  That sang as trumpets played;
I set it down against the step,
  And, though the door is wide,
The Lady of the Yarran-tree
  Dwells ever safe inside.

1939

Nationality

I have grown past hate and bitterness,
I see the world as one;
But though I can no longer hate,
My son is still my son.

All men at God's round table sit,
And all men must be fed;
But this loaf in my hand,
This loaf is my son's bread.

1954

Fourteen Men

Fourteen men,
And each hung down
Straight as a log
From his toes to his crown.

Fourteen men,
Chinamen they were,
Hanging on the trees
In their pig-tailed hair.

Honest poor men,
But the diggers said 'Nay!'
So they strung them all up
On a fine summer's day.

There they were hanging
As we drove by,
Grown-ups on the front seat,
On the back seat I.

That was Lambing Flat,
And still I can see
The straight up and down
Of each on his tree.

1954

C. J. DENNIS (1876-1938)

The Play

'Wot's in a name?' she sez . . . And then she sighs,
An' clasps 'er little 'ands, an' rolls 'er eyes.
'A rose,' she sez, 'be any other name
Would smell the same.
Oh, w'erefore art you Romeo, young sir?
Chuck yer ole pot, an' change yer moniker!'

Doreen an' me, we bin to see a show –
The swell two-dollar touch. Bong tong, yeh know
A chair apiece wiv velvit on the seat;
A slap-up treat.
The drarmer's writ be Shakespeare, years ago,
About a barmy goat called Romeo.

'Lady, be yonder moon I swear!' sez 'e.
An' then 'e climbs up on the balkiney;
An' there they smooge a treat, wiv pretty words,
Like two love-birds.
I nudge Doreen. She whispers, 'Ain't it grand!'
'Er eyes is shinin'; an' I squeeze 'er 'and.

Lambing Flat   on the Burragorang goldfields, near the present town of Young: the site
of riots directed against Chinese diggers in 1860-61. Although serious beatings occurred,
the suggestion of lynchings has not been verified.

'Wot's in a name?' she sez. 'Struth, I dunno.
Billo is just as good as Romeo.
She may be Juli-er or Juli-et – 'E loves 'er yet.
If she's the tart 'e wants, then she's 'is queen,
Names never count . . . But ar, I like 'Doreen!'

A sweeter, dearer sound I never 'eard;
Ther's music 'angs around that little word,
Doreen! . . . But wot was this I starts to say
About the play?
I'm off me beat. But when a bloke's in love
'Is thorts turn 'er way, like a 'omin' dove.

This Romeo 'e's lurkin' wiv a crew –
A dead tough crowd o' crooks – called Montague.
'Is cliner's push – wot's nicknamed Capulet –
They 'as 'em set.
Fair narks they are, jist like them back-street clicks,
Ixcep' they fights wiv skewers 'stid o' bricks.

Wot's in a name? Wot's in a string o' words?
They scraps in ole Verona wiv the'r swords,
An' never give a bloke a stray dog's chance,
An' that's Romance.
But when they deals it out wiv bricks an' boots
In Little Lon., they're low, degraded broots.

Wot's jist plain stoush wiv us, right 'ere to-day,
Is 'valler' if yer fur enough away.
Some time, some writer bloke will do the trick
Wiv Ginger Mick,
Of Spadger's Lane. 'E'll be a Romeo,
When 'e's bin dead five 'undred years or so.

Fair Juli-et, she gives 'er boy the tip.
Sez she: 'Don't sling that crowd o' mine no lip,
An' if you run agin a Capulet,
Jist do a get,'
'E swears 'e's done wiv lash; 'e'll chuck it clean.
(Same as I done when I first met Doreen.)

They smooge some more at that. Ar, strike me blue!
It gimme Joes to sit an' watch them two!
'E'd break away an' start to say good-bye,
An' then she'd sigh

'Ow, Ro-me-o!' an' git a strangle-holt,
An' 'ang around 'im like she feared 'e'd bolt.

Nex' day 'e words a gorspil cove about
A secrit weddin'; an' they plan it out.
'E spouts a piece about 'ow 'e's bewitched:
Then they git 'itched.
Now, 'ere's the place where I fair git the pip:
She's 'is for keeps, an' yet 'e lets 'er slip!

Ar! but 'e makes me sick! A fair gazob!
'E's jist the glarsey on the soulful sob,
'E'll sigh and spruik, an' 'owl a lovesick vow –
(The silly cow!)
But when 'e's got 'er, spliced an' on the straight,
'E crools the pitch, an' tries to kid it's Fate.

Aw! Fate me foot! Instid of slopin' soon
As 'e was wed, off on 'is 'oneymoon,
'un an' 'is cobber, called Mick Curio,
They 'ave to go
An' mix it wiv that push o' Capulets.
They look fer trouble; an' it's wot they gets.

A tug named Tyball (cousin to the skirt)
Sprags 'em an' makes a start to sling off dirt.
Nex' minnit there's a reel ole ding-dong go –
'Arf round or so.
Mick Curio, 'e gets it in the neck,
'Ar, rats!' 'e sez, an' passes in 'is check.

Quite natchril, Romeo gits wet as 'ell.
'It's me or you!' 'e 'owls, an' wiv a yell,
Plunks Tyball through the gizzard wiv 'is sword,
'Ow I ongcored!
'Put in the boot!' I sez. 'Put in the boot!'
'Ush!' sez Doreen . . . 'Shame!' sez some silly coot

Then Romeo, 'e dunno wot to do.
The cops gits busy, like they allwiz do,
An' nose around until 'e gits blue funk
An' does a bunk.
They wants 'is tart to wed some other guy.
'Ah, strike!' she sez. 'I wish that I could die!'

Now, this 'ere gorspil bloke's a fair shrewd 'ead.
Sez 'e, 'I'll dope yeh, so they'll *think* yer dead.'
(I tips 'e was a cunnin' sort, wot knoo
A thing or two).
She takes 'is knock-out drops, up in 'er room:
They think she's snuffed, an' plant 'er in 'er tomb.

Then things gits mixed a treat an' starts to whirl.
'Ere's Romeo comes back an' finds 'is girl
Tucked in 'er little coffing, cold an' stiff,
An' in a jiff
'E swallers lysol, throws a fancy fit,
'Ead over turkey, an' 'is soul 'as flit.

Then Juli-et wakes up an' sees 'im there,
Turns on the water-works an' tears 'er 'air,
'Dear love,' she sez, 'I cannot live alone!'
An', wif a moan,
She grabs 'is pockit knife, an' ends 'er cares . . .
'Peanuts or lollies!' sez a boy upstairs.   *1915*

Click Go the Shears

Out on the board the old shearer stands,
Grasping his shears in his long, bony hands,
Fixed is his gaze on a bare-bellied 'Joe',
Glory if he gets her, won't he make the ringer go.

> *Chorus*
> Click go the shears, boys, click, click, click,
> Wide is his blow and his hands move quick,
> The ringer looks around and is beaten by a blow,
> And curses the old snagger with the blue-bellied 'Joe.'

In the middle of the floor, in his cane-bottomed chair
Is the boss of the board, with eyes everywhere;
Notes well each fleece as it comes to the screen,
Paying strict attention if it's taken off clean.

---

board   *shearing floor*   Joe   *ewe*   ringer   *fastest shearer*
blow   *stroke of the shears*   snagger   *rough shearer*

[C. J. Dennis & Anonymous] 347

The colonial experience man, he is there, of course,
With his shiny leggin's, just got off his horse,
Casting round his eye like a real connoisseur,
Whistling the old tune, 'I'm the Perfect Lure.'

The tar-boy is there, awaiting in demand,
With his blackened tar-pot and his tarry hand;
Sees one old sheep with a cut upon its back,
Here's what he's waiting for, 'Tar, here, Jack!'

Shearing is all over and we've all got our cheques,
Roll up your swag for we're off on the tracks;
The first pub we come to, it's there we'll have a spree,
And everyone that comes along it's 'Come and drink with me!'

Down by the bar the old shearer stands,
Grasping his glass in his thin bony hands;
Fixed is his gaze on a green-painted keg,
Glory, he'll get down on it, ere he stirs a peg.

There we leave him standing, shouting for all hands.
Whilst all around him every 'shouter' stands;
His eyes are on the cask, which is now lowering fast,
He works hard, he drinks hard, and goes to hell at last!

JACK MATHIEU (1873-1949)

That Day at Boiling Downs

He was driving Irish tandem, but perhaps I talk at random –
I'd forgotten for a moment you are not all mulga-bred:
What I mean's he had his swag up through his having knocked his nag up;
He had come in off the Cooper – anyhow that's what he said.

And he looked as full of knowledge as a thirty-acre college
As he answered to the question – 'How's things look the way you comes
'Well, they *were* a trifle willing for a bit. There's been some killing;
In fact, I'm the sole survivor of the district . . . mine's a rum!'

Then we all got interested in the chap as he divested
Himself of a fat puppy that he carried in his shirt;
But he said no more until he had put down his swag and billy,
And had taken off his bluchers just to empty out the dirt.

Bits of cork were tied with laces round his hat in many places,
Out of which he gave the puppy some refreshment, and began –
'Sammy Suds was bound'ry-riding, quite content and law-abiding,
Till he bought some reading-matter one day off a hawker man.

'Then he started to go ratty, and began to fancy that he
Was an Injun on the warpath; so he plaited a lassoo,
Shaved and smeared his face with raddle, and knocked up a greenhide saddle,
After creeping on his belly through the grass a mile or two.

'Then he decked himself in feathers, and went out and scalped some wethers
Just to give himself a lesson in the sanguinary art;
Sammy then dug up the hatchet, chased a snake but couldn't catch it,
Killed his dog, lassooed a turkey, scalped the cat and made a start.

'And he caused a great sensation when he landed at the station;
And the boss said, "Hello! Sammy, what the devil's up with you?"
"I am Slimy Snake the Snorter! wretched pale-face, crave not quarter!"
He replied, and with a shot-gun nearly blew the boss in two.

'Next, the wood-and-water joey fell a victim to his bowie,
And the boss's weeping widow got a gash from ear to ear;
And you should have seen his guiver when he scalped the bullock-driver
And made openings for a horse-boy, servant-maid, and overseer.

'Counting jackaroos and niggers, he had put up double figures,
When ensued his awful combat with a party of new-chums,
All agog to do their duty, with no thought of home or beauty –
But he rubbed them out as rapid as a school-boy would his sums.

'Out across the silent river, with some duck-shot in his liver,
Went the store-man, and a lassooed lady left in the same boat.
Sam then solved the Chinese question – or at least made a suggestion –
For he dragged one from a barrel by the tail and cut his throat.

'But, with thus the job completed, Sammy he got over-heated
And dropped dead of apoplexy – I felt better when he did!
For I'd got an awful singein' while I watched this mulga engine
Doing all that I've related – through a cracked brick oven-lid.

'And when now I find men strangled, or I come across the mangled
Corpses of a crowd of people or depopulated towns,
Or ev'n a blood-stained river, I can scarce repress a shiver,
For my nerves were much affected that day out on Boiling Downs.'

(1899) 1927

[Jack Mathieu] 349

Bush Courtin'

When the milkin' music's ended, and the big cans stacked away,
An' the poddies have done drinkin', an' the neddies chew their hay,
Then I eat my snack while dressin', for Dad's always on the growl,
An' the cow-hairs from my love-lock brush, ere to my tryst I prowl.

Through my doss-room windy leavin', for the old man's ears are cocked,
I negotiate the pickets as the garden gate is locked;
For I hear the bittern's boomin' from the lily beds afar,
And my heart-strings are a-tingle to old Cupid's sweet guitar.

Jake is waitin' in the timber, where the lace-like shadows fall;
'Tis his signal that is stealin' like the mopoke's croakin' call;
Then he clasps me to his shirt-front with a bushman's brawny squeeze,
An' his whiskers sweep my freckles like soft tangles off the trees!

We discuss the price of sorghum; will there be a rise in wheat?
(Just a crumb or two of love-talk, for this fare is awful sweet!)
An' Jake's gettin' in his taters – half a patch a day he digs –
While his poddies feed themselves now; an' he's goin' to sell his pigs!

Then we let the world go hang there, as together close we cling
An' swear we'll love each other whate'er prices Fate may bring
(Jake's old trusty dog is watchin' where the shadows dim the track),
An' into Life's old, grey portmanteau a thousand joys we pack.

How the saucy moonbeams mock us, an' the grey bats tauntin' fly –
Seems they know that we are wanted, that we're courtin' on the sly;
We'll be married 'after harvest' if the wheat will only rise,
An' Dad will get what he's expectin' – that's a mighty big surprise!

(1904)

Wallaby Stew

Poor Dad, he got five years or more, as everybody knows,
And now he lives in Maitland gaol, broad arrows on his clothes;
He branded old Brown's cleanskins and he never left a tail
So I'll relate the family's fate since Dad got put in gaol.

Chorus
So stir the wallaby stew, make soup of the kangaroo tail
I tell you things is pretty tough since Dad got put in gaol.

Our sheep all died a month ago, of footrot and the fluke;
Our cow got shot last Christmas day by my big brother Luke;
Our mother's got a shearer cove forever within hail;
The family will have grown a bit when Dad gets out of gaol.

Our Bess got shook upon some bloke, but he's gone, we don't know where;
He used to act about the sheds, but he ain't acted square;
I sold the buggy on my own, and the place is up for sale;
That won't be all that has been junked when Dad comes out of gaol.

They let Dad out before his time to give us a surprise.
He came and slowly looked around, then gently blessed our eyes;
He shook hands with the shearer cove, and said that things seemed stale,
And left him here to shepherd us, and battled back into gaol.

ARTHUR H. ADAMS (1872-1936)

The Australian

Once more this Autumn-earth is ripe,
Parturient of another type.

While with the Past old nations merge
His foot is on the Future's verge;

They watch him, as they huddle pent,
Striding a spacious continent,

Above the level desert's marge
Looming in his aloofness large.

No flower with fragile sweetness graced –
A lank weed wrestling with the waste.

Pallid of face and gaunt of limb,
The sweetness withered out of him.

Sombre, indomitable, wan,
The juices dried, the glad youth gone.

A little weary from his birth;
His laugh the spectre of a mirth.

Bitter beneath a bitter sky,
To Nature he has no reply.

Wanton, perhaps, and cruel. Yes,
Is not his sun more merciless?

Joy has such niggard dole to give,
He laughs, a child, just glad to live.

So drab and neutral is his day
He gleans a splendour in the grey,

And from his life's monotony
He lifts a subtle melody.

When earth so poor a banquet makes
His pleasures at a gulp he takes.

The feast is his to the last crumb;
Drink while he can . . . the drought will come.

His heart a sudden tropic flower,
He loves and loathes within an hour.

Yet you who by the pools abide,
Judge not the man who swerves aside.

He sees beyond your hazy fears;
He roads the desert of the years.

Rearing his cities in the sand,
He builds where even God has banned.

With green a continent he crowns,
And stars a wilderness with towns.

His gyves of steel the great plain wears:
With paths the distances he snares.

A child who takes a world for toy,
To build a nation, or destroy.

His childish features frozen stern,
A nation's task he has to learn,

From feeble tribes to federate
One splendid peace-encompassed State.

But if there be no goal to reach?
The way lies open, dawns beseech!

Enough that he lay down his load
A little further on the road.

So, toward undreamt-of destinies
He slouches down the centuries.   *1899*

CHRISTOPHER BRENNAN (1870-1932)

from *Towards the Source*

The yellow gas is fired from street to street
past rows of heartless homes and hearths unlit,
dead churches, and the unending pavement beat
by crowds – say rather, haggard shades that flit

round nightly haunts of their delusive dream,
where'er our paradisal instinct starves: –
till on the utmost post, its sinuous gleam
crawls in the oily water of the wharves;

where Homer's sea loses his keen breath, hemm'd
what place rebellious piles were driven down –
the priestlike waters to this task condemn'd
to wash the roots of the inhuman town! –

where fat and strange-eyed fish that never saw
the outer deep, broad halls of sapphire light,
glut in the city's draught each nameless maw:
– and there, wide-eyed unto the soulless night,

methinks a drown'd maid's face might fitly show
what we have slain, a life that had been free,
clean, large, nor thus tormented – even so
as are the skies, the salt winds and the sea.

Ay, we had saved our days and kept them whole,
to whom no part in our old joy remains,
had felt those bright winds sweeping thro' our soul
and all the keen sea tumbling in our veins,

had thrill'd to harps of sunrise, when the height
whitens, and dawn dissolves in virgin tears,
or caught, across the hush'd ambrosial night,
the choral music of the swinging spheres,

or drunk the silence if nought else – But no!
and from each rotting soul distil in dreams
a poison, o'er the old earth creeping slow,
that kills the flowers and curdles the live streams,

that taints the fresh breath of re-risen day
and reeks across the pale bewilder'd moon:
– shall we be cleans'd and how? I only pray,
red flame or deluge, may that end be soon!   *1897*

from *The Forest of Night*

Fire in the heavens, and fire along the hills,
and fire made solid in the flinty stone,
thick-massed or scatter'd pebble, fire that fills
the breathless hour that lives in fire alone.

This valley, long ago the patient bed
of floods that carv'd its antient amplitude,
in stillness of the Egyptian crypt outspread,
endures to drown in noon-day's tyrant mood.

Behind the veil of burning silence bound,
vast life's innumerous busy littleness
is hush'd in vague-conjectured blur of sound
that dulls the brain with slumbrous weight, unless

some dazzling puncture let the stridence throng
in the cicada's torture-point of song.

(1899) 1914

from *The Wanderer*

When window-lamps had dwindled, then I rose
and left the town behind me; and on my way
passing a certain door I stopt, remembering
how once I stood on its threshold, and my life
was offer'd to me, a road how different
from that of the years since gone! and I had but
to rejoin an olden path, once dear, since left.
All night I have walk'd and my heart was deep awake,
remembering ways I dream'd and that I chose,
remembering lucidly, and was not sad,
being brimm'd with all the liquid and clear dark
of the night that was not stirr'd with any tide;
for leaves were silent and the road gleam'd pale,
following the ridge, and I was alone with night.
But now I am come among the rougher hills
and grow aware of the sea that somewhere near
is restless; and the flood of night is thinn'd
and stars are whitening. O, what horrible dawn
will bare me the way and crude lumps of the hills
and the homeless concave of the day, and bare
the ever-restless, ever-complaining sea?   (1902) 1914

from *The Wanderer*

I cry to you as I pass your windows in the dusk;

Ye have built you unmysterious homes and ways in the wood
where of old ye went with sudden eyes to the right and left;
and your going was now made safe and your staying comforted,
for the forest edge itself, holding old savagery
in unsearch'd glooms, was your houses' friendly barrier.
And now that the year goes winterward, ye thought to hide
behind your gleaming panes, and where the hearth sings merrily
make cheer with meat and wine, and sleep in the long night,
and the uncared wastes might be a crying unhappiness.
But I, who have come from the outer night, I say to you
the winds are up and terribly will they shake the dry wood:
the woods shall awake, hearing them, shall awake to be toss'd and riven,
and make a cry and a parting in your sleep all night
as the wither'd leaves go whirling all night along all ways.

And when ye come forth at dawn, uncomforted by sleep,
ye shall stand at amaze, beholding all the ways overhidden
with worthless drift of the dead and all your broken world:
and ye shall not know whence the winds have come, nor shall ye know
whither the yesterdays have fled, or if they were.

(1902) 1914

Because she would ask me why I loved her

If questioning could make us wise
no eyes would ever gaze in eyes;
if all our tale were told in speech
no mouths would wander each to each.

Were spirits free from mortal mesh
and love not bound in hearts of flesh
no aching breasts would yearn to meet
and find their ecstasy complete.

For who is there that lives and knows
the secret powers by which he grows?
Were knowledge all, what were our need
to thrill and faint and sweetly bleed?

Then seek not, sweet, the *If* and *Why*
I love you now until I die:
For I must love because I live
And life in me is what you give.

(written 1923) 1960

R. H. CROLL (1869-1947)

Australia (In Contemporary Literature)

Whalers, damper, swag and nosebag, Johnny-cakes and billy-tea,
Murrumburrah, Meremendicoowoke, Yoularbudgeree,
Cattle-duffers, bold bushrangers, diggers, drovers, bush race courses,
And on all the other pages horses, horses, horses, horses.

(1899)

The Keening

We are the women and children
    Of the men that mined for gold,
Heavy are we with sorrow,
    Heavy as heart can hold;
Galled are we with injustice,
    Sick to the soul of loss –
Husbands and sons and brothers
    Slain for the yellow dross!

We are the women and children
    Of the men that died like sheep,
'Stoping' the stubborn matrix,
    Piling the mullock heap,
Stifling in torrid 'rises',
    Stumbling with stupid tread
Along the Vale of the Shadow
    To the thud of the stamper-head!

We are the women and children
    Of the miners that delved below –
Main shaft and winze and crosscut –
    Opening the deadly 'show'.
Look at us! Yea, in our faces!
    God! Are ye not ashamed
In the sight of your godless fellows
    Of the men ye have killed and maimed?

They moiled like gnomes in the 'faces,'
    They choked in the "fracteur' fumes,
And your dividends paved the pathways
    That led to their early tombs.
With Death in the sleepless night-shifts
    They diced for the prize ye drew;
And the Devil loaded the pieces –
    But the stakes were held by you!

Ye were the lords of Labor;
    They were the slaves of Need.
Homes had they for the keeping,
    Children to clothe and feed!

Ye paid them currency wages –
    Shall it stand to your souls for shrift
That ye bought them in open market
    For 'seven-and-six a shift?'

Wise in your generation,
    Cunning are ye in your day!
But 'ware of the stealthy vengeance
    That never your wealth shall stay!
They won it – yea, with their life-blood;
    Ye laughed at the sacrifice;
But by every drop of your spilling
    We shall hold you to pay the price!

Ye have sown the wind, to your sorrow;
    Ye have sown by the coward's code,
Where the glimmering candles gutter,
    And the rock-drill bites on the lode!
Ye have sown to the jangle of stampers,
    To the brawl of the Stock Exchange,
And your children shall reap the whirlwind
    On the terms that the gods arrange.

And ye, who counsel the nation,
    Statesmen who rule the State!
Foolish are ye in your weakness,
    Wise are we in our hate!
Traitors and false that pander
    To the spillers of human life,
Slaying with swords of silence
    Who dared not slay with the knife!

And ye of the House of Pilate,
    Ye who gibber of Christ
At the foot of the golden crosses
    Where the sons of men are triced!
Ye who whimper of patience,
    Who slay with a loose-lipped lie
At the word of the fat blasphemers
    Whose poppet-heads mock the sky!

We are the women and children
    Of the men that ye mowed like wheat;
Some of us slave for a pittance –
    Some of us walk the street;

Bodies and souls, ye have scourged us;
   Ye have winnowed us flesh from bone:
But, by the God ye have flouted,
   We will come again for our own!   *1911*

J. K. McDOUGALL (1867-1957)

The White Man's Burden

Take up the White Man's Burden
   Lift high the blazing cross;
For Greed must have his guerdon,
   Whoever counts the loss.
Beneath the White Man's banner,
   Enlist, ye sons of blood,
Leave cot and peaceful manor
   And march by field and flood.

Let War and War's dread rumour
   Bring light and Christian hope
To crowds ye deftly humour
   With sword and gallow's rope.
Send forth, with blood anointed,
   The butchers that ye breed,
To push the frauds appointed
   To gild the hand of Greed.

Your sires were gods of slaughter;
   Where still their altars are,
On shudd'ring land and water,
   Be yours their bloody star.
Turn on the crouching savage
   Your cannon gorged with shot;
Let Might and Murder ravage,
   God sleeps and hears you not.

Spur on the war-horse plunging
   Proud crested o'er the slain;
With sword blades, fiercely lunging,
   Wet earth with rose red rain.

The White Man's Burden   *McDougall wrote this poem in 1902, naming it from the title of a poem (1899) on imperial responsibility by Rudyard Kipling.*

Let nations see your sabres
    Turn flashing in the sun,
Cut down your Christian neighbours
    High Mammon's will be done!

Ride down the rebel workers,
    Ride down their children, too;
Ye are the tools of shirkers,
    Whose red behests ye do.
Ye are the rich men's beagles,
    Kill while your hirers gloat;
Feed ye the wolves and eagles
    On dead men – till they bloat.

Ride down – ye have the horses –
    Strike down with lances keen;
Fill up the gaps with corses,
    Between each still machine.
Drive home the mob like cattle,
    Take ye the spoilers' pay;
Ride grimly into battle
    And slay, and slay, and slay.

Ye are the White Man's engines;
    Ye fight and force for him;
Fill up his cup of vengeance,
    Yea, fill it to the brim.
Paid bullies of the robbers,
    Your murders are not sin;
Kill for the Trusts and Jobbers –
    Sock ye the bay'nets in.

Take up the White Man's burden,
    Hired slaves march forth and slay;
The gear of battle gird on,
    Loose Hell and darken day.
Thrust brand at breast of brother,
    And hear above the strife
The wail of some White Mother,
    The sob of some White Wife.

Let conquest be your charter
    To force the rights of Trade;
(Arise ye rogues who barter,
    And track the conqu'ror's blade.)

Fresh plunder lies before you;
    Law quits the stricken land;
A Christian flag waves o'er you
    To back the thieving hand.

Ye are the sordid killers,
    Ye murder for a fee;
Ye prop like rotten pillars
    Trade's lust and treachery.
Hog souled and dirty handed
    Ye sell yourselves for gain,
And stand forever branded,
    Red felons after Cain.

Ye are the fools and flunkeys;
    Ye die to serve the great –
The rooks and gilded monkeys
    Who eat the fat of State.
Ye fall on alien places;
    On foreign wastes ye lie,
Stiff-limbed, with battered faces
    Turned livid to the sky.

The shouts of yobs and wenches –
    Loose cheer and blare of brass
Have died beyond the trenches,
    Have passed as echoes pass.
Long lines of helmets gleaming,
    A march in battle played,
Ye see and hear and dreaming
    Your lives swoon out in shade.

Fill up your foaming glasses
    With blood instead of wine,
And pledge the robber classes
    And kings as base as swine.
Drink to each paid defender,
    While loyal boozers rant;
And veil with flow'rs and splendour,
    The spectre face of Want.

Race ever race is spoiling;
    The strong hand triumphs still;
Let Progress cease her toiling,
    Man's mission is to kill.

Shed blood and let it curd on
  The patriot's tear-wet cheek
Take up the White Man's burden,
  And rob and wrong the weak.   *(written 1902) (1915) 1922*

HENRY LAWSON (1867-1922)

Middleton's Rouseabout

Tall and freckled and sandy,
  Face of a country lout;
This was the picture of Andy,
  Middleton's Rouseabout.

Type of a coming nation,
  In the land of cattle and sheep,
Worked on Middleton's station,
  'Pound a week and his keep'.

On Middleton's wide dominions
  Plied the stockwhip and shears;
Hadn't any opinions,
  Hadn't any 'idears'.

Swiftly the years went over,
  Liquor and drought prevailed;
Middleton went as a drover
  After his station had failed.

Type of a careless nation,
  Men who are soon played out,
Middleton was: – and his station
  Was bought by the Rouseabout.

Flourishing beard and sandy,
  Tall and solid and stout:
This is the picture of Andy,
  Middleton's Rouseabout.

Now on his own dominions
  Works with his overseers;
Hasn't any opinions,
  Hasn't any idears.   *(1890) 1896*

Freedom on the Wallaby

Our fathers toiled for bitter bread
    While idlers thrived beside them;
But food to eat and clothes to wear
    Their native land denied them.
They left their native land in spite
    Of royalties' regalia,
And so they came, or if they stole
    Were sent out to Australia.

They struggled hard to make a home,
    Hard grubbing 'twas and clearing.
They weren't troubled much with toffs
    When they were pioneering;
And now that we have made the land
    A garden full of promise,
Old greed must crook his dirty hand
    And come to take it from us.

But Freedom's on the Wallaby,
    She'll knock the tyrants silly,
She's going to light another fire
    And boil another billy.
We'll make the tyrants feel the sting
    Of those that they would throttle;
They needn't say the fault is ours
    If blood should stain the wattle.

                                  (1891) 1913

Up the Country

I am back from up the country – very sorry that I went –
Seeking for the Southern poets' land whereon to pitch my tent;
I have lost a lot of idols, which were broken on the track,
Burnt a lot of fancy verses, and I'm glad that I am back.
Further out may be the pleasant scenes of which our poets boast,
But I think the country's rather more inviting round the coast.
Anyway, I'll stay at present at a boarding-house in town,
Drinking beer and lemon-squashes, taking baths and cooling down.

---

on the Wallaby   *on the wallaby track: tramping the outback to find work*

'Sunny plains!' Great Scott! – those burning wastes of barren soil and sand
With their everlasting fences stretching out across the land!
Desolation where the crow is! Desert where the eagle flies,
Paddocks where the luny bullock starts and stares with reddened eyes;
Where, in clouds of dust enveloped, roasted bullock-drivers creep
Slowly past the sun-dried shepherd dragged behind his crawling sheep.
Stunted peak of granite gleaming, glaring like a molten mass
Turned from some infernal furnace on a plain devoid of grass.

Miles and miles of thirsty gutters – strings of muddy water-holes
In the place of 'shining rivers' – 'walled by cliffs and forest boles'.
Barren ridges, gullies, ridges! where the everlasting flies –
Fiercer than the plagues of Egypt – swarm about your blighted eyes!
Bush! where there is no horizon! where the buried bushman sees
Nothing – Nothing! but the sameness of the ragged, stunted trees!
Lonely hut where drought's eternal – suffocating atmosphere –
Where the God-forgotten hatter dreams of city life and beer.

Treacherous tracks that trap the stranger, endless roads that gleam and glare,
Dark and evil-looking gullies, hiding secrets here and there!
Dull dumb flats and stony rises, where the toiling bullocks bake,
And the sinister 'gohanna', and the lizard, and the snake.
Land of day and night – no morning freshness, and no afternoon,
When the great white sun in rising brings the summer heat in June.
Dismal country for the exile, when the shades begin to fall
From the sad heart-breaking sunset, to the newchum worst of all.

Dreary land in rainy weather, with the endless clouds that drift
O'er the bushman like a blanket that the Lord will never lift –
Dismal land when it is raining – growl of floods, and, O the woosh
Of the rain and wind together on the dark bed of the bush –
Ghastly fires in lonely humpies where the granite rocks are piled
In the rain-swept wildernesses that are wildest of the wild.

Land where gaunt and haggard women live alone and work like men,
Till their husbands, gone a-droving, will return to them again:
Homes of men! if homes had ever such a God-forgotten place,
Where the wild selector's children fly before a stranger's face.
Home of tragedy applauded by the dingoes' dismal yell,
Heaven of the shanty-keeper – fitting fiend for such a hell –
And the wallaroos and wombats, and, of course, the curlew's call –
And the lone sundowner tramping ever onward through it all!

I am back from up the country, up the country where I went
Seeking for the Southern poets' land whereon to pitch my tent;
I have shattered many idols out along the dusty track,
Burnt a lot of fancy verses – and I'm glad that I am back.
I believe the Southern poets' dream will not be realized
Till the plains are irrigated and the land is humanized.
I intend to stay at present, as I said before, in town
Drinking beer and lemon-squashes, taking baths and cooling down.

(1892) 1896

The Sliprails and The Spur

The colours of the setting sun
    Withdrew across the Western land –
He raised the sliprails, one by one,
    And shot them home with trembling hand;
Her brown hands clung – her face grew pale –
    Ah! quivering chin and eyes that brim! –
One quick, fierce kiss across the rail,
    And, 'Good-bye, Mary!'·'Good-bye, Jim!'

> *O he rides hard to race the pain*
>   *Who rides from love, who rides from home;*
> *But he rides slowly home again,*
>   *Whose heart has learnt to love and roam.*

A hand upon the horse's mane,
    And one foot in the stirrup set,
And, stooping back to kiss again,
    With 'Good-bye, Mary! don't you fret!
When I come back' – he laughed for her –
    'We do not know how soon 'twill be;
I'll whistle as I round the spur –
    You let the sliprails down for me.'

She gasped for sudden loss of hope,
    As, with a backward wave to her,
He cantered down the grassy slope
    And swiftly round the dark'ning spur.
Black-pencilled panels standing high,
    And darkness fading into stars,
And blurring fast against the sky,
    A faint white form beside the bars.

And often at the set of sun,
    In winter bleak and summer brown,
She'd steal across the little run,
    And shyly let the sliprails down,
And listen there when darkness shut
    The nearer spur in silence deep;
And when they called her from the hut
    Steal home and cry herself to sleep.

A great white gate where sliprails were,
    A brick house 'neath the mountain brow,
The 'mad girl' buried by the spur
    So long ago, forgotten now.

        And he rides hard to dull the pain
            Who rides from one that loves him best;
        And he rides slowly back again
            Whose restless heart must rove for rest.

                        (1899) 1900

To Victor Daley

I thought that silence would be best,
    But I a call have heard,
And, Victor, after all the rest,
    I well might say a word:
The day and work is nearly done,
    And ours the victory,
And we are resting, one by one,
    In graveyards by the sea.

You made a jest on that last night,
    I met it with a laugh:
You wondered which of us should write
    The other's epitaph.
We filled the glasses to the brim –
    'The land's own wine' you know –
And solemnly we drank to him
    Who should be first to go.

No ribald jest; we were but two –
    The royst'ring days were past –
And in our heart of hearts we knew
    That one was going fast.

We both knew who should win the race –
    Were rest or fame the prize –
As with a quaint smile on your face
    You looked into my eyes.

But then you talked of other nights,
    When, gay from dusk to dawn,
You wasted hours with other lights
    That went where you have gone.
You spoke not of the fair and 'fast',
    But of the pure and true –
'Sweet ugly women of the past'
    Who stood so well by you.

You talked about old struggles brave,
    But in a saddened tone –
The swindles editors forgave
    For laughter's sake alone.
You talked of humorous distress
    And bailiffs that you knew,
But with a touch of bitterness
    I'd never seen in you.

No need for tears or quick-caught breath –
    You sleep not in the sand –
No need for ranting song of death,
    With the death drink in our hand.
No need for vain invective hurled
    At 'cruel destiny';
Though you seem dead to all the world
    You are not dead to me.

I see you walk into the room –
    We aye remember how –
And, looking back into the gloom,
    You'll smile about it now.
'Twas Victor's entry, solemn style –
    With verse or paragraph:
Though we so often saw your smile
    How many heard you laugh?

They dare to write about the man
    That they have never seen:

The blustering false Bohemian
    That you have never been;
Some with the false note in their voice
    And with the false tear shed,
Who in their secret heart rejoice
    For one more rival – dead.

They miss the poems, real and true,
    Where your heart's blood was shed,
And rave of reckless things that you
    Threw out for bitter bread.
They 'weep' and 'worship' while you 'rest',
    They drivel and they dote –
But, Victor, we remember best
    The things we never wrote.

The things that lie between us two,
    The things I'll never tell.
A fool, I stripped my soul, but you –
    You wore your mask too well.
(How strangely human all men be,
    Though each one plays a part.)
You only dropped it once for me,
    But then I saw your heart.

A souls'-match, such as one might strike
    With or without intent
(How strangely all men are alike –
    With masks so different).
No need to drop the mask again,
    On that last night, I know –
It chanced when we were sober men,
    Some seven years ago.

They slander you, fresh in the sand,
    They slander me alive;
But, when their foul souls flee the land,
    Our spirits shall arrive.
In slime and envy let them rave,
    And let the worst be said:
'A drunkard at a drunkard's grave,'
    'A brilliant drunkard dead.'

Because we would not crawl to them,
    Their hands we would not shake,

Because their greed we would condemn,
    Their bribes we would not take:
Because unto the fair and true
    Our hearts and songs we gave –
But I forgot them when I threw
    My white flower on your grave.

So let us turn, and with a smile
    Let those poor creatures pass,
While we, the few who wait awhile,
    Drink to an empty glass.
We'll live as in the days gone by,
    To no god shall we bow –
Though, Victor, there are times when I
    Feel jealous of you now.

But I'll have done with solemn songs,
    Save for my country's sake;
It is not meet, for all the wrongs,
    That any heart should break.
So many need to weep and smile,
    Though all the rest should frown,
That I'd take your burden up awhile
    Where you have laid it down.   (1906) 1913

ANONYMOUS

The Bastard from the Bush

As night was falling slowly on city, town and bush,
From a slum in Jones's Alley came the Captain of the Push,
And his whistle, loud and piercing, woke the echoes of the Rocks,
And a dozen ghouls came slouching round the corners of the blocks.

Then the Captain jerked a finger at a stranger by the kerb,
Whom he qualified politely with an adjective and verb.
Then he made the introduction: 'Here's a covey from the bush;
Fuck me blind, he wants to join us, be a member of the Push!'

The Bastard from the Bush *has survived in several forms through oral transmission*
and fugitive publication. Its similarity to Henry Lawson's 'The Captain of the Push'
(1892) has fed speculation that he may be the author.

Then the stranger made this answer to the Captain of the lush:
'Why, fuck me dead, I'm Foreskin Fred, the Bastard from the Bush!
I've been in every two-up school from Darwin to the Loo;
I've ridden colts and blackgins; what more can a bugger do?'

'Are you game to break a window?' said the Captain of the Push.
I'd knock a fucking house down!' said the Bastard from the Bush.
'Would you out a man and rob him?' said the Captain of the Push.
'I'd knock him down and fuck him!' said the Bastard from the Bush.

'Would you dong a bloody copper if you caught the cunt alone?
Would you stoush a swell or Chinkie, split his garret with a stone?
Would you have a moll to keep you; would you swear off work for good?'
Said the Bastard: 'My colonial silver-mounted oath I would!'

'Would you care to have a gasper?' said the Captain of the Push.
I'll take that bloody packet!' said the Bastard from the Bush.
Then the Pushites all took council, saying, 'Fuck me, but he's game!
Let's make him our star basher; he'll live up to his name.'

So they took him to their hideout, that Bastard from the Bush,
And granted him all privileges appertaining to the Push.
But soon they found his little ways were more than they could stand,
And finally their Captain addressed the members of his band:

'Now listen here, you buggers, we've caught a fucking Tartar.
At every kind of bludging, that Bastard is a starter.
At poker and at two-up he's shook our fucking rolls;
He swipes our fucking likker and he robs our bloody molls!'

So down in Jones's Alley all the members of the Push
Laid a dark and dirty ambush for that Bastard from the Bush.
But against the wall of Riley's pub the Bastard made a stand,
A nasty grin upon his dial; a bike-chain in each hand.

They sprang upon him in a bunch, but one by one they fell,
With crack of bone, unearthly groan, and agonising yell,
Till the sorely battered Captain, spitting teeth and gouts of blood,
Held an ear all torn and bleeding in a hand bedaubed with mud.

'You low polluted Bastard!' snarled the Captain of the Push,
'Get back where your sort belongs – that's somewhere in the bush.
And I hope heaps of misfortunes may soon tumble down on you;
May some lousy harlot dose you till your ballocks turn sky-blue!

'May the itching piles torment you; may corns grow on your feet!
May crabs as big as spiders attack your balls a treat!
And when you're down and outed, to a hopeless bloody wreck,
May you slip back through your arsehole and break your fucking neck!'

(from 1880s–1914)

BARCROFT BOAKE (1866-92)

Where the Dead Men Lie

Out on the wastes of the Never Never –
   That's where the dead men lie!
There where the heat-waves dance for ever –
   That's where the dead men lie!
That's where the Earth's loved sons are keeping
Endless tryst: not the west wind sweeping
Feverish pinions can wake their sleeping –
   Out where the dead men lie!

Where brown Summer and Death have mated –
   That's where the dead men lie!
Loving with fiery lust unsated –
   That's where the dead men lie!
Out where the grinning skulls bleach whitely
Under the saltbush sparkling brightly;
Out where the wild dogs chorus nightly –
   That's where the dead men lie!

Deep in the yellow, flowing river –
   That's where the dead men lie!
Under the banks where the shadows quiver –
   That's where the dead men lie!
Where the platypus twists and doubles,
Leaving a train of tiny bubbles;
Rid at last of their earthly troubles –
   That's where the dead men lie!

East and backward pale faces turning –
   That's how the dead men lie!
Gaunt arms stretched with a voiceless yearning –
   That's how the dead men lie!

Oft in the fragrant hush of nooning
Hearing again their mothers' crooning,
Wrapt for aye in a dreamful swooning –
    That's how the dead men lie!

Only the hand of Night can free them –
    That's when the dead men fly!
Only the frightened cattle see them –
    See the dead men go by!
Cloven hoofs beating out one measure,
Bidding the stockman know no leisure –
That's when the dead men take their pleasure!
    That's when the dead men fly!

Ask, too, the never-sleeping drover:
    He sees the dead pass by;
Hearing them call to their friends – the plover,
    Hearing the dead men cry;
Seeing their faces stealing, stealing,
Hearing their laughter pealing, pealing,
Watching their grey forms wheeling, wheeling
    Round where the cattle lie!

Strangled by thirst and fierce privation –
    That's how the dead men die!
Out on Moneygrub's farthest station –
    That's how the dead men die!
Hardfaced greybeards, youngsters callow;
Some mounds cared for, some left fallow;
Some deep down, yet others shallow;
    Some having but the sky.

Moneygrub, as he sips his claret,
    Looks with complacent eye
Down at his watch-chain, eighteen-carat –
    There, in his club, hard by:
Recks not that every link is stamped with
Names of the men whose limbs are cramped with
Too long lying in grave mould, camped with
    Death where the dead men lie.   (1891) 1897

A. B. Paterson ('The Banjo') (1864-1941)

Clancy of the Overflow

I had written him a letter which I had, for want of better
   Knowledge, sent to where I met him down the Lachlan, years ago,
He was shearing when I knew him, so I sent the letter to him,
   Just on spec, addressed as follows, 'Clancy, of The Overflow.'

And an answer came directed in a writing unexpected,
   (And I think the same was written with a thumb-nail dipped in tar)
'Twas his shearing mate who wrote it, and *verbatim* I will quote it:
   'Clancy's gone to Queensland droving, and we don't know where he are.'

     *

In my wild erratic fancy visions come to me of Clancy
   Gone a-droving 'down the Cooper' where the Western drovers go;
As the stock are slowly stringing, Clancy rides behind them singing,
   For the drover's life has pleasures that the townsfolk never know.

And the bush has friends to meet him, and their kindly voices greet him
   In the murmur of the breezes and the river on its bars,
And he sees the vision splendid of the sunlit plains extended,
   And at night the wondrous glory of the everlasting stars.

     *

I am sitting in my dingy little office, where a stingy
   Ray of sunlight struggles feebly down between the houses tall,
And the foetid air and gritty of the dusty, dirty city
   Through the open window floating, spreads its foulness over all.

And in place of lowing cattle, I can hear the fiendish rattle
   Of the tramways and the buses making hurry down the street;
And the language uninviting of the gutter children fighting,
   Comes fitfully and faintly through the ceaseless tramp of feet.

And the hurrying people daunt me, and their pallid faces haunt me
   As they shoulder one another in their rush and nervous haste,
With their eager eyes and greedy, and their stunted forms and weedy,
   For townsfolk have no time to grow, they have no time to waste.

And I somehow rather fancy that I'd like to change with Clancy,
   Like to take a turn at droving where the seasons come and go,
While he faced the round eternal of the cash-book and the journal –
   But I doubt he'd suit the office, Clancy, of The Overflow.

                                 (1889) 1895

The Man from Snowy River

There was movement at the station, for the word had passed around
    That the colt from old Regret had got away,
And had joined the wild bush horses – he was worth a thousand pound,
    So all the cracks had gathered to the fray.
All the tried and noted riders from the stations near and far
    Had mustered at the homestead overnight,
For the bushmen love hard riding where the wild bush horses are,
    And the stock-horse snuffs the battle with delight.

There was Harrison, who made his pile when Pardon won the cup,
    The old man with his hair as white as snow;
But few could ride beside him when his blood was fairly up –
    He would go wherever horse and man could go.
And Clancy of the Overflow came down to lend a hand,
    No better horseman ever held the reins;
For never horse could throw him while the saddle-girths would stand –
    He learnt to ride while droving on the plains.

And one was there, a stripling on a small and weedy beast,
    He was something like a racehorse undersized,
With a touch of Timor pony – three parts thoroughbred at least –
    And such as are by mountain horsemen prized.
He was hard and tough and wiry – just the sort that won't say die –
    There was courage in his quick impatient tread;
And he bore the badge of gameness in his bright and fiery eye,
    And the proud and lofty carriage of his head.

But still so slight and weedy, one would doubt his power to stay,
    And the old man said, 'That horse will never do
For a long and tiring gallop – lad, you'd better stop away,
    Those hills are far too rough for such as you.'
So he waited sad and wistful – only Clancy stood his friend –
    'I think we ought to let him come,' he said;
'I warrant he'll be with us when he's wanted at the end,
    For both his horse and he are mountain bred.'

'He hails from Snowy River, up by Kosciusko's side,
    Where the hills are twice as steep and twice as rough,
Where a horse's hoofs strike firelight from the flint stones every stride,
    The man that holds his own is good enough.
And the Snowy River riders on the mountains make their home,
    'Where the river runs those giant hills between;

I have seen full many horsemen since I first commenced to roam,
    But nowhere yet such horsemen have I seen.'

So he went – they found the horses by the big mimosa clump –
    They raced away towards the mountain's brow,
And the old man gave his orders, 'Boys, go at them from the jump,
    'No use to try for fancy riding now.
'And, Clancy, you must wheel them, try and wheel them to the right.
    'Ride boldly, lad, and never fear the spills,
'For never yet was rider that could keep the mob in sight,
    'If once they gain the shelter of those hills.'

So Clancy rode to wheel them – he was racing on the wing
    Where the best and boldest riders take their place,
And he raced his stock-horse past them, and he made the ranges ring
    With the stockwhip, as he met them face to face.
Then they halted for a moment, while he swung the dreaded lash,
    But they saw their well-loved mountain full in view,
And they charged beneath the stockwhip with a sharp and sudden dash,
    And off into the mountain scrub they flew.

Then fast the horsemen followed, where the gorges deep and black
    Resounded to the thunder of their tread,
And the stockwhips woke the echoes, and they fiercely answered back
    From cliffs and crags that beetled overhead.
And upward, ever upward, the wild horses held their way,
    Where mountain ash and kurrajong grew wide;
And the old man muttered fiercely, 'We may bid the mob good day,
    'No man can hold them down the other side.'

When they reached the mountain's summit, even Clancy took a pull,
    It well might make the boldest hold their breath,
The wild hop scrub grew thickly, and the hidden ground was full
    Of wombat holes, and any slip was death.
But the man from Snowy River let the pony have his head,
    And he swung his stockwhip round and gave a cheer,
And he raced him down the mountain like a torrent down its bed,
    While the others stood and watched in very fear.

He sent the flint-stones flying, but the pony kept his feet,
    He cleared the fallen timber in his stride,
And the man from Snowy River never shifted in his seat –
    It was grand to see that mountain horseman ride.

Through the stringy barks and saplings, on the rough and broken ground,
    Down the hillside at a racing pace he went;
And he never drew the bridle till he landed safe and sound,
    At the bottom of that terrible descent.

He was right among the horses as they climbed the farther hill,
    And the watchers on the mountain, standing mute,
Saw him ply the stockwhip fiercely, he was right among them still,
    As he raced across the clearing in pursuit.
Then they lost him for a moment, where two mountain gullies met
    In the ranges – but a final glimpse reveals
On a dim and distant hillside the wild horses racing yet,
    With the man from Snowy River at their heels.

And he ran them single-handed till their sides were white with foam.
    He followed like a bloodhound on their track,
Till they halted cowed and beaten; then he turned their heads for home,
    And alone and unassisted brought them back.
But his hardy mountain pony he could scarcely raise a trot,
    He was blood from hip to shoulder from the spur;
But his pluck was still undaunted, and his courage fiery hot,
    For never yet was mountain horse a cur.

And down by Kosciusko, where the pine-clad ridges raise
    Their torn and rugged battlements on high,
Where the air is clear as crystal, and the white stars fairly blaze
    At midnight in the cold and frosty sky,
And where around the Overflow the reed-beds sweep and sway
    To the breezes, and the rolling plains are wide,
The man from Snowy River is a household word to-day,
    And the stockmen tell the story of his ride.   (1890) 1895

The Travelling Post Office

The roving breezes come and go, the reed-beds sweep and sway,
The sleepy river murmurs low, and loiters on its way,
It is the land of lots o' time along the Castlereagh.

        *

The old man's son had left the farm, he found it dull and slow,
He drifted to the great North-west, where all the rovers go.
'He's gone so long,' the old man said, 'he's dropped right out of mind,
But if you'd write a line to him I'd take it very kind;

He's shearing here and fencing there, a kind of waif and stray –
He's droving now with Conroy's sheep along the Castlereagh.

'The sheep are travelling for the grass, and travelling very slow;
They may be at Mundooran now, or past the Overflow,
Or tramping down the black-soil flats across by Waddiwong
But all those little country towns would send the letter wrong.
The mailman, if he's extra tired, would pass them in his sleep;
It's safest to address the note to "Care of Conroy's sheep",
For five and twenty thousand head can scarcely go astray,
You write to "Care of Conroy's sheep along the Castlereagh".'

     *

By rock and ridge and riverside the western mail has gone
Across the great Blue Mountain Range to take that letter on.
A moment on the topmost grade, while open fire-doors glare,
She pauses like a living thing to breathe the mountain air,
Then launches down the other side across the plains away
To bear that note to 'Conroy's sheep along the Castlereagh'.

And now by coach and mailman's bag it goes from town to town,
And Conroy's Gap and Conroy's Creek have marked it 'Further down'.
Beneath a sky of deepest blue, where never cloud abides,
A speck upon the waste of plain the lonely mailman rides.
Where fierce hot winds have set the pine and myall boughs asweep
He hails the shearers passing by for news of Conroy's sheep.
By big lagoons where wildfowl play and crested pigeons flock,
By camp-fires where the drovers ride around their restless stock,
And past the teamster toiling down to fetch the wool away
My letter chases Conroy's sheep along the Castlereagh.

1895

The Geebung Polo Club

It was somewhere up the country, in a land of rock and scrub,
That they formed an institution called the Geebung Polo Club.
They were long and wiry natives from the rugged mountain side,
And the horse was never saddled that the Geebungs couldn't ride;
But their style of playing polo was irregular and rash –
They had mighty little science, but a mighty lot of dash:
And they played on mountain ponies that were muscular and strong,
Though their coats were quite unpolished, and their manes and tails were
    long.

And they used to train those ponies wheeling cattle in the scrub:
They were demons, were the members of the Geebung Polo Club.

It was somewhere down the country, in a city's smoke and steam,
That a polo club existed, called 'The Cuff and Collar Team.'
As a social institution 'twas a marvellous success,
For the members were distinguished by exclusiveness and dress.
They had natty little ponies that were nice, and smooth, and sleek,
For their cultivated owners only rode 'em once a week.
So they started up the country in pursuit of sport and fame,
For they meant to show the Geebungs how they ought to play the game;
And they took their valets with them – just to give their boots a rub
Ere they started operations on the Geebung Polo Club.

Now my readers can imagine how the contest ebbed and flowed,
When the Geebung boys got going it was time to clear the road;
And the game was so terrific that ere half the time was gone
A spectator's leg was broken – just from merely looking on.
For they waddied one another till the plain was strewn with dead,
While the score was kept so even that they neither got ahead.
And the Cuff and Collar Captain, when he tumbled off to die,
Was the last surviving player – so the game was called a tie.

Then the Captain of the Geebungs raised him slowly from the ground,
Though his wounds were mostly mortal, yet he fiercely gazed around;
There was no one to oppose him – all the rest were in a trance,
So he scrambled on his pony for his last expiring chance,
For he meant to make an effort to get victory to his side;
So he struck at goal – and missed it – then he tumbled off and died.

                    *

By the old Campaspe River, where the breezes shake the grass,
There's a row of little gravestones that the stockmen never pass,
For they bear a crude inscription saying, 'Stranger, drop a tear;
'For the Cuff and Collar players and the Geebung boys lie here.'
And on misty moonlit evenings, while the dingoes howl around,
You can see their shadows flitting down that phantom polo ground;
You can hear the loud collisions as the flying players meet,
And the rattle of the mallets, and the rush of ponies' feet,
Till the terrified spectator rides like blazes to the pub –
He's been haunted by the spectres of the Geebung Polo Club.

1895

Waltzing Matilda

Carrying a Swag

Oh! there once was a swagman camped in a Billabong,
    Under the shade of a Coolabah tree;
And he sang as he looked at his old billy boiling,
    'Who'll come a-waltzing Matilda with me?'

    Who'll come a-waltzing Matilda, my darling,
        Who'll come a-waltzing Matilda with me?
    Waltzing Matilda and leading a water-bag –
        Who'll come a-waltzing Matilda with me?

Down came a jumbuck to drink at the water-hole.
    Up jumped the swagman and grabbed him in glee;
And he sang as he stowed him away in his tucker-bag,
    You'll come a-waltzing Matilda with me!'

Down came the Squatter a-riding his thoroughbred;
    Down came Policemen – one, two, and three.
'Whose is the jumbuck you've got in the tucker-bag?
    You'll come a-waltzing Matilda with me.'

But the swagman, he up and he jumped in the water-hole,
    Drowning himself by the Coolabah tree;
And his ghost may be heard as it sings in the Billabong
    'Who'll come a-waltzing Matilda with me?'

(written 1895) 1917

W. T. GOODGE (1862-1909)

Federation

    Let us sing of Federation
        ('T is the theme of every cult)
    And the joyful expectation
        Of its ultimate result.
    'Twill confirm the jubilation
        Of protection's expectation,

Waltzing Matilda   *The words sung today, which differ slightly from Paterson's poem, are from the musical adaptation by Marie Cowan of 1903*

And the quick consolidation
Of freetrade with every nation;
And teetotal legislation
Will achieve its consummation
And increase our concentration
On the art of bibulation.
We shall drink to desperation,
And be quite the soberest nation
We'll be desperately loyal
Unto everything that's royal,
And be ultrademocratic
In a matter most emphatic.
We'll be prosperous and easeful,
And pre-eminentlY peaceful,
And we'll take our proper station
As a military nation!
We shall show the throne affection,
Also sever the connection,
And the bonds will get no Fainter
And we'll also cut the painter.
We'll proclaim with lute and tabor
The millennium of labour,
And we'll bow before the gammon
Of plutocracy and Mammon.
We'll adopt all fads and fictions
And their mass of contradictions
If all hopes are consummated
When Australia's federated;
For the Federation speeches
This one solid moral teach us –
That a pile of paradoxes are expected to result!   *1899*

Life

Infant; teething,
Thrush and croup.
Schoolboy; marbles,
Top and hoop.
Youth; sweet picnics,
Cigarettes,
Cricket, football,
Sundry bets!

Young man; courtship
Lovely she!
Married; youngsters
Two or three
Worry, trouble,
Smile and frown.
'In memoriam
William Brown!'

1899

VICTOR DALEY (1858-1905)

The Woman at the Washtub

The Woman at the Washtub,
    She works till fall of night;
With soap, and suds and soda
    Her hands are wrinkled white.
Her diamonds are the sparkles
    The copper-fire supplies;
Her opals are the bubbles
    That from the suds arise.

The Woman at the Washtub
    Has lost the charm of youth;
Her hair is rough and homely,
    Her figure is uncouth;
Her temper is like thunder,
    With no one she agrees –
The children of the alley
    They cling around her knees.

The Woman at the Washtub,
    She too had her romance;
There was a time when lightly
    Her feet flew in the dance.
Her feet were silver swallows,
    Her lips were flowers of fire;
Then she was Bright and Early,
    The Blossom of Desire.

O Woman at the Washtub,
    And do you ever dream
Of all your days gone by in

Your aureole of steam?
From birth till we are dying
    You wash our sordid duds,
O Woman of the Washtub!
    O Sister of the Suds!

One night I saw a vision
    That filled my soul with dread,
I saw a Woman washing
    The grave-clothes of the dead;
The dead were all the living,
    And dry were lakes and meres,
The Woman at the Washtub
    She washed them with her tears.

I saw a line with banners
    Hung forth in proud array –
The banners of all battles
    From Cain to Judgment Day.
And they were stiff with slaughter
    And blood, from hem to hem,
And they were red with glory,
    And she was washing them.

'Who comes forth to the Judgment,
    And who will doubt my plan?'
'I come forth to the Judgment
    And for the Race of Man.
I rocked him in his cradle,
    I washed him for his tomb,
I claim his soul and body,
    And I will share his doom.'

                                    (1902) 1947

The Dove

Within his office, smiling,
    Sat JOSEPH CHAMBERLAIN,
But all the screws of Birmingham
    Were working in his brain.

Joseph Chamberlain   (1836–1914) *British politician: mayor of Birmingham, and later
Secretary of State for the Colonies 1895–1903, where he was an advocate of Empire. His
period in office encompassed the Boer War.*

The heart within his bosom
    Was as a millstone hard;
His eye was cold and cruel,
    His face was frozen lard.

He had the map of Africa
    Upon his table spread:
He took a brush, and with the same
    He painted it blood-red.

He heard no moan of widows,
    But only the hurrah
Of charging lines and squadrons
    And 'Rule Britannia.'

A white dove to his window
    With branch of olive sped –
He took a ruler in his hand,
    And struck the white dove dead.

(1902) 1947

LOUISA LAWSON (1848-1920)

In Memoriam

White and all waxen a fair maiden lay,
White as the snowdrift her beautiful clay.
White raiment clothed her, and over her bier
White lilies faded, sweet emblems they were.
White was her record, and where she is gone
White is the stone that her new name is on.

1905

Back Again

Oh, my boy, come in, do.
    You are back at last:
Years since last we saw you
    How the time has passed!

In Memoriam   *for the poet's daughter, Annette, who died at eight months in 1878*

Have a bath and shave first?
    No? A cup of tea?
Think you want a rest worst?
    Dear, oh deary me.

Look, dear, at your boots, too,
    All cut with the rocks;
And you haven't, have you,
    Any mended socks?

They are always tearing?
    Threw them all away?
Alberts you are wearing?
    Goodness, what are they?
Felt that you were coming,
    So I wrote to Bob;
He says things are humming,
    And you'll get a job.

Now, dear, don't come near me,
    You're all over dust;
Can you smoke? Oh, dear me,
    If you really must.   *1905*

God Give Me Gold

God give me gold that I may test
The blessed sweets of perfect rest,
For I am ill and hotly pressed.
    God give me gold!

God give me gold that I may ease
The sorrow that the city sees –
I cannot help the least of these.
    God give me gold!

God give me gold that I may buy
The thing for which my soul doth sigh –
For human love, else, Lord, I die.
    God give me gold!   *1905*

MARY HANNAY FOOTT (1846-1918)

Where the Pelican Builds

The unexplored parts of Australia are sometimes spoken of by the bushmen of
Western Queensland as the home of the pelican, a bird whose nesting place, so
far as the writer knows is seldom, if ever found.

The horses were ready, the rails were down,
   But the riders lingered still, –
      One had a parting word to say,
   And one had his pipe to fill.
Then they mounted, one with a granted prayer,
   And one with a grief unguessed.
      'We are going' they said, as they rode away –
   'Where the pelican builds her nest!'

They had told us of pastures wide and green,
   To be sought past the sunset's glow;
      Of rifts in the ranges by opal lit;
   And gold 'neath the river's flow.
And thirst and hunger were banished words
   When they spoke of that unknown West;
      No drought they dreaded, no flood they feared,
   Where the pelican builds her nest!

The creek at the ford was but fetlock deep
   When we watched them crossing there;
      The rains have replenished it thrice since then
   And thrice has the rock lain bare.
But the waters of Hope have flowed and fled,
   And never from blue hill's breast
      Come back – by the sun and the sands devoured –
   Where the pelican builds her nest!   *(written 1881) 1885*

'AUSTRALIE' (EMILY MANNING) (1845-90)

From the Clyde to Braidwood

A Winter morn. The blue Clyde river winds
'Mid sombre slopes, reflecting in clear depths
The tree-clad banks or grassy meadow flats
Now white with hoary frost, each jewell'd blade
With myriad crystals glistening in the sun.

Thus smiles the Vale of Clyde, as through the air
So keen and fresh three travellers upward ride
Toward the Braidwood heights. Quickly they pass
The rustic dwellings on the hamlet's verge,
Winding sometimes beside the glassy depths
Of Nelligen Creek, where with the murmuring bass
Of running water sounds the sighing wail
Of dark swamp-oaks, that shiver on each bank;
Then winding through a shady-bower'd lane,
With flickering streaks of sunlight beaming through
The feathery leaves and pendant tassels green
Of bright mimosa, whose wee furry balls
Promise to greet with golden glow of joy
The coming spring-tide.

                    Now a barren length
Of tall straight eucalyptus, till again
A babbling voice is heard, and through green banks
Of emerald fern and mossy boulder rocks,
The Currawong dances o'er a pebbly bed,
In rippling clearness, or with cresting foam
Splashes and leaps in snowy cascade steps.
Then every feature changes – up and down,
O'er endless ranges like great waves of earth,
Each weary steed must climb, e'en like a ship
Now rising high upon some billowy ridge
But to plunge down to mount once more, again
And still again.

                    Naught on the road to see
Save sullen trees, white arm'd, with naked trunks,
And hanging bark, like tatter'd clothes thrown off,
An undergrowth of glossy zamia palms
Bearing their winter store of coral fruit,
And here and there some early clematis,
Like starry jasmine, or a purple wreath
Of dark kennedea, blooming e'er their time,
As if in pity they would add one joy
Unto the barren landscape.

                    But at last
A clearer point is reach'd, and all around
The loftier ranges loom in contour blue,
With indigo shadows and light veiling mist
Rising from steaming valleys. Straight in front

towers the Sugarloaf, pyramidal King
Of Braidwood peaks.

Impossible it seems
To scale that nature-rampart, but where man
Would go he must and will; so hewn from out
The mountain's side, in gradual ascent
Of league and half of engineering skill
There winds the Weber pass.

A glorious ride!
Fresher and clearer grows the breezy air,
Lighter and freer beats the quickening pulse
As each fair height is gain'd. Stern, strong, above
Rises the wall of mountain; far beneath,
In sheer precipitancy, gullies deep
Gloom in dark shadow, on their shelter'd breast
Cherishing wealth of leafage richly dight
With tropic hues of green.

No sound is heard
Save the deep soughing of the wind amid
The swaying leaves and harp-like stems, so like
A mighty breathing of great mother earth,
That half they seem to see her bosom heave
With each pulsation as she living sleeps.
And now and then to cadence of these throbs
There drops the bell-bird's knell, the coach-whip's crack,
The wonga-pigeon's coo, or echoing notes
Of lyre-tail'd pheasants in their own rich tones
Mocking the song of every forest bird.

Higher the travellers rise – at every turn
Gaining through avenued vista some new glimpse
Of undulating hills, the Pigeon-house
Standing against the sky like eyrie nest
Of some great dove or eagle. On each side
Of rock hewn road, the fern trees cluster green,
Now and then lighted by a silver star
Of white immortelle flower, or overhung
By crimson peals of bright epacris bells.

Another bend, a shelter'd deepening rift,
And in the mountain's very heart they plunge –
So dark the shade, the sun is lost to view.

Great silver wattles tremble o'er the path,
Which overlooks a glen one varying mass
Of exquisite foliage, full-green sassafras,
The bright-leaf'd myrtle, dark-hued Kurrajong
And lavender, musk-plant, scenting all the air,
Entwined with clematis or bignonia vines,
And raspberry tendrils hung with scarlet fruit.

The riders pause some moments, gazing down,
Then upward look. Far as the peeping sky
The dell-like gully yawns into the heights;
A tiny cascade drips o'er mossy rocks,
And through an aisle of over-arching trees,
Whose stems are dight with lichen, creeping vines,
A line of sunlight pierces, lighting up
A wealth of fern trees; filling every nook
With glorious circles of voluptuous green,
Such as, unview'd, once clothed the silent earth
Long milliards past in Carboniferous Age.

A mighty nature-rockery! Each spot
Of fertile ground is rich with endless joys
Of leaf and fern; now here a velvet moss,
And there a broad asplenium's shining frond
With red-black veinings or a hart's-tongue point,
Contrasting with a pale-hued tender brake
Or creeping lion's-foot. See where the hand
Of ruthless man hath cleft the rock, each wound
Is hidden by thick verdure, leaving not
One unclothed spot, save on the yellow road.

Reluctant the travellers leave the luscious shade
To mount once more. But now another joy –
An open view is here! Before them spreads
A waving field of ranges, purple grey,
In haze of distance with black lines of shade
Marking the valleys, bounded by a line
Of ocean-blue, o'er whose horizon verge
The morning mist-cloud hangs. The distant bay
Is clear defined. The headland's dark arms stretch
(Each finger-point white-lit with dashing foam)
In azure circlet, studded with rugged isles –
A picturesque trio, whose gold rock sides glow
In noonday sunlight, and round which the surf
Gleams like a silvery girdle.

> The grand Pass
Is traversed now, the inland plateau reach'd,
The last sweet glimpse of violet peaks is lost,
An upland rocky stream is pass'd, and naught
But same same gum-trees vex the wearied eye
Till Braidwood plain is reach'd.

> A township like
All others, with its houses, church, and school –
Bare, bald, prosaic – no quaint wild tower,
Nor ancient hall to add poetic touch,
As in the dear old land – no legend old
Adds softening beauty to the Buddawong Peak,
Or near-home ranges with too barbarous names.
But everything is cold, new, new, too new
To foster poesy; and famish'd thought
Looks back with longing to the mountain dream.   *1877*

ADA CAMBRIDGE (1844-1926)

By The Camp Fire

Ah, 'twas but now I saw the sun flush pink on yonder placid tide;
The purple hill-tops, one by one, were strangely lit and glorified;
And yet how sweet the night has grown, with palest starlights dimly sown!

Those mountain ranges, far and near, enclasp me, – sharply pencilled there,
Like blackest sea-waves, – outlined here, like phantoms in the luminous air,
Between that cold and quiet sky, and the calm river running by.

The gum-trees whisper overhead, and, delicately dark and fine,
Their lovely shadow-patterns shed across the paths of white moonshine.
The golden wattles glimmer bright, scenting this cool, transparent night.

What spirits wake when earth is still? I hear wild wood-notes softly swell.
There's the strange clamour, hoarse and shrill, that drowns the bull-frogs'
     hollow bell;
And there's the plaintive rise and fall of the lone mopoke's cuckoo-call.

And nearer, an opossum flits above the firelight, pauses, peers –
I see a round ball where he sits, with pendant tail and pointed ears;
And two are gruffly snarling now in hollows of yon upper bough.

Hark! that's the curlew's thrilling scream. What mountain echoes it has
    stirred!
The sound goes crying down the stream, the wildest bird-note ever heard.
And there's a crane, with legs updrawn, gone sailing out to meet the dawn.

It croaks its farewell, like a crow, beating the air with soft, wide wings.
On the white water down below its vague grey shadow-shape it flings,
And, dream-like, passes out of sight, a lonely vision of the night.

Ah me! how weird the undertones that thrill my wakeful fancy through!
The river softly creeps and moans; the wind seems faintly crying too.
Such whisperings seem to come and pass across the orchis-flower'd grass.

The darkness gather'd all around is full of rustlings, strange and low,
The dead wood crackles on the ground, and shadowy shapes flit to and fro;
I think they are my own dim dreams, wandering amongst the woods and
    streams.

The tangled trees seem full of eyes, – still eyes that watch me as I sit;
A flame begins to fall and rise, their glances come and go with it.
And on the torn bark, rough and brown, I hear soft scratchings up and down.

Sometimes I hear a sound of feet, – a slow step through the darkness steals;
And then I think of yours, my sweet, in spirit following at my heels;
For leagues before, around, behind, part me from all my human-kind.

Coo-ey! – the long vibration throbs in countless echoes through the hills.
The lonely forest wakes and sobs, and then no sound the silence fills, –
Only the night-frogs' bubbling shriek in every water-hole and creek;

Only a rush of wind in flight, as startled wild-ducks flutter past,
Quivering and twinkling in the light, skimming the shining water fast;
And ripples from a black swan's breast, darting from out its rushy nest.

How is't in England? – Sunday morn, and organ-music, love, with you.
That breath of memory, idly born, like a great storm-wind shakes me through.
Ah darling! bend your head and pray, – it cannot touch you far away.

Why do I care? My house of God, beyond all thought, is grand and great!
My prayerful knees, upon the sod, its flowers and grasses consecrate.
And I can see Him in the stars, undimmed by walls and window-bars.

Great Nature spreads her wondrous book, and shows me all her pages fair;
To me the language, when I look, seems but a letter here and there –
The very stones beneath me teach a lore beyond my utmost reach.

For all my pain, and toil, and strife, I see so dimly what is true!
O Art! O Science! O great Life! I grasp thee by so faint a clue!
No more of ocean tides I dream than minnows in their shallow stream.

Sea without bottom, without shore, where is the plumb to fathom thee?
O mystery! as I learn thee more, the more thy deeps are dark to me!
But who am I, that I should scan the Divine Maker's mighty plan?

And yet, oh yet, if I could hear that organ-music once again,
My soul, methinks, would lose its fear; and on this troubled heart and brain
Some light of knowledge would be shed, and some few riddles would be read.

1875

Fallen

For want of bread to eat and clothes to wear –
    Because work failed and streets were deep in snow,
    And this meant food and fire – she fell so low,
Sinning for dear life's sake, in sheer despair.
Or, because life was else so bald and bare,
    The natural woman in her craved to know
    The warmth of passion – as pale buds to blow
And feel the noonday sun and fertile air.

And who condemns? She who, for vulgar gain
    And in cold blood, and not for love or need,
        Has sold her body to more vile disgrace –
        The prosperous matron, with her comely face –
Wife by the law, but prostitute in deed,
In whose gross wedlock womanhood is slain.   1887

Influence

As in the mists of embryonic night,
    Out of the deep and dark obscurities
    Of Nature's womb, the little life-germs rise,
Pushing by instinct upward to the light;
As, when the first ray dawns on waking sight,
    They leap to liberty, and recognize
    The golden sunshine and the morning skies
Their own inheritance by inborn right; –

So do our brooding thoughts and deep desires
    Grow in our souls, we know not how or why;
      Grope for we know not what, all blind and dumb.
So, when the time is ripe, and one aspires
    To free his thought in speech, ours hear the cry,
      And to full birth and instant knowledge come.   *1887*

HENRY KENDALL (1839-82)

Prefatory Sonnets

I

I purposed once to take my pen and write
    Not songs like some tormented and awry
    With Passion, but a cunning harmony
Of words and music caught from glen and height,
And lucid colours born of woodland light,
    And shining places where the sea-streams lie;
But this was when the heat of youth glowed white,
    And since I've put the faded purpose by.
I have no faultless fruits to offer you
    Who read this book; but certain syllables
    Herein are borrowed from unfooted dells,
And secret hollows dear to noontide dew;
And these at least, though far between and few,
    May catch the sense like subtle forest spells.

II

So take these kindly, even though there be
    Some notes that unto other lyres belong:
    Stray echoes from the elder sons of Song;
And think how from its neighbouring, native sea
The pensive shell doth borrow melody.
    I would not do the lordly masters wrong,
    By filching fair words from the shining throng
Whose music haunts me, as the wind a tree!
    Lo, when a stranger, in soft Syrian glooms
Shot through with sunset, treads the cedar dells,
And hears the breezy ring of elfin bells
    Far down by where the white-haired cataract booms,
He, faint with sweetness caught from forest smells,
    Bears thence, unwitting, plunder of perfumes.   *1869*

A Death in the Bush

The hut was built of bark and shrunken slabs
That wore the marks of many rains, and showed
Dry flaws, wherein had crept and nestled rot.
Moreover, round the bases of the bark
Were left the tracks of flying forest-fires,
As you may see them on the lower bole
Of every elder of the native woods.

For, ere the early settlers came and stocked
These wilds with sheep and kine, the grasses grew
So that they took the passing pilgrim in,
And whelmed him, like a running sea, from sight.

And therefore, through the fiercer summer months,
While all the swamps were rotten – while the flats
Were baked and broken; when the clayey rifts
Yawned wide, half-choked with drifted herbage past,
Spontaneous flames would burst from thence, and race
Across the prairies all day long.

                              At night
The winds were up, and then with fourfold speed,
A harsh gigantic growth of smoke and fire
Would roar along the bottoms, in the wake
Of fainting flocks of parrots, wallaroos,
And 'wildered wild things, scattering right and left,
For safety vague, throughout the general gloom.

Anon, the nearer hill-side growing trees
Would take the surges; thus, from bough to bough,
Was borne the flaming terror! Bole and spire,
Rank after rank, now pillared, ringed, and rolled
In blinding blaze, stood out against the dead
Down-smothered dark, for fifty leagues away.

For fifty leagues! and when the winds were strong,
For fifty more! But, in the olden time,
These fires were counted as the harbingers
Of life-essential storms; since out of smoke
And heat there came across the midnight ways
Abundant comfort, with upgathered clouds,
And runnels babbling of a plenteous fall.

So comes the Southern gale at evenfall
(The swift 'brickfielder' of the local folk)
About the streets of Sydney, when the dust
Lies burnt on glaring windows, and the men
Look forth from doors of drouth, and drink the change
With thirsty haste and that most thankful cry
Of, 'here it is – the cool, bright, blessed rain!'

The hut, I say, was built of bark and slabs,
And stood, the centre of a clearing, hemmed
By hurdle-yards, and ancients of the blacks:
These moped about their lazy fires, and sang
Wild ditties of the old days, with a sound
Of sorrow, like an everlasting wind,
Which mingled with the echoes of the noon,
And moaned amongst the noises of the night.

From thence a cattle-track, with link to link,
Ran off against the fishpools, to the gap,
Which sets you face to face with gleaming miles
Of broad Orara, winding in amongst
Black, barren ridges, where the nether spurs
Are fenced about by cotton-scrub, and grass
Blue-bitten with the salt of many droughts.

'Twas here the shepherd housed him every night,
And faced the prospect like a patient soul;
Borne up by some vague hope of better days,
And God's fine blessing in his faithful wife;
Until the humour of his malady
Took cunning changes from the good to bad,
And laid him lastly on a bed of death.

Two months thereafter, when the summer heat
Had roused the serpent from his rotten lair,
And made a noise of locusts in the boughs,
It came to this, that, as the blood-red sun
Of one fierce day of many slanted down
Obliquely past the nether jags of peaks
And gulfs of mist, the tardy night came vexed
By belted clouds, and scuds that wheeled and whirled
To left and right about the brazen clifts
Of ridges, rigid with a leaden gloom.

Then took the cattle to the forest camps
With vacant terror, and the hustled sheep
Stood dumb against the hurdles, even like
A fallen patch of shadowed mountain snow;
And ever through the curlew's call afar
The storm grew on, while round the stinted slabs
Sharp snaps and hisses came, and went, and came,
The huddled tokens of a mighty blast
Which ran with an exceeding bitter cry
Across the tumbled fragments of the hills,
And through the sluices of the gorge and glen.

So, therefore, all about the shepherd's hut
That space was mute, save when the fastened dog,
Without a kennel, caught a passing glimpse
Of firelight moving through the lighted chinks;
For then he knew the hints of warmth within,
And stood, and set his great pathetic eyes,
In wind and wet, imploring to be loosed.

Not often now the watcher left the couch
Of him she watched; since, in his fitful sleep,
His lips would stir to wayward themes, and close
With bodeful catches. Once she moved away,
Half-deafened by terrific claps, and stooped,
And looked without; to see a pillar dim
Of gathered gusts and fiery rain.

                              Anon,
The sick man woke, and, startled by the noise,
Stared round the room, with dull delirious sight,
At this wild thing and that; for, through his eyes,
The place took fearful shapes, and fever showed
Strange crosswise lights about his pillow-head.
He, catching there at some phantasmic help,
Sat upright on the bolster, with a cry
Of, 'Where is Jesus? – it is bitter cold!'
And then, because the thundercalls outside
Were mixed for him with slanders of the Past,
He called his weeping wife by name, and said,
'Come closer, darling! we shall speed away
Across the seas, and seek some mountain home,
Shut in from liars, and the wicked words
That track us day and night, and night and day.'

So waned the sad refrain. And those poor lips,
Whose latest phrases were for peace, grew mute,
And into everlasting silence passed.

As fares a swimmer who hath lost his breath
In 'wildering seas afar from any help –
Who, fronting Death, can never realise
The dreadful Presence, but is prone to clutch
At every weed upon the weltering wave;
So fared the watcher, poring o'er the last
Of him she loved, with dazed and stupid stare;
Half conscious of the sudden loss and lack
Of all that bound her life, but yet without
The power to take her mighty sorrow in.

Then came a patch or two of starry sky;
And through a reef of cloven thunder-cloud
The soft Moon looked: a patient face beyond
The fierce impatient shadows of the slopes,
And the harsh voices of the broken hills!
A patient face, and one which came and wrought
A lovely silence like a silver mist
Across the rainy relics of the storm.

For in the breaks and pauses of her light
The gale died out in gusts; yet, evermore
About the roof-tree, on the dripping eaves,
The damp wind loitered; and a fitful drift
Sloped through the silent curtains, and athwart
The dead.

          There, when the glare had dropped behind
A mighty ridge of gloom, the woman turned
And sat in darkness face to face with God,
And said – I know,' she said, 'that Thou art wise;
That when we build and hope, and hope and build,
And see our best things fall, it comes to pass
For evermore that we must turn to Thee!
And therefore now, because I cannot find
The faintest token of Divinity
In this my latest sorrow, let Thy light
Inform mine eyes, so I may learn to look
On something past the sight which shuts, and blinds,
And seems to drive me wholly, Lord, from Thee.'

Now waned the moon beyond complaining depths;
And, as the dawn looked forth from showery woods
(Whereon had dropt a hint of red and gold),
There went about the crooked cavern-eaves
Low flute-like echoes with a noise of wings
And waters flying down far-hidden fells.
Then might be seen the solitary owl,
Perched in the clefts; scared at the coming light,
And staring outward (like a sea-shelled thing
Chased to his cover by some bright fierce foe)
As at a monster in the middle waste.

At last the great kingfisher came and called
Across the hollows loud with early whips,
And lighted, laughing, on the shepherd's hut,
And roused the widow from a swoon like death.

This day, and after it was noised abroad,
By blacks, and straggling horsemen on the roads
That he was dead 'who had been sick so long,'
There flocked a troop from far-surrounding runs
To see their neighbour and to bury him.
And men who had forgotten how to cry
(Rough flinty fellows of the native bush)
Now learned the bitter way, beholding there
The wasted shadow of an iron frame
Brought down so low by years of fearful pain;
And marking, too, the woman's gentle face,
And all the pathos in her moaned reply
Of 'masters, we have lived in better days.'

One stooped – a stockman from the nearer hills –
To loose his wallet-strings, from whence he took
A bag of tea, and laid it on her lap;
Then, sobbing, 'God will help you, missus, yet,'
He sought his horse with most bewildered eyes,
And, spurring swiftly, galloped down the glen.

Where black Orara nightly chafes his brink,
Midway between lamenting lines of oak
And Warra's gap, the shepherd's grave was built,
And there the wild-dog pauses, in the midst
Of moonless watches: howling through the gloom
At hopeless shadows flitting to and fro,
What time the East Wind hums his darkest hymn,
And rains beat heavy on the ruined leaf.

There, while the Autumn in the cedar trees
Sat cooped about by cloudy evergreens,
The widow sojourned on the silent road,
And mutely faced the barren mound, and plucked
A straggling shrub from thence, and passed away,
Heart-broken on to Sydney, where she took
Her passage in an English vessel bound
To London, for her home of other years.

At rest! Not near, with Sorrow on his grave,
And roses quickened into beauty – wrapt
In all the pathos of perennial bloom;
But far from these, beneath the fretful clay
Of lands within the lone perpetual cry
Of hermit plovers and the night-like oaks,
All moaning for the peace which never comes.

At rest! And she who sits and waits behind
Is in the shadows; but her faith is sure,
And *one* fine promise of the coming days
Is breaking, like a blessed morning, far
On hills 'that slope through darkness up to God.'

(1865) 1869

On a Street

I dread that street! its haggard face
    I have not seen for eight long years –
A mother's curse is on the place:
    (There's blood, my reader, in her tears.)
No child of man shall ever track
    Through filthy dust the singer's feet;
A fierce old memory drags me back –
    I hate its name – I dread that street.

Upon the lap of green sweet lands,
    Whose months are like your English Mays,
I try to hide in Lethe's sands
    The bitter old Bohemian days.

On a Street   *Charlotte Kendall wrote in a private note dated 1882: 'The whole of this poem is correct and our own case except with the exception of hunting for chips of wood in the alley. I never did only that my husband begged me not to suppress a single line'.*

But Sorrow speaks in singing leaf,
  And trouble talketh in the tide;
The skirts of a stupendous grief
  Are trailing ever at my side.

I will not say who suffered there:
  'Tis best the name aloof to keep,
Because the world is very fair –
  Its light should sing the dark to sleep.
But – let me whisper – in that street
  A woman, faint through want of bread,
Has often pawned the quilt and sheet,
  And wept upon a barren bed.

How gladly would I change my theme,
  Or cease the song and steal away
But on the hill, and by the stream
  A ghost is with me night and day!
A dreadful darkness full of wild
  Chaotic visions comes to me:
I seem to hear a dying child –
  Its mother's face I seem to see.

Here surely on this bank of bloom
  My verse with shine should overflow;
But ah, it comes – the rented room,
  With man and wife who suffered so!
From flower and leaf there is no hint –
  I only see a sharp distress:
A lady in a faded print,
  A careworn writer for the Press.

I only hear the brutal curse
  Of landlord clamouring for his pay;
And yonder is the pauper's hearse
  That comes to take a child away.
Apart, and with the half-grey head
  Of sudden age, again I see
The father writing by the dead
  To earn the undertaker's fee.

No tear at all is asked for him –
  A drunkard well deserves his life;
But voice will quiver – eyes grow dim
  For her, the patient, pure young wife,

The gentle girl of better days,
  As timid as a mountain fawn,
Who used to choose untrodden ways,
  And place at night her rags in pawn.

She could not face the lighted square,
  Or show the street her poor thin dress;
In one close chamber, bleak and bare,
  She hid her burden of distress.
Her happy schoolmates used to drive
  On gaudy wheels the town about:
The meal that keeps a dog alive
  She often had to go without.

I tell you this is not a tale
  Conceived by me, but bitter truth!
Bohemia knows it pinched and pale
  Beside the pyre of burnt-out Youth!
These eyes of mine have often seen
  The sweet girl-wife, in winters rude,
Steal out at night through courts unclean,
  To hunt about for chips of wood.

Have I no word at all for him
  Who used down fetid lanes to slink,
And squat in taproom corners grim,
  And drown his thoughts in dregs of drink?
This much I'll say, that, when the flame
  Of Reason re-assumed its force,
The hell the Christian fears to name
  Was heaven to his fierce remorse.

Just think of him – beneath the ban,
  And steeped in sorrow to the neck!
Without a friend – a feeble man
  In failing health – a human wreck!
With all his sense and scholarship,
  How could he face his fading wife?
The devil never lifted whip
  With stings like those that scourged his life!

But He, in whom the dying thief
  Upon the Cross did place his trust,
Forgets the sin and feels the grief,
  And lifts the sufferer from the dust.

And now because I have a dream
    The man and woman found the light,
A glory burns upon the stream –
    With gold and green the woods are bright.

But – still I hate that haggard street –
    Its filthy courts, its alleys wild!
In dreams of it I always meet
    The phantom of a wailing child.
The name of it begets distress –
    Ah, Song, be silent! show no more
The lady in the perished dress –
    The scholar on the taproom floor!   (1879) 1886

The Song of Ninian Melville

Sing the song of noisy Ninny – hang the Muses – spit it out!
(Tuneful Nine ye needn't help me – poet knows his way about!)
Sling me here a penny whistle – look alive, and let me slip
Into Ninny like a father – Ninny with the nimble lip.
Mister Melville, straight descendant from Professor Huxley's ape,
Started life as mute for daddy – pulling faces, sporting crape;
But, alas, he didn't like it – lots of work and little pay!
Nature whispered, 'you're a windbag – play your cards another way.'

Mister Melville picked the hint up – pitched the coffin 'biz' to pot:
Paid his bills, or didn't pay them – 'doesn't matter now a jot–
Twigging how the bread was buttered, he commenced a 'waiting game':
Pulled the strings upon the quiet – no one 'tumbled' to his aim.
Paine, he purchased, Strauss, he borrowed – read a page or two of each:
Posed before his father's porkers – made to them his maiden speech.
Then he spluttered, 'Ninny has it! Nin will keep himself in clothes,
Like that gutter Tully, Bradlaugh, leading noodles by the nose!'

In the fly-blown village pothouse, where a dribbling bag of beer
Passes for a human being, Nin commenced his new career –
Talked about the 'Christian swindle' – cut the Bible into bits –
Shook his fist at Mark and Matthew – give the twelve Apostles fits:
Slipped into the priests and parsons – hammered at the British Court –
Boozy boobies were astonished: lubbers of the Lambton sort!
Yards of ear were cocked to listen – yards of mouth began to shout,
'Here's a cove as is long-headed – Ninny knows his way about!'

Ninian Melville   (1843–97) member of parliament, New South Wales, 1880–94

Mister Melville was delighted – game in hand was paying well:
Fools and coin don't hang together – Nin became a howling swell!
Took to 'stumping' on the Racecourse – cut the old debating club:
Wouldn't do for mighty Ninny now to mount a local tub!
Thornton's Column was his platform: here our orator began
Hitting at the yellow heathen – cracking up the 'working man' –
Spitting out at Immigration: roaring, like a worried bull,
At the lucre made on tallow – at the profit raised on wool!

Said our Ninny to our Ninny, 'I have not the slightest doubt
Soaping down the "'orny-'anded" is the safest "bizness" out!
Little work for spanking wages – this is just the thing they like,
So I'll prop the eight hours swindle – be the boss in every strike.
In the end, I'll pull a pot off – what I'm at is bound to take:
Ninny sees a bit before him – Ninny's eyes are wide-awake!
When the boobies make me member, Parkes, of course, will offer tip –
I will take the first fat billet – then my frouzy friends may rip!'

So it came to pass that Melville – *Mister* Melville, I should say –
Dodged about with deputations, half a dozen times a day!
Started strikes and bossed the strikers – damned employers, every one,
On the Column – off the Column – in the shanty – in the sun!
'Down with masters – up with wages! keep the "pigtail" out of this!'
This is what our Ninny shouted – game, you see, of hit or miss!
World, of course, is full of noodles – some who bray at Wallsend sent
Thing we know to be a windbag bouncing into Parliament!

Common story, this of Ninny! many fellows of his breed
Prowl about to bone the guinea, up to dirty tricks indeed!
Haven't now the time to tan them; but, by Jove, I'd like to tan
Back of that immense impostor that they call the 'working man'!
Drag upon our just employers – sponger on a worn-out wife –
Boozing in some alley pothouse every evening of his life!
Type he is of Nin's supporters: tot him up and tot him down,
He would back old Nick to-morrow for the sake of half a crown!

House with high, august traditions – Chamber where the voice of Lowe,
And the lordly words of Wentworth sounded thirty years ago –
Halls familiar to our fathers, where, in days exalted, rang
All the tones of all the feeling which ennobled Bland and Lang –
We in ashes – we in sackcloth, sorrow for the insult cast
By a crowd of bitter boobies on the grandeur of your past!
Take again your penny whistle – boy, it is no good to me:
Last invention is a bladder with the title of M.P.!   (1880)

Cui Bono

Oh! wind that whistles o'er thorns and thistles,
    Of this fruitful earth like a goblin elf;
Why should he labour to help his neighbour
    Who feels too reckless to help himself?
The wail of the breeze in the bending trees
    Is something between a laugh and a groan;
And the hollow roar of the surf on the shore
    Is a dull, discordant monotone;
I wish I could guess what sense they express,
    There's a meaning, doubtless, in every sound,
Yet no one can tell, and it may be as well –
    Whom would it profit? the world goes round!

On this earth so rough, we know quite enough,
    And, I sometimes fancy, a little too much;
The sage may be wiser than clown or than kaiser,
    Is he more to be envied for being such?
Neither more nor less, in his idleness,
    The sage is doom'd to vexation sure;
The kaiser may rule, but the slippery stool
    That he calls his throne, is no sinecure;
And as for the clown, you may give him a crown,
    Maybe he'll thank you, and maybe not,
And before you can wink, he may spend it in drink –
    To whom does it profit? – We ripe and rot!

Yet under the sun much work is done
    By clown and kaiser, by serf and sage;
All sow and some reap, and few gather the heap
    Of the garner'd grain of a by-gone age.
By sea or by soil man is bound to toil,
    And the dreamer, waiting for time and tide,
For awhile may shirk his share of the work,
    But he grows with his dream dissatisfied;
He may climb to the edge of the beetling ledge,
    Where the loose crag topples and well-nigh reels
'Neath the lashing gale, but the tonic will fail, –
    What does it profit? – Wheels within wheels!

Cui Bono   *Latin: to what good?*

Aye! work we must, or with idlers rust,
    And eat we must our bodies to nurse;
Some folk grow fatter – what does it matter?
    I'm blest if I do – quite the reverse;
'Tis a weary round to which we are bound,
    The same thing over and over again;
Much toil and trouble, and a glittering bubble,
    That rises and bursts, is the best we gain;
And we murmur, and yet, 'tis certain we get
    What good we deserve – can we hope for more? –
They are roaring, those waves in their echoing caves, –
    To whom do they profit? – Let them roar!   *1867*

The Sick Stockrider

Hold hard, Ned! Lift me down once more, and lay me in the shade.
    Old man, you've had your work cut out to guide
Both horses, and to hold me in the saddle when I sway'd
    All through the hot, slow, sleepy, silent ride.
The dawn at 'Moorabinda' was a mist rack dull and dense,
    The sunrise was a sullen, sluggish lamp;
I was dozing in the gateway at Arbuthnot's bound'ry fence,
    I was dreaming on the Limestone cattle camp.
We crossed the creek at Carricksford, and sharply through the haze,
    And suddenly the sun shot flaming forth;
To southward lay 'Katâwa' with the sandpeaks all ablaze
    And the flush'd fields of Glen Lomond lay to north.
Now westward winds the bridle path that leads to Lindisfarm,
    And yonder looms the double-headed Bluff;
From the far side of the first hill, when the skies are clear and calm,
    You can see Sylvester's woolshed fair enough.
Five miles we used to call it from our homestead to the place
    Where the big tree spans the roadway like an arch;
'Twas here we ran the dingo down that gave us such a chase
    Eight years ago – or was it nine? – last March.

'Twas merry in the glowing morn, among the gleaming grass
    To wander as we've wander'd many a mile,
And blow the cool tobacco cloud, and watch the white wreaths pass,
    Sitting loosely in the saddle all the while.
'Twas merry 'mid the blackwoods when we spied the station roofs,
    To wheel the wild scrub cattle at the yard,

With a running fire of stockwhips and a fiery run of hoofs;
 Oh! the hardest day was never then too hard!

Aye! we had a glorious gallop after 'Starlight' and his gang,
 When they bolted from Sylvester's on the flat;
How the sun-dried reed-beds crackled, how the flint-strewn ranges rang
 To the strokes of 'Mountaineer' and 'Acrobat.'
Hard behind them in the timber, harder still across the heath,
 Close beside them through the tea-tree scrub we dash'd;
And the golden-tinted fern leaves, how they rustled underneath!
 And the honeysuckle osiers, how they crash'd!

We led the hunt throughout, Ned, on the chestnut and the grey,
 And the troopers were three hundred yards behind,
While we emptied our six-shooters on the bushrangers at bay,
 In the creek with stunted box-tree for a blind!
There you grappled with the leader, man to man and horse to horse,
 And you roll'd together when the chestnut rear'd;
He blaz'd away and missed you in that shallow watercourse –
 A narrow shave – his powder singed your beard!

In these hours when life is ebbing, how those days when life was young
 Come back to us; how clearly I recall
Even the yarns Jack Hall invented, and the songs Jem Roper sung;
 And where are now Jem Roper and Jack Hall?

Ay! nearly all our comrades of the old colonial school,
 Our ancient boon companions, Ned, are gone;
Hard livers for the most part, somewhat reckless as a rule,
 It seems that you and I are left alone.

There was Hughes, who got in trouble through that business with the cards,
 It matters little what became of him;
But a steer ripp'd up MacPherson in the Cooraminta yards,
 And Sullivan was drown'd at Sink-or-swim;

And Mostyn – poor Frank Mostyn – died at last a fearful wreck,
 In 'the horrors' at the Upper Wandinong,
And Carisbrooke the rider at the Horsefall broke his neck,
 Faith! the wonder was he saved his neck so long!
Ah! those days and nights we squandered at the Logans' in the Glen –
 The Logans, man and wife, have long been dead.
Elsie's tallest girl seems taller than your little Elsie then;
 And Ethel is a woman grown and wed.

I've had my share of pastime, and I've done my share of toil,
    And life is short – the longest life a span;
I care not now to tarry for the corn or for the oil,
    Or for the wine that maketh glad the heart of man.
For good undone and gifts misspent and resolutions vain,
    'Tis somewhat late to trouble. This I know –
I should live the same life over, if I had to live again;
    And the chances are I go where most men go.

The deep blue skies wax dusky and the tall green trees grow dim,
    The sward beneath me seems to heave and fall;
And sickly, smoky shadows through the sleepy sunlight swim,
    And on the very sun's face weave their pall.
Let me slumber in the hollow where the wattle blossoms wave,
    With never stone or rail to fence my bed;
Should the sturdy station children pull the bush flowers on my grave,
    I may chance to hear them romping overhead.

1870

ANONYMOUS

The Banks of the Condamine

Oh, hark the dogs are barking, love,
I can no longer stay,
The men are all gone mustering
And it is nearly day.
And I must off by the morning light
Before the sun doth shine,
To meet the Sydney shearers
On the banks of the Condamine.

Oh Willie, dearest Willie,
I'll go along with you,
I'll cut off all my auburn fringe
And be a shearer, too,
I'll cook and count your tally, love,
While ringer-o you shine,
And I'll wash your greasy moleskins
On the banks of the Condamine.

Oh, Nancy, dearest Nancy,
With me you cannot go,
The squatters have given orders, love,
No woman should do so;
Your delicate constitution
Is not equal unto mine,
To stand the constant tigering
On the banks of the Condamine.

Oh Willie, dearest Willie,
Then stay back home with me,
We'll take up a selection
And a farmer's wife I'll be:
I'll help you husk the corn, love,
And cook your meals so fine
You'll forget the ram-stag mutton
On the banks of the Condamine.

Oh, Nancy, dearest Nancy,
Please do not hold me back,
Down there the boys are waiting,
And I must be on the track;
So here's a good-bye kiss, love,
Back home here I'll incline
When we've shorn the last of the jumbucks
On the banks of the Condamine.   *(from 1860's)*

The Eumerella Shore

There's a happy little valley on the Eumerella shore,
    Where I've lingered many happy hours away,
On my little free selection I have acres by the score,
    Where I unyoke the bullocks from the dray.

    To my bullocks then I say
    No matter where you stray,
        You will never be impounded any more;
    For you're running, running, running on the duffer's piece of land,
        Free selected on the Eumerella shore.

---

tigering   *roughing it*
free selection   *(or simply, 'selection') the low-price allocation, mainly from the late
1850s to the 1870s, of crown land for small farms: a policy opposed by the* squatters,
*pastoralists with large land-holdings already established. The poem has been read both
as a selector's snub to the squatter and as a squatter's satire on the selector.*

When the moon has climbed the mountains and the stars are shining bright,
　　Then we saddle up our horses and away,
And we yard the squatters' cattle in the darkness of the night,
　　And we have the calves all branded by the day.

　　Oh, my pretty little calf,
　　At the squatter you may laugh.
　　　　For he'll never be your owner any more;
　　For you're running, running, running on the duffer's piece of land,
　　　　Free selected on the Eumerella shore.

If we find a mob of horses when the paddock rails are down,
　　Although before they're never known to stray,
Oh, quickly will we drive them to some distant inland town,
　　And sell them into slav'ry far away.

To Jack Robertson we'll say
You've been leading us astray
　　And we'll never go a'farming anymore;
For it's easier duffing cattle on the little piece of land
　　Free selected on the Eumerella shore.

(from 1860s) 1905

CHARLES HARPUR (1831-78)

The Beautiful Squatter

Where the wandering Barwin delighteth the eye,
Befringed with the myall and golden-bloomed gorse,
Oh a beautiful Squatter came galloping by,
With a beard on his chin like the tail of his horse!
And his locks trained all round to so equal a pitch,
That his mother herself, it may truly be said,
Had been puzzled in no small degree to find which
Was the front, or the back, or the sides of his head.

Beside a small fire, 'neath a fair-spreading tree
(A cedar I think, but perhaps 'twas a gum)
What vision of Love did that squatter now see,
In the midst of a catch so to render him dumb?

Jack Robertson　*Sir John Robertson, responsible for two parliamentary land bills that established selection in NSW in 1861*

Why, all on the delicate herbage asquat,
And smiling to see him so flustered and mute,
'Twas the charming Miss Possumskin having a chat
With the elegant Lady of Lord Bandycoot.

The Squatter dismounted – what else could he do?
And, meaning her tender affections to win,
'Gan talking of dampers, and blankets quite new
With a warmth that soon ruined poor Miss Possumskin!
And Lord Bandycoot also, whilst dining that day
On a baked kangaroo of the kind that is red,
At the very third bite to King Dingo did say –
O how heavy I feel all at once in the head!

But alas for the Belles of the Barwin! the youth
Galloped home, to forget all his promises fair!
Whereupon Lady Bandycoot told the whole truth
To her Lord, and Miss Possumskin raved in despair!
And mark the result! royal Dingo straightway,
And his Warriors, swore to avenge them in arms:
And that Beautiful Squatter one beautiful day,
Was waddied to death in the bloom of his charms.

(1845) 1984

A Flight of Wild Ducks

Far up the River – hark! 'tis the loud shock
Deadened by distance, of some Fowler's gun:
And as into the stillness of the scene
It wastes now with a dull vibratory boom,
Look where, fast widening up at either end
Out of the sinuous valley of the waters,
And o'er the intervenient forest, – up
Against the open heaven, a long dark *line*
Comes hitherward stretching – a vast Flight of Ducks!
Following the windings of the vale, and still
Enlarging lengthwise, and in places too
Oft breaking into solitary dots,
How swiftly onward comes it – till at length,
The River, reaching through a group of hills,
Off leads it, – out of sight. But not for long:
For, wheeling ever with the water's course,
Here into sudden view it comes again

Sweeping and swarming round the nearest point!
And first now, a swift airy rush is heard
Approaching momently; – then all at once
There passes a keen-cutting, gusty tumult
Of strenuous pinions, with a streaming mass
Of instantaneous skiey streaks; each streak
Evolving with a lateral flirt, and thence
Entangling as it were, – so rapidly
A thousand wings outpointingly dispread
In passing tiers, seem, looked at from beneath,
With rushing intermixtures to involve
Each other as they beat. Thus seen o'erhead
Even while we speak – ere we have spoken, – lo!
The living cloud is onward many a rood,
Tracking as 'twere in the smooth stream below
The multifarious shadow of itself.
Far coming – present – and far gone at once!
The senses vainly struggle to retain
The impression of an Image (as the same)
So swift and manifold: For now again
A long dark *line* upon the utmost verge
Of the horizon, steeping still, it sinks
At length into the landscape; where yet seen
Though dimly, with a wide and scattering sweep
It fetches eastward, and in column so
Dapples along the steep face of the ridge
There banking the turned River. Now it drops
Below the fringing oaks – but to arise
Once more, with a quick circling gleam, as touched
By the slant sunshine, and then disappear
As instantaneously, – there settling down
Upon the reedy bosom of the water.

The Creek of the Four Graves

Part I

I verse a Settler's tale of olden times –
One told me by our sage friend, Egremont,
Who then went forth, meetly equipt, with four
Of his most trusty and adventurous men
Into the wilderness, – went forth to seek
New streams and wider pastures for his fast

Augmenting flocks and herds. On foot were all,
For horses then were beasts of too great price
To be much ventured upon mountain routes,
And over wild wolds clouded up with brush,
Or cut with marshes, perilously pathless.

So went they forth at dawn: and now the sun
That rose behind them as they journeyed out,
Was firing with his nether rim a range
Of unknown mountains that, like rampires, towered
Full in their front; and his last glances fell
Into the gloomy forest's eastern glades
In golden masses, transiently, or flashed
Down on the windings of a nameless Creek,
That noiseless ran betwixt the pioneers
And those new Appennines; – ran, shaded up
With boughs of the wild willow, hanging mixed
From either bank, or duskily befringed
With upward tapering feathery swamp-oaks –
The sylvan eyelash always of remote
Australian waters, whether gleaming still
In lake or pool, or bickering along
Between the marges of some eager stream.

Before them, thus extended, wilder grew
The scene each moment – and more wilder.
For when the sun was all but sunk below
Those barrier mountains, – in the breeze that o'er
Their rough enormous backs deep fleeced with wood
Came whispering down, the wide upslanting sea
Of fanning leaves in the descending rays
Danced interdazzlingly, as if the trees
That bore them, were all thrilling, – tingling all
Even to the roots for very happiness:
So prompted from within, so sentient, seemed
The bright quick motion – wildly beautiful.

But when the sun had wholly disappeared
Behind those mountains – O what words, what hues
Might paint the wild magnificence of view
That opened westward! Out extending, lo,
The heights rose crowding, with their summits all
Dissolving, as it seemed, and partly lost
In the exceeding radiancy aloft;

And thus transfigured, for awhile they stood
Like a great company of Archeons, crowned
With burning diadems, and tented o'er
With canopies of purple and of gold!

    Here halting wearied, now the sun was set,
Our travellers kindled for their first night's camp
The brisk and crackling fire, which also looked
A wilder creature than 'twas elsewhere wont,
Because of the surrounding savageness.
And soon in cannikins the tea was made
Fragant and strong; long fresh-sliced rashers then
Impaled on whittled skewers, were deftly broiled
On the live embers, and when done, transferred
To quadrants from an ample damper cut,
Their only trenchers, – soon to be dispatched
With all the savoury morsels they sustained,
By the keen tooth of healthful appetite.

    And as they supped, birds of new shape and plume,
And wild strange voice, nestward repairing by,
Oft took their wonder; or betwixt the gaps
In the ascending forest growths they saw
Perched on the bare abutments of the hills,
Where, haply, yet some lingering of gleam fell through,
The wallaroo look forth: till eastward all
The view had wasted into formless gloom,
Night's front; and westward, the high massing woods
Steeped in a swart but mellowed Indian hue –
A deep dusk loveliness, – lay ridged and heaped
Only the more distinctly for their shade
Against the twilight heaven – a cloudless depth
Yet luminous from the sunset's fading glow;
And thus awhile, in the lit dusk, they seemed
To hang like mighty pictures of themselves,
In the still chambers of some vaster world.

    The silent business of their supper done,
The Echoes of the solitary place,
Came as in sylvan wonder wide about
To hear, and imitate tentatively,
Strange voices moulding a strange speech, as then
Within the pleasant purlieus of the fire
Lifted in glee – but to be hushed ere long,
As with the night in kindred darkness came

O'er the adventurers, each and all, some sense –
Some vague-felt intimation from without
Of danger, lurking in its forest lairs.

  But nerved by habit, and all settled soon
About the well-built fire, whose nimble tongues
Sent up continually a strenuous roar
Of fierce delight, and from their fuming pipes
Full charged and fragrant with the Indian weed,
Drawing rude comfort, – typed without, as 'twere,
By tiny clouds over their several heads
Quietly curling upward; – thus disposed
Within the pleasant firelight, grave discourse
Of their peculiar business brought to each
A steadier mood, that reached into the night.

  The simple subject to their minds at length
Fully discussed, their couches they prepared
Of rushes, and the long green tresses pulled
Down from the boughs of the wild willows near.
Then four, as pre-arranged, stretched out their limbs
Under the dark arms of the forest trees,
That mixed aloft, high in the starry air,
In arcs and leafy domes whose crossing curves
And roof-like features, – blurring as they ran
Into some denser intergrowth of sprays, –
Were seen in mass traced out against the clear
Wide gaze of heaven; and trustful of the watch
Kept near them by their thoughtful Master, soon
Drowsing away, forgetful of their toil,
And of the perilous vast wilderness
That lay around them like a spectral world,
Slept, breathing deep; – whilst all things there as well
Showed slumbrous, – yea, the circling forest trees,
Their foremost boles carved from a crowded mass
Less visible, by the watchfire's bladed gleams,
As quick and spicular, from the broad red ring
Of its more constant light they ran in spurts
Far out and under the umbrageous dark;
And even the shaded and enormous mountains,
Their bluff brows glooming through the stirless air,
Looked in their quiet solemnly asleep:
Yea, thence surveyed, the Universe might have seemed
Coiled in vast rest, – only that one dim cloud,

Diffused and shapen like a huge spider,
Crept as with scrawling legs along the sky;
And that the stars, in their bright orders, still
Cluster by cluster glowingly revealed
As this slow cloud moved on, – high over all, –
Looked wakeful – yea, looked thoughtful in their peace.

Part II

Meanwhile the cloudless eastern heaven had grown
More and more luminous – and now the Moon
Up from behind a giant hill was seen
Conglobing, till – a mighty mass – she brought
Her under border level with its cone,
As thereon it were resting: when, behold
A wonder! Instantly that cone's whole bulk,
Erewhile so dark, seemed inwardly a-glow
With her instilled irradiance; while the trees
That fringed its outline, their huge statures dwarfed
By distance into brambles, and yet all
Clearly defined against her ample orb, –
Out of its very disc appeared to swell
In shadowy relief, as they had been
All sculptured from its substance as she rose.

Thus o'er that dark height her great orb arose,
Till her full light, in silvery sequence still
Cascading forth from ridgy slope to slope,
Like the dropt foldings of a lucent veil,
Chased mass by mass the broken darkness down
Into the dense-brushed valleys, where it crouched,
And shrank, and struggled, like a dragon doubt
Glooming some lonely spirit that doth still
Resist the Truth with obstinate shifts and shows,
Though shining out of heaven, and from defect
Winning a triumph that might else not be.

There standing in his lone watch, Egremont
On all this solemn beauty of the world
Looked out, yet wakeful; for sweet thoughts of home
And all the sacred charities it held,
Ingathered to his heart, as by some nice
And subtle interfusion that connects

The loved and cherished (then the most, perhaps,
When absent, or when passed, or even when *lost*)
With all serene and beautiful and bright
And lasting things of Nature. So then thought
The musing Egremont: when sudden – hark!
A bough crackt loudly in a neighbouring brake,
And drew at once, as with a 'larum, all
His spirits thitherward in wild surmise.

But summoning caution, and back stepping close
Against the shade-side of a bending gum,
With a strange horror gathering to his heart,
As if his blood were charged with insect life
And writhed along in clots, he stilled himself,
Listening long and heedfully, with head
Bent forward sideways, till his held breath grew
A pang, and his ears rang. But Silence there
Had recomposed her ruffled wings, and now
Brooded it seemed even stiller than before
Deep nested in the darkness: so that he,
Unmasking from the cold shade, grew ere long
More reassured from wishing to be so,
And to muse, Memory's suspended mood,
Though with an effort, quietly recurred.

But there again – crack upon crack! And hark!
O Heaven! have Hell's worst fiends burst howling up
Into the death-doom'd world? Or whence, if not
From diabolic rage, could surge a yell
So horrible as that which now affrights
The shuddering dark! Beings as fell are near!
Yea, Beings, in their dread inherited hate
And deadly enmity, as vengeful, come
In vengeance! For behold, from the long grass
And nearer brakes, a semi-belt of stript
And painted Savages divulge at once
Their bounding forms! – full in the flaring light
Thrown outward by the fire, that roused and lapped
The rounding darkness with its ruddy tongues
More fiercely than before, – as though even *it*
Had felt the sudden shock the air received
From those dire cries, so terrible to hear!

A moment in wild agitation seen
Thus, as they bounded up, on then they came
Closing, with weapons brandished high, and so
Rushed in upon the sleepers! three of whom
But started, and then weltered prone beneath
The first fell blow dealt down on each, by three
Of the most stalwart of their pitiless foes!
But one again, and yet again, heaved up –
Up to his knees, under the crushing strokes
Of huge-clubbed nulla-nullas, till his own
Warm blood was blinding him! For he was one
Who had with Misery nearly all his days
Lived lonely, and who therefore, in his soul,
Did hunger after hope, and thirst for what
Hope still had promised him, – some taste at least
Of human good however long deferred,
And now he could not, even in dying, loose
His hold on life's poor chances of to-morrow –
Could not but so dispute the terrible fact
Of death, even in Death's presence! Strange it is:
Yet oft 'tis seen that Fortune's pampered child
Consents to his untimely power with less
Reluctance, less despair, than does the wretch
Who hath been ever blown about the world
The straw-like sport of Fate's most bitter blasts,
Vagrant and tieless; – ever still in him
The craving spirit thus grieves to itself:

'I never yet was happy – never yet
Tasted unmixed enjoyment, and I would
Yet pass on the bright Earth that I have loved
Some season, though most brief, of happiness;
So should I walk thenceforward to my grave,
Wherever in her green maternal breast
It might await me, more than now prepared
To house me in its gloom, – resigned at heart,
Subjected to its certainty and soothed
Even by the consciousness of having shaped
Some personal good in being; – strong myself,
And strengthening others. But to have lived long years
Of wasted breath, because of woe and want,
And disappointed hope, – and now, at last,
To die thus desolate, is horrible!'

And feeling thus through many foregone moods
Whose lines had in the temper of his soul
All mixed, and formed *one* habit, – that poor man,
Though the black shadows of untimely death,
Inevitably, under every stroke,
But thickened more and more, – against them still
Upstruggled, nor would cease: until one last
Tremendous blow, dealt down upon his head,
As if in mercy, gave him to the dust
With all his many woes and frustrate hope.

Struck through with a cold horror, Egremont,
Standing apart, – yea, standing as it were
In marble effigy, saw this, saw all!
And when outthawing from his frozen heart
His blood again rushed tingling, – with a leap
Awaking from the ghastly trance which there
Had bound him, as with chill petrific bonds,
He raised from instinct more than conscious thought
His death-charged tube, and at that murderous crew
Firing! saw one fall ox-like to the earth; –
Then turned and fled! Fast fled he, but as fast
His deadly foes went thronging on his track!
Fast! for in full pursuit, behind him yelled
Wild men whose wild speech hath no word for *mercy*!
And as he fled, the forest beasts as well,
In general terror, through the brakes a-head
Crashed scattering, or with maddening speed athwart
His course came frequent. On – still on he flies –
Flies for dear life! and still behind him hears,
Nearer and nearer, the so rapid dig
Of many feet, – nearer and nearer still!

Part III

So went the chase! And now what should he do?
Abruptly turning, the wild Creek lay right
Before him! But no time was there for thought:
So on he kept, and from a bulging rock
That beaked the bank like a bare promontory,
Plunging right forth and shooting feet-first down,
Sunk to his middle in the flashing stream –
In which the imaged stars seemed all at once

To burst like rockets into one wild blaze
Of interwrithing light. Then wading through
The ruffled waters, forth he sprang and seized
A snake-like root that from the opponent bank
Protruded, and round which his earnest fear
Did clench his cold hand like a clamp of steel,
A moment, – till as swiftly thence he swung
His dripping form aloft, and up the dark
O'erjutting ledge went clambering in the blind
And breathless haste of one who flies for life:
When in its face – O verily our God
Hath those in his peculiar care for whom
The daily prayers of spotless Womanhood
And helpless Infancy, are offered up! –
When in its face a cavity he felt,
The upper earth of which in one rude mass
Was held fast bound by the enwoven roots
Of two old trees, – and which, beneath the mould,
Just o'er the clammy vacancy below,
Twisted and lapped like knotted snakes, and made
A natural loft-work. Under this he crept,
Just as the dark forms of his hunters thronged
The bulging rock whence he before had plunged.

    Duskily visible, thereon a space
They paused to mark what bent his course might take
Over the farther bank, thereby intent
To hold upon the chase, which way soe'er
It might incline, more surely. But no form
Amongst the moveless fringe of fern was seen
To shoot up from its outline, – up and forth
Into the moonlight that lay bright beyond,
In torn and shapeless blocks, amid the boles
And mixing shadows of the taller trees,
All standing now in the keen radiance there
So ghostly still, as in a solemn trance.
But nothing in the silent prospect stirred –
No fugitive apparition in the view
Rose, as they stared in fierce expectancy:
Wherefore they augured that their prey was yet
Somewhere between, – and the whole group with that
Plunged forward, till the fretted current boiled
Amongst their crowding trunks from bank to bank;

And searching thus the stream across, and then
Lengthwise, along the ledges, – combing down
Still, as they went, with dripping fingers, cold
And cruel as inquisitive, each clump
Of long-flagged swamp-grass where it flourished high, –
The whole dark line passed slowly, man by man,
Athwart the cavity – so fearfully near,
That as they waded by the Fugitive
Felt the strong odor of their wetted skins
Pass with them, trailing as their bodies moved
Stealthily on, – coming with each, and going.

But their keen search was keen in vain. And now
Those wild men marvelled, – till, in consultation,
There grouped in dark knots standing in the stream
That glimmered past them, moaning as it went,
His vanishment, so passing strange it seemed,
They coupled with the mystery of some crude
Old fable of their race; and fear-struck all,
And silent, then withdrew. And when the sound
Of their receding steps had from his ear
Died off, as back to the stormed Camp again
They hurried to despoil the yet warm dead,
Our Friend slid forth, and springing up the bank,
Renewed his flight, nor rested from it, till
He gained the welcoming shelter of his Home.

Return we for a moment to the scene
Of recent death. There the late flaring fire
Now smouldered, for its brands were strewn about,
And four stark corses, plundered to the skin
And brutally mutilated, seemed to stare
With frozen eyeballs up into the pale
Round visage of the Moon, who, high in heaven,
With all her stars, in golden bevies, gazed
As peacefully down as on a bridal there
Of the warm Living – not, alas! on them
Who kept in ghastly silence through the night
Untimely spousals with a desert death.

O God! and thus this lovely world hath been
Accursed for ever by the bloody deeds
Of its prime Creature – Man. Erring or wise,
Savage or civilised, still hath he made

This glorious residence, the Earth, a Hell
Of wrong and robbery and untimely death!
Some dread Intelligence opposed to Good
Did, of a surety, over all the earth
Spread out from Eden – or it were not so!
For see the bright beholding Moon, and all
The radiant Host of Heaven, evince no touch
Of sympathy with Man's wild violence; –
Only evince in their calm course, their part
In that original unity of Love,
Which, like the soul that dwelleth in a harp
Under God's hand, in the beginning, chimed
The sabbath concord of the Universe;
And look on a gay clique of maidens, met
In village tryst, and interwhirling all
In glad Arcadian dances on the green –
Or on a hermit, in his vigils long,
Seen kneeling at the doorway of his cell –
Or on a monster battle-field where lie
In sweltering heaps, the dead and dying both,
On the cold gory ground, – as they that night
Looked in bright peace, down on the doomful Wild.

Afterwards there, for many changeful years,
Within a glade that sloped into the bank
Of that wild mountain Creek – midway within,
In partial record of a terrible hour
Of human agony and loss extreme,
Four grassy mounds stretched lengthwise side by side,
Startled the wanderer; – four long grassy mounds
Bestrewn with leaves, and withered spraylets, stript
By the loud wintry wingéd gales that roamed
Those solitudes, from the old trees which there
Moaned the same leafy dirges that had caught
The heed of dying Ages: these were all;
And thence the place was long by travellers called
The Creek of the Four Graves. Such was the Tale
Egremont told us of the wild old times.

1853

Early and Late Art

When Art is young, it slighteth Nature;
When old, it loves her every feature.

1984

To Myself, June 1855

What's the Crimean War to thee,
    Its craft and folly, blame and blunder?
Its aims are dodges plain to see,
    Its victories shams with all their thunder.

Heed not its proud but passing things,
    The royal mischiefs of their day;
But give thou Thought's immortal wings
    To glories of a purer ray:

To Freedom in her future prime,
    To Nature's everlasting lore,
To Science from her tower in Time
    Surveying the Eternal's shore.

Be such the subjects of thy thought,
    Not Old World Kings and ruling sets,
And liberties that flounder, caught
    Like fish in diplomatic nets.

For these, if pondered, can but hurt
    The straightness of thy moral view,
And foul as with the Old World's dirt
    The virgin nature of the New.   *1984*

A Mid-Summer Noon in the Australian Forest

Not a bird disturbs the air,
There is quiet everywhere;
Over plains and over woods
What a mighty stillness broods.

    Even the grasshoppers keep
Where the coolest shadows sleep;
Even the busy ants are found
Resting in their pebbled mound;
Even the locust clingeth now
In silence to the barky bough:
And over hills and over plains
Quiet, vast and slumbrous, reigns.

Only there's a drowsy humming
From yon warm lagoon slow coming:
'Tis the dragon-hornet – see!
All bedaubed resplendently
With yellow on a tawny ground –
Each rich spot nor square nor round,
But rudely heart-shaped, as it were
The blurred and hasty impress there,
Of a vermeil-crusted seal
Dusted o'er with golden meal:
Only there's a droning where
Yon bright beetle gleams the air –
Gleams it in its droning flight
With a slanting track of light,
Till rising in the sunshine higher,
Its shards flame out like gems on fire.

Every other thing is still,
Save the ever wakeful rill,
Whose cool murmur only throws
A cooler comfort round Repose;
Or some ripple in the sea
Of leafy boughs, where, lazily,
Tired Summer, in her forest bower
Turning with the noontide hour,
Heaves a slumbrous breath, ere she
Once more slumbers peacefully.

O 'tis easeful here to lie
Hidden from Noon's scorching eye,
In this grassy cool recess
Musing thus of Quietness.

(1858) 1883

Modern Poetry

How I hate those modern Poems
    Vaguer, looser than a dream!
Those pointless things that look like proems,
    Only, to some held-back theme!
Wild, unequal, agitated
As by steam ill-regulated –
    Balder-dashic steam!
And if (in fine) not super-lyrical,
Then vapid, almost to a miracle.

1984

Water Beaux

'Hist! grave-eyed frogs!

Demurely squatting upon floating leaves,
And greener than their couches. Their round backs
Of many-shaded chrysoprase, all moist,
Change with each throbbing inner pulse, that waves
And varies that rare pattern in gold thread,
Till to our puzzled eyes it seems to fuse
And run in other shapes. Anon, a note,
Deep, full and thrilling, as a harp-string, twanged
I' the bass by a firm finger, rings along,
And after a due interval – all's done
With marvellous dignity – another voice,
In bell-like monosyllable, replies;
Then, up and down the brook, the solemn tones,
In quaint, uneven melody, resound;
Else, all is still.'

Ah! do you laugh, because I say these frogs
Are Water Beaux? In sooth, I do not know
That mortal exquisite, who pranks himself
In comparable bravery of garb.
Broadcloth and velvet are prosaic, dull,
Nowhere in competition! Even those
Supreme high-priests of Nature's mysteries
The scientists, who usually delight
In giving hardest names to fairest things,
Calling a butterfly by such a string
Of big, rough, heavy Greek and Latin words
As well might overweight an elephant; –
E'en they, throned high in professorial chairs
Have gracefully unbending, recognised
My frog-friend's right to an illustrious name,
And dubbed him Hylas, after the fair youth
Beloved and stol'n by water-nymphs of yore.
Brightly he wears his honours. Not a bird
Floating on radiant pinions to the sun,
Nor fish illumining the azure deeps

Water Beaux   *The first sixteen lines are self-quoted from* 'A Summer Sketch', *first
published in 1860.*

Of ocean with rich iridescent hues,
Nor tropic fly's superbest pencilled wings
May venture rivalry. I have said it oft,
A 'thrice-told tale' indeed. A tale, told first
When Austral climes and forms to me were new,
And life, all throbbing and aglow with youth
And newly wedded love and cloudless hope,
Seemed more of Heaven than earth.
                              One day I stood
Amidst an arid, grassless plain, beside
The well-nigh dried-up river-pools, and saw –
For the first time – with eager, wondering eyes
The Water Beaux! 'Tis fifty years ago!
Life, then so bright, is wan and weary now;
And I – left all alone – grey, feeble, old –
Saddened by sorrow, worn and bent with pain,
Await the nearing end – the sleep below the sod.
Yet – you may deem it childish – so to dream –
'Tis as a written story of the past,
The chequered – shadowed – but most happy past –
To fancy that I even now look down
Once more, in hushed and cautious silence, where
On the still waters, broad leaves lie afloat
And drooping streamers of fair sweet wild flowers
Wave in the sunlit air above the forms
Of these – dear friends for half a century –
My peerless Water Beaux!   *1891*

ROBERT LOWE (1811-92)

from *Songs of the Squatters*

2

The Commissioner bet me a pony – I won,
So he cut off exactly two thirds of my run,
For he said I was making a fortune too fast;
And profit gained slower, the longer would last.

He remarked as, devouring my mutton, he sat,
That I suffered my sheep to grow sadly too fat;
That they wasted waste land, did prerogative brown,
And rebelliously nibbled the droits of the Crown.

That the creek that divided my station in two
Showed that Nature design'd that two fees should be due.
Mr Riddell assured me 'twas paid but for show,
But he kept it, and spent it – that's all that I know.

The Commissioner fined me, because I forgot
To return an old ewe that was ill of the rot,
And a poor wry-necked lamb that we kept for a pet,
And he said it was treason such things to forget.

The Commissioner pounded my cattle, because
They had mumbled the scrub with their famishing jaws
On the part of the run he had taken away,
And he sold them by auction the costs to defray.

The Border Police they were out all the day
To look for some thieves who had ransack'd my dray,
But the thieves they continued in quiet and peace,
For they'd robb'd it themselves had the Border Police.

When the white thieves were gone, next the black thieves appeared,
My shepherds they waddied, my cattle they speared;
But for fear of my License I said not a word,
For I knew it was gone if the Government heard.

The Commissioner's bosom with anger was filled
Against me, because my poor shepherd was killed;
So he straight took away the last third of my run,
And got it transferred to the name of his son.

The son had from Cambridge been lately expell'd,
And his license for preaching most justly withheld;
But this is no cause, the Commissioner says,
Why he should not be fit for my license to graze.

The cattle that had not been sold at the pound
He took with the run, at five shillings all round,
And the sheep the blacks left me, at sixpence a head –
And a very good price, the Commissioner said.

The Governor told me I justly was served,
That Commissioners never from duty had swerved;
But that if I'd a fancy for any more land,
For one pound an acre he'd plenty on hand.

I'm not very proud, I can dig in a bog,
Feed pigs, or for firewood can split up a log,
Clean shoes, riddle cinders, or help to boil down,
Any thing that you please – but graze lands of the Crown!

3

The Gum has no shade,
And the Wattle no fruit;
The parrot don't warble
In trolls like the flute;
The Cockatoo cooeth
Not much like a dove,
Yet fear not to ride
To my station, my love.
Four hundred miles off
Is the goal of our way,
It is done in a week,
At but sixty a day.
The plains are all dusty,
The creeks are all dried,
'Tis the fairest of weather
To bring home my bride.
The blue vault of heaven
Shall curtain thy form,
One side of a Gum tree
The moonbeam *must* warm;
The whizzing Mosquito
Shall dance o'er thy head,
And the Guana shall squat
At the foot of thy bed;
The brave Laughing Jackass
Shall sing thee to sleep,
And the Snake o'er thy slumber
His vigils shall keep!
Then sleep, lady, sleep,
Without dreaming of pain,
Till the frost of the morning
Shall wake thee again.
Our brave bridal bower
I built not of stones,
Though like old Doubting Castle,
'Tis paved with bones:
The bones of the sheep
On whose flesh I have fed,

Where thy thin satin slipper
Unshrinking may tread;
For the dogs have all polished
Them clean with their teeth,
And they're better, believe me,
Than what lies beneath.
My door has no hinge,
And the window no pane –
They let out the smoke,
But they let in the rain!
The frying pan serves us
For table and dish,
And the tin pot of tea stands
Still filled to your wish;
The sugar is brown,
The milk is all done,
But the stick it is stirred with
Is better than none.
The stockmen *will* swear,
And the shepherds *won't* sing,
But a dog's a companion
Enough for a king.
So fear not, fair Lady,
Your desolate way,
Your clothes will arrive
In three months with my dray.
Then mount, lady, mount, to the wilderness fly –
My stores are laid in, and my shearing is nigh;
And our steeds that through Sydney exultingly wheel,
Must graze in a week on the banks of the Peel.   *(1845) 1885*

'FRANK THE POET' (FRANCIS MACNAMARA) (*b ?1811*)

For the Company Under Ground

Francis MacNamara of Newcastle to J. Crosdale Esq. greeting

When Christ from Heaven comes down straightway
All his Father's laws to expound
MacNamara shall work that day
For the Company under ground.

J.Crosdale   *probably William Croasdill, superintendent of the Australian Agricultural
Company's mines in the Newcastle area in the late 1830s*

When the man in the moon to Moreton Bay
Is sent in shackles bound
MacNamara shall work that day
For the Company under ground.

When the Cape of Good Hope to Twofold Bay
Comes for the change of a pound
MacNamara shall work that day
For the Company under ground.

When cows in lieu of milk yield tea
And all lost treasures are found
MacNamara shall work that day
For the Company under ground.

When the Australian Company's heaviest dray
Is drawn 80 miles by a hound
MacNamara shall work that day
For the Company under ground.

When a frog a caterpillar and a flea
Shall travel the globe all round
MacNamara shall work that day
For the Company under ground.

When turkey cocks on Jews harps play
And mountains dance at the sound
MacNamara shall work that day
For the Company under ground.

When milestones go to church to pray
And whales are put in the Pound
MacNamara shall work that day
For the Company under ground.

When Christmas falls on the 1st of May
And O'Connell's King of England crown'd
MacNamara shall work that day
For the Company under ground.

When thieves ever robbing on the highway
For their sanctity are renowned
MacNamara shall work that day
For the Company under ground

When the quick and dead shall stand in array
Cited at the last trumpet's sound
Even then, damn me if I'd work a day
For the Company under ground

    Nor over ground.   *(written late 1830s)*

'HUGO'

The Gin

'Where spreads the sloping shaded turf
    By Coodge's smooth and sandy bay,
And roars the ever-ceaseless surf,
    I've built my gunya for to-day.

'The gum-tree with its glitt'ring leaves
    Is sparkling in the sunny light,
And round my leafy home it weaves
    Its dancing shade with flow'rets bright.

'And beauteous things around are spread
    The burwan, with its graceful bend
And cone of nuts, and o'er my head
    The flowering vines their fragrance lend.

'The grass-tree, too, is waving there,
    The fern-tree sweeping o'er the stream,
The fan-palm, curious as rare,
    And warretaws with crimson beam.

'Around them all the glecinae
    Its dainty tendrils careless winds,
Gemming their green with blossoms gay,
    One common flower each bush-shrub finds.

'Fresh water, too, is tumbling o'er
    The shell-strewn rocks into the sea;
'Midst them I seek the hidden store,
    To heap the rich repast for thee.

'But where is Bian? – where is he? –
    My husband comes not to my meal:
Why does he not the white man flee,
    Nor let their god his senses steal?

'Lingers he yet in Sydney streets?
    Accursed race! to you we owe,
No more the heart contended beats,
    But droops with sickness, pain, and woe.

'Oh! for the days my mother tells,
    Ere yet the white man knew our land;
When silent all our hills and dells,
    The game was at the huntsman's hand.

'Then roamed we o'er the sunny hill,
    Or sought the gully's grassy way,
With ease our frugal nets could fill
    From forest, plain, or glen, or bay.

'Where sported once the kangaroo,
    Their uncouth cattle tread the soil,
Or corn-crops spring, and quick renew,
    Beneath the foolish white man's toil.

'On sunny spots, by coast and creek,
    Near the fresh stream we sat us down;
Now fenced, and shelterless, and bleak,
    They're haunted by the white man's frown.'

She climbed the rock – she gazed afar –
    The sun behind those mountains blue
Had sunk; faint gleamed the Western star,
    And in the East a rainbow hue

Was mingling with the darkling sea;
    When gradual rose the zodiac light,
And over rock, and stream, and tree,
    Spread out its chastened radiance bright.

So calm, so soft, so sweet a ray,
    It lingers on the horizon's shore;
The echo of the brighter day,
    That bless'd the world an hour before.

But sudden fades the beam that shone,
    And lit the earth like fairy spell;
Whilst in the East, the sky's deep tone
    Proclaims the daylight's last farewell.

'Fast comes the night, and Bian yet
      Returns not to his leafy bed;
My hair is with the night-dew wet –
      Sleep comes not to this aching head.

'The screeching cockatoo's at rest;
      From yonder flat the curlew's wail
Comes mournful to this sorrowing breast,
      And keenly blows the Southern gale.

'Avaunt ye from our merry land!
      Ye that so boast our souls to save,
Yet treat us with such niggard hand:
      We have no hope but in the grave.'

Thus sung Toongulla's wretched child,
      As o'er her sleeping babe she hung,
Mourning her doom, to lead a wild
      And cheerless life the rocks among.

Their health destroyed – their sense depraved –
      The game, their food, for ever gone;
Let me invoke religion's aid
      To shield them from this double storm

Of physical and moral ill;
      We owe them all that we possess –
The forest, plain, the glen, the hill,
      Were theirs; – to slight is to oppress.   (1831)

                                              ANONYMOUS

   Australian Courtship

The Currency Lads may fill their glasses,
And drink to the health of the Currency Lasses;
But the lass I adore, the lass for me,
Is a lass in the Female Factory.

Currency Lads   Currency Lasses   *Australian-born (in the sense of local currency as opposed to British sterling)*
Female Factory   *a place where female convicts manufactured cloth. Several existed in the Australian colonies; the best known was at Parramatta.*

O! Molly's her name, and her name is Molly,
Although she was tried by the name of Polly;
She was tried and was cast for death at Newry,
But the Judge was bribed and so were the Jury.

She got 'death recorded' in Newry town
For stealing her mistress's watch and gown;
Her little boy Paddy can tell you the tale,
His father was turnkey of Newry jail.

The first time I saw this comely lass
Was at Parramatta, going to mass;
Says I, 'I'll marry you now in an hour,'
Says she, 'Well, go and fetch Father Power.'

But I *got into trouble* that very same night!
Being drunk in the street I got into a fight;
A constable seized me – I gave him a box –
And was put in the watch-house and then in the stocks.

O! It's very unaisy as I remember,
To sit in the stocks in the month of December;
With the north wind so hot, and the hot sun right over,
O! sure, and it's no place at all for a lover!

'It's worse than the tread-mill,' says I, 'Mr Dunn,
To sit here all day in the *hate* of the sun!'
'Either that or a dollar,' says he, 'for your folly', –
But if I had a dollar I'd drink it with Molly.

But now I am out again, early and late
I sigh and I cry at the Factory gate.
'O! Mrs Reordan, late Mrs Farson,
O! won't you let Molly out very soon?'

'Is it Molly McGuigan?' says she to me,
'Is it not?' says I, for she know'd it was she.
'Is it her you mean that was put in the stocks
For beating her mistress, Mrs Cox?'

'O! yes and it is, madam, pray let me in,
I have brought her a half-pint of Cooper's best gin.
She likes it as well as she likes her own mother,
O! now let me in, madam, I am her brother.'

So the Currency Lads may fill their glasses,
And drink the health of the Currency Lasses;
But the lass I adore, the lass for me,
Is a lass in the Female Factory.   *(1831)*

ELIZA HAMILTON DUNLOP *(1796-1880)*

The Aboriginal Mother
from Myall's Creek

Oh! hush thee – hush my baby,
    I may not tend thee yet.
Our forest-home is distant far,
    And midnight's star is set.
Now, hush thee – or the pale-faced men
    Will hear thy piercing wail,
And what would then thy mother's tears
    Or feeble strength avail!

Oh, could'st thy little bosom,
    That mother's torture feel,
Or could'st thou know thy father lies
    Struck down by English steel;
Thy tender form would wither,
    Like the *kniven* on the sand,
And the spirit of my perished tribe
    Would vanish from our land.

For thy young life, my precious,
    I fly the field of blood,
Else had I, for my chieftain's sake,
    Defied them where they stood;
But basely bound my woman arm,
    No weapon might it wield:
I could but cling round him I loved,
    To make my heart a shield.
I saw my firstborn treasure
    Lie headless at my feet,
The goro on this hapless breast,
    In his life-stream is wet!

Myall's Creek   *a place in the NSW northern tablelands, where 28 Aboriginal people*
were shot, and their bodies burned, by a party of twelve white stockmen on 9 June 1838

And thou! I snatch't thee from their sword,
    It harmless pass'd by thee!
But clave the binding cords – and gave,
    Haply, the power to flee.

To flee! my babe – but whither?
    Without my friend – my guide?
The blood that was our strength is shed!
    He is not by my side!
Thy sire! oh! never, never
    Shall *Toon Bakra* hear our cry:
My bold and stately mountain-bird!
    I thought not he could die.

Now who will teach thee, dearest,
    To poise the shield, and spear,
To wield the *koopin*, or to throw
    The *boommerring*, void of fear;
To breast the river in its might;
    The mountain tracks to tread?
The echoes of my homeless heart
    Reply – the dead, the dead!

And ever must their murmur
    Like an ocean torrent flow:
The parted voice comes never back,
    To cheer our lonely woe:
Even in the region of our tribe,
    Beside our summer streams,
'Tis but a hollow symphony –
    In the shadow-land of dreams.

Oh hush thee, dear – for weary
    And faint I bear thee on –
His name is on thy gentle lips,
    My child, my child, *he's gone!*
Gone o'er the golden fields that lie
    Beyond the rolling cloud,
To bring thy people's murder cry
    Before the Christian's God.

Yes! o'er the stars that guide us,
    He brings my slaughter'd boy:
To shew their God how treacherously
    The stranger men destroy;

To tell how hands in friendship pledged
    Piled high the fatal pire;
To tell – to tell of the gloomy ridge!
    And the *stockmen's human fire.*   (*1838*)

FIDELIA S. T. HILL (*1790-1854*)

Recollections

Yes, South Australia! three years have elapsed
Of dreary banishment, since I became
In thee a sojourner; nor can I choose
But sometimes think on thee; and tho' thou art
A fertile source of unavailing woe,
Thou dost awaken deepest interest still. –
Our voyage past, we anchor'd in that port
Of our New Colony, styled Holdfast Bay.
In part surrounded by the range sublime
Of mountains, with Mount Lofty in their centre: –
Beautiful mountains, which at even-tide
I oft have gazed upon with raptur'd sense,
Watching their rose-light hues, as fleeting fast
Like fairy shadows o'er their verdant sides
They mock'd the painter's art, and to pourtray
Defied the utmost reach of poet's skill! –
The new year open'd on a novel scene, –
New cares, new expectations, a new land! –
Then toil was cheer'd, and labour render'd light,
Privations welcom'd, every hardship brav'd,
In the blest anticipation of reward: –
(Which some indeed deserv'd, but ne'er obtain'd)
Some who unceasingly, had lent their aid,
And time, and information, to promote
The interests of the rising Colony –
Still flattering hope on the dark future smil'd,
Gilding each object with fallacious dyes,
And picturing pleasure, that *was not to be!*
They bore me to the future Capitol,

---

*Hill and her husband arrived with the first main party of colonists at Holdfast Bay
(now Glenelg) on 28 December 1836, and moved to the site of Adelaide soon after.*

Ere yet 'twas more than desart – a few tents,
Scatter'd at intervals, 'mid forest trees,
Marked the abode of men. 'Twas a wide waste,
But beauteous in its wildness. – Park-like scenery
Burst on the astonish'd sight; for it did seem
As tho' the hand of art, had nature aided,
Where the broad level walks – and verdant lawns,
And vistas grac'd that splendid wilderness!
'Twas then they hail'd me as the *first* white lady
That ever yet had enter'd Adelaide. –
Can time e'er teach me to forget the sound,
Of gratulations that assail'd me then,
And cheer'd me at the moment, or efface
The welcome bland of the distinguish'd one –
Who fixed the site, and form'd the extensive plan
Of that young City? – He hath passed away
To the dark cheerless chambers of the tomb!
But Adelaide if crown'd with fortune, shall
To after age perpetuate his name! –

   *

One tent was pitch'd upon the sloping bank
Of the stream Torrens, in whose lucid wave
Dipp'd flow'ring shrubs – the sweet mimosa there
Wav'd its rich blossoms to the perfum'd breeze,
High o'er our heads – amid the stately boughs
Of the tall gum tree – birds of brightest hues
Or built their nests, or tun'd 'their wood-notes wild,'
Reposing on the rushes, fresh and cool,
Which a lov'd hand had for my comfort strew'd: –
This, this methought shall be my happy home!
Here may I dwell, and by experience prove,
That tents with love, yield more substantial bliss
Than Palaces without it, can bestow.   *1840*

John Dunmore Lang (1799-1878)

D'Entrecasteaux Channel, Van Dieman's Land

Now D'Entrecasteaux Channel opens fair,
    And Tasman's Head lies on your starboard bow;
Huge rocks and stunted trees meet you where e'er
    You look around; 'tis a bold coast enow.
With foul wind and crank ship 'twere hard to wear:
    A reef of rocks lies westward long and low.
At ebb tide you may see the Aetœon lie
A sheer hulk o'er the breakers, high and dry.

'Tis a most beauteous Strait. The Great South Sea's
    Proud waves keep holiday along its shore,
And as the vessel glides before the breeze,
    Broad bays and isles appear, and steep cliffs hoar
With groves on either hand of ancient trees
    Planted by Nature in the days of yore:
Van Dieman's on the left and Brunè's isle
Forming the starboard shore for many a mile.

But all is still as death! Nor voice of man
    Is heard, nor forest warbler's tuneful song.
It seems as if this beauteous world began
    To be but yesterday, and the earth still young
And unpossessed. For though the tall black swan
    Sits on her nest and sails stately along,
And the green wild doves their fleet pinions ply,
And the grey eagle tempts the azure sky,

Yet all is still as death! Wild solitude
    Reigns undisturbed along that voiceless shore,
And every tree seems standing as it stood
    Six thousand years ago. The loud wave's roar
Were music in these wilds. The wise and good
    That wont of old, as hermits, to adore
The God of Nature in the desert drear,
    Might sure have found a fit sojourning here.

(written 1823) 1872

Colonial Nomenclature

'Twas said of Greece two thousand years ago,
    That every stone i' the land had got a name.
Of New South Wales too, men will soon say so too;
    But every stone there seems to get the same.
'Macquarie' for a name is all the go:
    The old Scotch Governor was fond of fame,
Macquarie Street, Place, Port, Fort, Town, Lake, River:
    'Lachlan Macquarie, Esquire, Governor,' for ever!

I like the native names, as Parramatta,
    And Illawarra, and Woolloomoolloo;
Nandowra, Woogarora, Bulkomatta,
    Tomah, Toongabbie, Mittagong, Meroo;
Buckobble, Cumleroy, and Coolingatta,
    The Warragumby, Bargo, Burradoo;
Cookbundoon, Carrabaiga, Wingecarribbee,
    The Wollondilly, Yurumbon, Bungarribbee.

I hate your Goulburn Downs and Goulburn Plains,
    And Goulburn River and the Goulburn Range,
And Mount Goulburn and Goulburn Vale! One's brains
    Are turned with Goulburns! Vile scorbutic mange
For immortality! Had I the reins
    Of Government a fortnight, I would change
These Downing Street appellatives, and give
    The country names that should deserve to live.

I'd have Mount Hampden and Mount Marvell, and
    Mount Wallace and Mount Bruce at the old Bay.
I'd have them all the highest in the land,
    That men might see them twenty leagues away,
I'd have the Plains of Marathon beyond
    Some mountain pass yclept Thermopylœ,
Such are th' immortal names that should be written
    On all thy new discoveries, Great Britain!

Yes! let some badge of liberty appear
    On every mountain and on every plain
Where Britain's power is known, or far or near,
    That freedom there may have an endless reign!
Then though she die, in some revolving year,
    A race may rise to make her live again!
The future slave may lisp the patriot's name
    And his breast kindle with a kindred flame!

I love thee, Liberty, thou blue-eyed maid!
    Thy beauty fades not in the hottest clime!
In purple or plebeian garb arrayed
    I love thee still! The great in olden time,
Roman and Greek, worshipped thy very shade
    And sung thy beauty in their song sublime.
'Tis Paradise to live beneath thy smile,
    Thou patron Goddess of my native isle.

But he that loves fair Liberty must be
    Virtue's sworn friend. The vicious is a slave
And serves a tyrant, nor can e'er be free.
    Of old her wooers were like Brutus, brave;
Like Marvell, incorrupt; Milton, like thee!
    A recreant race wooes now and digs her grave;
Byron their leader, whose high-lineaged muse
    Walks a vile pimp and caters for the stews!

Choice work for British Peers! Baser alliance
    Than Austria's with her band of despot kings!
For he who setteth virtue at defiance
    And holds her dread commands as paltriest things,
Whate'er his rank, learning, or wit, or science,
    Or high pretence of love for freedom, brings
A tyrant worse than Slavery in his train
    And binds men with a more ignoble chain.

On Freedom's altar ere I place strange fire
    Be my arm withered from its shoulder-blade!
Yea! were I lord of Great Apollo's lyre,
    I'd sooner rend its chords than e'er degrade
Its sweet seraphic music to inspire
    One vicious thought! When built on vice, fair maid,
Thy temple's base is quicksand; on the rock
    Of virtue reared, it braves the whirlwind's shock.

(written 1824) 1872

The Female Transport

Come all young girls, both far and near, and listen unto me,
While unto you I do unfold what proved my destiny,
My mother died when I was young, it caused me to deplore,
And I did get my way too soon upon my native shore.

Sarah Collins is my name, most dreadful is my fate,
My father reared me tenderly, the truth I do relate,
'Till enticed by bad company along with many more,
It led to my discovery upon my native shore.

My trial it approached fast, before the judge I stood,
And when the judge's sentence passed it fairly chill'd my blood,
Crying, you must be transported for fourteen years or more,
And go from hence across the seas unto Van Dieman's shore.

It hurt my heart when on a coach I my native town passed by,
To see so many I did know, it made me heave a sigh,
Then to a ship was sent with speed along with many more,
Whose aching hearts did grieve to go unto Van Dieman's shore.

The sea was rough, ran mountains high, with us poor girls 'twas hard,
No one but God to us came nigh, no one did us regard.
At length, alas! we reached the land, it grieved us ten times more,
That wretched place Van Dieman's Land, far from our native shore.

They chained us two by two, and whipp'd and lashed along,
They cut off our provisions if we did the least thing wrong,
They march us in the burning sun until our feet are sore,
So hard's our lot now we are got to Van Dieman's shore.

We labour hard from morn to night until our bones do ache,
Then every one they must obey, their mouldy beds must make,
We often wish when we lay down we ne'er may rise no more,
To meet our savage governor upon Van Dieman's shore.

Every night when I lay down I wet my straw with tears,
While wind upon that horrid shore did whistle in our ears,
Those dreadful beasts upon that land around our cots do roar,
Most dismal is our doom upon Van Dieman's shore.

Come all young men and maidens, do bad company forsake,
If tongue can tell our overthrow it will make your heart to ache;
Young girls I pray be ruled by me, your wicked ways give o'er.
For fear like us you spend your days upon Van Dieman's shore.

(from a broadside, c.1820s)

Van Dieman's Land

Come all you gallant poachers, that ramble void of care
That walk out on moonlight night with your dog, gun and snare,
The lofty hare and pheasants you have at your command,
Not thinking of your last career upon Van Dieman's land.

Poor Tom Brown, from Nottingham, Jack Williams, and poor Joe,
We are three daring poachers, the country does well know,
At night we were trepan'd by the keepers hid in sand,
Who for 14 years, transported us unto Van Dieman's land.

The first day that we landed upon that fatal shore,
The planters they came round us full twenty score or more,
They rank'd us up like horses, and sold us out of hand
They yok'd us unto ploughs, my boys, to plough Van Dieman's land.

Our cottages that we live in were built of clod and clay,
And rotten straw for bedding, & we dare not say nay,.
Our cots were fenc'd with fire, we slumber when we can,
To drive away wolves and tigers upon Van Dieman's land.

It's often when I slumber I have a pleasant dream,
With my sweet girl a setting down by a purling stream,
Thro' England I've been roaming with her at command,
Now I awaken broken-hearted on Van Dieman's land.

God bless our wives and families likewise that happy shore,
That isle of great contentment which we shall see no more,
As for our wretched females, see them we seldom can,
There's twenty to one woman upon Van Dieman's land.

There was a girl from Birmingham, Susan Summers was her name,
For fourteen years transported we all well know the same,
Our planter bought her freedom and married her out of hand,
She gave to us good usage upon Van Dieman's land.

So you gallant poachers give ear unto my song
It is a bit of good advice altho' it is not long.
Throw by your dogs & snare for to you I speak plain,
For if you know our hardships you'd never poach again.

(from c.1820s)

BARRON FIELD (1786-1846)

Sonnet

On visiting the spot where Captain Cook and Sir Joseph Banks first landed in
Botany Bay

Here fix the tablet. This must be the place
Where our Columbus of the South did land;
He saw the Indian village on that sand,
And on this rock first met the simple race
Of Australasia, who presum'd to face
With lance and spear his musquet. Close at hand
Is the clear stream, from which his vent'rous band
Ref resh'd their ship; and thence a little space
Lies Sutherland, their shipmate; for the sound
Of Christian burial better did proclaim
Possession, than the flag, in England's name.
These were the *commelinæ* Banks first found;
But where's the tree with the ship's wood-carv'd fame?
Fix then th' Ephesian brass. 'Tis classic ground.   1819

---

commelinæ   *plural of 'commelina', an order of herbaceous plants, a number of species of*
which are native to Australia
The Ephesians were the first who erected brazen trophies. The Greeks and Romans
preferred wood, as not perpetuating hostility (author's note).

On Reading the Controversy Between Lord Byron
and Mr. Bowles

Anticipation is to a young country what antiquity is to an old.

Whether a ship's poetic? – Bowles would own,
If here he dwelt, where Nature is prosaic,
Unpicturesque, unmusical, and where
Nature-reflecting Art is not yet born; –
A land without antiquities, with one,
And only one, poor spot of classic ground,
(That on which Cook first landed) – where, instead
Of heart-communings with ancestral relicks,
Which purge the pride while they exalt the mind,
We've nothing left us but anticipation,
Better (I grant) than utter selfishness,
Yet too o'erweening – too American;
Where's no past tense; the ign'rant present's all;
Or only great by the *All hail, hereafter!*
One foot of Future's glass should rest on Past;
Where Hist'ry is not, Prophecy is guess –
If here he dwelt, Bowles (I repeat) would own
A ship's the only poetry we see.
For, first, she brings us 'news of human kind,'
Of friends and kindred, whom perchance she held
As visitors, that she might be a link,
Connecting the fond fancy of far friendship,
A few short months before, and whom she may
In a few more, perhaps, receive again.
Next is a ship poetic, forasmuch
As in this spireless city and prophane,
She is to my home-wand'ring phantasy,
With her tall anch'ring masts, a three-spir'd minster,
Vane-crown'd; her bell our only half-hour chimes.
Lastly, a ship is poetry to me,
Since piously I trust, in no long space,
Her wings will bear me from this prose-dull land.

1823

Controversy   Byron's 'Letter . . . on the Rev. W. L. Bowles's Strictures on the Life and
Writings of Pope' (1821) contested Bowles's view that figures of nature and passion are
more 'poetical' than others. Bowles claimed that a ship is not in itself poetical; Byron
replies in effect that no image is poetical in itself.

Song Cycle of the Moon-Bone

1

The people are making a camp of branches in that country at Arnhem Bay:
With the forked stick, the rail for the whole camp, the *Mandjigai* people
    are making it.
Branches and leaves are about the mouth of the hut: the middle is clear
    within.
They are thinking of rain, and of storing their clubs in case of a quarrel,
In the country of the Dugong, towards the wide clay pans made by
    the Moonlight.
Thinking of rain, and of storing the fighting sticks.
They put up the rafters of arm-band-tree wood, put the branches on to
    the camp, at Arnhem Bay, in that place of the Dugong . . .
And they block up the back of the hut with branches.
Carefully place the branches, for this is the camp of the Morning-
    Pigeon man,
And of the Middle-of-the-Camp man; of the Mangrove-Fish man; of
    two other head-men,
And of the Clay-pan man; of the *Baiini*-Anchor man, and of the
    Arnhem Bay country man;
Of the Whale man and of another head-man; of the Arnhem Bay Creek
    man;
Of the Scales-of-the-Rock-Cod man; of the Rock Cod man, and of the
    Place-of-the-Water man.

2

They are sitting about in the camp, among the branches, along the
    back of the camp:
Sitting along in lines in the camp, there in the shade of the paperbark
    trees:
Sitting along in a line, like the new white spreading clouds:
In the shade of the paperbarks, they are sitting resting like clouds.
People of the clouds, living there like the mist; like the mist sitting
    resting with arms on knees,

The Wonguri Mandjigai people *are from north-eastern Arnhem Land. The poem is*
translated by Ronald M. Berndt.

In here towards the shade, in this Place, in the shadow of paperbarks.
Sitting there in rows, those *Wonguri-Mandjigai* people, paperbarks
    along like a cloud.
Living on cycad-nut bread; sitting there with white-stained fingers,
Sitting in there resting, those people of the Sandfly clan . . .
Sitting there like mist, at that place of the Dugong . . . and of the
    Dugong's Entrails . . .
Sitting resting there in the place of the Dugong . . .
In that place of the Moonlight Clay Pans, and at the place of the Dugong . . .
There at that Dugong place they are sitting all along.

    3

Wake up from sleeping! Come, we go to see the clay pan, at the place of
    the Dugong . . .
Walking along, stepping along, straightening up after resting:
Walking along, looking as we go down on to the clay pan.
Looking for lily plants as we go . . . and looking for lily foliage . . .
Circling around, searching towards the middle of the lily leaves to
    reach the rounded roots.
At that place of the Dugong . . .
At that place of the Dugong's Tail . . .
At that place of the Dugong; looking for food with stalks,
For lily foliage, and for the round-nut roots of the lily plant.

    4

The birds saw the people walking along.
Crying, the white cockatoos flew over the clay pan of the Moonlight;
From the place of the Dugong they flew, looking for lily-root food;
    pushing the foliage down and eating the soft roots.
Crying, the birds flew down and along the clay pan, at that place of the
    Dugong . . .
Crying, flying down there along the clay pan . . .
At the place of the Dugong, of the Tree-Limbs-Rubbing-Together, and
    of the Evening Star.
Where the lily-root clay pan is . . .
Where the cockatoos play, at that place of the Dugong . . .
Flapping their wings they flew down, crying, 'We saw the people!'
There they are always living, those clans of the white cockatoo
And there is the Shag woman, and there her clan:
Birds, trampling the lily foliage, eating the soft round roots!

5

An animal track is running along: it is the track of the rat . . .
Of the male rat, and the female rat, and the young that hang to her
    teats as she runs,
The male rat hopping along, and female rat, leaving paw-marks as a sign . . .
On the clay pans of the Dugong, and in the shade of the trees,
At the Dugong's place, and at the place of her Tail . . .
Thus, they spread paw-mark messages all along their tracks,
In that place of the Evening Star, in the place of the Dugong . . .
Among the lily plants and into the mist, into the Dugong place, and
    into the place of her Entrails.
Backwards and forwards the rats run, always hopping along . . .
Carrying swamp-grass for nesting, over the little tracks, leaving their
    signs.
Backwards and forwards they run on the clay pan, around the place of
    the Dugong.
Men saw their tracks at the Dugong's place, in the shade of the trees,
    on the white clay;
Roads of the rats, paw-marks everywhere, running into the mist.
All around are their signs; and there men saw them down on the clay
    pan, at the place of the Dugong.

6

A duck comes swooping down to the Moonlight clay pan, there at the
    place of the Dugong . . .
From far away. 'I saw her flying over, in here at the clay pan . . .'
Floating along, pushing the pool into ripples and preening her feathers.
                                         (the duck speaks)
'I carried these eggs from a long way off, from inland to Arnhem
    Bay . . .'
Eggs, eggs, eggs; eggs she is carrying, swimming along.
She preens her feathers, and pulls at the lily foliage,
Drags at the lily leaves with her claws for food.
Swimming along, rippling the water among the lotus plants
Backwards and forwards: she pulls at the foliage, swimming along,
    floating and eating.
This bird is taking her food, the lotus food in the clay-pan,
At the place of the Dugong there, at the place of the Dugong's Tail . . .
Swimming along for food, floating, and rippling the water, there at the
    place of the Lilies.

Taking the lotus, the rounded roots and stalks of the lily; searching and
    eating there as she ripples the water.
'Because I have eggs, I give to my young the sound of the water.'
Splashing and preening herself, she ripples the water, among the lotus . . .
Backwards and forwards, swimming along, rippling the water,
Floating along on the clay pan, at the place of the Dugong.

7

People were diving here at the place of the Dugong . . .
Here they were digging all around, following up the lily stalks,
Digging into the mud for the rounded roots of the lily,
Digging them out at that place of the Dugong, and of the Evening Star,
Pushing aside the water while digging, and smearing themselves with
    mud . . .
Piling up the mud as they dug, and washing the roots clean.
They saw arm after arm there digging: people thick like the mist . . .
The Shag woman too was there, following up the lily stalks.
There they saw arm after arm of the *Mandjigai* Sandfly clan,
Following the stalks along, searching and digging for food:
Always there together, those *Mandjigai* Sandfly people.
They follow the stalks of the lotus and lily, looking for food.
The lilies that always grow there at the place of the Dugong . . .
At that clay-pan, at the place of the Dugong, at the place of the lilies.

8

Now the leech is swimming along . . . It always lives there in the
    water . . .
It takes hold of the leaves of the lily and pods of the lotus, and climbs
    up on to their stalks.
Swimming along and grasping hold of the leaves with its head . . .
It always lives there in the water, and climbs up on to the people.
Always there, that leech, together with all its clan . . .
Swimming along towards the trees, it climbs up and waits for people.
Hear it swimming along through the water, its head out ready to grasp
    us . . .
Always living here and swimming along.
Because that leech is always there, for us, however it came there:
The leech that catches hold of those *Mandjigai* Sandfly people . . .

9

The prawn is there, at the place of the Dugong, digging out mud with
   its claws . . .
The hard-shelled prawn living there in the water, making soft little noises.
It burrows into the mud and casts it aside, among the lilies . . .
Throwing aside the mud, with soft little noises . . .
Digging out mud with its claws at the place of the Dugong, the place of
   the Dugong's Tail . . .
Calling the bone invocation, the catfish invocation, the frog invocation,
   the sacred tree invocation . . .
The prawn is burrowing, coming up, throwing aside the mud, and
   digging . . .
Climbing up on to the lotus plants and on to their pods . . .

10

Swimming along under the water, as bubbles rise to the surface, the
   tortoise moves in the swamp grass.
Swimming among the lily leaves and the grasses, catching them as she
   moves . . .
Pushing them with her short arms. Her shell is marked with designs,
This tortoise carrying her young, in the clay pan, at the place of the
   Dugong . . .
The short-armed *Madarba* tortoise, with special arm-bands, here at the
   place of the Dugong . . .
Backwards and forwards she swims, the short-armed one of the
   Madarba, and the *Dalwongu*.
Carrying eggs about, in the clay pan, at the place of the Dugong . . .
Her entrails twisting with eggs . . .
Swimming along through the grass, and moving her patterned shell.
The tortoise with her young, and her special arm-bands,
Swimming along, moving her shell, with bubbles rising;
Throwing out her arms towards the place of the Dugong . . .
This creature with the short arms, swimming and moving her shell;
This tortoise, swimming along with the drift of the water . . .
Swimming with her short arms, at the place of the Dugong . . .

11

Wild-grape vines are floating there in the billabong:
Their branches, joint by joint, spreading over the water.
Their branches move as they lie, backwards and forwards,
In the wind and the waves, at the Moonlight clay pan, at the place of
    the Dugong . . .
Men see them lying there on the clay pan pool, in the shade of the
    paperbarks:
Their spreading limbs shift with the wind and the water:
Grape vines with their berries . . .
Blown backwards and forwards as they lie, there at the place of the Dugong.
Always there, with their hanging grapes, in the clay pan of the
    Moonlight . . .
Vine plants and roots and jointed limbs, with berry food, spreading
    over the water.

12

Now the New Moon is hanging, having cast away his bone:
Gradually he grows larger, taking on new bone and flesh.
Over there, far away, he has shed his bone: he shines on the place of
    the Lotus Root, and the place of the Dugong,
On the place of the Evening Star, of the Dugong's Tail, of the
    Moonlight clay pan . . .
His old bone gone, now the New Moon grows larger;
Gradually growing, his new bone growing as well.
Over there, the horns of the old receding Moon bent down, sank into
    the place of the Dugong:
His horns were pointing towards the place of the Dugong.
Now the New Moon swells to fullness, his bone grown larger.
He looks on the water, hanging above it, at the place of the Lotus.
There he comes into sight, hanging above the sea, growing larger and
    older . . .
There far away he has come back, hanging over the clans near
    Milingimbi . . .
Hanging there in the sky, above those clans . . .
'Now I'm becoming a big moon, slowly regaining my roundness . . .'
In the far distance the horns of the Moon bend down, above Milingimbi,
Hanging a long way off, above Milingimbi Creek . . .
Slowly the Moon Bone is growing, hanging there far away.
The bone is shining, the horns of the Moon bend down.

First the sickle Moon on the old Moon's shadow; slowly he grows,
And shining he hangs there at the place of the Evening Star . . .
Then far away he goes sinking down, to lose his bone in the sea;
Diving towards the water, he sinks down out of sight.
The old Moon dies to grow new again, to rise up out of the sea.

13

Up and up soars the evening Star, hanging there in the sky.
Men watch it, at the place of the Dugong and of the Clouds, and of the
    Evening Star,
A long way off, at the place of Mist, of Lilies and of the Dugong.
The Lotus, the Evening Star, hangs there on its long stalk, held by the
    Spirits.
It shines on that place of the Shade, on the Dugong place, and on to the
    Moonlight clay pan . . .
The Evening Star is shining, back towards Milingimbi, and over the
    Malag people . . .
Hanging there in the distance, towards the place of the Dugong,
The place of the Eggs, of the Tree-Limbs-Rubbing -Together, and of the
    Moonlight clay pan . . .
Shining on its short stalk, the Evening Star, always there at the
    clay pan, at the place of the Dugong . . .
There, far away, the long string hangs at the place of the Evening Star,
    the place of Lilies.
Away there at Milingimbi . . . at the place of the Full Moon,
Hanging above the head of that *Wonguri* tribesman:
The Evening Star goes down across the camp, among the white gum
    trees . . .
Far away, in those places near Milingimbi . . .
Goes down among the *Ngurulwulu* people, towards the camp and the
    gum trees,
At the place of the Crocodiles, and of the Evening Star, away towards
    Milingimbi . . .
The Evening Star is going down, the Lotus Flower on its stalk . . .
Going down among all those western clans . . .
It brushes the heads of the uncircumcised people . . .
Sinking down in the sky, that Evening Star, the Lotus . . .
Shining on to the foreheads of all those headmen . . .
On to the heads of all those Sandfly people . . .
It sinks there into the place of the white gum trees, at Milingimbi.

Oceania, xix, September 1948

Biographical Notes

Arthur H Adams 1872-1936 Born in NZ, he arrived in Australia in his twenties. He worked in Sydney as a journalist and literary editor.

Robert Adamson b 1944 Sydney. A poetry editor and former publisher, he lives in the Hawkesbury River district.

Adam Aitken b 1960 in London to Thai and Australian parents. He grew up in Bangkok, Kuala Lumpur, Perth and Sydney, where he now teaches writing.

'Australie' (Emily Manning) 1845-90 Born in Sydney, she worked as a journalist there from the early 1870s. Her poetry and some of her journalism were published under the pseudonym 'Australie'.

Coral Hull b 1965 Sydney. Also photographer and a visual and conceptual artist, and a long-term campaigner for animal rights, she grew up in Sydney's west and currently lives in Darwin.

Jordie Albiston b 1961 Melbourne, where she lives. She is also a musician and works as an editor.

Dorothy Auchterlonie 1915-91 Born in Sunderland, England, she arrived in Australia in her teens. A broadcaster and journalist in Sydney during the 1940s, she subsequently taught literature at several universities, latterly in Canberra. She published literary studies under her married name, Green.

Catherine Bateson b 1960 in Sydney. She grew up in Brisbane, moved to Melbourne in 1985, and now lives in the Dandenongs. She is a novelist in prose and verse for younger, and young adult, readers.

Bruce Beaver 1928-2004 Born in Manly, where he lived. He worked in various manual and clerical jobs, and from the early 1960s was a freelance journalist.

Judith Beveridge b 1956 in London; moved to Sydney in 1960. She has worked there as a researcher, librarian and teacher. Currently she is a poetry editor and teaches creative writing at Sydney University.

John Blight 1913-95 Born in Adelaide, he grew up in Brisbane. He worked variously as an orchardist, an accountant, and part-owner of timber mills in the coastal areas of south-east Queensland. From 1968 he lived in Brisbane.

Barcroft Boake 1866-92 Born in Sydney, he worked as a surveyor's assistant, drover and boundary rider from 1886-91. Beset by personal and financial problems, he committed suicide shortly after returning to Sydney. A book of his bush ballads was published in 1897.

Peter Boyle b 1951 Melbourne. He moved to Sydney in 1962, where he works as a teacher.

Christopher Brennan 1870-1932 Born in Sydney, he spent two formative years studying in Berlin from 1892-94. He was a cataloguer in the Sydney Public Library from 1895, then taught modern comparative literature at Sydney University, 1909-25.

Vincent Buckley 1925-88 Born in Romsey, central Victoria, of Irish lineage. A critic and literary editor, he taught literature at the University of Melbourne.

Kevin Brophy b 1949 in Melbourne. He studied psychology and worked for many years with intellectually disabled people. He now teaches creative writing at the University of Melbourne.

Caroline Caddy b 1944 in WA. Her early childhood was spent in the USA and Japan. She worked in Road Dental Units throughout WA, and then as a farmer on the state's south coast, where she now lives.

Ada Cambridge 1844-1926 Born in Norfolk, she arrived in Australia in 1870 and lived with her clergyman husband in several Victorian country towns before settling in Melbourne in 1893. She was also novelist.

David Campbell 1915-79 Born on Ellerslie Station near Adelong, south-eastern NSW (now ACT). He farmed in the district after wartime service as a pilot.

Elizabeth Campbell b 1980 in Melbourne, where she lives. She is a reviewer and teaches English in a secondary school.

Nancy Cato 1917-2000 Born in Adelaide, where she lived, she was a literary editor and a historical novelist.

Julian Croft b 1941 in Newcastle, where he grew up. Since 1970 he has lived in Armidale, where he taught literature at the University of New England.

Alison Croggon b 1962 Carltonville in Transvaal. She moved to England in 1966 and to a property near Ballarat in 1969. A novelist for young adults and also a theatre critic, she lives in Melbourne.

R H Croll 1869-1947 Born in Stawell, western Victoria, he worked as a literary editor and education administrator in Melbourne.

Zora Cross 1890-1964 Born in Brisbane, she was also a novelist, and worked as a freelance journalist in Sydney.

Lidija Cvetkovic b 1967 in the former Yugoslavia. She arrived in Brisbane in 1980 and works there as a psychologist.

Victor Daley 1858-1905 Born in Co. Meath, Ireland, he arrived in Australia in 1878 and worked as a journalist in Adelaide, Melbourne and Sydney.

Jack Davis 1917-2000 Born in Perth of Aboriginal, Sikh and Irish lineage, his many occupations included stockman, lay preacher and actor. A playwright based in Fremantle, he was a prominent advocate of Aboriginal rights.

Bruce Dawe b 1930 in Geelong. He was in the RAAF from 1959-68, and taught from 1972 in Toowoomba at Darling Downs IAE, which became the University of Southern Queensland.

Sarah Day b 1958 in Lancashire; arrived in Hobart as a young child. She has worked as a teacher of English and as a poetry editor.

C J Dennis 1876-1938 Born in Auburn, SA, he worked in poorly paid jobs until his ballad series, *Songs of a Sentimental Bloke* (1915) sold 60,000 copies in eighteen months. Settling in Melbourne, he became staff poet with the *Herald*.

Rosemary Dobson b 1920 in Sydney. She has also been an art historian and literary editor, and worked in Sydney in publishing in the 1940s. After a period in London, she has lived in Canberra since 1972.

Michael Dransfield 1948-73 Born in Sydney, he worked briefly in the public service, then led an itinerant life, mainly in NSW. A prolific poet in his early twenties, he died of complications from drug use and a road injury.

Eliza Hamilton Dunlop 1790-1854 Born in Ireland, she arrived in Sydney in February 1838 and moved to Wollombi in the Hunter Valley in 1839 when her husband was appointed magistrate and protector of Aborigines for the area. She maintained a close interest in Aboriginal people and their culture.

'E' (Mary E Fullerton) 1868-1946 Born in Glenmaggie, Gippsland, she was also a novelist, and a campaigner on feminist issues. She lived in England from 1922, where her last two books of poetry were published under the pseudonym 'E'.

Stephen Edgar b 1951 in Sydney. From 1974 he lived in Hobart, where he worked as a librarian, before returning to Sydney in 2005. He is a freelance editor and proofreader.

Rebecca Edwards b 1969 in Batlow, south-eastern NSW. She grew up in places north, including Papua New Guinea, Nambucca Heads and Darwin, and has lived in Brisbane and Townsville. Also a visual artist and reviewer, she is currently based in Jakarta.

Anne Elder 1918-76 Born in Auckland, she arrived in Australia at the age of three. In the early 1940s she was a soloist with the Borovansky Ballet. She lived in Melbourne, and later on a farm near Macedon, central Victoria.

Brook Emery b 1949 in Sydney. He has been a teacher of history and English in secondary schools, and currently works as an arts administrator.

Diane Fahey b 1945 in Melbourne, where she grew up. She has worked as a teacher in secondary and tertiary education. After several years based in England, then in Adelaide, she now lives on the Bellerine peninsula.

Barron Field 1786-1846 Born in England, he spent 1817-24 in Australia as a judge of the Supreme Court of NSW, then returned home. His *First Fruits of Australian Poetry* (1819) was the first book of poetry published in Australia.

Robert D FitzGerald 1902-87 Born in Sydney, he was a professional surveyor, and lived for most of his life there.

Lionel G Fogarty b 1959 in Barambah, south-east Queensland, on Wakka Wakka tribal land. An activist in Aboriginal rights and culture, he is based in Brisbane.

Mary Hannay Foott 1846-1918 Born in Glasgow, she arrived in Australia in 1853. She trained as an artist in Melbourne, and worked as a journalist. From 1877 she farmed in south-east Queensland, then moved to Brisbane, where she founded a private school in 1884, and worked as a journalist for a decade from 1887.

John Forbes 1950-98. Born in Melbourne, he grew up in New Guinea, Malaya and Sydney. He did various manual and literary work in Sydney, and then in Melbourne from 1989.

Claire Gaskin b 1966 in Melbourne, where she teaches creative writing.

'Frank the Poet' (Francis MacNamara) Born c.1811 in Ireland, he was transported to NSW in 1832 and spent time at several penal settlements. A recalcitrant prisoner, he was sent to Port Arthur in 1842, finally receiving his freedom in 1849. His life thereafter is unknown, and rumour. He may be the balladeer seen by the writer Marcus Clarke in a doss-house in Melbourne in 1868.

Leon Gellert 1892-1977 Born in Adelaide, he was a schoolteacher there before the 1914-18 war. He took part in the landing at Gallipoli, and was wounded and evacuated in July 1915. Moving to Sydney, he worked again as a schoolteacher and later became an arts journalist and literary editor.

Jane Gibian b 1972 She lives in Sydney where she works as a librarian and ESL teacher.

Kevin Gilbert 1933-93 Born in Condobolin, central NSW, to an Irish father and a part-Wiradjuri mother. He left school early, worked as a labourer and spent time in gaol. Also a playwright and a visual artist, he became a leading advocate of Aboriginal rights and culture.

Barbara Giles 1912-2006 Born in Manchester, she arrived in Australia in 1923. She worked as a teacher and literary editor and wrote children's fiction. She published the first of several books of poetry in 1978.

Mary Gilmore 1865-1962 Born in Cotta Walla near Goulburn, she taught in country schools and then in Sydney from 1890-95. A socialist, she joined William Lane's utopian 'New Australia' community in Paraguay (1896-1902), then farmed in western Victoria, and finally settled in Sydney in 1912. As a journalist, and especially as editor of the Women's Page of the Sydney *Worker* (1908-31), she was a radical social campaigner.

Peter Goldsworthy b 1951 in Minlaton on the Yorke peninsula. Living in Adelaide, he is a medical doctor and also a writer of fiction and a librettist.

W T Goodge 1862-1909 Born in London, he arrived in Australia in 1882 and worked for twelve years in outback NSW. He then settled in Orange, working as a journalist and newspaper editor.

Adam Lindsay Gordon 1833-70 Born in the Azores to British parents, he arrived in Australia in 1853. He worked in South Australia as a mounted policeman, and then as an itinerant horse dealer and steeplechase rider before settling near Mt Gambier. In 1867-68 he ran a livery stable in Ballarat. He died by suicide.

Alan Gould b 1949, London, to British and Icelandic parents. He lived in Ireland, Iceland, Germany and Singapore before arriving in Australia in 1966. Also a novelist, he lives in Canberra.

Robert Gray b 1945 in Coffs Harbour, and grew up there. He lives in Sydney, where he has worked in advertising and as a bookseller.

Lesbia Harford 1891-1927 Born in Melbourne, she studied at the University of Melbourne from 1912-16, graduating in law and philosophy. Poor in health from a heart defect, she worked as a teacher and as an office worker, and for a time in a clothing factory. Her association with radical social groups in Melbourne is reflected in her poetry and one novel, all published well after her death.

Charles Harpur 1813-68 Born in Windsor outside Sydney to emancipist parents, he grew up in the Hawkesbury River district. He worked as a clerk in Sydney from 1837-39, then moved to the Hunter Valley where he worked at farming and for a time as a schoolteacher. From 1859 to 1866 he was a Gold Commissioner for the Tuross River area south of Sydney, then settled on a farm at Eurobodalla. He dedicated himself to becoming the first major poet of Australia in terms both of landscape and of emerging nation.

Robert Harris 1951-93 He was born in Melbourne, and lived there. He worked at a variety of jobs, including teaching creative writing, and was active in Christian lay ministry.

Jennifer Harrison b 1955 in Sydney, where she grew up. She spent 1980-91 in Asia, Europe, NZ and the USA, and now practises as a child psychiatrist in Melbourne.

Martin Harrison b 1949 He was born in England. Also a critic and reviewer, he currently teaches creative writing at the University of Technology Sydney.

J S Harry b 1939 in Adelaide and educated there. She has lived in Sydney since the late 1960s, where she has worked as a bookseller.

Kevin Hart b 1954 in London; arrived in Brisbane aged eleven and grew up there. He has taught literature and literary theory at Monash and Notre Dame, and currently at the University of Virginia.

William Hart-Smith 1911-90 Born in Tunbridge Wells, England, he went to NZ in 1924 and from there to Australia in 1936. He lived in NZ again after the war, in Sydney from 1962, Perth from 1970-78, and then settled in NZ. He worked mainly in advertising and in radio.

Gwen Harwood 1920-95 Born in Brisbane, she moved to Hobart in 1945, where she lived at Oyster Cove. She was also a librettist and a musician.

Jill Hellyer b 1925 in Sydney. She was the founding executive secretary of the Australian Society of Authors 1963-71.

Dorothy Hewett 1923-2002 Born in Perth, she grew up on a wheat farm at Wickepin, southwest WA. She was a member of the Communist Party 1942-68. Also a playwright, she lived in Sydney 1949-60, then returned to Perth and taught literature at the University of WA. She lived in Sydney from 1974.

Fidelia S T Hill 1790-1854 Born in Yorkshire, she arrived in Australia with the first settlers in the Adelaide area in 1836. She moved briefly to Sydney in 1840, then settled in Tasmania from 1841. Her *Poems and Recollections of the Past* (1840) was the first book of poetry by a woman published in Australia.

Philip Hodgins 1959-95 Born near Shepparton, where he grew up on a dairy farm. He worked in publishing in Melbourne, then lived near Maryborough, central Victoria, from 1990. From his mid-twenties until his death he was under treatment for leukemia.

Sarah Holland-Batt b 1982 in Southport. She teaches literary studies at the University of Queensland.

L K Holt b 1982 in Melbourne. She grew up in Adelaide, and now works in Melbourne as a poetry editor and publisher.

Yvette Holt b 1971 in Brisbane. She is a member of the Bidjara Nation, Queensland, and currently lectures on Aboriginal women's studies at the University of Queensland.

A D Hope 1907-2000 Born in Cooma, he taught literature at Sydney Teachers College from 1938, then from 1945 at the University of Melbourne, and from 1951 at Canberra University College, later ANU.

John Jenkins b 1949 in Melbourne, where he lives just outside the city. He is a journalist.

Martin Johnston 1947-90 Born in Sydney, he grew up on the Greek island of Hydra from 1954 and was based in Sydney again from 1964. Also the author of a novel, he worked as a journalist and a translator.

Emma Jones b 1977 in Sydney, and educated there, she is currently studying literature in the UK.

Evan Jones b 1931 in Melbourne. He taught literature at the University of Melbourne from 1963-89 and lives in that city.

Nancy Keesing 1923-93 Born in Sydney, she worked there as a social worker, then as a literary editor, critic, children's novelist and arts administrator.

Aileen Kelly b 1939 in Portsmouth; arrived in Melbourne in1962. She has worked as an adult educator in a number of fields, including poetry and creative writing.

Henry Kendall 1839-82 Born near Milton, NSW south coast, he grew up in the Clarence River district, northern NSW, and then near Wollongong. He worked on a whaling ship 1855-57, and in the public service in Sydney in 1862-69. In Melbourne from 1869-70, problems of unemployment and alcoholism led to a five-year rift with his wife and family, and treatment in a mental hospital. From 1876, restored to family and health, he settled in Camden Haven, NSW north coast, where he worked for a timber company. Kendall consciously followed Harpur in embracing the vocation of poetry as contributing to the emerging sense of a new nation.

John Kinsella b 1963 Perth. An editor and publisher of poetry, he has taught extensively in the UK and USA, and now lives near York in south-west WA.

Peter Kirkpatrick b 1955 in Sydney. He teaches Australian literature at Sydney University.

John Dunmore Lang 1799-1878 Born in Greenock, Scotland, he arrived in Australia in 1823. Based in Sydney, he was a Presbyterian minister and became a member of the NSW parliament. He wrote poetry, and voluminous essays on religion, politics and history. He was a stirrer in the intellectual life of the colony, advocating the abolition of transportation, as well as the institution of a system of national education, federation and a republic.

Anthony Lawrence b 1957 Tamworth, NSW. He has worked as a jackeroo and in various manual and teaching occupations across the country, and currently lives in Newcastle.

Henry Lawson 1867-1922 Born on the Grenfell goldfields, NSW, he was the eldest child of Louisa Lawson. He grew up mainly at New Pipeclay (later Eurunderee) near Mudgee. Also a writer of short fiction, he lived principally in Sydney from 1883.

Louisa Lawson 1848-1920 Born near Mudgee, she was the mother of Henry Lawson. She moved to Sydney in 1883 and became a journalist, campaigning on radical social issues. She founded and edited the feminist journal *The Dawn* from 1888-1905.

Bronwyn Lea b 1969 in Tasmania. She grew up in Queensland and Papua New Guinea. After studies in the USA, she now teaches at the University of Queensland.

Geoffrey Lehmann b 1940 in Sydney, where he has worked as a lawyer, and lecturing and writing on taxation law.

Emma Lew b 1962 in Melbourne, where she lives and writes.

Tony Lintermans b 1948 in Melbourne, and lives there. He grew up on a farm at Lysterfield. He works as a scriptwriter and a speechwriter.

Kathryn Lomer b 1958 in north-west Tasmania. She lives in Hobart, and is also a novelist.

Robert Lowe 1811-92 Born in Nottinghamshire, he arrived in Australia in 1842. A barrister, and a member of the NSW parliament (1843-50), he initially supported, then from 1847 opposed, the land monopoly of the squatters. He wrote political satires and founded a newspaper, the *Atlas*. Returning to England in 1850, he entered the British parliament and was made Viscount Sherbrooke in 1880.

James McAuley 1917-76 Born in Sydney, he worked as a government adviser on New Guinea and Pacific affairs in the 1940s and 50s. He worked as a literary editor, and from 1961 taught literature in Hobart at the University of Tasmania.

Dennis McDermott b 1946. Although he grew up on Gamilaroi land, Tamworth, NSW, his mother's mob is from inner Sydney, Gadigal country, and his father's from Donegal. He works as a psychologist and lives in Adelaide.

Roger McDonald b 1941 in Young. He worked in radio and television in Sydney, and as a poetry editor with UQP. Already known as a poet, he turned to novel-writing from 1976.

J K McDougall 1867-1957 Born in Learmonth, western Victoria, for much of his life he farmed near Ararat. He also wrote political prose, and was the Labor member for Wannon in the federal parliament 1906-13.

Dorothea Mackellar 1885-1968 Born in Sydney, where she lived for most of her life, she was also the author of three novels. She wrote little after the mid-1920s.

Geraldine McKenzie b 1954 in Sydney. She grew up mainly in Grenfell, central west NSW. A teacher of English and history, she lives in the Blue Mountains.

Kenneth Mackenzie 1913-55 Born in Perth, he grew up there and in the country town of Pinjarra. He was also a novelist. Working occasionally as a journalist and publisher's reader, he lived in Sydney from 1934.

Paul Magee b 1970 in Melbourne, where he studied and taught classics. He currently teaches creative writing at the University of Canberra.

'Ern Malley' '1918-43' Born in Liverpool, England, he arrived in Australia about 1920 and grew up in Sydney, where he worked briefly as a mechanic. From about 1935 he was an insurance salesman in Melbourne. After his death, a collection of his poems submitted by his sister was accepted and published as modernist work in the Autumn 1944 issue of the arts and literary journal *Angry Penguins*. James McAuley and Harold Stewart subsequently identified themselves as the hoax creators of author and work, intended as parody.

David Malouf b 1934 in Brisbane, to English and Lebanese parents. After living for a decade in Europe, he taught literature at the University of Sydney from 1968-77. Also novelist and a librettist, he lives in Sydney.

John Manifold 1915-85 Born in Melbourne, he grew up on the family pastoral property in western Victoria. He joined the Communist Party in the 1930s. After war service, he lived in Brisbane and worked as a freelance writer. He was a noted scholar of Australian folk song and ballad.

Philip Martin 1931-2005 Born in Melbourne, he taught literature at Monash University from 1964-88, and was also a writer and presenter of literary programmes on radio.

John Mateer b 1971 in Roodeport, South Africa. He grew up there and, briefly, in Canada. He arrived in Perth in 1989. Since then, he has been based in Melbourne and in Perth, while travelling widely.

Jack Mathieu 1873-1949 Born in the Goulburn Valley, Victoria, he was a writer of bush ballads and short fiction, and worked as a sailor, shearer, drover and digger. He lived in Brisbane for the latter part of his life.

'Furnley Maurice' (Frank Wilmot) 1881-1942 Born in Melbourne, he worked there as a bookseller from 1895, and from 1932 as publisher at Melbourne University Press.

Louisa Anne Meredith 1812-95 Born in Birmingham, she was already established as a poet in England when she arrived in Sydney in 1839. She settled in Tasmania from 1840; a botanist and botanic artist, she illustrated several of her own books of poetry and prose.

Graeme Miles b 1976 in Perth. He lived there mainly until moving to Hobart in 2008, where he teaches classics at the University of Tasmania.

Les Murray b 1938 in Nabiac. He grew up on a dairy farm at Bunyah, between Forster and Gloucester. He was based in Sydney from 1957 to 1985, when he returned to Bunyah. Also an essayist and a literary editor, he has been a full-time writer since 1971.

David Musgrave b 1965 in Sydney. He is a poetry editor, publisher, novelist and critic.

John Shaw Neilson 1872-1942 Born in Penola, south-eastern SA, he grew up there and at Minimay, western Victoria. He worked as an itinerant agricultural labourer, mainly in western Victoria, until 1928, when in recognition of his literary merit and needs he was given a sinecure with the Country Roads Board in Melbourne. From about 1905 his vision was impaired so that he could only read large print.

Mark O'Connor b 1945 in Ararat; grew up there and in Melbourne. An environmentalist who has travelled in and written poetry about many of the regions of Australia, he is based in Canberra.

Oodgeroo of the tribe Noonuccal 1920-93 Born on Stradbroke Island, she lived there for much of her life. Formerly known as Kath Walker, she was an influential national voice for the Aboriginal people.

Jan Owen b 1940 in Adelaide. She has worked as a librarian, literary editor and teacher of creative writing, and now lives on the coast south of Adelaide.

Π O b 1951 in Katerini, Greece. He arrived in Australia in 1954, and lives in Fitzroy in inner Melbourne. He is active in promoting and performing poetry, and also works in the state public service.

Geoff Page b 1940 in Grafton. He grew up on a cattle station on the Clarence. Also a novelist and a reviewer, he taught English at secondary schools in Canberra.

AB Paterson 1864-1941 He was born on Narambla Station near Orange and grew up near Yass. He settled in Sydney and gained a law degree, but worked mainly as a journalist, becoming a newspaper editor and war correspondent. His pseudonym, 'The Banjo', was adopted only in his earliest publications in the *Bulletin*.

Marie E J Pitt 1869-1948 She was born in Doherty's Corner, Gippsland, and grew up there. She lived in rural Tasmania from 1893-1905, and subsequently in Melbourne. She was an office worker and journalist, and active in socialist and feminist causes.

Marcella Polain b 1958 in Singapore, to Irish and Armenian parents. She arrived in Perth in 1960. Also a novelist, she has taught creative writing at universities since the mid-1990s.

Dorothy Porter 1954-2008 Born in Sydney, she was a teacher of creative writing and wrote book-length verse narratives, as well as shorter poems and libretti. She lived in Melbourne from the end of the 1990s.

Peter Porter b 1929 in Brisbane. He has lived in London since 1951, at first working in advertising, and then as a freelance writer and reviewer. He has visited Australia regularly since 1974.

Elizabeth Riddell 1910-98 Born in Napier, NZ, she arrived in Australia in 1928. She worked as a professional journalist in Australia, the USA and Europe, including a period as a war correspondent. She later settled in Sydney.

Nick Riemer b 1972 in Sydney, where he lives and works.

Roland Robinson 1912-92 Born in Co. Clare, Ireland, to English parents, he arrived in Australia in 1921. He left school early, and seems to have worked in most of the jobs available in rural Australia, from rouseabout to crocodile catcher. He was also a ballet dancer, and ballet and literary reviewer. Much of his work in poetry and prose reflects a deep familiarity with Aboriginal culture.

Judith Rodriguez b 1936 in Perth. She grew up in Brisbane and has worked as a teacher at universities in Melbourne since 1969.

Peter Rose b 1955. He grew up in Wangaratta. Based mainly in Melbourne, he has worked in publishing and currently is a literary editor.

Gig Ryan b 1956 in Melbourne, where she works as a poetry editor. She spent the 1980s in Sydney and has been an office worker and a songwriter.

Philip Salom b 1950 Perth. He grew up in south-west WA and worked in farming and cattle research. He has taught creative writing in Perth and, from 1999 until recently, in Melbourne where he lives.

Dipti Saravanamuttu b 1960 in Sri Lanka; moved to Sydney in 1972, where she now lives after a time in Melbourne. She has worked as a scriptwriter and academic.

John A Scott b 1948 in Sussex. He arrived in Melbourne in 1959, where he worked as a scriptwriter and as a teacher in media studies. Also a writer of prose fiction, he taught creative writing at the University of Wollongong until recently, and now writes full-time.

Margaret Scott 1934-2005 Born in Bristol, she arrived in Australia in 1959. She taught literature in Hobart at the University of Tasmania from 1966-89, and was also a novelist.

Thomas Shapcott b 1935 in Ipswich. He worked there as an accountant, and was later a literary editor and arts administrator in Sydney, then taught at the University of Adelaide. Also a novelist, he lives in Melbourne.

Michael Sharkey b 1946 in Sydney. After five years postgraduate study in Auckland, he taught literature at a succession of Australian universities from 1977. Based at Armidale since 1992, he is a critic and reviewer.

Alex Skovron b 1948 in Katowice, Poland. He arrived in Sydney in 1958, after fifteen months in Israel. He moved in 1979 to Melbourne, where he works as a book editor.

Kenneth Slessor 1901-71 Born in Orange, from 1920 he worked as a journalist in Sydney, becoming a newspaper and literary editor, and in 1940-44 an official war correspondent.

Vivian Smith b 1933 in Hobart. He taught French at the University of Tasmania, and from 1967 taught English at Sydney University.

Peter Steele b 1939 in Perth. Since 1957 he has been based mainly in Melbourne. A Jesuit priest, he teaches literature at the University of Melbourne.

Douglas Stewart 1913-85 Born in Eltham, Taranaki Province, NZ, he settled in Australia in 1938. Also a writer of verse plays for radio, he was influential as the literary editor of the *Bulletin* in Sydney from 1940-61, and then as poetry editor with the publishers Angus & Robertson from 1961-71.

Randolph Stow b 1935 in Geraldton. Also a novelist, he has taught literature at several universities, and since 1966 has lived in England.

Jennifer Strauss b 1933 in Heywood, south-western Victoria. She taught literature at Monash University from 1964, and lives in Melbourne.

John Tranter b 1943 in Cooma. He has worked in publishing, as a radio producer, and as a literary editor. He lives in Sydney.

Dimitris Tsaloumas b 1921 on the island of Leros, Greece. He arrived in Australia in 1952 and taught in schools in Melbourne, where he lives. He writes poems in Greek, published in Greece, as well as poems in English.

Vicki Viidikas 1948-98 Born in Sydney, where she lived and worked, to Australian and Estonian parents. She travelled extensively in India.

Chris Wallace-Crabbe b 1934 in Melbourne. Also a critic, he taught literature and Australian studies at the University of Melbourne from 1961.

Ania Walwicz b 1951 in Świdnica Ślaska, Poland. She arrived in Australia in 1963 and lives in Melbourne. She is a noted performer of her own writing, and is also a visual artist.

Samuel Wagan Watson b 1972 in Brisbane, of Bundjalung, Birri Gubba, German, Irish and Scots descent. He lives and works in Brisbane.

John Watson b 1939 in West Wyalong. After teaching for a number of years in secondary schools, he now writes full-time.

Alan Wearne b 1948 in Melbourne, where he grew up. Much of his work in poetry has been in novelistic sequences. He now teaches creative writing at the University of Wollongong.

Francis Webb 1925-73 Born in Adelaide, he grew up in Sydney. He lived in Canada and England in the mid to late 1940s and again in England from 1953-60. Diagnosed as schizophrenic in 1949, he spent much of his subsequent life in psychiatric hospitals.

Simon West b 1974 in Melbourne. He currently teaches Italian at Monash University.

Petra White b 1975 in Adelaide. She moved to Melbourne in 1998 and works there as a public servant.

Judith Wright 1915-2000 Born near Armidale, she grew up there on her family's pastoral property. She later lived at Mt Tamborine in south-east Queensland and moved in the early 1970s to Braidwood. She was also a critic, historian, and writer of fiction, and a prominent activist in the areas of conservation and Aboriginal rights.

Morgan Yasbincek b 1964 in Sydney; moved to Perth in 1972. A second-generation Australian of Croatian background, she is also a novelist.

Fay Zwicky b 1933 in Melbourne. She was a concert pianist for several years, and subsequently taught literature at the University of WA from 1972-87. She lives in Perth.

Acknowledgements

ROBERT ADAMSON: 'Into Forest', 'Canticle for the Bicentennial Dead', 'The Language of Oysters', and 'The Goldfinches of Baghdad' from *The Golden Bird: New & Selected Poems* (2008), Black Inc. ADAM AITKEN: 'S21' from *eighth habitation* (2009), Giramondo. JORDIE ALBISTON: 'Headcount (1788)' from *Botany Bay Document* (1996), Black Pepper; 'The Fall' from *The Fall* (2003), White Crane Press; 'maximus' from *the sonnet according to 'm'* (2009), John Leonard Press. DOROTHY AUCHTERLONIE: 'Night at the Opera' from *The Dolphin* (1957), ANU Press. CATHERINE BATESON: 'Learning to Swim' from *Marriage for Beginners* (2009), John Leonard Press. BRUCE BEAVER: 'Anima XIII' from *Anima and Other Poems* (1994), UQP; 'Something for the Birds' from *The Long Game and Other Poems* (2005), UQP. JUDITH BEVERIDGE: 'The Domesticity of Giraffes' from *The Domesticity of Giraffes* (1987) Black Lightning Press and 'Yachts' from *Accidental Grace* (1996), UQP, to the author; 'Bahadour', from *Wolf Notes* (2003), Giramondo. JOHN BLIGHT: 'Pearl Perch' and 'Down from the Country' from *Selected Poems 1939 - 1990* (1992), UQP. PETER BOYLE: 'Everyday' from *What the painter saw in our faces* (2001), Five Islands Press, to the author. KEVIN BROPHY: 'What I Believe' and 'Walking towards sunset' from *Portrait in Skin* (2002), Five Islands Press. VINCENT BUCKLEY: 'Stroke', 'Give me time and I'll tell you', 'Golden Builders I, XIX', 'A Tincture of Budapest' and 'Small Brown Poem for Grania Buckley' from *Collected Poems* (2009), John Leonard Press, to the estate of Vincent Buckley. CAROLINE CADDY: 'Solitude' from *Esperance: New and Selected Poems* (2007), Fremantle Press. DAVID CAMPBELL: 'Ariel', 'Windy Gap', 'On Frosty Days', 'We Took the Storms to Bed', 'The Australian Dream' and 'Snake' from *Collected Poems* (1989), Angus & Robertson, to Judy Campbell. ELIZABETH CAMPBELL: 'Inferno' to the author; 'Proverb' from *Letters to the Tremulous Hand* (2007), John Leonard Press. NANCY CATO: 'The Dead Swagman' from *The Dancing Bough* (1957), Angus & Robertson; 'Great Aunt Ada' from *Australian Poetry 1965* (1965), Angus & Robertson. JULIAN CROFT: 'Sandworm' and 'Labour and Capital' from *Ocean Island* (2006), John Leonard Press. ALISON CROGGON: 'The Elwood Organic Fruit and Vegetable Shop' from *The Blue Gate* (1997), Black Pepper; 'Language' from *Attempts at Being* (2002), Salt; 'Ode' from *Theatre* (2008), Salt. ZORA CROSS: 'Love Sonnets III, XLIX' from *The Lilt of Life* (1918), Angus & Robertson. LIDIJA CVETKOVIC: 'The Fugitive' from *war is not the season for figs* (2004), UQP. JACK DAVIS: 'Camped in the Bush' from *The First Born and Other Poems* (1983), Dent; 'John Pat' from *John Pat and Other Poems* (1988), Dent, to Curtis Brown. BRUCE DAWE: 'Drifters', 'Homecoming', 'Going', 'Doctor to Patient', 'Betrayers', and 'A Park in the Balkans' from *Sometimes Gladness: Collected Poems 1954 - 2005* (6th ed., 2006), Longman Cheshire. SARAH DAY: 'Olive Grove' from *A Hunger to be Less Serious* (1987), Angus & Robertson and 'Navigator' from *Quickening* (1997), Penguin, to the author. ROSEMARY DOBSON: 'The Bystander', 'Cock Crow', 'The Rape of Europa' and 'Folding the Sheets' from *Collected Poems* (1992), Angus & Robertson, to the author. MICHAEL DRANSFIELD: 'Fix' from *Collected Poems* (1987), UQP. STEPHEN EDGAR: 'Destiny' from *Ancient Music* (1988), Angus & Robertson, to the author; 'Made to Measure' from *History of the Day* (2009), Black Pepper. REBECCA EDWARDS: 'Draw a Lion', and 'The Mothers' from *Scar Country* (2000), UQP and 'The Young Milton Moon Throws His Pots into the Brisbane River', to the author. ANNE ELDER: 'The Love Fight' from *For The Record* (1972), Hawthorn Press; 'The White Spider' from *Crazy Woman and Other Poems* (1976), Angus & Robertson, to Catherine Elder. BROOK EMERY: 'Approaching the Edge' and 'Postscript: like Picasso' from *Misplaced Heart* (2003), Five Islands Press, to the author. DIANE FAHEY: 'Andromeda' from *Metamorphoses* (1988) Dangaroo; 'Dressmaker' from *Turning the Hourglass* (1990), Dangaroo; 'Earwigs' from *Mayflies in Amber* (1993), Angus & Robertson, to the author. ROBERT D. FITZGERALD: 'The Face of the Waters', 'In Personal Vein' and 'The Wind at Your Door' from *Forty Years' Poems* (1965), Angus & Robertson. LIONEL G. FOGARTY: 'Frisky Poem and Risky' from *New and Selected Poems* (1995), Hyland House. JOHN FORBES: 'Four Heads & how to do them', 'Speed, a Pastoral', 'Love Poem', and 'Ode to Karl Marx' from *Collected Poems* (3rd ed., 2004), Brandl & Schlesinger, to Mick Forbes. CLAIRE GASKIN: 'The evening is loud with life' and 'all the blue rushing through the pinpoint of an iris' from *a bud* (2006), John Leonard Press. JANE GIBIAN: 'Parts of the tongue' from *Ardent* (2007), Giramondo. KEVIN GILBERT: 'Consultation' and 'The Soldier's Reward' from *The Blackside: people are legends and other poems* (1990), Hyland House. MARY GILMORE: 'Eve-Song', 'The Hunter of the Black', 'The Yarran-tree', 'Nationality' and 'Fourteen Men' courtesy of the publishers, ETT Imprint, Sydney.

PETER GOLDSWORTHY: 'Alcohol' from *This Goes With That: Selected Poems 1970 - 1990* (1991), Angus & Robertson. ALAN GOULD: 'The Move from Shelter', 'Intently', and 'An Interrogator's Opening Remarks' from *The Past Completes Me: Selected Poems 1973-2003* (2005), UQP. ROBERT GRAY: 'Journey: the North Coast' from *New Selected Poems* (1998), Duffy & Snellgrove; 'In Departing Light' from *Afterimages* (2002), Duffy & Snellgrove, to the author. JENNIFER HARRISON: 'Cancer Poem' from *Michelangelo's Prisoners* (1994), Black Pepper; 'Electra' from *Cabramatta/Cudmirrah* (1996), Black Pepper; 'Fauna of Mirrors' and 'Museum Flute' from *Folly & Grief* (2006), Black Pepper. MARTIN HARRISON: 'Late Western Thought' from *Wild Bees: Selected Poems* (2008), UWA Press. J. S. HARRY: 'honesty-stones' and 'wind painting' from *Selected Poems* (1995), Penguin, to the author. KEVIN HART: 'The Calm', 'The Bird is Close' and 'Beneath the Ode' from *Flame Tree: Selected Poems* (2002), Paperbark, to Golvan Arts Management. WILLIAM HART-SMITH: 'Biamai's Never-Failing Stream' and 'Relativity' from Brian Dibble ed. William Hart-Smith: *Selected Poems, 1936-1984* (1985), Angus & Robertson. GWEN HARWOOD: 'In the Park', 'Carnal Knowledge I', 'Oyster Cove', 'Night Thoughts: Baby & Demon', 'An Impromptu for Ann Jennings', 'The Sea Anemones', 'Death Has No Features of His Own', 'A Simple Story' and 'The Twins' from *Selected Poems* (2001), Penguin, to Penguin Books and John Harwood. JILL HELLYER: 'Living With Aunts' from *Song of the Humpbacked Whales: Selected Verse* (1981), Sisters, to the author. DOROTHY HEWETT: 'Grave Fairytale' from *Collected Poems 1940-1995* (1995), Fremantle Arts Centre Press, and 'The Runner' from *Halfway up the Mountain* (2001), Fremantle Arts Centre Press, to the estate of Dorothy Hewett. PHILIP HODGINS: 'Apologies', 'Shooting the Dogs' and 'The Land Itself' from *New and Selected Poems* (2000), Duffy & Snellgrove, to Janet Shaw. SARAH HOLLAND-BATT: 'Mythos' from *Aria* (2008), UQP; 'Winter Harmonica' to the author. L. K. HOLT: 'Waking: for Kafka' to the author; 'Man is Wolf to Man' from *Man Wolf Man* (2007), John Leonard Press. YVETTE HOLT: 'Storyteller' from *Anonymous Premonitions* (2008), UQP. A. D. HOPE: 'Australia', 'Ascent into Hell' 'Imperial Adam', 'Crossing the Frontier', 'On An Engraving by Casserius', 'Moschus Moschiferus', 'Inscription for a War' and 'The Mayan Books' reprinted by permission of Curtis Brown. CORAL HULL: 'Liverpool' from *The Wild Life* (1996), Penguin, to the author. JOHN JENKINS: 'Six O'clock Swill' and 'Push This Wall Back' from *Growing up with Mr Menzies* (2008), John Leonard Press. MARTIN JOHNSTON: 'The typewriter, considered as a beetrap', 'Esprit de l'escalier', and 'The recidivist' from *The typewriter, considered as a beetrap* (1984), Hale & Iremonger, to Roseanne Bonney and Barbara Mobbs. EMMA JONES: 'Winnowing' from *The Striped World* (2009), Faber. EVAN JONES: 'Generations', 'Eurydice Remembered' and 'Him' from *Understandings* (1967), MUP, to the author. NANCY KEESING: 'Old Hardware Store, Melbourne' and 'Olympus' from *Hails and Farewells and Other Poems* (1977), Angus & Robertson. AILEEN KELLY: 'Encounters with my mother's ghost' and 'They flee from me' from *The Passion Paintings: Poems 1983 – 2006* (2007), John Leonard Press. JOHN KINSELLA: 'Visitant Eclogue' from *Visitants* (1999), Bloodaxe; 'Yellow' to the author. PETER KIRKPATRICK: 'Texas, Queensland' and 'Wally, Wally' from *Westering* (2006), Puncher & Wattmann. ANTHONY LAWRENCE: 'The Drive' from *The Darkwood Aquarium* (1993), Penguin and 'Mark and Lars' from *Selected Poems* (1998), UQP, to the author; 'Bait Ball' from *Bark* (2008), UQP. BRONWYN LEA: 'The Cairn' and 'The Place' from *The Other Way Out* (2008), Giramondo. GEOFFREY LEHMANN: 'The Two Travellers', 'The Old Rifle' and 'Parenthood' from *Collected Poems* (1997), Heinemann, to the author. EMMA LEW: 'The Tale of Dark Louise' and 'Pursuit' from *Anything the Landlord Touches* (2002), Giramondo. TONY LINTERMANS: 'The Escape from Youth' and 'Heat' from *The Shed Manifesto* (1989), Scribe, to the author. KATHRYN LOMER: 'Bats' from *Two Kinds of Silence* (2007), UQP. DOROTHEA MACKELLAR: 'My Country' and 'Heritage' reprinted by permission of Curtis Brown. GERALDINE MCKENZIE: 'the honey-pit' from *Duty* (2001), Paperbark, to the author. PAUL MAGEE: 'Study' and 'Elegy' to the author. Kenneth Mackenzie: 'The Snake' and 'Two Trinities' from *The Poems of Kenneth Mackenzie* (1972), Angus & Robertson. ERN MALLEY: 'Petit Testament' from *Collected Poems* (1993), ETT Imprint. DAVID MALOUF: 'Confessions of An Only Child' from *Revolving Days: Selected Poems* (2008), UQP; 'Into the Blue' from *Typewriter Music* (2007), UQP. J. S. MANIFOLD: 'The Tomb of Lt John Learmonth AIF' from *Selected Verse* (1946), John Day (NY); 'Making Contact', and 'Incognito' from *Collected Verse* (1978), UQP. PHILIP MARTIN: 'Nursing Home' from *New & Selected Poems* (1988), Longman reprinted by permission of Jennifer Gribble. JOHN MATEER: 'The Monkey-Seller's Stall' and 'Autumn is Everywhere' from *Elsewhere* (2008), Salt; 'Cémiterio da Ajuda' from *Southern Barbarians* (2007), Zero Press. JAMES MCAULEY: 'Celebration of Love', 'Because', 'Pietà', 'Childhood Morning, Homebush', and 'The Hazard and the Gift' from *Collected Poems* (1994), Angus & Robertson. DENNIS MCDERMOTT: 'Dorothy's Skin' and 'The Up Train' from *Dorothy's Skin* (2003), Five Islands Press, to the author. ROGER MCDONALD: 'Two

Summers in Moravia' from *Airship* (1975), UQP, to the author. LES MURRAY: 'Once in a Life-time, Snow', 'The Broad Bean Sermon', 'The Future', 'The Dream of Wearing Shorts Forever', 'The Last Hellos', 'It Allows a Portrait in Line-Scan at Fifteen' and 'The Instrument' from *Collected Poems* (2006), Black Inc; 'On the North Coast Line' from *The Biplane Houses* (2006), Black Inc. DAVID MUSGRAVE: 'Lagoon' from *To Thalia* (2004), Five Islands Press, to the author. MARK O'CONNOR: 'The Beginning', 'The Sun Hunters' and 'Nemargon, the Lightning Grass-hopper' from *The Olive Tree: Collected Poems 1972 - 2000* (2000), Hale & Iremonger, to the au-thor. OODGEROO OF THE TRIBE NOONUCCAL: 'Municipal Gum', 'No More Boomerang', 'Gifts', 'Ballad of the Totem' and, 'Biami' from *My People* (4th ed., 2007), John Wiley. JAN OWEN: 'Seascape with Young Girl', 'The Kiss', 'Horizon', 'Freesias', 'Port Lincoln' from *Poems 1980 – 2008* (2008), John Leonard Press. GEOFF PAGE: 'The Poem That You Haven't Seen' and 'Adulterers' from *Darker and Lighter* (2001), Five Islands Press. Π.O.: 'He:Her' from *24 Hours: the day the language stood still* (1996), Collective Effort Press, to the author. MARCELLA POLAIN: 'writer's subject' and 'Marathon' from *Therapy like Fish: New & Selected Poems* (2008), John Leonard Press. DOROTHY PORTER: 'Bull-leaping' and 'The Water' from Crete (1996), Hyland House © Dorothy Porter, 1996. PETER PORTER: 'The Sadness of the Creatures', 'The Lying Art', 'Non Piangere, Liù', 'An Exequy', 'How Important is Sex?', 'Both Ends Against the Middle' and 'Basta Sangue' from *Collected Poems*, (1999), OUP, to the author. NICK RIEMER: 'The Fence' from *James Stinks (and so does Chuck)* (2005), Puncher & Wattmann. ELIZABETH RIDDELL: 'The Letter' and 'The Children March' from *Selected Poems* (1992), ETT Imprint. ROLAND ROBINSON: 'The Dancers' from *Selected Poems 1944 – 1982* (1983), Angus & Rob-ertson; 'The Two Sisters', 'Mapooram', and 'Billy Bamboo' from *The Nearest White Man Gets: Aboriginal Poems and Narratives of New South Wales* (1989), Hale & Iremonger. JUDITH ROD-RIGUEZ: 'The mud-crab eaters' and 'In-flight note' from *New & Selected Poems: the House by Water* (1988), UQP, to the author. PETER ROSE: 'Vantage' from *Rattus Rattus: New & Selected Poems* (2005), Salt, to the author. GIG RYAN: 'The Cross/The Bay' from *Excavation* (1990), Picador, to the author. PHILIP SALOM: 'Driving to Bury His Ashes' from *A Cretive Life* (2001), Fremantle Arts Centre Press; 'The Composer Shostakovich Orders His Funeral' to the author. DÎPTI SARAVANAMUTTU: 'Autumn Sonata' and 'Talk of Angels' from *Language of the Icons* (1993), Angus & Robertson; 'Dingo Trails' from *The Colosseum* (2004), Five Islands Press, to the author. JOHN A. SCOTT: 'Pride of Erin' and 'Polka' from *Selected Poems* (1995), UQP, to the author. MARGARET SCOTT: 'Grandchild' and 'Surfers' from *Collected Poems* (2000), Montpe-lier Press, to Australian Literary Management. THOMAS SHAPCOTT: 'Those who have seen visions' from *Welcome!* (1983), UQP and 'Australian Horizons' from *Chekhov's Mongoose* (2000), Salt, to the author; 'The City of Empty Rooms' from *The City of Empty Rooms* (2006), UQP. MICHAEL SHARKEY: 'Lucky for Some' and 'Signs and Wonders' from *The Sweeping Plain* (2007), Five Islands Press, to the author. ALEX SKOVRON: 'The Note' from *Infinite City: 100 Sonnetinas* (1999), Five Islands Press; 'Some Precepts of Postmodern Mourning' and 'Supper Song' from *The Man and the Map* (2003), Five Islands Press, to the author. KENNETH SLES-SOR: 'Nuremberg', 'The Night-Ride', 'Country Towns', 'South Country', 'Captain Dobbin', 'Out of Time', 'Five Bells' and 'Beach Burial' from *Collected Poems* (1994), Angus & Robertson. VIV-IAN SMITH: 'For My Daughter' and 'Night Life' from *Along the Line* (2007), Salt, to the author. PETER STEELE: 'Hats', 'Dreaming the Bridge', and 'Word' from *White Knight with Bee-box: New and Selected Poems* (2008), John Leonard Press. DOUGLAS STEWART: 'Two Englishmen' from *Selected Poems* (1973), Angus & Robertson, courtesy of Curtis Brown. RANDOLPH STOW: 'Ruins of the City of Hay' and 'This Land's Meaning' from *A Counterfeit Silence: Selected Poems of Randolph Stow* (1969), Angus & Robertson © Randolph Stow 1969, reproduced by permission of Sheil Land Associates Ltd. JENNIFER STRAUSS: 'Tending the Graves' and 'Wife to Horatio' from *Tierra Del Fuego: New & Selected Poems* (1997), Pariah, to the author. JOHN TRANTER: 'The Alphabet Murders 23', 'Voodoo', 'Fine Arts' and 'Lavender Ink' from *Urban Myths: 210 Poems: New & Selected* (2006), UQP. DIMITRIS TSALOUMAS: 'The Return' and 'The Rain' from *New & Selected Poems* (2000), UQP. VICKI VIIDIKAS: 'Going down. With no permanence' and 'The country as an answer' from *Condition Red* (1973), UQP, to Ingrid Lisners. CHRIS WALLACE-CRABBE: 'Melbourne', 'Other People', ' There', 'Genius Loci' and 'The Bush' from *Selected Poems 1956 – 1994* (1995), OUP; 'Good Friday Seder at Separation Creek' from *Rungs of Time* (1993), OUP; 'Erstwhile' from *Whirling* (1998), OUP; 'Modern Times: X, XIV' from *By And Large* (2001), Brandl & Schlesinger; 'It Sounds Different Today' from *Telling a Hawk from a Handsaw* (2008), Carcanet. ANIA WALWICZ: 'Australia' to the author; 'Little Red Riding Hood' from *Travel / Writing* (1989), Angus & Robertson, to the author. JOHN WATSON: 'At the Grotto Double Pool', 'From His Parapet' and 'In Tidal Baths' from *Montale: A Biographical An-thology: Collected Works Volume 1* (2006), Puncher & Wattmann. SAMUEL WAGAN WATSON:

'for the wake and skeleton dance', 'white stucco dreaming' and 'the golden skin of cowgirls' from *smoke encrypted whispers* (2004), UQP. ALAN WEARNE: 'Legend: Jack, the Barman' and 'Carrie, Wal' from *The Lovemakers* (2008), Shearsman Books (Essex), to the author. FRANCIS WEBB: 'Morgan's Country', 'Five Days Old', 'Back Street in Calcutta', 'Harry', 'Old Timer', 'A Man' and 'The Old Women' from *Collected Poems* (1977), Angus & Robertson. SIMON WEST: 'Flight' from *First Names* (2006), Puncher & Wattmann; 'The Translation' to the author. PETRA WHITE: 'Trampolining' to the author; 'Kangaroos' from *The Incoming Tide* (2007), John Leonard Press. JUDITH WRIGHT: 'Woman to Man', 'Woman to Child', 'Train Journey', 'At Cooloolah', 'Request to a Year', 'A Document', 'To Another Housewife', 'Australia, 1970', 'Lament for Passenger Pigeons' and 'For a Pastoral Family' from *A Human Pattern: Selected Poems* (2008), ETT Imprint. MORGAN YASBINCEK: 'nineleven' from *firelick* (2004), Fremantle Arts Centre Press. 'echo' from *white camel* (2009), John Leonard Press. FAY ZWICKY: 'Tiananmen Square June 4, 1989' and 'Letting Go' from *Poems 1970 – 1992* (1992), UQP and 'The Witnesses', to the author. 'Song Cycle of the Moon-Bone', translated by Ronald M Berndt, from *Oceania xix, September 1948*, reproduced courtesy of the Estate of RM and CH Berndt, JE Stanton Literary Executor of the Estate.

Index of Titles

Index of Poets

472